Borrowing Credibility

Nations with credible monetary regimes borrow at lower interest rates in international markets and are less likely to suffer speculative attacks and currency crises. Whereas scholars typically attribute credibility to either domestic institutions or international agreements, Jana Grittersová argues that when reputable multinational banks, headquartered in Western Europe or North America, open branches and subsidiaries within a nation, they enhance its monetary credibility.

Such multinational banks enhance credibility in several ways. First, they promote financial transparency in the local financial system. Second, they improve the quality of banking regulation and supervision in host countries. Finally, the banks serve as private lenders of last resort. Reputable multinational banks provide an enforcement mechanism, ensuring that publicized economic policies will be carried out. Therefore the presence of these banks signals to the international financial markets that the host government is committed to low inflation and stable currency.

Grittersová examines actual changes in government behavior in nations trying to gain legitimacy in international financial markets and the ways international perceptions of these nations change because of the presence of multinational banks. In addition to quantitative analysis of more than eighty emerging-market countries, she offers extensive case studies of credibility building in the transition countries of Eastern Europe, Argentina in 2001, and the global financial crisis of 2008. Grittersová illuminates the complex interactions between multinational banks and national policymaking that characterize the process of financial globalization. The book reveals the importance of market confidence in a world of mobile capital.

Jana Grittersová is Associate Professor of Political Science and Cooperating Faculty at the Department of Economics at the University of California–Riverside.

Michigan Studies in International Political Economy

SERIES EDITORS: Edward Mansfield, Lisa Martin, and William Clark

For a complete list of titles, please see www.press.umich.edu

Borrowing Credibility

Global Banks and Monetary Regimes

JANA GRITTERSOVÁ

University of Michigan Press
Ann Arbor

Published in the United States of America by the
University of Michigan Press
Printed and bound by CPI Group (UK) Ltd, Croydon, CR0 4YY

2020   2019   2018   2017   4   3   2   1

A CIP catalog record for this book is available from the British Library.

Library of Congress Cataloging-in-Publication Data

Names: Grittersová, Jana, author.
Title: Borrowing credibility : global banks and monetary regimes / Jana Grittersová.
Description: Ann Arbor : University of Michigan Press, [2017] | Series: Michigan studies
    in international political economy | Includes bibliographical references and index.
Identifiers: LCCN 2017011111| ISBN 9780472130467 (hardcover : alk. paper) | ISBN
    9780472123087 (e-book)
Subjects: LCSH: International finance. | Banks and banking, International. | Financial
    institutions, International.
Classification: LCC HG3881 .G7258   2017 | DDC 332.1/5—dc23
LC record available at https://lccn.loc.gov/2017011111

CONTENTS

CONTENTS

PREFACE

This is a book about credibility building in the global economy. I embarked on this project in my attempt to understand the ways countries with a meager reputational track record to build credibility on can achieve policy credibility in the eyes of international markets. This question seemed important to me because my native country, Slovakia, was confronted with a severe credibility deficit after the demise of the communist regime. The intellectual lineage of the ideas of this book can be traced back to my experience working as an economist at the central bank of Slovakia. It was an interesting period during which the nation faced crucial decisions about its economic policies. The decision over the exchange rate regime was one of the most important macroeconomic policy decisions in the country as it underwent sweeping economic, social, and political changes. I observed how the powerful public banks, private financial groups with political ties, and the political elites that came to depend on them challenged the political autonomy of a new central bank, the guardian of sound money and stable currency. It became apparent to me that the role of banks in an economy goes well beyond financial intermediation. This blatant contradiction between what I observed and the economic literature I was acquainted with piqued my curiosity.

My interest in understanding the relationship between banks and politics intensified when I was working in the European Commission's Directorate-General for Competition in Brussels. My work focused on assessing banking privatizations and reforms in the new member states from the former communist bloc, which allowed me to learn a great deal about the global banks that led institutional change in these countries' emerging banking sectors. The vulnerability of the banking sectors of transition countries created the opportunity for large international banks to play the role of "money doctors," helping local governments reform their financial systems and improve market confidence. But the 2008 global financial crisis sparked debate on the role these banks had in originating and transmitting the crisis.

This course of events inspired my intellectual interest in understanding the different roles banks—domestic and foreign—can play in a world of mobile capital. I have never been confined by narrow disciplinary boundaries and thus felt extraordinarily well-situated to explore these issues while exploiting my invaluable working experience. This book broadens our understanding of reputation formation of emerging-market governments by sharpening our understanding of the role of global banks. The novelty of this book is that it considers the role of private actors in building the credibility of emerging nations, whereas scholars typically attribute credibility to either domestic institutions or international agreements. I hope this book opens new avenues of research on the politics of financial globalization.

Bankers and those who write about them are familiar with debts, and I have inevitably accumulated a large amount of debt in crafting this book. Since this book is the outgrowth of my doctoral dissertation at Cornell concentrating on the topic of government choices of exchange rate regimes, my first round of thanks goes to my superb advisors. Peter Katzenstein, my dissertation committee chair, was an ideal advisor and remains a source of inspiration, trenchant criticism, and high standards. Valerie Bunce, Jonathan Kirshner, and Chris Way provided me with profound insights and advice drawing on their diverse areas of expertise. I can hardly imagine a more helpful set of people to teach, inspire, and guide me.

I asked Barry Eichengreen to serve on my dissertation committee more than a decade ago, and I continue to seek his counsel regularly. Barry graciously took me under his intellectual wing at the University of California–Berkeley, at his resident Economics Department. Barry's own work and his enthusiasm for international finance were inspirations for this book. He threw his support behind this project, listened to every idea I had, and steered me into the right direction at crucial moments. Barry deserves recognition for substantially improving the clarity of my ideas and the rigor of my argument. I am eternally grateful for his excellent guidance, friendship, and above all, unwavering support through the years. Barry is still my intellectual hero.

Most of the writing took place at the University of California–Riverside, which provided me with a friendly and wonderfully supportive environment. I owe particular debts to Shaun Bowler and Indridi Indridason for their valuable feedback, support, and occasional reality checks. Shaun has set an unparalleled standard for collegiality. Without his frequent encouragements I would not have dared to try this book, and his humor made much of the hard work fun. Although working in a different field of political science, Indridi provided extensive and penetrating comments on draft after draft of book chapters (often on very short notice). He has the ability to put his finger on the weak spots in the arguments and propose ways to improve them in a constructive manner. Our frequent discussions resulted in many improvements in this manuscript. I could not have asked for a more generous colleague and friend. I also owe my profuse thanks to Georgia Warnke for valuable professional and personal advice, friendship, and dinners proffered at crucial moments. Julian Allison, Marcelle Chauvet, John Cioffi, Bronwyn Leebaw, Matthew Mahutga, Sharon Oselin, and John Medearis graciously offered keen insights and encouragements and gave me much-appreciated advice on the publication process.

This project has benefited from several grants and fellowships that helped to fund my field research and make writing possible. I am grateful for funding from the Einaudi Center for International Studies and its Institute for European Studies, the Government Department, and the Graduate School at Cornell. An Austrian Marshall Plan Fellowship gave me time to think about and write this book as a resident at the School of Advanced and International Studies at Johns Hopkins University, during which it changed in radically new ways. I offer profuse thanks to the SAIS's Center for Transatlantic Relations and its director Dan Hamilton for providing a hospitable and stimulating environment. I benefited greatly from the rich and vibrant academic community at Johns Hopkins, Georgetown, and UC Berkeley, where I was a visiting scholar, and I am grateful to those who involved me in their seminars and gave me a chance to present my work. Special thanks go to Gordon Bodnar, Marc Busch, Henry Hale, Kate McNamara, Mitchell Orenstein, and Barbara Voytek. The Regents Fellowship from the Academic Senate at the University of California–Riverside also supported my research.

In researching this book, I spent time as a visiting scholar in the research departments of the Bulgarian National Bank, Czech National Bank, and National Bank of Poland. I owe all three central banks my warmest thanks and appreciation for opening their excellent facilities to me, providing me with office space and with research and archival assistance, and helping with interviews. Special thanks to Nikolay Nenovsky of the Bulgarian National Bank for being such a gracious host. I also benefited from my discussions with the European Commission's officials during my work assignment there. I am especially grateful to Mary McCarthy, director of the Structural Reform Support Service. I also offer my genuine thanks to the central bankers and policymakers from the National Bank of Slovakia, Bank of Estonia, European Bank for Reconstruction and Development, Oesterreichische Nationalbank, and the World Bank, as well as those in private financial communities, finance ministries, and universities, who graciously dedicated their time to answer my questions and share their reflections. I learned an extraordinary amount from these discussions.

I was fortunate to discuss my research with many mentors, colleagues, and friends who provided insightful suggestions and comments on this project in its various iterations and incarnations. I am deeply indebted to Marc Flandreau, whose work on prestigious nineteenth-century financial intermediaries influenced the argument of this book in profound ways. While I cannot hope to thank everyone who has influenced my work, I especially want to thank to Rawi Abdelal, Cristina Bodea, Hein Bogaard, Lawrence Broz, Marcos Chamon, Bill Clark, Jerry Cohen, Patrick Crowley, Richard Deeg, Rui Pedro Esteves, Steve Fish, Jesse Fried, Jeff Frieden, Timothy Frye, Davide Furceri, Pedro Gomes, Daniel Gros, Ilene Grabel, Anna Grzymala-Busse, Rachel Epstein, Galina Hale, Mark Hallerberg, Ray Hicks, Stefan Huemer, Juliet Johnson, Ethan Kaplan, Evžen Kočenda, Jacek Kugler, David Leblang, Gerald McDermott, Thomas Oatley, Peter Rosendorff, Dennis Quinn, Jay Shambaugh, Jan Švejnar, Daniel Treisman, Tom Willett, Robert Wade, John Zysman, and others whose names have been lost to the mists of time. David Freedman, Charles Franklin, Greg Wawro, and Chris Zorn all answered various technical questions. Cristina Bodea, Ray Hicks, Axel Dreher, Armand Fouejieu, Scott Roger, Linda Goldberg, Julia Gray, Ben Graham, Jim Vreeland, and Ugo Panizza graciously shared their data. Cheryl Applewood provided invaluable help compiling the index. Tony Roberts also merits recognition for his outstanding research assistance.

I offer my gratitude to anonymous referees for their highly constructive and encouraging comments about this book. I am grateful to Bill Clark, editor of the Michigan Studies in International Political Economy, for his support, insight, and enthusiasm for this project. Melody Herr has patiently accompanied the writing process and shepherded me through the peer review. Working with Melody, her successor Mary Francis, Kevin Rennells and their team has made publishing with the University of Michigan Press a great pleasure.

I received some of the most helpful comments and reactions to preliminary presentations of my ideas and arguments at various conferences, seminars, workshops, and presentations along the way. I am especially grateful to participants in seminars and workshops at Cornell University, University of California–Berkeley, Georgetown University, George Washington University, Johns Hopkins University, University of Cambridge, University of Pittsburgh, University of Miami, Claremont Graduate School, University of Denver, University of California–Riverside, University of Washington, the European Bank for Reconstruction and Development, the Bulgarian National Bank, and the National Bank of Slovakia, as well as attendees of the annual meetings of the American and Midwest Political Science Associations, American Economic Association, International Political Economy Society, International Studies Association, European Union Studies Association, and the Society for Institutional and Organizational Economics.

My greatest thanks go to my family. Words are not enough to express my gratitude toward my parents, who instilled in me the desire to learn and study and taught me the importance of determination and hard work. My mother has my heartfelt thanks for so much encouragement and the innumerable sacrifices she made as she watched me moving around the globe far away from the family. I am certain that my late father, although skeptical about my decision to pursue an academic career, would have been proud to see my accomplishments. I am also indebted to my wonderful brothers and sisters for their warm and constant support and encouragement. My brother Jozef took a personal interest in my project and provided valuable help with the tables and figures. Finally, my greatest debt is to my husband, Jérôme, who lived throughout the highs and lows of this project with love, patience, and enthusiasm, and my son Adrian, who is a constant source of delight, amazement, and pure joy. This book is dedicated to them.

ACRONYMS

BANK PEKAO	Bank Polska Kasa Opieki
BCRA	Central Bank of Argentina (Banco Central de la República Argentina)
BIS	Bank for International Settlements
BOE	Bank of Estonia (Eesti Pank)
BPH	Bank Przemysłowo-Handlowy
BRE	Bank Rozwoju Eksportu
BNB	Bulgarian National Bank (Blgarska Narodna Banka)
CS	Česká Spořitelna
CSOB	Československá Obchodní Banka
CNB	Czech National Bank (Česká národní banka)
DSK	Darzhavna Spestovna Kasa
EMBI	The J. P. Morgan Emerging Market Bond Index
EBRD	European Bank for Reconstruction and Development
GMM	generalized method of moments
IMF	International Monetary Fund
IPB	Investiční a Poštovní Banka
IPFs	Investment privatization funds
KB	Komerční Banka Praha
NBP	National Bank of Poland (Bank Narodowy Polski)
OECD	Organization for Economic Cooperation and Development
PKO BP	Powszechna Kasa Oszczędności Bank Polski
PBK	Powszechny Bank Kredytowy
SEB	Skandinaviska Enskilda Banken
ZB	Živnostenská banka

CHAPTER 1

The Puzzle of Credibility in International Markets

> CAS: Reputation, reputation, reputation! Oh, I have lost my reputation!
> I have lost the immortal part of myself, and what remains is bestial.
> My reputation, Iago, my reputation!
> IAGO: As I am an honest man, I thought you had received some bodily
> wound. There is more sense in that than in reputation. Reputation
> is an idle and most false imposition, oft got without merit and lost
> without deserving. You have lost no reputation at all unless you
> repute yourself such a loser. What, man! There are ways to recover
> the General again.
> —William Shakespeare, *Othello*, Act 2, Scene 3[1]

In this book I explore a question that has preoccupied scholars for decades: How do governments establish a reputation in international markets? The advantages to governments of having a reputation for being reliable and credible are well known. It is much less clear how those reputations can be established, especially in countries whose histories and institutions are too new or weak to provide adequate signals about the credibility of their chosen policies. Since World War II, the number of states in the world has grown from roughly fifty to just under two hundred. The vast majority of states, including postcolonial regimes and new democracies, cannot rely on historical interactions as a basis for their reputations.

Countries can rely on external actors for help in acquiring international legitimacy. In May 2013, the Ministry of Finance of the Russian Federation hired J. P. Morgan, Goldman Sachs, and other reputable international banks to advise it about how to improve the country's international reputation in order to attract foreign investments (Corcoran 2013). Another way countries can gain credibility is by importing the monetary policy of an anchor nation. In the wake of the 2014 crisis in Ukraine, some U.S. policymakers have suggested creating a currency board to increase the nation's monetary credibility in the eyes of international investors and to help stabilize the national currency as an aid in its political and economic transformation.[2] In addition to countries that are now rising in reputation, there are numerous examples of countries whose reputations have declined. The ongoing debt crisis in Greece and southern European countries and the recurring turmoil in financial markets have seriously weakened the credibility of the European monetary union and its member countries. Thus, history abounds with examples of governments that lack or have lost credibility in the eyes of international markets.

In tackling this issue, I focus on the credibility of monetary regimes, a topic that despite its centrality for understanding international monetary cooperation, inflationary expectations (Kydland and Prescott 1977; Barro and Gordon 1983), and currency crises (Krugman 1979; Obstfeld 1986), has largely been neglected.[3] The advantage of credibility is especially important when we consider international monetary relations in the post–Bretton Woods era, which are characterized by a variety of exchange rate regimes that range from full floats to currency boards and monetary unions. The exchange rate is the most important asset price in an economy.[4] Exchange rates have also been endowed with symbolic importance and prestige. As Charles Kindleberger (1970, 198) has said, "A country's exchange rate is more than a number. It is an emblem of its importance to the world, a sort of international status symbol." A credible monetary regime, in turn, confers significant reputational effects on governments.

What makes a government's monetary regime credible in the eyes of international market participants? In this book I offer a novel account of credibility building in international finance. I argue that in effect, governments may borrow credibility from third-party actors. I develop a theory of *borrowing credibility* through financial integration via multinational banks. Multinational banks with established reputations enhance the credibility of institutions and policies in host nations that is necessary for the credibility of their monetary regimes. Reputable foreign bank investors can thus serve as *external anchors*, alleviating the credibility problems of emerging-market governments.

The origin of the credibility of monetary regimes can be traced to the classical gold standard, which was the prevalent regime in the international monetary system from the 1870s until World War I.[5] Under this standard, all currency prices were fixed in terms of gold, so all national currencies were also fixed against one another. In his magisterial study of the gold standard, Barry Eichengreen (1992, 5) defines credibility as "the confidence invested by the public in the government's commitment to a policy." The main responsibility of central banks was preserving the official parity between their own currencies and gold. Eichengreen (1992, 5) further remarks that "the very credibility of the official commitment to gold meant that this commitment was rarely tested." Therefore, in the era of the classical gold standard, the adherence by the central banks to the rule of convertibility of national currencies into a fixed weight of gold provided a credible nominal anchor, as Michael Bordo and Ronald Mac-Donald (2012, 3) explain.

In the postwar era, the Bretton Woods system (1945–1973) established an asymmetrical system of fixed exchange rates. It was based on fixed exchange rates, as the gold standard was, but only the U.S. dollar was pegged to gold; other currencies were fixed to the dollar. In other words, the United States pledged to redeem dollars for gold. In this arrangement, exchange rates were fixed but adjustable because governments could devalue their currencies when they faced a fundamental disequilibrium. Since 1973, when gold ceased to be an anchor in the international monetary system, fixed monetary arrangements—under which the central bank declares the value of the exchange rate that it will act to maintain—raise particularly serious problems of credibility. Bordo and MacDonald (2012, 4) argue that a key underlying factor behind the sustainability of a fixed exchange rate regime is the credibility of the peg. The credibility of fixed exchange rate regimes, in turn, derives from the credibility of a government's commitment not to increase the money supply and not to devalue the national currency (Bordo and MacDonald 2012).

A credible fixed exchange rate regime is less likely to suffer speculative attacks (Bordo and MacDonald 2012, 3). If a monetary regime is credible, expectations of market participants will remain well anchored even in the face of bad economic conditions (Fergusson and Schularick 2012). Credible monetary arrangements will prevent the population and investors from engaging in currency substitution and speculations against the local currency and will reduce the probability of rumor-based reversals in capital flows (Edwards 2003; Grabel 2003). In addition, countries with credible monetary regimes borrow at lower interest rates in international markets. Bordo and Rockoff (1996) portray the gold standard as a kind of Good Housekeeping Seal of Approval that conferred significant credibility on its adherents. They argue that the financial markets considered adherence to the gold standard to be a sign of financial discipline and loaned at lower rates to countries on gold. The rate on a gold bond was forty basis points lower for countries on the gold standard than it was for otherwise comparable countries (Bordo and Rockoff 1996, 413).

In contrast, a monetary regime that lacks credibility suffers currency volatility, devaluations, and financial crises with devastating domestic and international consequences. When a government does not observe the rules of the game inherent in a monetary strategy, speculators will lose confidence in the currency, an intervention by the central bank in support of the currency will drain international reserves, and the government will be forced to abandon the peg (Krugman 1979). The post–Bretton Woods history of the world's monetary system has included a number of spectacular collapses of exchange rates and currency crises that have imposed enormous political, economic, and social costs. These include several crisis episodes in Latin America (e.g., Mexico in 1982 and 1994), the collapse of the European Monetary System in 1992, the 1997–98 crises in Asia, the 1998 Russian crisis and the similar financial turmoil in Argentina in 2001.[6] The 1998 financial crisis in Russia serves as a clear example of how an exchange rate regime that lacks credibility can prove disastrous. The crisis created a panic in international financial markets, the ruble lost more than 80 percent of its value, the Russian government defaulted on its debt, and a political crisis erupted. Even hard pegs such as currency boards—monetary regimes similar to a gold standard—can fail, as in Argentina in 2001. Currency unions may break up too. Rising sovereign bond spreads and the prospect of a disorderly default were at the heart of the debate over Greece's potential exit from the eurozone. Currency crises are very costly; they reduce national output by about 5 percent to 8 percent over two to four years (Hutchison and Noy 2005).

Building credibility thus is an important task for monetary policymakers around the world. Re-establishing credibility after a financial collapse that has bred uncertainty among investors and the public is also difficult and often requires radical institutional reforms. Achieving credible monetary regimes is particularly important for emerging markets that suffer from the high borrowing costs, which hinder investment and economic growth. Many emerging markets are still confronted with a severe "credibility deficit" stemming from histories of high inflation, failed economic policies, weak domestic institutions, and unstable financial systems. They have little endogenously created reputational capital. The general public and international markets have limited confidence in the technical abilities and commitments of the monetary authorities of these countries to undertake politically unpopular anti-inflationary policies (Schmieding 1992). As a consequence, emerging-market countries that lack credibility are subject to currency speculation, high interest rates, and a host of other problems that make the task of governing more difficult and the development path more uncertain. Yet the standard means of gaining legitimacy on the international stage—having established domestic institutions and depth of international integration—are unavailable to many emerging market democracies.

The argument I advance makes a distinct contribution to the debate on credibility in international markets. It challenges the prevailing scholarship in economics and political science, which depicts credibility building as being the result of domestic institutions (such as autonomous central banks or fixed exchange rate regimes) or international agreements and institutions. The problem with the first instance of this reasoning is that many countries lack the institutional setup that could assure market participants that the government will not renege on its promises. Central banks in emerging-market countries lack credibility and the ability to conduct their monetary policies independently of government fiscal needs, and thus inflation expectations are not firmly anchored. The focus on the credibility-enhancing effect of the presence of foreign banks also contrasts with much of the research that emphasizes international institutions. The existing studies that explore credibility enhancement by delegating powers internationally ignore private-market agents, such as foreign investors or lenders, as external anchors.

Ultimately, the theory and evidence presented in the book presents an alternative to the claim that reputation can serve as a substitute for a commitment mechanism. Tomz (2007) provides impressive empirical evidence that countries' reputations are a function of their own behavior. In his account, in their efforts to preserve their country's reputation, policymakers will stick to their commitments. Many emerging markets, however, have little reputation to protect. Whereas Tomz's (2007) theory of reputation centers on the role of political instability in creating room for reputational destruction and recovery, I highlight the importance of the degree of financial integration through multinational banks.

Toward a Borrowing Credibility Argument

Taking insights from international economics and global banking, I posit that expectations of market participants about government policies center on the presence of reputable multinational banks. When multinational banks head-quartered in Western Europe and North America locate branches and affiliates within a nation, investors take the reputation of these banks into account as a signal of the host government's monetary rectitude. Put differently, foreign bank ownership serves as a proxy for the commitment of host governments to pursuing macroeconomic policies compatible with a credible monetary regime. The credibility of monetary policy depends not only on monetary policy but also on the perceived coherence of the overall macroeconomic program (Blackburn and Christensen 1989, 4). Openness to foreign bank entry serves as shorthand for a country's intentions.

Nonetheless, it is not enough to provide initial credibility. Market participants also observe governments' initiatives, looking for signals of the policy agenda that is likely to be advanced. In my theory of credibility, the presence of foreign banks not only generates expectations about a government's policy commitments to low inflation and stable currency, but it also provides a commitment mechanism: foreign banks can punish governments that deviate from sound monetary policies. The presence of foreign banks thus gives assurance to financial markets that the policies a government has announced will be carried out.

The ability of reputable multinational banks to reduce information asymmetries in financial markets (when one party in a transaction has more or superior information than the other party), combined with their ability to punish revealed bad behavior, provides a credible commitment device in the eyes of international audiences. The presence of multinational banks *creates* the credibility of currency policies, rather than simply revealing it. The theory I propose is thus concerned with both actual changes in government behavior in emerging-market countries that are trying to gain legitimacy on the international stage and changes in how these countries are perceived as a function of the presence of foreign banks. This book moves beyond approaches that focus on passive third-party perceptions of government reputations instead of active transformation of government behavior.

I focus on the decisions large multinational banks make about where to locate and the influence they have in the countries where they establish their presence. The finance literature on the role of financial intermediaries in international credit markets has long argued that when information about sovereign borrowers is scarce, investors rely on the reputation of prestigious bank underwriters (Riley 1980; Fang 2005; Flandreau and Flores 2009, 2012). I extend this strand of research by examining multinational bank investors as enhancers of the perceived credibility of governments. In my theory there is scope for a *transfer of reputation* from a reputable multinational bank to host governments. Like leading European investment banks in the nineteenth century, modern global banks have assumed the role of "money doctors," or private and public foreign financial advisers.[7] Money doctors are "brokers" between local governments and international markets who speak "the price language" of market players and so are in a good position to convey accurate signals and assess the economic situation of an emerging-market country, and additionally are well placed to push for economic reforms (Flandreau 2003a, 3).[8]

Why and How Foreign Banks Matter for Credibility

My argument offers three novel channels that link multinational banks to credibility outcomes. Foreign banks contribute to the consistency between monetary and macroprudential policies (policies safeguarding financial stability) through these channels. This study highlights the benefits that multinational banks confer for financial stability. As Sylvia Maxfield notes (1997, 88), maintaining price stability, a cornerstone of credibility, requires "the ability to control credit." This focus on the interaction between the goals of monetary policy and financial stability is distinct from the traditional focus on the mix of monetary and fiscal policies.[9] Various policy targets of the overall economic program should be compatible; otherwise a monetary regime will be neither credible nor sustainable.

First, foreign banks increase transparency in the financial system by tightening up accounting standards and disclosure rules so governments will have greater difficulty concealing their actions in financial policies (such as granting political loans to their constituents through state-owned banks). The best starting point for a discussion is the influential work of J. Lawrence Broz (2002, 861), who defines transparency in political systems as "the ease with which the public can monitor the government with respect to its commitments." When the political process is transparent, the public and the political opposition are able to observe whether a government has violated its commitment to low inflation. Broz argues that the transparency of a fixed exchange rate regime and the transparency of political systems are substitutes in ensuring that inflation expectations are anchored.[10] While this argument highlights the fundamental importance of the transparency of the political system, a similar logic can be extended to transparency in the financial system, which has received less attention.

Financial transparency and information sharing have important implications for the level of risk a bank takes and consequently for the likelihood of a financial crisis (Houston et al. 2010). In the presence of information asymmetries in financial markets, contagion—where the collapse of a bank may cast doubt on the solvency of other banks—may lead to a systemic banking crisis (Hagendorff, Keasey, and Vallascas 2013). This book emphasizes that foreign banks can help establish institutions that promote the availability and exchange of transparent credit information, such as credit-reporting institutions and accounting and auditing firms. When projects that generate domestic currency are financed with foreign currency, banks and firms accumulate dollar-denominated debt and thus face severe currency mismatches in their balance sheets (Eichengreen and Hausmann 1999; Calvo and Reinhart 2002). Multinational banks can improve transparency in financial reporting by, for example, promoting international accounting standards. In emerging economies where capital markets are underdeveloped, multinational banks can play a particularly important role in promoting transparency of financial reporting related to the banks' balance sheets.

Information-sharing institutions promote the exchange of credit information in the financial system. Therefore, they mitigate information asymmetries and serve as a disciplining device for borrowers by increasing the incentive to repay loans if they want to remain creditworthy (Houston et al. 2010). Furthermore, financial reporting also helps the authorities to strengthen supervision of regulated financial institutions. In this way, credit reporting institutions support the supervisory role of the state (World Bank 2013). In sum, transparency and the availability of credit information allow economic agents to monitor and assess financial stability and the credibility of monetary policies.

Second, foreign banks can improve the quality of regulation and the stability of local banking sectors by exporting regulation and supervision from home countries and by promoting regulatory reforms in host markets. Integration with multinational banks allows a government of an emerging-market nation to import best practices in financial regulation that are commonly in place in the developed countries, where multinational banks are headquartered. Foreign banks promote the harmonization of regulations with host countries so that common standards are imposed on banks. A prominent example of this are memoranda of understanding (regional agreements) between home and host supervisory institutions in the Nordic-Baltic region and elsewhere that provide a framework for cross-border supervision, cooperation, and information sharing (see chapters 4 and 5). A robust regulatory and supervisory framework in emerging market countries will help rein in the financial instability that is inherent in financial markets and institutions. Financial regulation and supervision is also an important complement to monetary policy in efforts to counter rapid expansion of bank credit (Schoenmaker 2013).

Third, multinational banks can act as private lenders of last resort by providing emergency liquidity facilities to their affiliates. The argument and evidence presented in this book suggest that by providing lender-of-last resort facilities to their affiliates overseas, parent banks can prevent bank runs and panics in host countries. Foreign banks can thus strengthen financial stability in host countries by improving the liquidity and solvency of their affiliates (Vogel and Winkler 2010). The ability of multinational banks to raise funds in international markets allows them to operate their own internal market, thus providing their subsidiaries with access to capital and liquidity in times of crisis. The legal structure multinational banks adopt—in particular whether they organize their cross-border operations through branches or subsidiaries—may affect expectations about bailouts, but in practice concerns about maintaining a global brand blur the differences between branches and subsidiaries.

This is important because although an international lender of last resort is desirable in today's international financial system (Obstfeld 2009), the International Monetary Fund (IMF) is not yet equipped financially to play this role fully (Frieden 2016). Recognizing the importance of global banks in the international financial system, the IMF has only recently broadened its support from sovereign countries to include global banks. In sum, like their nineteenth-century predecessors, multinational banks not only support "good policies" but they can also fulfill some "proto-IMF" policies (Flandreau 2003a, 6).

Evidently, global banks may recapitalize their affiliates abroad using bailouts from their home governments or from the IMF, or foreign central banks may extend swap lines. It is worth noting that as a consequence of the increase in the international activities of global banks, the responsibility for national central banks in their role as lenders of last resort has become blurred (Obstfeld 2009, 5). Who the capital supplier of last resort is, however, is not consequential for the theory of monetary credibility put forward here. What matters most is the expectations of market participants that branches and subsidiaries of multinational banks have access to additional liquidity when in need, to avoid a destabilizing systemic banking crisis in emerging markets with negative implications for the credibility of their monetary regimes.

I test the independent effects of these three mechanisms in detailed case studies presented in chapters 4 through 6. In assessing the risk premium, market participants look at macroeconomic indicators, including inflation, foreign exchange reserves, public finances, and external debt to assess whether monetary and fiscal policies are compatible. But my argument implies that market participants also look at indicators of financial stability. To gauge the importance of foreign banks for financial stability, I analyze information-sharing mechanisms (credit reporting institutions) as a measure of the transparency in a banking system. I also examine banking sector reforms, credit allocation process, credit quality (volume of nonperforming loans), banking sector capitalization, and progress in the process of harmonizing banking laws and regulations with international bank safety standards (e.g., capital adequacy standards) when I assess the strength of banking regulations and supervision *before* and *after* a foreign bank enters a market. Finally, by comparing financial crises in host and home countries (chapter 6), I show how foreign banks act as international lenders of last resort in difficult economic times. The 2008 global financial crisis provides an opportune "stress test" for my theory, particularly in terms of commitments of foreign banks to emerging Europe, since tighter funding constraints raised concerns about large, uncoordinated withdrawals of these banks (Bonin 2010). But what people feared did not happen, as the subsequent chapters of this book demonstrate. As Allen et al. (2011, 5) note, "Multinational banks have been the *face*, but not necessarily the *cause* of the crisis."

The main insight that can be extracted from this discussion is that foreign banks can decrease the currency-risk (and country-risk) premium of emerging economies because international markets envision lower financial vulnerability and fewer bank rescues financed by host governments in times of financial distress. Also due to foreign bank presence, governments of these countries are able to keep inflation, public spending, and external debt in check. It is worth noting that the benefits of the presence of global banks I identify here are different from the benefits usually attributed to financial globalization such as increased international risk sharing and more efficient allocation of capital.

Credibility and Moral Hazard

It is plausible that multinational banks per se do not have a direct effect on credibility. Instead, it may be the case that the presence of large global banks merely signals the likelihood that creditor-country governments and the IMF will bail out a national economy if a crisis occurs.[11] This potential alternative channel of global bank influence highlights the moral hazard problem: financial-market participants reward countries where large global banks have established their operations because they expect that these banks will extract the benefits of a financial safety net because they are "too big to fail."

Admittedly, some multinational banks are likely to be systemically important banks because of their size, their complexity, and their interconnectedness with the global financial system. The list of global systemically important banks, which is published annually by the Financial Stability Board,[12] includes major internationally active banks such as HSBC, Deutsche Bank, Barclays, Citigroup, and JPMorgan Chase.[13] If a global systemically important bank were to fail, that might impose significantly higher costs on the global financial system than would be the case if a domestic bank failed. Thus the presence of global bank affiliates in emerging market nations may raise expectations that the taxpayers of creditor countries will provide lending to these nations.

Not all multinational banks, however, are systemically important. Many reputable multinational banks with long traditions in international banking have an extensive web of branches and subsidiaries located in a particular region. These banks include Raiffeisen of Austria, Intesa Sao Paolo of Italy, KBC of Belgium, and Swedbank of Sweden, each of which has sizeable international operations in emerging Europe. It is reasonable to assume that these regional multinational banks might not engender the same expectations with regards to international bailouts as systemically important banks would. And yet, as we will see, these banks conferred substantial credibility

benefits on host countries in emerging Europe. In contrast, some systemically important global banks are headquartered in developing countries,
most notably large Chinese banks: the Bank of China, the China Construction Bank, and the Industrial and Commercial Bank of China Limited. The
analysis in chapter 3 shows that financial market participants are prudent
and do not reduce the currency risk premiums of countries in which nonreputable multinational banks have a substantial presence. Yet the moral
hazard argument, which focuses on the systemic size of banks, would predict a similar credibility-enhancing effect for all large banks, whether they
were reputable or nonreputable.

Another implication of the moral hazard argument suggests that expectations of bailouts may incentivize big global banks to take on more risk.
This is how the story of the ongoing crisis in the eurozone has been told:
German, Dutch, and French banks lent excessively to peripheral European
countries before 2007 because they were relying on government bailouts if
their loans became nonperforming. But Hagendorff, Keasey, and Vallascas
(2013) find that with the exception of the 2008 global crisis, no general risk-
increasing effect was linked to size of global banks during earlier financial
crises (or during periods of noncrisis). This is in line with the findings by
Demirgüç-Kunt and Huizinga (2010) that systemically large banks actually
engage in less risk taking because of the perception that they are "too big to
save" and hence subject to more market discipline. But even if one accepts
that large global banks engage in excessive risk taking, this irresponsible
behavior should reduce the value of the credibility signal associated with
the entry of these banks into emerging markets.

Large international banks can increase the risk of contagion through
common-lender effects, transmitting financial crises that start in one country. This raises problems for cross-border externalities and global financial
stability. The risk of contagion can be reduced, however, if foreign banks
have a subsidiary presence in host markets and not just portfolio capital
(Goldberg 2004). Indeed, the statistical findings in chapter 3 indicate that
large cross-border loan exposures of global banks that do not have an affiliate presence in an emerging market and are solely providers of cross-border
bank credit are associated with increased risk premium. By contrast, the
presence of multinational banks as foreign strategic investors (investors
that manage the banks) reduces risk. The analysis also shows that lending
through local subsidiaries of multinational banks has proven to be more
stable in times of crisis than direct cross-border lending. The moral hazard

argument, however, would not have predicted that credibility outcomes associated with global banks as external creditors would be different from the ones associated with global banks as foreign strategic owners.

More generally, some may find objectionable the claim that multinational banks are "prestigious," particularly in the post-2008 crisis world.[14] Historically, since the Latin American debt crises of the 1980s, global banks seem to have miscalculated and heightened the risks of lending to developing countries and generated ruinous boom-and-bust cycles of foreign lending. During the boom phase, the banks became euphoric about the future and less risk-averse, and herd behavior amplified the capital-inflow bonanza.[15] When random events drew attention to the previously ignored risks, banks suddenly became extremely cautious in their lending, which precipitated the panic and the crisis. After the sudden stop in lending, the very global banks that caused the crisis in the first place were bailed out by taxpayers. As this book shows, however, multinational banks can provide an insurance mechanism against "sudden stops" of capital (large drops in capital flows) (Calvo 1998) and panic in financial markets. Indeed, for all the worries about global banks, their liquidity support during the 2008 global crisis increased banking stability in emerging countries.

It is also worth noting that there may be two different types of bank reputations.[16] The first is a general reputation among the interested public that is related to transparency and ethical behavior. The second is the professional reputation of global banks among peers that is important for currency and other types of financial risks. It is plausible to assume that a club mentality exists with regard to the reputations of multinational banks in international financial circles. By this logic, even though large multinational banks may suffer a decline in reputation in the eye of the public and big fines may be levied against them, their reputation among participants in the financial market can remain intact.

The moral hazard argument does not represent a threat to the inferences in the analyses of this book. The use of the count ratio of foreign to domestic banks as the principal measure of foreign bank presence should alleviate the fears that a single large systemically important multinational bank with a large market share can provide the biggest credibility boost because of expectations of international bailouts. Instead, my analysis suggests that the entry of each reputable multinational bank can be a vote of confidence that signals a government's commitment to sound economic policies.

Overall, I argue and empirically demonstrate that as shrewd assessors of risk and drivers of improved transparency and governance in the host banking system, foreign banks can directly improve monetary credibility independent of moral hazard. If the presence of large global banks was associated only with expectations of international bailouts, we would not have observed these benefits in the financial systems of emerging markets.

On Selection and Endogeneity

One might also argue that multinational banks decide to enter countries with responsible governments and good institutions. In other words, foreign banks enter a market only after they feel confident that a government will provide a safe environment for long-term investments. Therefore, examining the effect of foreign banks on credibility outcomes does bring up concerns about reverse causation. I recognize the theoretical possibility that multinational banks may be motivated to establish affiliates in countries with more credible institutions and monetary regimes. Nonetheless, an increased presence of foreign banks reinforces a host country's monetary credibility. There are many arguments about the benefits foreign banks bring; for example, they are seen as promoting institutional and regulatory reforms in local financial systems and as disciplining the monetary and fiscal policies of host-country governments (Goldberg 2004; Mishkin 2006).

Because credibility can be both a cause and a consequence of foreign bank presence, disentangling the nature of the relationship between the two can be difficult. I address the problem of reverse causation in chapter 3 using an instrumental-variable approach. In chapters 4 through 6 I further attempt to disentangle the consequences from the determinants of foreign bank presence through qualitative evidence from case studies that shows the independent effect of foreign banks on credibility. The existing literature identifies several factors that influence location decisions of foreign banks, including host-country economic growth and the degree of efficiency of local financial institutions (Focarelli and Pozzolo 2001), information costs and regulations (Buch 2003), and geographical, cultural, trade, and investment ties between home and host countries (Brealey and Kaplanis 1996; Focarelli and Pozzolo 2005). When a multinational bank decides to invest in a particular host country, it does not appear to take into consideration the credibility of its monetary regime. My interviews with senior executives at large European multinational banks also support and give credence to the claim that causality runs from the presence of foreign banks to monetary credibility, not the other way around.

Defining the Credibility of a Monetary Regime

It is useful to start the conceptual discussion with the definition of a monetary regime. I follow Rose's (2014) conceptualization, in which a fixed exchange rate regime has a well-defined monetary policy while a flexible regime does not. How do market participants express their confidence in a country and its monetary regime? A credible monetary regime reduces the premium that countries are charged to borrow in international markets. This premium, which measures the risk market participants face, has two components: currency risk and country risk (Edwards 1986; Domowitz, Glen, and Madhavan 1998). When assessing the credibility of monetary regimes, some researchers focus on currency risk while others examine country risk.

Currency risk pertains to market perceptions regarding the probability of currency devaluation. The magnitude of the anticipated devaluation of the nominal exchange rate or the obstacles to devaluation are embodied in the nature of the exchange rate regime. In the modern era, a variety of alternative exchange rate regimes can be arranged along a spectrum by the degree of fixity, from a full float to currency union (Frankel 1999; Bordo 2003). At the fixed-rate end of the spectrum is the option of a currency union in which members share a common currency, as in the eurozone. In currency board arrangements, a country retains a separate currency but only when it is fully backed by hard currency reserves. Intermediate regimes, or soft pegs, run from adjustable pegs (in which the nominal exchange rate is fixed but governments can periodically adjust the parity) to crawling pegs (in which the peg is regularly reset in a series of devaluations) to basket pegs (in which the exchange rate is fixed in terms of a weighted basket of foreign currencies) to target zones or bands (in which the nominal exchange rate is allowed to fluctuate within a band while the center of the band is a fixed rate). Flexible regimes are divided into two groups. In managed floats, the central bank sporadically intervenes in foreign exchange markets by buying or selling foreign exchange reserves. At the opposite end of the spectrum are free floats, in which monetary authorities allow the value of the foreign exchange rate to be determined in the market.[17]

Hard pegs—currency boards, dollarization, and currency unions—eliminate exchange rate fluctuations and decrease the probability of devaluation because the legal framework makes it difficult to change the rules of the monetary regime (Bleaney, Lee, and Lloyd 2013). As a consequence, hard pegs should reduce or even eliminate the currency risk premium and hence lower domestic interest rates. This is not because of changes in the behavior of monetary authorities following the irrevocable fixing of exchange rates (for instance by joining a monetary union), but is rather the immediate impact of pegging on the beliefs of market participants (Ravenna 2012).

Only a handful of studies look at the currency-risk premium as an indicator of the credibility of a monetary regime (Schmukler and Servén 2002; Mitchener and Weidenmier 2009). Currency risk can be measured through the differentials between short-term interest rates on local and foreign currency credits of the same maturity offered in the same market (Schmukler and Servén 2002). Fixed exchange rate regimes that financial markets do not consider to be perfectly credible cause domestic interest rates to move independently of foreign ones (Bleaney, Lee, and Lloyd 2013).[18] Inflation differential is another potential measure of currency risk (Bleaney, Lee, and Lloyd 2013). A low inflation differential relative to the anchor currency indicates a more credible monetary regime.

The country-risk premium is associated with the risk that a country will default on its debt. Sovereign bond yields reflect market perceptions concerning the country and returns on investments. There are common factors in foreign exchange and sovereign debt markets, but there are also differences. Movements in foreign exchange markets anticipate inflation. Movements in sovereign credit markets primarily take into account political risk (Bailey and Chung 1995). It is important to note that a lower currency-risk premium translates into a lower country-risk premium and thus a lower cost of capital (Edwards 2003, 55). Country-risk premium, measured by sovereign bond yield spreads, has been studied more extensively (Edwards 1986; Eichengreen and Mody 1998; Mauro, Sussman, and Yafeh 2002). A few studies explore the relationship between the currency-risk premium and the country-risk premium (Domowitz, Glen, and Madhavan 1998). Recall Bordo and Rockoff's (1996) finding that the gold standard lowered the sovereign default risk of its members. By contrast, countries that frequently suspended their membership in the gold standard suffered reputational costs by reneging on exchange rate commitments, and these costs were reflected in a higher risk premium on their bonds. In subsequent chapters, I use these measures of country and currency risk to test the predictions of my theory of foreign bank advantage.

Fix or Float?

Rose (2011) notes that choosing an exchange rate regime is tantamount to choosing a monetary policy.[19] An explanation of the credibility of the monetary regime thus requires an understanding of decisions of governments regarding exchange rate regimes.[20] A government makes tradeoffs between exchange rate (currency) stability and monetary autonomy (flexibility) across the spectrum of exchange rate regimes (Frankel 1995; Edwards 1996). According to optimum currency area theory—a central theoretical framework that informs our understanding of what informs the decisions countries make about exchange rate regimes—the benefits of fixed exchange rate regimes and monetary unification include transparent prices, lower transaction costs, and greater certainty for investors.[21] A fixed exchange rate regime encourages monetary discipline associated with lower rates of inflation. Restrictions on governments, imposed by the objective of maintaining a peg, discipline policymakers and discourage their propensity toward erratic policies (such as monetary financing of fiscal deficits) (Eichengreen and Rose 1998). In addition to monetary stability, fixed exchange rate regimes are associated with currency stability. Fixing reduces transaction costs and exchange rate risk for cross-border exchanges and foreign investments, thus increase trade and capital flows. For example, the positive impact of exchange rate stability on international trade was provided as the main justification for monetary integration in Europe.[22]

The weakness of a fixed exchange rate regime is a loss of monetary autonomy and thus a loss of flexibility in using interest rates to achieve domestic economic goals (such as those related to employment and growth) and to respond to exogenous shocks.[23] Fixed exchange rate regimes also reduce the ability of policymakers to respond to distributional pressures of interest groups, their constituencies. The monetary authorities cannot devalue currency to address the demands of exporters for a more competitive currency or lower interest rates to satisfy debtors (Frieden and Stein 2001).[24] In a world of full capital mobility, fixed exchange rate regimes cannot be sustained without giving up an independent monetary policy according to the "impossible trinity" hypothesis (or the Mundell-Fleming model of an open economy) (Mundell 1961; Fleming 1962; Obstfeld and Taylor 2002;

Obstfeld, Schambaugh, and Taylor 2005). Yet when monetary policy is credible, countries can gain short-term flexibility to pursue some (albeit limited) countercyclical monetary policies (Svensson 1994).

Why Emerging Markets?

The dynamics of reputations I analyze here are most relevant in emerging markets. The similar level of economic development of these countries makes it possible to compare them with one another. For the most part, the monetary authorities of these countries lack credibility and have only limited access to international markets. Compared to developed countries, emerging markets suffer from more pronounced adverse effects of currency volatility on trade, high-liability dollarization, and high exchange rate pass-through (the effect of exchange rate changes on inflation) (Vives 2006; Eichengreen and Hausmann 1999). Fighting against high inflation and establishing credibility within international markets have been the top priorities of policymakers in most emerging markets for most of their histories. Poor developing nations and war-torn countries are not included in the sample I analyze because they do not issue their debt publicly and because they are less attractive to multinational banks as investment opportunities.

Historically, the important distinction between core (developed) and peripheral (emerging and developing) countries has been "financial maturity" (e.g., sound public finance, healthy banking system, developed securities market) (Bordo and Flandreau 2003). This is evidenced by the inability of developing countries to issue bonds denominated in domestic currency, referred to as the "original sin" (Eichengreen and Hausman 1999). Interestingly, Bordo and Flandreau (2003) observe that the group of "peripheral" countries today is similar to the pre-1914 period. It includes emerging market countries in Latin America, central and eastern Europe, Russia, and, to a certain degree, Asia (with the exception of Japan). Emerging markets are powerful test cases for many of the theories about international monetary relations.

I test my credibility theory by combining statistical analyses of more than eighty emerging markets with comparative case studies of credibility building in Estonia, Bulgaria, the Czech Republic, Poland, Argentina, and Ukraine. I also conducted extensive semistructured interviews with more than 120 central bankers, commercial and investment bankers, finance ministers and other government officials, local academics, and staff members in international institutions, credit rating agencies, and think tanks in Poland, the Czech Republic, Bulgaria, Estonia, and Austria, as well as in Brussels, Washington, Paris, and London. I also draw upon a wide variety of other source materials, including archival material; internal documents from central banks, commercial banks, and international institutions; and other primary written material in five languages.

I made decisions about which countries in emerging Europe to study based on several methodological criteria. Eastern European countries started the postcommunist transformation in the early 1990s with common legacies of authoritarianism and central planning.[25] In addition to political and economic reforms, nation and state building have been central to post-communist development. Virtually all Eastern European states gained national independence, either from the Soviet bloc or from domination by a federal state. These states were unknown entities on the international stage in the early 1990s, although a handful of them had some credit history (record of repayment) in international markets. The majority of Eastern European countries thus faced a severe credibility deficit in international markets.[26] At the same time, many of these countries are small and open economies and thus have been highly dependent on international markets. These are also the countries that have faced several external constraints and pressures from international institutions (such as the IMF) that influenced the policy autonomy of their governments to a great extent. Under the circumstances, establishing an international reputation was the top priority of most policymakers in Eastern Europe in order to stabilize domestic economies and gain access to foreign capital.

Eastern European countries emerged from communist regimes with authoritarian political systems and without clear property rights and fundamental market institutions. The development of financial systems in this region provides a quasi-experimental setting because all Eastern European countries started the postcommunist transition process with a financial system in which money supply and credit allocation functions were located within a single institution. Consequently, they went through a transformation from a state-owned monobank system to a market-oriented banking system. In addition, emerging Europe has witnessed the most significant growth of foreign ownership in local banking systems of all emerging market countries.[27]

The combination of several methods of inquiry in this book means that deficiencies in one area may be compensated for by other modes. This makes the research rigorous, testable, and generalizable. Statistical analysis can establish the empirical validity of the theoretical assumptions, but without contextual knowledge it may miss key causal variables and can produce unreliable conclusions. Qualitative analysis can generate a case for causation in a few cases by tracing the causal processes, but it is difficult to establish the generality of its conclusions or to refute false hypotheses.

Outline of the Book

The credibility theory I advance explains how countries establish reputation on the international stage in relation to the presence of reputable multinational banks. The story of credibility building is told in seven chapters. Chapter 2 lays out the theoretical underpinnings of the central argument. I first discuss in detail the problem of information asymmetries in financial markets. I then explain how multinational banks can address this problem. When banks have the ability to both address information asymmetries and punish bad behavior, international audiences perceive them as providing a credible commitment device. I then examine the three mechanisms of foreign bank influence: foreign banks increasing financial transparency through stricter accounting standards and disclosure rules; foreign regulatory structures acting as surrogates for local authorities; and foreign parent banks serving as the international lenders of last resort. In this chapter I also introduce alternative perspectives on credibility in international finance that depict reputation formation as a result of either domestic institutions or membership in international institutions. I test these perspectives in subsequent chapters.

Chapter 3 presents the statistical tests of the predictions of my theory and the leading rival hypotheses. The battery of statistical tests I conducted provides evidence to support my credibility theory, that the credibility of a country's monetary regime is enhanced when foreign ownership of its banking sector is substantial. This finding holds up against the two alternate hypotheses discussed earlier. The presence of foreign banks has an independent effect on a country's reputation in international markets, as measured in terms of both currency risk and country risk. This effect is not the result of financial reforms that were undertaken before the foreign bank entered an economy. I also use instrumental variables to measure factors that push foreign banks to enter emerging markets. This chapter further explores cases in which credibility building does not occur by focusing on the reputation of the parent bank. By presenting a mix of statistical analysis and an illustration of Ukraine's struggle to establish international credibility, I demonstrate that less reputable multinational banks do not significantly influence the credibility of their host countries.

Chapters 4 through 6 present case studies that delve into the key mechanisms through which monetary credibility is established. The empirical analysis in these chapters is based on semistructured interviews and other primary sources of evidence. In chapters 4 and 5, I demonstrate the importance of foreign banks to the commitment of governments to monetary regimes of currency boards and inflation targeting. The case studies show that the adoption of currency boards and inflation targeting alone was not sufficient to bring down inflation expectations and interest rate differentials. Only when foreign banks emerged on the domestic scene as significant players did the uncertainty premium decline. For each country study, I evaluate the evolution of the domestic banking structures, central banking, and international credibility qualitatively as part of the historical narrative that compares and contrasts financial integration both before and after multinational banks entered a country. My analysis indicates that although governments and societies in emerging Europe in search of capital were generally receptive to foreign financiers, they also differed in terms of their receptiveness to foreign presence. For instance, while Estonia engaged in a radical exercise in opening its banking sector from the outset of its transition, the governments of Bulgaria and the Czech Republic were reluctant to open their markets to foreign banks until they experienced severe banking and currency crises in the second half of the 1990s. Furthermore, case studies capture the theoretically important variation in the reputation of multinational banks, ranging from reputable banks from the Nordic countries, Austria, and Italy to nonreputable Russian banks.

Chapter 4 traces the different trajectories of Estonia and Bulgaria to analyze their experiences with establishing credible currency boards. Estonia can be used as the paradigmatic case of a newly established country in which the transformation of the financial system from state-owned to predominantly foreign-owned rendered the government's commitment to a currency board credible over time. In contrast, financial market participants demanded a significant currency-risk premium from the Bulgarian government. Neither the left nor the right factions of the Bulgarian government proved able to cut their ties with incumbent banks, and thus Bulgarian financial policies lacked credibility. Market participants decided to cover their risks until the government let foreign banks in following the severe financial crisis in 1996–97. This shift in policy signaled a government commitment to financial and monetary stability. In both countries, foreign banks have built the foundations for a strong and resilient banking system by increasing transparency in financial reporting and strengthening banking regulation, supervision, and risk management. The resulting financial stability is the source of the credibility of the currency boards in these countries.

Chapter 5 looks at Poland and the Czech Republic, which started the postcommunist transition with more favorable international reputations than most countries in Eastern Europe. The chapter shows how reputation changes when governments act contrary to their perceived type and how reputation can be restored. The Czech case illustrates this dynamic particularly well. The Czech center-right governments squandered their initial credibility by pursuing a national model of capitalism that favored domestic state-owned banks over foreign capital in banking. The consequence of the resulting banking sector instability was the devastating financial crisis in 1997 that led to a devaluation of and then the collapse of the fixed exchange rate regime. The Czech case also shows that an independent central bank is a necessary but not a sufficient condition for the credibility of monetary commitments. Although the Czech central bank was internationally praised for its high degree of independence from the government, its monetary authority did not match the quality of its regulatory oversight.

The Polish route to reputation enhancement was not linear either. The Polish government took a positive stance toward foreign investments in the banking sector at the outset of transition but then reversed its position before again opening the banking sector to foreign banks. The case of Poland shows that countries that behave as expected should not suffer much reputational loss if they do not fully liberalize their banking sectors. In contrast to the Czech case, the central bank in Poland, though independent, had a firm domestic political mandate for its mission to ensure national competitiveness. In both countries, however, foreign banks made it possible to build the credibility of inflation-targeting regimes by fostering confidence in the stability of the banking sector. Foreign banks weakened the political influence of incumbent state-owned banks, improved information sharing, reduced the risks banks took, and improved national financial regulation. In

Poland, as in Bulgaria, the entry of foreign banks coincided with institutional reforms that increased the autonomy of their central banks.

Chapter 6 focuses on the third channel foreign banks use to exert influence: as an international lender of last resort. The chapter examines the implications of a multinational banking presence on the credibility of their hosts during boom and bust phases in both host and home countries. I look at the 2001 financial crisis in Argentina as a crisis in the host country. I also examine the 2008 global financial crisis that erupted in developed countries, where the headquarters of most multinational banks are located. Through a cross-regional investigation and a detailed analysis of these crises episodes, we can gauge the importance of foreign banks as lenders of last resort for their affiliates in emerging Europe, Latin America, and Asia. I show how access to capital, liquidity, and funding from the parent bank may vary depending on the business model that a multinational bank pursues, the extent of foreign bank ownership, and, in some instances, the logic of politics. Cross-regional comparisons between emerging Europe and Latin America illustrates that foreign banks may matter more under certain circumstances (such as political integration of emerging European states into the European Union) than in others.

Taken together, the quantitative and qualitative evidence in this study presents a novel approach to analysis of reputation building in the emerging market democracies facing severe credibility deficits. The evidence points overwhelmingly in one direction: global banks profoundly influenced the monetary credibility of emerging markets by increasing their financial stability and reducing the vulnerability of their banking systems. Chapter 7 discusses the theoretical and policy implications of these findings and identifies the main avenues for further research.

CHAPTER 2
A Theory of Credibility through Financial Integration

Governments of countries with a history of chronic inflation and new or weak institutions find it difficult to signal a credible commitment to sound economic policies. As Gros (2003) observes, these countries can fall into a "low liquidity trap" that is associated with a high risk premium in the form of high interest rates, which subsequently results in high debt burden. Under these circumstances, policymakers may be easily tempted to reduce the real value of the debt through surprise inflation. This will further increase the risk premium and will eventually lead to a spiral of rising interest rates and rising inflation.

This chapter lays out a theory of the advantage of foreign bank presence for credibility building with international audiences. What causes bond investors and currency traders to take countries more seriously when reputable multinational banks have penetrated their financial sectors? In environments of high uncertainty, market participants face the problem of information asymmetry and have difficulty detecting whether policymakers will adhere to announced policies. Market participants cope with the problem of information asymmetry by looking for transparent signals of the probability that a government will inflate the economy or devalue the currency. When a country announces that a reputable multinational bank has invested in its economy, it borrows the reputation of that bank and its home country to some extent. In my theory, foreign banks not only influence third-party perceptions but also serve as a form of credible commitment. A foreign bank also becomes a political actor with distinct economic interests vis-à-vis the local economy and can thereby have a direct effect on a government's commitment to sound monetary and financial policies. Currency risk stems from uncertainty, and a substantial presence of reputable foreign banks creates a more predictable environment.

I suggest three plausible mechanisms for how foreign banks influence credibility. Multinational banks increase transparency in local financial systems through better accounting standards and disclosure rules, which allows better monitoring of economic policies. Foreign banks transfer regulation and supervision from their home country to the host country and contribute to the soundness of the financial system of their hosts. Finally, foreign bank entry involves the transfer of the role of lender of last resort from the local central bank to the foreign parent bank.

Before laying out the details of my theory of credibility through financial integration, I outline what multinational banks typically do and then examine the events and debates that have contributed to an increased interest in global banking among academics and policymakers. I then examine the standard models of monetary policy credibility and discuss the problems of asymmetric information and time-inconsistency in monetary policy. Following that, I define the specific mechanisms that link global banks to improvements in macroeconomic performance. Finally, I distinguish my theory from alternative perspectives on credibility in international finance. I consider theories that focus on domestic institutions. I also discuss research that explores whether delegation of competencies to international organizations increases the credibility of member states.

Multinational Banks: Why the Interest?

A multinational bank is a type of multinational corporation,[1] and multinational banking contains an element of foreign direct investment.[2] An important aspect of multinational banking is geographical diversification, which can help reduce the vulnerability of multinational banks to developments in their home country and increase their profit margins. Multinational banks are divided into three groups: global banks, regional banks, and semi-international banks. Both global and regional banks have less than 50 percent of their business in their home country. Whereas global banks do the largest portion of their international business in various countries of the world, regional banks concentrate their international activities in the region in which they are located. Semi-international banks do between 50 and 75 percent of their business in the home country (Schoenmaker 2013, 50).

Multinational banks follow two main models of banking: the centralized (integrated) model and the decentralized model. In the centralized model, the top management makes almost all the key decisions for the entire banking group; Citigroup, Deutsche Bank, and ING are typical examples. In the decentralized model, the bank's holding company owns separate bank subsidiaries in different host countries and the subsidiaries have substantial autonomy; HSBC and Santander are examples (Schoenmaker 2013, 38).[3]

History and Trends in Multinational Banking

The rise of multinational banking is closely linked to the development of international trade.[4] In the fifteenth and sixteenth centuries, the Medici, the bank of the famous Italian banking family, had branches in Avignon, Brugge, Geneva, and London. It can be considered the first international bank (Schoenmaker 2013, 34). The Medici provided the financial services needed for international trade. The first big wave of multinational banking in the nineteenth and early twentieth centuries was associated with the expansion of colonial firms and was concentrated heavily in developing countries. Britain, the largest colonial power, dominated this wave. In 1830, British banks opened branches in their colonies in Australasia, the Caribbean, sub-Saharan Africa, and North America. In the 1880s, French and German banks started to expand abroad.[5] Often large banks would expand abroad by practicing the "follow the client" principle, thus supporting the activities of their national industrial champions. A good example is the expansion of Deutsche Bank in Asia and Latin America in the 1890s (Schoenmaker 2013, 35). The second wave took place in the late 1950s and was concentrated in developed countries. It was linked to the emergence of Eurodollar markets and the expansion of financial centers such as New York and London. U.S. banks led the second wave of multinational banking. But during the 1980s, Japanese banks became more and more prominent.

Multinational banks saw their expansion abroad as originating in their search for yield, international risk sharing, and portfolio diversification following regulatory changes or as a result of trade and investment agreements (Goldberg 2009). The presence of foreign banks in emerging markets has allowed these banks to take advantage of higher profits.[6] Multinational banks face saturated and highly competitive banking markets in their developed-country home economies. In addition, in many countries, the notion of an open banking sector is politically contested; many countries still have highly protectionist regimes. This limits opportunities for multinational banks to expand internationally.[7]

Why has concern about multinational banks reached new heights today? The presence of foreign banks has sharply increased over the past two decades.[8] In contrast with the previous two waves of foreign bank expansion, the scope and speed of this latest wave is quite remarkable. By the end of 2006, almost nine hundred foreign banks had a presence in the developing world and controlled combined assets of more than $1.2 trillion (World Bank 2008, 86). From 1995 to 2009, the number of foreign banks increased by 72 percent in emerging markets and by 122 percent in developing countries (Claessens and van Horen 2012, 11).[9]

As I will show in chapter 6, while aggregate international banking statistics suggest a small decline in cross-border banking operations after the 2008 global financial crisis, individual bank data show a different picture. Most large banks have preserved a strong international orientation, and some have even expanded their international business after the crisis. For example, Citigroup increased its international operations from 39 percent in 2000 to 64 percent in 2011 (Schoenmaker 2013, 53).

What Do Multinational Banks Do?

Multinational banks are involved in various activities, such as trading in foreign securities markets, borrowing and lending in foreign currencies, and financing international trade. Traditionally, global banks that engaged in cross-border expansion were looking to follow their customers abroad (mainly multinational corporations) to provide them with financial services.[10] Facing growing competitive pressures in their home markets, multinational banks sought to penetrate foreign retail banking markets to increase their profitability and diversify risks (Martinez-Diaz 2009, 24). Multinational banks play an important role in financial intermediation in emerging and developing countries; they got control of nearly 50 percent of market shares, on average, in these countries in terms of loans, deposits, and profits (Claessens and van Horen 2012, 5). Multinational banks have been driving foreign currency lending (mostly to corporate clients) because of their easier access to foreign wholesale funding (Brown and DeHaas 2012). Prior to the 2008 global financial crisis, cross-border lending amounted to $515 billion and accounted for 38 percent of gross private capital flows to emerging markets (Herrmann and Mihaljek 2013, 480).

Multinational banks have a great potential to influence the national economies of their hosts. Consequently, one of the liveliest debates in global banking involves the implications of the growing foreign bank presence in developing countries. The literature presents diverging views of foreign banks. The supporters of global banking argue that foreign banks can accelerate the development of a host country's financial market by increasing competition and improving the efficiency of the banking sector, by stimulating reforms in banking supervision and regulation, and by improving access to international markets. Critics contend that foreign banks can destabilize a host country's banking sector by exposing it to credit shocks transmitted from their home countries, by threatening the survival of local banks that are unable to withstand fierce competition from these new entrants, and by cherry-picking the most profitable customers while squeezing the majority of domestic firms and customers out of credit markets (see, e.g., Detragiache, Tressel, and Gupta 2008; Cull and Martínez Pería 2010).[11]

Although the number of foreign banks in emerging and developing economies has grown steadily in the past decades, the effects are far from understood. Over the past two decades, foreign banks have emerged as significant players in many less-developed economies. Yet the literature on multinational banking remains silent about how foreign bank entry affects how the credibility of host governments and their policies are perceived in international markets. The subsequent sections examine how multinational banks can improve a country's monetary credibility.

Sources of Credibility Problems

As Rose (2011, 669) notes, "acquiring monetary credibility is difficult, especially for poor countries." Inflation expectations depend on the market's perception of the type of government and the degree to which a government is tempted to inflate its economy (Holden and Vikøren 1996). It follows that there are two main sources of credibility problems in monetary policy: information asymmetries and time inconsistency (policymakers can improve welfare by announcing one policy and then implementing a different policy after people have made their decisions based on the announcement).[12] International market agents cannot directly observe the identity and preferences of governments. Thus a government with a preference for low inflation has an incentive to eliminate this information asymmetry quickly by signaling its true identity. I treat government as a single entity: the composite of the authorities who are responsible for determining monetary policy and managing the economy. This convenient abstraction is not uncommon in models of monetary policy. I recognize that a central bank is in charge of monetary policy and that a separate authority is responsible for other aspects of macroeconomic policies (e.g., fiscal policy). But I agree with Alesina and Drazen (1991), who argue that it is not realistic to assume that an autonomous central bank can set monetary policy without regard for the fiscal authority's objectives in economically and politically unstable countries. Monetary policy can never be completely free from political influence. A government grants the central bank autonomy in the first place and can abolish it if the monetary authority conducts policies that the government significantly disagrees with (Blackburn and Christensen 1989, 33).

I contend that where great uncertainties about a government's intentions exist, the entry of reputable foreign banks may convincingly signal that the government is determined to carry through on its policy commitments. Governments that are serious about stabilizing their economies commit to both nominal exchange rate targets (such as currency boards) and openness to foreign investments in banking. The key insight of my argument is that international market participants make inferences based on the attributes of the reputable global banks that enter or are already present in the economy in question. The entry or presence of a foreign bank indicates a government's intention to pursue sound monetary and financial policies.

Credibility has also been identified with time inconsistency. Governments encounter a fundamental difficulty in establishing the credibility of their announced policies because of their short-term incentives to engineer surprise monetary expansions in order to generate a temporary boost in employment and in seigniorage revenues (government revenue received through creating money). A government without reputational capital cannot convince markets by proclamations alone when previous attempts to stabilize inflation have failed. I argue that foreign banks are a credible external mechanism that ensures compliance with the rules. My theory of credibility thus involves a signaling factor and the effect of foreign banks in bringing about credible changes in monetary policy and in the banking regulations of host nations.[13] It would be wrong to assume that the "seal of approval" granted by entry of foreign banks is independent of the actual impact of foreign banks on the policies of their hosts.[14]

Asymmetric Information

In standard models of monetary policy, assessing the credibility of monetary commitments requires making assumptions about the government's type on the basis of the relative weight it puts on low inflation and unemployment. Under the assumption of incomplete information about the policymaker's preferences, credibility of monetary policy is a measure of the private sector's belief that the policymaker is committed to low inflation (type 1) (Blackburn and Christensen 1989, 19–20).

Uncertainty about a policymaker's resolve to combat inflation is a crucial consideration in theories on monetary credibility (Barro and Gordon 1983; Backus and Driffill 1985).[15] Keefer and Stasavage (2002) point to two types of information asymmetries that complicate the efforts of governments to establish the credibility of their monetary commitments. First, private agents have incomplete information about governments' preferences and thus about their incentives to act opportunistically and renege on their monetary commitments.[16] Second, as a consequence, it is difficult to determine whether national governments will carry out their announced policies. Private agents thus look for clear signals of likelihood that a government will not inflate its economy or devalue its currency.

Asymmetric information and uncertainty are more acute in emerging markets. Monetary institutions are immature in these economies, so market participants will have limited confidence in the technical abilities and commitment of governments to implement politically unpopular anti-inflationary policies (Grabel 2000).[17] There is no doubt that policymakers in these countries have a strong incentive to signal their policy preferences to international markets in order to eliminate this uncertainty. Yet because governments in many countries lack credible domestic institutions and have histories of failed economic policies, they find it difficult to signal credible policy commitments. As a consequence, assessments of credibility by agents in international markets can be particularly subjective in environments of high uncertainty, depending on the agents' preconceived ideas.

Flandreau and Flores (2009, 2012) note that because of the scarcity of information about governments in nineteenth-century sovereign debt markets, investors relied on the reputation of prestigious bank underwriters to guide their investments. These underwriters had monopoly power and the capacity to implement conditional lending and to punish defaulters. The leading creditor banks of the nineteenth century (such as Rothschild or

Barings) "owned a 'brand' that could grant market access on favorable terms" (Flandreau and Flores 2009, 647). In their subsequent work, Flandreau and Flores (2012, 223) remark,

> The world we consider is one in which investors use the signals from certain prestigious brands to make inferences about countries' types. Investors cannot tell which countries' debt would be a good investment, but they know that credible delegated monitors have that knowledge and the capacity to enforce; hence investors react not to news about a country's behavior but rather to the presence (or absence!) of a prestigious underwriter.

My analysis focuses on multinational banks as strategic investors. Can multinational banks help reduce the uncertainty that is commonplace in financial markets? In emerging-market countries, where information is scarce and unreliable, investors pay attention to signals and events—such as the entry of a multinational bank—that can be easily interpreted. I contend that reputable multinational banks can be a powerful driver of market sentiment in these high-uncertainty environments. Governments can use foreign banks to signal their commitment to sound monetary and financial policies. The entry of these banks into emerging markets is thus a visible and public signal of the sustainability of a country's policy commitments.

Time Inconsistency

In standard models of monetary policy, credibility is interpreted as the extent to which economic actors' beliefs about future economic policies are consistent with the program a government has publicly announced (see Kydland and Prescott 1977; Barro and Gordon 1983; Drazen and Masson 1994). According to these rational-expectation theories, the fundamental problem of credibility is time inconsistency. The logic of a time-inconsistency problem in monetary policy is as follows: Policymakers may renege on their promise of maintaining low inflation policies in order to achieve short-term improvements in employment and growth. Because private actors anticipate this behavior, the attempt of policymakers to create inflationary surprise is neutralized and the economic outcome is higher inflation without additional output. Thus the rational expectations of private actors introduce an inflationary bias into wage bargaining and price setting.

In many emerging markets, the source of a credibility problem is the inability of policymakers to precommit to low inflation (Blackburn and Christensen 1989). Much of the literature on this focuses on the preferences of the policymaker trying to signal toughness and commitment to anti-inflationary policies to build reputation (Backus and Driffill 1985). The problem of policy credibility may arise when the current government discounts the future and implements suboptimal macroeconomic policies.[18] The government may have incentives to obtain short-term gains by reneging on previously announced policies. Obstfeld (1996) argues that in the Barro-Gordon model, it is likely that a policymaker will have an incentive to devalue the currency in order to generate a higher inflation rate. Assessing policy credibility, therefore, involves market participants' perceptions about the viability and effectiveness of announced policies and policymakers' commitment to sustaining them. When market participants doubt that policymakers are committed to following through on sound macroeconomic policies, they will request compensation for this risk.

A Fixed Exchange Rate Regime as a Solution to Time Inconsistency

One prominent institutional mechanism that governments use to establish the credibility of their monetary policy involves fixing the value of their national currency to that of another country that has a credible monetary regime. Introducing a fixed exchange rate regime as a nominal anchor involves an effort to import the credibility of low-inflation policies from a reputable foreign central bank (Giavazzi and Pagano 1988; Fratiani and von Hagen 1992; Alesina and Barro 2002). Fixing the exchange rate ties the hands of the domestic central bank. It is equivalent to indirectly appointing a foreign central banker. It can increase the credibility of a government's announcements of anti-inflatory policies and reinforce its commitment to macroeconomic stabilization.[19] In this respect, an exchange rate peg is seen as a form of credible commitment in countries with a legacy of high inflation and previously unsuccessful attempts to achieve price stability. These theoretical insights have informed policy reforms in many developing countries that have been advised to adopt fixed exchange rate regimes in order to import credibility from abroad (Calvo and Mishkin 2003).[20]

It is easy to see how this logic could make the exchange rate peg a form of a credible commitment. When private actors do not have complete information about the true preferences of a government, they may have doubts about the government's willingness or ability to halt inflation (Canavan and

Tommasi 1997, 102). A fixed exchange rate regime is a transparent and easily verifiable target that makes it easier for market participants to evaluate
whether the government has deviated from an announced commitment
(Canavan and Tommasi 1997). The adoption of a rigid parity, such as a currency board, that legally requires a country not to print local currency without backing in hard currency reserves is reassuring to international markets. The abandonment of a peg is a highly visible indicator of a government's
inflationary agenda. Such a move is typically associated with high political
costs (Broz 2002). As Sachs, Tornell, and Velasco (1996, 8) write, "Governments that commit to a peg and then renege on the promise typically face
costs—loss of pride, voter disapproval, maybe even removal from office—
that need not be proportional to the size of the devaluation."

Merely fixing the exchange rate does not solve the credibility problem
vis-à-vis international markets, however, because a weak government is
more likely to renege on its commitment than to carry out a strict monetary
policy (De Grauwe 1992, 53). Since economic actors expect this, they do
not take seriously the commitment to low inflation and a fixed exchange
rate rule of a government that lacks credibility. Countries with poor institutional quality, weak protection of property rights, and high levels of corruption often lack the capability to maintain macroeconomic stability. These
countries are more likely to renege on their official international monetary
obligations (Alesina and Wagner 2006).

Although the empirical research on the topic is not extensive, the available evidence on the credibility effect of fixed exchange rate regimes is quite
revealing (Eichengreen and Hausman 1999; Guidotti and Végh 1999; Carlson and Valev 2001). Exchange rate pegs, even currency boards, suffer from
the "incomplete credibility" problem: they seldom achieve full credibility
even after delivering low inflation and currency stability for many years
(Valev and Carlson 2007).[21] This is particularly true when governments do
not have an established reputation for a sound monetary policy. Not even
the gold standard could assure credibility for all its adherents. Eichengreen
(1992) reminds us that the credibility of the gold standard was significantly
greater in the core European countries than at the periphery. Most scholars
agree that joining the gold standard did not buy immediate credibility for
peripheral countries such as Chile, Greece, Portugal, Italy, and Russia,
which continued to face relatively high short-term interest rates and large
currency premiums long after they joined the gold bloc (Bordo and Flandreau 2003; Mitchener and Weidenmier 2009). Chile is a particularly in-

structive case; its decision to return to gold in 1895 was accompanied by a sharp increase in interest rates and an economic recession because its commitment to gold lacked credibility in the eyes of international markets (Subercaseaux 1926; cited in Bordo and Flandreau 2003, 436). Flandreau and Zumer (2004) raise doubts about the importance of adherence to the gold standard for country risk; they find a negligible effect of the gold standard on sovereign yields.

In all likelihood, the classic gold standard has been more credible than modern fixed exchange rate arrangements, given the ability of central banks to prioritize exchange rate parity over reducing unemployment.[22] The problem with modern currency pegs is that central banks often succumb to political pressures and abandon the peg (Obstfeld and Taylor 2003). The fixed exchange rate regime can serve as a commitment device only as long as the costs of abandoning it (higher inflation expectations and borrowing costs) exceed the benefits of engineering surprise inflation. The erosion of a fixed exchange rate regime's credibility creates inflationary expectations, and such a regime becomes unsustainable as a result.

The efficiency of a fixed regime as a target for monetary policy depends on its ability "to anchor the public's expectations of future monetary-policy adjustments" (Guisinger and Singer 2010, 316). Persistent expectations of currency devaluation in contexts, in which financial instability and high inflation is a chronic problem, is embedded in Calvo's (1986) model of "temporary stabilizations." The model accounts for the slow decline in inflation in countries that adopted exchange-rate-based stabilization programs because the expectations of market participants are conditioned by their recollections of monetary authorities' past unsuccessful efforts to reduce inflation.[23] The credibility of stabilization programs is an essential part of the success of these programs (Alesina and Drazen 1991). All in all, the absence of full credibility appears to be the norm for fixed exchange rate regimes, particularly in emerging markets (Obstfeld and Rogoff 1995). This leaves us with a puzzle. How do fixed exchange rate regimes gain credibility in the first place?

Mechanisms of Foreign Bank Influence

From this discussion, it can be extracted that the government can address its credibility deficit in monetary policy with a nominal anchor—a fixed exchange rate regime. Alternatively, the government can introduce inflation targeting as a nominal anchor in a pure floating regime.[24] Adopting the exchange rate peg can be done "overnight" (Guidotti and Végh 1999, 24). A government that lacks reputational capital, however, cannot convince international markets of its determination to remain committed to the goal of low inflation simply by announcing a nominal anchor. The challenge for a government is to convince market agents of the credibility of its monetary policy announcements.[25] This book is thus concerned with the second stage of the credibility game: how to establish the credibility of the peg by implementing financial reforms through integration with multinational banks.[26]

My credibility theory takes into account both information asymmetries and time inconsistency.[27] Lack of credibility is attributed to the uncertainty of market agents about the true preferences (or "type") of a government. Information asymmetries are more acute in emerging markets because of their histories of high inflation, their general state of political and economic instability, and their lack of reliable and transparent information about their economic policies. The entry of a reputable foreign bank into such economies can act as an information-revealing mechanism by providing and disseminating information about a government type. It is a signal that the government is a low-inflation type. Market participants can make inferences from the presence of a foreign bank about the government's type and future behavior and about the perceptions of other economic agents of that nation's future policies. From this perspective, the success of this signal depends on the commonality of interpretation of the significance of the entry of a foreign bank or banks. Scholars in international finance and banking have long championed the importance of foreign banks for ensuring all sorts of positive outcomes, from bringing new, stable sources of capital to improving the development and efficiency of host financial markets to bringing stability during periods of financial distress (see, e.g., Mishkin 2006; Goldberg 2009). The behavior of financial markets should thus reflect the thinking that foreign banks encourage better policies and institutions in their hosts. Publicizing a commitment to monetary discipline is an important psychological element of that policy's effectiveness (Lohmann 1992; Posen 1995).

A "soft" type government may, however, seek short-term gain by reneging on its announced policy. The source of the credibility problem at this stage lies in time inconsistency. Foreign banks can provide commitment mechanisms that prevent such a government from altering its policy in the period $t + 1$, thus mitigating the problem of time inconsistency. They can also impose costs directly by withdrawing their investments or by not investing. Even if the type of government is known, markets know that there may be external circumstances that could force even a "hard" type government to abandon its monetary commitments (Drazen and Masson 1994; Obstfeld 1997),[28] particularly if markets anticipate that a country's foreign exchange reserves will soon be exhausted.[29] Foreign banks, acting as private lenders of last resort, can assure market participants that a monetary regime will remain in place for the foreseeable future.

The three mechanisms of increasing transparency in local financial systems, importing home-country banking regulations and supervision, and serving as a lender of last resort highlight the impact of foreign banks on financial stability, which is as important as price stability for the credibility of monetary commitments in open economies.[30] A common goal of both those who seek monetary stability and those who seek financial stability is to prevent excessive credit expansion that may lead to inflationary pressures and asset bubbles (Schoenmaker 2013). The monetary regime cannot become fully credible if monetary policies aimed at price stability and banking regulations aimed at financial stability are at cross-purposes.[31] I now examine these three mechanisms in detail.

Transparency

Debt and financial crises in emerging markets in the 1980s and 1990s, and the 2008 global credit crisis, have underlined the importance of transparent financial reporting and have renewed interest in the role of opacity within a financial system in exacerbating shocks. One implication of opaque financial policies is inescapable: a high percentage of public debt (government bonds) ends up in the hands of banks. Governments may also use local banks as a tool for providing directed credit to their political constituencies and to underperforming sectors of the economy. The accumulation of uncollectible debt is not immediately apparent in banks' accounts. But when this debt is unveiled, it is so high that a government has no choice but to bail out a bank to prevent its failure (Gros 2003). Furthermore, a central bank without a credible commitment to price stability will have incentives to induce inflation in order to reduce the real value of nominal debt when domestic banks or enterprises face difficulties (Vives 2006). To the extent that there are information asymmetries in the market, the lack of transparency makes these countries vulnerable to highly risky investing based on rumors and on the herd instinct (Calvo and Mendoza 2000).

The presence of foreign banks can increase the transparency in the banking system, which should reduce the accumulation of debt in the balance sheets of banks (Gros 2003). Reputable multinational banks from developed countries tend to have more transparent accounts than most domestic banks in developing countries (Gros 2003, 11). Much empirical evidence suggests that foreign banks contribute to the overall development of the financial system in emerging markets by rigorously screening out bad credit risks, monitoring borrowers to avoid taking on excessive risk, and treating bad loans more aggressively (Mishkin 2006; Crystal, Dages, and Goldberg 2001).

Foreign banks do not have access to the same insider information as domestic banks because they lack a previous lending relationship with and information about potential borrowers. Therefore, as Mishkin (2006) notes, it is likely that foreign banks will be a constituency for institutional reforms in host countries aimed at improving the transparency and quality of information, including better accounting standards and disclosure requirements. More specifically, banks have an incentive to establish credit bureaus in host countries that lack transparent corporate reporting (Pagano and Jappelli 1993).[32] The available evidence indicates that foreign banks encourage the establishment of credit bureaus and improve the quality of financial reporting in host countries.[33] A credit reporting system is the institutional mechanism that mitigates information asymmetry in credit markets by helping banks collect information on borrowers from member banks or other sources (e.g., tax authorities, courts, financial reports) and evaluate the financial health of borrowers (Tsai, Chang, and Hsiao 2011, 589).[34]

Information sharing may diminish informational advantage of incumbent banks by improving knowledge of borrowers' creditworthiness and imposing market discipline in the banking system. Credit bureaus tend to reduce excessive bank lending in cases where some borrowers have developed special relationships with incumbent banks. They also discipline borrowers to repay their loans because information about defaults becomes available to all creditors (Padilla and Pagano 2000). Information sharing through credit registries and bureaus helps curtail corruption in bank lending (Barth et al. 2009) and reduces default rates (Jappelli and Pagano 2002).

Research in business finance has empirically demonstrated that information sharing among creditors also reduces risk taking and the likelihood of crises (Houston et al. 2010). When there is greater transparency within financial systems, countries benefit from financial globalization without being hurt by excessive volatility in the capital market (Gelos and Wei 2005). Transparent credit information is of paramount importance for financial stability because it makes it easier for regulatory authorities to evaluate and monitor the loan portfolios of banks and assess the associated risks (World Bank 2013). Greater transparency decreases asymmetries of information and enables market participants to monitor government policies and evaluate policy changes (Hauner, Jonas, and Kumar 2007). Specifically, greater transparency with regard to financial policies makes it easier for private agents to observe whether a government has violated its monetary commitments by engaging in inflationary practices. The presence of foreign banks can thus be a visible signal to international markets regarding the financial policies of countries about which these markets may have insufficient information. Countries with transparent economic policies have an advantage in international markets that is reflected in a reduced risk premium.[35] In contrast, opacity at the country level amplifies the transmission of financial shocks internationally. The 2008 global financial crisis exemplifies this; the decrease in equity prices and the increase in sovereign bond spreads in emerging-market countries were most pronounced in nontransparent countries (Brandao-Marques, Gelos, and Melgar 2013, 3).

Financial Regulation

The second way foreign banks can enhance the monetary policy credibility of emerging markets is through the quality of financial regulation and supervision[36] they bring and the overall institutional development of financial systems.[37] The banking regulation and supervision that host countries import from the bank's home country regulators provide credible restrictions on the host government's ability to behave irresponsibly.[38] The involvement of foreign banks can thus have a disciplining effect in countries with central banks that lack capacity for disciplining banks. The home supervisors of foreign parent banks provide an additional layer of prudential supervision to foreign branches and subsidiaries (Boss et al. 2007, 121).[39] For example, Gedeon (2010) argues that in countries with currency board arrangements, monetary policy and banking regulation and supervision have been "decentralized" and "privatized" to foreign banks.

Foreign banks can also serve as a "push factor" that bring about institutional reforms in financial systems in emerging countries (Grabel 2003, 45). Improved prudential regulation and better market discipline can reduce excessive risk taking of banks. Because they conduct their operations in a safe and sound manner and bring about regulatory improvements, foreign banks can decrease the probability of crises associated with financial under-development (Dages, Goldberg, and Kinney 2000). Empirical studies find that a substantial foreign bank presence is a stabilizing factor in host markets. Crystal, Dages, and Goldberg (2001) show that foreign banks have higher loan-loss provisioning and reserves than domestic banks and that they address the deterioration of loan quality more aggressively. A better-capitalized foreign subsidiary (being guaranteed further provision of necessary liquidity from the parent bank) offers greater protection to local depositors than does a locally owned bank (Tschoegl 2003). Haber and Musacchio (2005) conclude that when foreign banks entered Mexico in the aftermath of the 1995 Tequila crisis, bank capitalization improved and nonperforming loans declined. Similarly, the strong financial position of banking sectors in emerging European countries appears to be the outcome of high foreign bank penetration (Herrmann and Mihaljek 2013; Grittersová 2014b). The presence of reputable and experienced foreign banks sends signals to international markets about the solvency and regulatory quality of a host country's financial sector (Mehl, Vespro, and Winkler 2006).

When the branches and subsidiaries of multinational banks are managed and supervised according to the standards of the regulatory authorities in developed countries, they can also directly prevent host country monetary or fiscal irresponsibility by being less open to political interference than domestic banks are (Andrianova, Demetriades, and Shortland 2008). It has been argued that domestic banks tend to be more amenable to forced purchases of government bonds issued to finance fiscal deficits or to forced lending to favored political constituents. Governments often use state-owned banks to finance money-losing state-owned enterprises and to direct credit based on political connections rather than on risk assessment (Andrews 2005, 3).[40] Political interference in the banking sector and the moral hazards that stem from soft budget constraints result in bad lending decisions and high volumes of nonperforming loans that make a banking system financially fragile. In the end, a government must take responsibility for the resulting accumulation of bad debt by bailing out banks that are politically connected with the ruling elite, an action that has negative consequences for the country's fiscal position (Gros 2003).

Velasco (1996, 1034) emphasizes that whether or not a government will devalue its currency depends on the accumulated stock of government debt, because "for stocks that are beyond a certain threshold, the temptation to devalue in a surprise manner may outweigh the costs of doing so," and speculative attacks against fixed exchange rate regimes often occur at high thresholds of government debt.[41] Foreign banks can break the entrenched relationship between politically connected domestic—often government-owned—banks and firms, thus breaking the vicious cycle of banking sector and monetary fragility (Allen et al. 2011). Their presence mitigates relational lending problems (Giannetti and Ongena 2009). Foreign banks can thus help the host government solve its commitment problem by limiting the scope for discretionary increases in inflation. Furthermore, foreign banks with deep pockets cannot as easily pressure governments to bail them out because it is politically difficult to convince the public that a foreign bank needs to be saved (Gros 2003, 12). Foreign bank presence can thus mitigate the incentives to bail out banks connected with political elites.

International Lender of Last Resort

I argue here that in addition to increasing transparency and the overall institutional strength of the local banking system, reputable multinational banks with access to international sources of capital can act as de facto international lenders of last resort.[42] Domestically, central banks play the role of lenders of last resort by providing an insurance mechanism aimed at stabilizing the financial system (Goodhart and Illing 2002, 1). Multinational banks can increase a host economy's resilience to withstand shocks and reduce the vulnerability to sudden stops of capital flows (Cardenas, Graf, and O'Dogherty 2003; Vogel and Winkler 2012). Internal capital transfers between parent banks and their affiliates reduce the volatility of destabilizing capital flows and thus the incidence of financial crises (Goldberg 2013). Multinational banks can, therefore, act as crisis managers.

Historically, private bankers in one country often relied on their counterparts in other countries for assistance in addressing a sudden outflow of capital. Central banks were absent from many of the major countries adhering to the gold standard in the nineteenth century. Consequently, the responsibility for maintaining the gold standard rested with a system of private commercial banks. The clearinghouses in the United States before the establishment of the Federal Reserve are good examples of this mechanism. When European bond prices collapsed during the financial crisis of 1846–48, a private banker, Nathan Rothschild in London, with the assistance of

Rothschild's representative in New York (Auguste Belmont), acted as the effective lender of last resort to the Rothschild houses in Paris, Vienna, and Frankfurt (Kindleberger and Aliber 2005, 249). Similarly, in the 1930s, the bankers Paul and Felix Warburg of Kuhn, Loeb in New York fulfilled the function of lender of last resort for their brother Max Warburg's bank in Hamburg by extending credit lines of more than $9 million (Kindleberger and Aliber 2005, 249). These prestigious private banks acting as international lenders of last resort imposed strict conditions on their bailouts, justifying them on the grounds that they were risking their own and their depositors' money. For instance, during the speculative attack on the franc in the 1920s, J. P. Morgan & Co. provided a stabilization loan to the French government that was accompanied by a government reform program exacted by the regents of the Banque de France that incorporated Rothschild and de Wendel banks (Kindleberger and Aliber 2005, 257).

More recently, when the brokerage subsidiaries of foreign banks in Hungary encountered large losses during the 1998 Russian financial crisis, parent banks provided the necessary recapitalizations (Cardenas, Graf, and O'Dogherty 2003). The 2008 global financial crisis, examined in detail in chapter 6, illustrates this point further. There was a widespread perception that foreign bank affiliates would be bailed out by their parent banks. This perception was certainly correct. A consortium of Western European multinational banks functioned as "big bank lender of last resort," ensuring provision of international reserves to countries in crisis and hence the stability of their monetary regimes (Gedeon 2010, 18). Foreign banks in emerging European countries in particular have acted as "shock absorbers" (Winkler 2014), which has proved to be the key to these countries' macroeconomic stability, as will be shown in subsequent chapters. Gedeon (2010) notes that in Eastern European countries with a currency board arrangement—a rule-bound monetary regime in which a domestic lender of last resort to banks is absent—a "quasi central bank intermediation" has been invented in which multinational bank groups act as "private central banks," fulfilling the function of lenders of last resort in their host countries. This echoes and extends the argument made by Edwards (2003) that in currency board arrangements banks may need to secure agreements with foreign financial institutions through the interbank market with which contingent credit lines can be contracted. Sufficient international reserves allow governments to defend their exchange rate peg.

The market perception is that the subsidiary will benefit from the support of the parent bank, which would assure the solvency of the subsidiary and cover its losses (Tschoegl 2003). Parent banks may support subsidiaries as they would support branches, so international market perception should not be affected along these lines. Although the parent bank does not have the legal obligation to stand behind its subsidiary (contrary to branches and agencies), the expectation is that concerns about a loss of reputation will lead a parent bank to provide financial support to its subsidiaries (Cerutti, Dell'Ariccia, and Martínez Pería 2007, 1671). Nonetheless, the bailout mechanism may be dependent on the type of model under which a multinational bank operates. Foreign subsidiaries are financially more independent from their parents in a decentralized model of funding (e.g., Spanish banking groups in Latin America) than in a centralized model (e.g., Austrian banking groups in emerging Europe) (Impavido, Rudolph, and Ruggerone 2013). The section that follows identifies additional conditions underlying the effect of foreign banks on the credibility of the policies of the governments of emerging markets.

Reputation of Multinational Banks

I contend that the impact of multinational banks varies along two dimensions: the reputation of the parent bank and the level of international banking integration. The first component of the perception of financial markets of foreign bank entry is that these banks have a well-established observable reputation. In the finance literature, a commonly used empirical measure of the reputation of a bank (as an underwriter of sovereign bonds) is its relative market share (DeLong 1991; Megginson and Weiss 1991; Fang 2005; Flandreau and Flores 2009). From the economic point of view, market share means profits at stake, and bigger banks have more to lose from a tarnished reputation (Fang 2005, 2734). When discussing the reputation of an investment bank underwriter, DeLong (1991, 209–10) notes:

> If reputations as honest brokers are sufficiently fragile, a firm with a large market share will find it most profitable in the long run to strive to be above suspicion in every short run: it will not imperil its reputation for the sake of higher short-run profits on any one deal. . . . With a small market share, the future returns expected from a reputation as an honest broker may be also small, and might be less than the benefits from exploiting to the fullest one unsound deal in the present.

A reputable multinational bank with a large market share needs to protect its brand name and reputation and is unlikely to behave opportunistically because a risky decision would affect its market share and, thus, its profits (Fang 2005). Gorton (1996) shows that the concern with retaining their reputations may have deterred U.S. banks from behaving as "wildcats" (i.e., issuing banknotes and subsequently disappearing) in the nineteenth-century free-banking era. Therefore, a large multinational bank's economic stake in a local economy incentivizes good behavior because the return on its investment depends critically on the local economy's stability and growth.

In Latin America and the Caribbean, more than 60 percent of foreign banks are from the United States and Spain, whereas in Eastern Europe more than 90 percent of foreign banks are headquartered in Austria and other European Union countries (fig. 2.1). The Spanish banks Santander and Banco Bilbao Vizcaya Argentaria are the top foreign investors in Latin America. Italy's UniCredit and Austria's Erste Bank and Raiffeisen have the largest market shares in Eastern Europe. Major European banks hold a large percentage of foreign assets (of total assets), representing 82 percent for Deutsche Bank, 64 percent for Santander, 62 percent for UniCredit, 41 percent for BNP Paribas, and 29 percent for Société Générale (Allen et al. 2011, 2).

I use several criteria as measures of reputation of multinational banks. The majority of large, reputable multinational banks (63 percent) are headquartered in Western Europe and North America. They engage in what is known as north-south multinational banking (Claessens and van Horen 2012, 11). These are the biggest banks, occupying the first places for total value of assets, in the Top 1,000 World Banks published by *The Banker* (the world's premier banking and finance resource) and rated globally by credit rating agencies. The largest international banks in Europe and in the American region documented on the basis of Tier 1 capital and published by *The Banker* in 2015 are shown in tables 2.1 and 2.2.[43] European banks have more significant international operations than their American or Asian counterparts. Europe houses most of the international banks—in the United Kingdom, France, Germany, Spain, Switzerland, and the Netherlands—that have a significant part of their operations abroad. Banks from the United States and Canada are also global powerhouses, particularly Citigroup, which is a truly global bank with operations in all regions of the world. HSBC is the largest European group with 65 percent of its business abroad (Schoenmaker 2013, 57).

In light of this, it is reasonable to assume that large global banks have

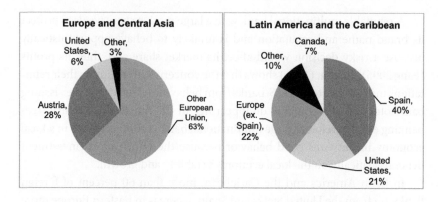

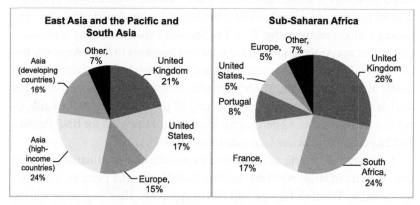

Fig. 2.1. Home Countries of Foreign Banks in Emerging and Developing Countries
Source: World Bank, *Global Development Finance 2008.*

strong incentives not to tarnish their reputations for the sake of higher short-term profit opportunities via their subsidiaries in various host countries. In the case of emerging Europe, the long-term business models of multinational banking groups involve "making a commitment to a transition economy host country, so as to build up the requisite reputational capital necessary for further expansion in the region," as Bonin (2010, 467) puts it. This focus on reputation puts constraints on the parent bank that makes it unable to withdraw its support for its subsidiaries without damaging the reputation of the entire banking group and its long-term investment opportunities. These banks with international standing usually possess information capital, substantial managerial resources, accumulated international experience, and access to financial resources at favorable conditions.

There are banks from several emerging markets, however, that started to invest abroad, particularly in small developing countries. These banks engage in what is known as south-south multinational banking (Claessens et al. 2008). By 2006, Panama, South Africa, and Brazil owned the largest number of affiliates in other developing countries (representing 28 percent of all south-south banks) (Claessens et al. 2008, 20). Two Brazilian banks—Itaú Unibanco Holding and Banco de Brazil—now occupy places in the global Top 50 listing in *The Banker*. Chinese banks are also becoming stronger. China now has three banks in the top places in *The Banker's* latest rankings (ICBC, China Construction Bank, and Bank of China), but Chinese

TABLE 2.1. The Biggest European Banks in 2015

Banking Groups	Capital Strength (in $ billions)	Total Assets (in $ billions)
HSBC Holdings (UK)	153	2,634
Crédit Agricole (France)	89	2,139
BNP Paribas (France)	85	2,522
Barclays (UK)	81	2,118
Banco Santander (Spain)	78	1,537
Deutsche Bank (Germany)	78	2,074
Royal Bank of Scotland (UK)	74	1,639
Lloyds Banking Group (UK)	62	1,334
Groupe BPCE (France)	61	1,485
Société Générale (France)	58	1,588
UniCredit (Italy)	55	1,025
BBVA (Spain)	51	767
Credit Suisse Group (Switzerland)	50	932
Intesa Sanpaolo (Italy)	46	784
Crédit Mutuel (France)	46	858

Source: The Banker (2015), available at http://www.thebanker.com/

TABLE 2.2. The Biggest Banks in the Americas in 2015

Banking Groups	Capital Strength (in $ billions)	Total Assets (in $ billions)
JPMorgan Chase & Co. (US)	187	2,573
Bank of America (US)	169	2,107
Citigroup (US)	167	1,843
Wells Fargo & Co. (US)	155	1,687
Goldman Sachs (US)	78	856
Morgan Stanley (US)	67	801
Royal Bank of Canada (Canada)	37	834
US Bancorp (US)	36	403
PNC Financial Services Group (US)	36	345
Scotiabank (Canada)	34	714

Source: The Banker (2015), available at http://www.thebanker.com/

banks tend to be more domestically oriented. Chapter 3 looks in depth at the trends and the implications for credibility of both north-south and south-south multinational banking.

Level of Financial Integration

For foreign banks to exert influence in any substantial way, their presence in the local banking system has to be substantial. This suggests some threshold effect. The positive effects of foreign bank presence can be constrained if they have a relatively low market share (Tschoegl 2003, 222). In other words, foreign banks can favorably influence a host country's banking development and the credibility of its monetary regime only after they attain a sufficient market share. The case of Argentina (examined in chapter 6) illustrates this point. It is also plausible that if foreign banks are relatively important in a country, it is likely that the country's institutional environment is suitable for the operations of these banks. Claessens and van Horen (2014, 315) argue that in countries where foreign bank presence is more substantial, these banks tend to play a more consequential role in enhancing local financial development. In contrast, when the number of foreign banks is small, the affiliates are usually niche players in the host countries, focusing on specific customers.

In summary, the argument advanced in this book is that reputable multinational banks can exogenously enhance the international reputation of emerging markets by making those countries' policies and commitments more credible. Their presence can reduce currency and country risks and decrease uncertainty surrounding an emerging-market country. The mechanisms behind this relationship are that foreign banks increase transparency and financial strength of a host economy and act as a lender of last resort. The reputation of multinational banking groups and the level of foreign bank ownership in emerging markets matter too.

Alternative Theories of Credibility

I now contrast my theory of borrowed credibility with two alternative views on credibility in international finance. The first maintains that the establishment of an autonomous central bank is paramount for the credibility of a government's monetary commitment to low inflation. The second focuses on the importance of international agreements in increasing government credibility in the eyes of international audiences.

Central Bank Independence

Beginning with Rogoff (1985), scholars have argued that an independent central bank can serve as an institutional mechanism for a government trying to reduce inflationary bias in its monetary policy while enhancing the credibility of its anti-inflationary announcements. A politically insulated central bank with the legal stipulation of maintaining price stability can tie the hands of governments, preventing them from pursuing an activist monetary policy of low interest rates to stimulate employment before elections (Cukierman, Webb, and Neyapti 1992). Having a politically insulated central bank that is free to conduct monetary policy without interference from the government has thus been offered as a solution to the time-inconsistency problem in monetary policy.

This view of the beneficial effects of an independent central bank has been internalized by policymakers. Maxfield (1997) argues that many developing country governments, in an attempt to establish credibility for their monetary policies, granted independence to their central banks as a signal to international investors of their preferences for inflation stabilization. But why does central bank independence have a greater signaling value than other sorts of policy announcements in the monetary realm? Politicians could instead announce monetary growth rules or inflation targets that are directly observable by market participants. Moreover, central bank procedures are opaque: it is quite difficult for the public to monitor government–central bank relations and identify the sources of inflationary pressures (Broz 2002; Keefer and Stasavage 2002). Yet credible commitment to low inflation requires transparency to detect and punish government opportunism. Broz (2002) suggests that when a political system is transparent, as in democracies, an independent central bank is rendered transparent indirectly through active monitoring and sanctioning by private and political actors. Others have shown that the effectiveness of central bank independence for solving the credibility problem of monetary policy depends on the presence of political institutions, such as multiple governmental veto players (Keefer and Stasavage 2002).[44]

Another difficulty is the assumption in the literature that a central bank operates with full and irreversible autonomy. Formal delegation of monetary authority to an independent central bank and respecting its operational independence are not the same thing. The actual turnover of central bank governors is a good example. For instance, in Argentina in the 1980s, the average term in office for a central bank governor was less than a year even though the legal term was four years (Cukierman 1992). Scholars have recognized the potential for political reversals of a decision to delegate monetary policy to an autonomous central bank (Lohmann 1992; Moser 1999). Monetary policy can never be divorced from government influence. Policymakers may be tempted to interfere with the decisions of a central bank, to change its personnel, or to revise the central bank law to restrict its legal independence.

The central bank independence argument seems problematic not only in theory but also in practice. There is ambiguous empirical support for the claim that a central bank accounts for price stability (see Alesina and Summers 1993). Whatever the reason, countries with a central bank that has less well-established credibility will have difficulties conducting a credible anti-inflationary monetary policy, and alternative mechanisms of securing commitment may be necessary. Monetary institutions of countries with poor records of accomplishment will inspire little confidence that monetary policy will be insulated from political interference (Grabel 2003). Moreover, a difficulty with this approach to monetary credibility is that it assumes that the fight against inflation is the only goal of monetary policy. Central banks also have a financial stability function, which has regained attention since the 2008 crisis. The goals of financial stability and low inflation may be at cross-purposes. For example, the provision of bailouts to banks to prevent a banking crisis may be at the cost of giving up the low inflation goal (Alesina and Stella 2010). Not all governments and their constituencies have the same level of tolerance for inflation.[45] Still others think that rather than independence, it is transparency of central bank operations and procedures that help to overcome the problem of asymmetric information in monetary policy (Faust and Svensson 2001).

International Delegation of Powers

Some governments may encounter difficulty in establishing the credibility of their policy commitments through domestic institutional reforms. Especially in countries with histories of conflict or transitioning from communism, an inherent public trust in domestic institutions is lacking. Additional research concurs that national governments can achieve credibility by delegating powers internationally. Put differently, governments and central banks need to be subjected to additional, externally imposed, constraints and guarantees.

A government can buy credibility through membership in international monetary arrangements by abandoning its ability to follow an independent monetary policy (the hand-tying effect) (Giavazzi and Pagano 1988). This could involve joining multilateral target zones (such as the former European Monetary System) or a monetary union (such as the eurozone). The institutional costs of the breakdown of a monetary union are higher than abandoning a fixed exchange rate regime; hence, the former may be a more effective credibility-enhancing device (Alesina and Stella 2010, 46). Stasavage and Guillaume (2002) suggest that the existence of parallel international agreements (in trade, aid, or security) increases the costs of exit from a monetary union. But they further argue that for a monetary union to provide credibility to its member countries, there should be a credible threat of punishment for members that "seek to break the rules of a monetary union without exiting" (Stasavage and Guillaume 2002, 126).

As De Grauwe (1994) points out, the main reason behind the fragility of a multilateral pegging arrangement is the lack of credibility of its members' promise to sustain fixed exchange rate regimes and avoid opportunism.[46] According to what has come to be known as the hegemonic stability theory (Kindleberger 1986), the credibility and stability of the prewar gold standard resulted from the effective engagement of the anchor country, Great Britain, to monitor, manage, and stabilize the system. Others have proposed that the IMF could play the role of a provider of credibility (Dhonte 1997; Cottarelli and Giannini 1997). External monitoring by the IMF via conditionality might enhance the transparency necessary to make monetary commitments credible. The IMF monitors and enforces reform policies and thus acts as an "agency of restraint" that minimizes program reversal and increases the credibility of governments' policy announcements (Dhonte 1997, 6–7). The costs for noncompliant behavior come in the form of restricted access to IMF financing in the future.

In the same vein, Dreher and Voight (2011) argue that national governments can enhance their creditworthiness by delegating power to various multilateral institutions. More specifically, Hauner, Jonas, and Kumar (2007) and Gray (2009) suggest that EU accession improves the credibility of economic reforms and policies of a country that joins the club, which is associated with lower sovereign bond spreads. Ultimately, though, the credibility-enhancing effect of international agreements and organizations depends on whether the agreement changes the payoffs of governments in such a way that the government cannot make itself better off by reneging on its commitments. The credibility of international institutions to impose direct costs on countries for a defection from a multilateral agreement may be reduced because political interests of donor countries often interfere with the economic decisions of the institutions (Stone 2002).[47] Gray (2013) thinks that international organizations may be simply a "shorthand for a country's intentions," decreasing uncertainty about government preferences. She acknowledges that too many international organizations fail to enforce their rules and make countries fulfill their promises. Ironically, the international delegation argument may solve one credibility problem by creating another.

Conclusion

Although we have learned much from scholarship on the role of domestic institutions and international organization, there is more to understand. Reputation can be infused exogenously not only by international institutions but also by foreign direct investors or lenders that existing studies ignore. My research indicates that multinational banks are well endowed to monitor government behavior, given their greater familiarity with local political circumstances and experience dealing with local political and monetary authorities. Large foreign bank investors can directly impose audience costs, as they may withdraw their investments or cut off a country from future loans (Hirschman 1970). This view represents a departure from the current research in political science and economics. It demonstrates the importance of modern finance theory for the study of international monetary regimes.

This chapter has developed a theoretical framework for analyzing credibility building in emerging markets. The task ahead in subsequent chapters is to bring statistical and case study evidence to bear on the principal hypothesis.

CHAPTER 3

Foreign Bank Advantage in Comparative Perspective

The main goal of this chapter is the empirical investigation of the relationship between the presence of foreign banks and policy credibility in emerging markets. The credibility theory predicts that reputable multinational banks enhance the credibility of institutions and policies of host nations, which is essential for the credibility of those nations' monetary regimes. A credible monetary regime, in turn, confers a significant effect on the creditworthiness of governments. Put differently, countries with credible monetary arrangements are rewarded with lower borrowing costs in sovereign debt markets.

The central proposition is that expectations of market participants take a cue from the presence of multinational banks. There is, in other words, a transfer of reputation from reputable multinational banks to host countries. To test the principal hypothesis, I examine the effects of foreign banks, both reputable and less reputable, on monetary credibility across the emerging world. Furthermore, I find that the *reputation* of foreign banks has distinct implications for credibility outcomes. All else equal, a country that has a substantial presence of reputable Western banks, headquartered in Western Europe and North America, will gain in reputation. My statistical analysis and the case study of Ukraine, however, show that credibility building does not occur when nonreputable—the so-called south-south banks—enter the financial systems of emerging markets. I show that international markets evaluate what types of multinational banks are present in a country and how substantial their presence is, in addition to considering a host country's progress in economic, financial, and political reforms.

Regression analysis using cross-country data for more than eighty emerging economies over the period from 1995 to 2009 tests the proposition that a substantial foreign bank presence will have a positive impact on both the currency and country risks of these countries. The approach of combining different time periods and regions into one analysis has the advantage of providing generalizable results across a range of emerging markets. The first restriction that needed to be imposed is that the analysis had to be focused on the period after the collapse of communism in the early 1990s given the inclusion of the transition countries in the sample. This time coverage is, however, consistent with the scope of the theory: both the involvement of emerging market countries in sovereign debt markets and international banking activity began to increase steadily from the early 1990s. The second restriction is that the statistical analysis must stop in 2009 due to two reasons. First, the cross-national data on foreign bank ownership are not available after 2009. Second, the 2008 global financial crisis changed the risk climate and the dynamics of the reputational game. I examine the consequences of foreign bank behavior during the 2008 financial turmoil in detail in chapter 6.

I test my principal hypothesis against the alternate explanations that are concerned with domestic institutions (independent central banks) and memberships in international organizations in explaining reputation formation on the international stage. I also take into account the possibility that international markets do not react to the presence of foreign banks per se, but to reforms undertaken by host countries. Finally, I test for the possibility that foreign banks self-select into countries with responsible governments and good institutions.

My investigation proceeds in four steps. The chapter begins by explaining the way in which the main variable of interest—the currency risk—will be operationalized. I then describe the dataset, including key explanatory and control variables. The subsequent sections consider macroeconomic and political factors at the country level to pin down precisely what matters in the international credibility game. Economic and financial indicators control not only for reforms that a country might undertake as a consequence of foreign bank entry, but also for macroeconomic fundamentals that determine a country's ability to keep its monetary commitments and repay its debts. The final section investigates the dynamics of country-risk premium by testing whether countries with credible monetary regimes and foreign bank ownership are rewarded with lower borrowing costs in sovereign debt markets.

Operationalizing Currency Risk

I use two measures to empirically distinguish credible monetary regimes from others. The currency-risk premium (or more popularly, currency risk) represents a straightforward indicator that captures the beliefs of markets as to the credibility of monetary policy commitments. It represents a compensation that an investor receives in case of an adverse movement in the exchange rate (Domowitz, Glen, and Madhavan 1998). The standard way to measure the currency-risk premium is through the differentials between the domestic currency and foreign currency short-term interest rates for each country (Schmukler and Servén 2002).[1]

Mitchener and Weidenmier (2009) examine the credibility of hard pegs during the classical gold standard era by looking at interest rate differentials between the short-term, gold-denominated bills of the United Kingdom and the trade bills of the largest emerging-market borrowers. For Drazen and Masson (1994, 744, 752), interest rate differentials between member countries of the European Monetary System and Germany, the anchor country, provide a measure of "the perceived credibility of a country's pledge to maintain a fixed parity." In the same vein, Weber (1991) and Knot, Sturm, and de Haan (1998) employ short-term money market interest rate differentials in their analysis of the credibility of monetary regimes of small European countries.

Advocates of hard pegs posit that the adherence to a rigid monetary framework would reduce the currency-risk premium, perhaps eliminate it altogether. But Edwards (2001) and other critics argue that the proclaimed fixed exchange rate regime, even a currency board, is not credible because market participants continuously expect devaluation. If financial markets do not consider a hard peg to be fully credible, the currency-risk premium (that is, interest rate differentials) will remain significantly positive. Higher interest rate differentials reflect higher concerns over potential realignment of the exchange rate (devaluation). Put differently, the persistence of the large currency-risk premium for an emerging economy signals that international markets do not consider its monetary regime credible.[2]

I use two types of short-term interest rates: money market rates and Treasury bill rates. Money market rates are considered to be a purer measure of market interest rates because they represent the rates at which banks lend to each other (Bleaney, Lee, and Lloyd 2013). Money market rates are indicative of a policy rate in a country, similar to the federal funds rate in the United States (Klein and Shambaugh 2013). Treasury bill rates are the rates of interest on short-term risk-free government securities. If both interest rates are available and have the same time span, money market rates are set as the default, as in Goldberg (2013).[3]

For the foreign interest rate, base currencies have to be identified. Whereas much empirical research uses the U.S. dollar as the universal base currency, the currencies of the United Kingdom, Germany, France, Belgium, South Africa, Australia, Malaysia, and India also serve as base currencies for emerging markets. The German mark or the euro are the base currencies for 20 percent of countries and the French franc for 13 percent (Klein and Shambaugh 2013). The interest rate used for the base country is always the same type of rate (money market or Treasury bill) used for the local country.[4] I use Goldberg's (2013) and Klein and Shambaugh's (2013) assignment of base currencies for each country. I then subtract the domestic and foreign (base) interest rates.

Following Shambaugh (2004); Frankel, Schmukler, and Servén (2004); Obstfeld, Shambaugh, and Taylor (2005); and Bleaney, Lee, and Lloyd (2013), I transformed both domestic and foreign interest rates as $\ln(1 + \text{interest rate}/100)$. I employ uncovered interest rate parity (UIP) to examine interest rate differentials.[5] The difference between the short-term interest rates between two countries can be expressed as the sum of two risk premiums (Alper, Ardic, and Fendoglu 2009, 127):[6]

$$(i_{t,k} - i_{t,k}^*) = (i_{t,k} - i_{t,k}^f) + (i_{t,k}^f - i_{t,k}^*) = (i_{t,k} - i_{t,k}^f) + (i_{t,k}^{EB} - i_{t,k}^*) + (i_{t,k}^f - i_{t,k}^{EB})$$

where k denotes the maturity of short-term interest rates; $i_{t,k}$ are the interest rates on a domestic asset denominated in domestic currency; $i_{t,k}^f$ denotes a domestic asset denominated in foreign currency under domestic jurisdiction, $i_{t,k}^{EB}$ is a domestic asset denominated in foreign currency under foreign jurisdiction; and $i_{t,k}^*$ are the interest rates on a foreign asset denominated in foreign currency. The first term in parentheses is the *currency-risk* premium. It reflects the risk associated with movements in the exchange rate. In other words, the currency-risk premium is the compensation that an investor requests because of the possibility of a movement in the exchange rate. The second term is the *default-risk* premium (the assets differ only in terms of the issuer country). It represents the risk that a country will default on its debt obligations. The third term is the *political-risk* premium: the difference between the yields on debt instruments, which are identical in terms of issuer and currency but differ in their jurisdiction, reflects the cost of shifting them across jurisdictions. The sum of default risk and political risk is traditionally called the *country-risk* premium.

Alper, Ardic, and Fendoglu (2009) argue that although the country-risk premium is negligible for developed countries, it is significant for emerging markets. Risk-averse investors request political- and default-risk premium from emerging markets because of their weaker institutions, worse macroeconomic fundamentals, more volatile economic conditions, and underdeveloped capital markets compared to developed nations. It should be noted, however, that there is no real way to disaggregate these two components of interest rate differentials due to the absence of cross-national data on the forward exchange rate in a cross-country setting. Forward foreign exchange markets are undeveloped in most emerging economies.[7] The existing studies that decompose the interest rate differential to examine currency and country risks focus on one or a very few countries or examine the time series properties of the risk premium (Schmukler and Servén 2002; Domowitz, Glen, and Madhavan 1998). Mitchener and Weidenmier (2009) set political-risk premium at zero under the assumption that the default risk for the short-term interest rates is the same for the two countries.[8] I follow this approach and relate interest rate differentials to foreign bank presence and various macroeconomic and political factors often cited as potential determinants of the currency risk.[9]

My second measure of the credibility of monetary regimes is based on the inflation differentials of the emerging market country relative to the base country, as in Bleaney, Lee, and Lloyd (2013). A small inflation differential is an indicator of a credible monetary regime. A credible fixed exchange rate regime has an implicit inflation target, which is equal to the inflation target of the anchor country. Accordingly, if a systematic inflation differential persists, the fixed exchange rate regime is not perceived as credible. Beyond that, it is important to consider that the inflation rate, consistent with the maintenance of a peg, depends on how rapidly the economy is growing. This regularity is known as the Balassa-Samuelson effect.[10] To capture the Balassa-Samuelson effect, I regress the inflation differential on output per capita, and then use the residuals from this regression as my measure of the credibility of a monetary regime.[11]

Principal Explanatory Variable: Multinational Banks

The principal hypothesis is that the substantial presence of reputable multinational banks should enhance the international reputation of host countries, while the presence of nonreputable foreign banks should not translate into a better reputation. The primary measure of multinational bank influence used in this book is the percentage of foreign banks among all banks (that is, the relative count of foreign banks out of all banks) in each country in each year.[12] The data on foreign banks come from Claessens and van Horen (2014). To my knowledge, this is the most comprehensive database of bank ownership, which contains information on 5,324 banks in 137 countries over the period from 1995 to 2009 at an annual level. The database includes commercial banks, savings banks, cooperative banks, bank holdings, and holding companies. The average share of foreign banks among all banks across my sample is 37 percent.

Claessens and van Horen (2014) document a sizable (69 percent) increase in the number of foreign-owned banks between 1995 and 2009. The increase in foreign bank penetration was particularly pronounced in the late 1990s and early 2000s, and then again in the period from 2006 to 2007, reflecting primarily extensive privatizations and banking sector opening in Eastern Europe and East Asia. The foreign bank expansion peaked in 2007 before slowing down during the global financial crisis. Yet for the most part, parent banks did not close or sell their foreign affiliates during the crisis (Claessens and van Horen 2014, 303).

As table 3.1 illustrates, the increase in the number of foreign banks was the highest in Eastern Europe (225 percent), reaching 47 percent in 2009 (Claessens and van Horen 2014, 306). In some countries of emerging Europe—Croatia, Estonia, Lithuania, Bosnia-Herzegovina—more than 90 percent of banking assets are currently owned by foreigners. Foreign bank penetration in Latin America, at 39 percent in 2009, is also substantial. Foreign bank presence in sub-Saharan Africa is high mainly due to past colonial links.[13] Even more importantly though, south-south banking represents a high component of foreign banking in sub-Saharan Africa (the highest of all regions) (Claessens et al. 2008). This trend has not been mirrored in East Asia and the Middle East, which have embraced foreign bank presence less enthusiastically (Cull and Martínez Pería 2010). In China and India, state-owned banks still play a major role in domestic financial intermediation (Goldberg 2009). My theory proposes that international markets

TABLE 3.1. Number of Foreign Banks by Host Country, Aggregates by Income Level and Region, 1995–2009

	1995		2000		2005		2009	
	N	Share	N	Share	N	Share	N	Share
East Asia and Pacific	56	0.18	64	0.19	68	0.19	93	0.24
Eastern Europe	115	0.15	235	0.28	310	0.38	374	0.47
Latin America and Caribbean	197	0.25	254	0.34	215	0.35	233	0.39
Middle East and North Africa	32	0.18	40	0.23	46	0.28	57	0.36
South Asia	10	0.07	15	0.09	15	0.09	22	0.13
Sub-Saharan Africa	100	0.31	143	0.37	158	0.42	181	0.52
OECD	238	0.18	280	0.20	311	0.22	329	0.24

Source: Adapted from Claessens and van Horen (2014, 302).
Note: The regions represent the regional classification as used by the World Bank.

should make inferences about the credibility of policy commitments of governments of emerging countries based on the degree of their financial integration involving multinational banks.

Alternative Explanatory Variables

As discussed in chapter 2, the principal alternative perspectives on the credibility of government's policy commitments emphasize fixed exchange rate regimes, independent central banks, and the delegation of authority from national governments to international organizations. It is widely believed that exchange rate pegs (particularly currency boards) are associated with transparency and price stability. Studies find that countries pegging their currencies to the U.S. dollar have their interest rates moving in step with U.S. interest rates (Di Giovani and Shambaugh 2008; Frankel, Schmukler, and Servén 2004). Likewise, a rule-based framework of inflation targeting is associated with enhanced transparency, implying that the central banks have become more accountable for their policies (Fouejieu and Roger 2013). Consequently, inflation-targeting countries have enjoyed lower inflation (Mishkin and Schmidt-Hebbel 2007).

The International Monetary Fund (2013) classified 25 countries as pursuing hard pegs and 101 countries as pursuing soft pegs, as opposed to 65 practicing floating exchange rates. Instead of the nineteenth-century peg to gold, exchange rates are now usually fixed to one of two major anchor currencies: the U.S. dollar (44 countries) or the euro (27 countries). At this point, it is also useful to distinguish between a country's de jure and de facto exchange rate regime. The former refers to the regime officially announced by the government, but recent empirical studies reveal that adjustments in central parities and foreign-exchange market interventions can generate exchange rates quite different from official arrangements.[14]

Rose (2014) argues that while a fixed exchange rate regime constitutes a well-defined monetary policy, a flexible regime does not. Accordingly, I divide monetary regimes into three categories—hard pegs, soft pegs, and inflation targeting—and create dummies for each of them. I do so using the latest update of the Ilzetzki, Reinhart, and Rogoff (2008) de facto exchange-rate regime classification.[15] Using data on official and dual (parallel and black) foreign exchange markets, Ilzetzki, Reinhart, and Rogoff (2008) produce a "fine" classification of fifteen regimes.[16] I define their categories (1) through (2) as a *hard peg*, which are monetary regimes with no separate legal tender and a currency board arrangement. The categories (4) through (11) correspond to a *soft peg*. The categories (12) and (13) are defined as floats and include managed floats and free floats. I treat *inflation targeting* as a distinct monetary regime. I rely on Rose (2014) and Fouejieu and Roger (2013) for the list of inflation-targeting countries and their effective adoption dates. Almost all inflation targeters are classified as flexible regimes, with only a few exceptions classified as intermediate regimes.

Another rival explanation is that an independent central bank, associated with better inflation outcomes, should increase the credibility of monetary commitments. I use the measure of legal *central bank independence* developed by Bodea and Hicks (2015),[17] who expand the index constructed originally by Cukierman, Webb, and Neyapti (1992) that runs only up to 1989. The index of central bank independence is based on sixteen characteristics of central bank statutes that pertain to the allocation of authority over monetary policy, the relative importance of price stability in central bank objectives, the term of office for the governor, limits on central bank lending to the government, and procedures for resolution of conflicts between the central bank and the government. The index ranges between 0 and 1, where 1 stands for the maximum level of independence.

Inasmuch as the membership in international organizations (IO) can be used by governments to signal their commitments to follow certain policies, this should enhance the international reputation of member states. I use the Dreher and Voigt's (2011) measure of international delegation of competences to international organizations. The authors have collected data on membership in numerous international organizations and the ratification of the conventions, including GATT/World Trade Organization, International Finance Corporation, the International Center for the Settlement of Investment Disputes, the International Convention for Civil and Political Rights, the International Convention for Economic, Social, and Cultural Rights, the UN's so-called Optional Protocol, the UN Convention on the Recognition and Enforcement of Foreign Arbitral Awards, the UN Convention against Torture and Other Cruel, Inhuman or Degrading Treatment or Punishment, and the International Court of Justice. They first construct binary dummy variables that indicate for every individual organization whether or not a country is a member. Then they add the dummy variables for all organizations and construct a country-specific index of *membership in IOs*, which was normalized to range between 0 and 1, with higher values indicating higher levels of membership.[18]

Control Variables

Identifying determinants of a credible monetary regime is important not only for model specification objectives, but also for testing rival hypotheses. The available empirical models of the determinants of interest rate differentials are inconclusive, so they can be suggestive at best (see Mitchener and Weidenmier 2009; Knot, Sturm, and de Haan 1998; Goldberg 2013; Klein and Shambaugh 2013; Schmukler and Servén 2002; and Bearce 2003, 2007).

One explanation maintains that interest rate differentials originate from impediments to international capital movements. Capital controls thus result in a higher cost of capital. I capture the restrictions on international capital flows by using the Chinn and Ito (2006) *capital account openness* measure. This measure reports a variety of capital controls, including current account transactions, capital account transactions, and multiple exchange rates. The index takes a higher value when these restrictions are few and a lower (or negative) value when the restrictions are extensive. The index reflects de jure restrictions on international movements of capital. Fewer capital controls imposed by an emerging market government should be associated with a lower currency-risk premium. Obstfeld (1998) argues that increased capital mobility could have a "disciplinary effect "on monetary policy because in the conditions of international substitutability of assets, governments have fewer incentives to use inflation as a source of revenues. As a consequence, this should result in a decline in price levels. High and volatile inflation creates uncertainty, and hence increases risk.[19] *Inflation* is measured by the annual percentage change in consumer price index. Following standard practice (Cukierman, Webb, and Neyapti 1992), I transform inflation using $\pi/(1 + \pi)$ that represents the depreciation rate in the real value of money. Using the depreciation rate of money rather than the logarithm of inflation attenuates the bias caused by heteroskedasticity and hyperinflationary observations without deleting them from the sample.[20] The probability of devaluation tends to be inversely related to the stock of international reserves taking the form of hard currency (Schmukler and Servén 2002). The variable *reserves* represents the log of total reserves without gold (in current U.S. dollars). I further control for the level of economic development by including per capita income. Including the per capita level of gross domestic product (the log of *GDP per capita*) also addresses concerns that some variables are merely a proxy for a country's level of economic development. To account for the national business cycle, I include the real *growth* rate as a ratio of GDP. The macroeconomic data come from the World Bank's World Development Indicators and the IMF's International Financial Statistics.

Following Bearce (2003), I include two domestic political factors in the regression analysis that uses short-term interest rate differentials as the dependent variable. The first political variable captures the partisan character of the government in power. Left-wing governments tend to be associated with higher inflation and interest rates than are right-wing governments. The variable *left government* used here measures the partisan orientation of the cabinet in power with respect to economic policy. I employ the national election results reported in the World Bank's Database of Political Institutions (Beck et al. 2001), which classifies the three largest government parties according to whether they have a left-wing, centrist, or right-wing ideological orientation (right is coded as 1, center as 2, and left as 3). To account for the effect of different power-sharing arrangements, I also use a measure of government *fractionalization*. The variable is continuous between 0 and 1, with higher values indicating greater power sharing among different political parties. This variable also comes from the World Bank's Database of Political Institutions (Beck et al. 2001).

The regression analysis using inflation differentials as the dependent variable takes its clue from the central bank models in the time inconsistency literature (reviewed in chapter 2) and the recent empirical models of inflation outcomes (Keefer and Stasavage 2002, 2003; Broz 2002; Cukierman, Webb, and Neyapti 1992; Spiegel 2008; Crowe and Meade 2008). I incorporate the measure of *trade openness*, which is the average of the sum of exports and imports as a share of GDP. Romer (1993) suggests that as imports increase as a share of total consumption, the government has less of an *ex post* incentive to inflate the economy. From the methodological point of view, countries that eliminated barriers on their capital account are also likely to be open to trade, so there is a risk that the financial openness measure may be capturing the effect of trade openness, if the latter is not included (Spiegel 2008). The log of *government expenditures* as a share of GDP indicates the government's spending. With an increase in government spending, the central bank may be compelled to resort to the inflation tax to fill the fiscal gap (Spiegel 2008). Private credit held by deposit money banks as a share of GDP, capturing credit allocation, has been traditionally used as an indicator of the level of the *banking system development*. International financial flows are expected to have a smaller impact on inflation performance in countries with developed banking systems (Spiegel 2008). Also, if a country has a weak and underdeveloped banking system, its central bank may need to loosen monetary policy to promote faster credit growth (Hammermann and Flanagan 2009, 305). This implies that as financial system develops, markets should expect lower inflation. Data on trade openness and government expenditures come from the World Bank's World Development Indicators. Data on private credit come from the Financial Development and Structure Dataset (Beck, Demirgüç-Kunt, and Levine 2000).

I further incorporate the key political explanations of inflation outcomes as controls. Keefer and Stasavage (2002, 2003) find that the effectiveness of pegs and independent central banks in reducing inflation increases with the number of veto players. To control for the effect of veto players, I employ the log of *checks* from the World Bank's Database of Political Institutions (Beck et al. 2001). This measure of checks and balances counts the number of veto players in a political system (presidential or parliamentary), adjusting for whether these veto players are independent of each other, as determined by the level of electoral competitiveness in a political system, their respective party affiliations, and electoral rules.[21] Previous studies also linked inflation with political instability (Broz 2002; Keefer and Stasavage 2002). Politically unstable governments—governments with tenuous political support and short horizons—may reduce time horizons of central banks and their ability to precommit to inflation goals (Hammermann and Flanagan 2009). Following Keefer and Stasavage (2002), I employ the *political instability* variable from the World Bank's Database of Political Institutions (Beck et al. 2001) that measures the share of veto players who drop from the government from the previous period. In authoritarian regimes with only one veto player, this measures the rate of government turnover. The next section describes in greater detail the sample and the econometric methods chosen.

Analyzing Credibility of Monetary Regimes: Empirical Tests

To test the principal hypothesis and rival explanations, I collected data for more than eighty emerging-market countries from 1995 to 2009. This time frame corresponds to foreign bank investment activity, which was particularly high in the late 1990s. The end date of this analysis coincides with the advent of the 2008 global financial crisis. All models reported here employ annual data because measures of foreign bank ownership in each country—the principal explanatory variable—are only available on an annual basis.

To ensure the comparability of my econometric approach with previous studies, I estimate fixed-effects regression models and include time fixed effects, which allow controlling for heterogeneity in my panel.[22] Individual country dummies capture the effects of time invariant but unmeasured country characteristics, such as geography or culture. Time fixed effects allow us to capture common worldwide or regional shocks (for instance, contagion during financial crises).

As previously discussed, the statistical analysis employs two measures of credibility of monetary regimes as the dependent variable. Therefore, I run separate analyses for the effects of multinational banks on interest rate differentials and inflation differentials. The results can be seen in tables 3.2 and 3.3. The first column of each table presents the baseline model. The subsequent models introduce dummy variables for monetary regimes (hard pegs, soft pegs, and inflation targeting), the index of central bank independence, and an indicator of membership in international organizations.

It can readily be seen that the results are quite stable across specifications, as are the coefficients. Starting with table 3.2, in which the dependent variable is the interest rate differentials, the multinational bank variable is statistically significant in all models. It bears repeating that negative values on the multinational bank variable indicate reduced interest rate differentials, whereas positive values indicate higher differentials. Consistent with my theoretical expectations, the greater penetration of host banking systems by foreign banks is associated with decreased interest differentials. The coefficient on the multinational bank variable is highly significant, at the 1 percent level. To put it another way, monetary regimes of countries that are financially integrated with reputable multinational banks are perceived as more credible by international markets than those that are not.

Most macroeconomic control variables have the expected signs and a powerful impact on interest rate differentials. Strong economic growth and

TABLE 3.2. Foreign Banks and Interest Rate Differentials

	(1)	(2)	(3)	(4)	(5)
Constant	0.805***	0.620***	0.635***	0.782***	0.895***
	(0.150)	(0.193)	(0.189)	(0.149)	(0.148)
Multinational Banks	−0.001***	−0.001***	−0.001***	−0.001***	−0.001***
	(0.000)	(0.000)	(0.000)	(0.000)	(0.000)
GDP Per Capita (log)	−0.034*	0.019	0.021	−0.036**	−0.091***
	(0.017)	(0.023)	(0.023)	(0.018)	(0.020)
Growth	−0.004***	−0.005***	−0.005***	−0.003***	−0.003***
	(0.000)	(0.001)	(0.001)	(0.000)	(0.000)
Capital Account Openness	−0.005**	−0.003	−0.002	−0.002	−0.008***
	(0.003)	(0.003)	(0.003)	(0.003)	(0.003)
Inflation	0.581***	0.582***	0.575***	0.568***	0.585***
	(0.028)	(0.034)	(0.034)	(0.029)	(0.028)
Reserves (log)	−0.020***	−0.030***	−0.032***	−0.017***	−0.019***
	(0.004)	(0.006)	(0.006)	(0.004)	(0.004)
Left Government	0.002	0.004	0.004	0.002	0.003
	(0.002)	(0.003)	(0.003)	(0.002)	(0.002)
Government	0.020**	0.021**	0.018*	0.020**	0.014*
Fractionalization	(0.008)	(0.010)	(0.010)	(0.008)	(0.008)
Central Bank Independence		−0.046**	−0.046**		
		(0.022)	(0.022)		
Hard Peg		−0.023			
		(0.014)			
Soft Peg		0.002			
		(0.008)			
Inflation Targeting			−0.024***		
			(0.008)		
Membership in IOs				−0.021	
				(0.031)	
Cross-Border Bank Loans					0.019***
(log)					(0.004)
N	858	577	577	843	858

Note: Dependent variable is interest rate differentials. This table reports the results of fixed effects regression. All models include fixed effects for year.

Standard errors are in parentheses. * Significant at 10%; ** significant at 5%; and *** significant at 1%.

large holdings of international reserves in foreign currency reduce interest rate differentials, while high inflation increases currency risk. As expected, capital controls are associated with greater interest rate differentials, although this variable attains statistical significance only in two specifications. Out of the proxies used here to attempt to capture political and institutional considerations, the governments with the large extent of political power sharing are associated with greater interest rate differentials. Market participants do not seem to react to the left-wing governments being in power, though.

It is commonplace in the political economy literature to assume that an independent central bank is a commitment mechanism that can assist governments in acquiring credibility for monetary policy objectives. Thus international markets would be reacting to changes in central bank statuses that would increase the legal independence of a central bank when assessing a currency risk. The results of models 2 and 3 show that central bank autonomy is indeed associated with reduced interest rate differentials. A drawback of introducing the variable representing central bank independence is that it is only available for a subsample of fifty-two countries, thus the sample size is reduced considerably. The results associated with the different types of monetary regimes are mixed: while inflation targeting reduces interest rate differentials, the effects of hard and soft pegs are not statistically different from zero (models 2 and 3).[23] Thus the alternate hypothesis of a reduced currency risk as a result of the adoption of fixed exchange-rate regimes does not seem to be confirmed.[24] The next specification incorporates a measure of membership in international organizations, which does not appear to influence interest rate differentials (model 4).

The final specification (model 5) controls for privately held foreign-currency-denominated debt by introducing a measure of cross-border claims of all Bank for International Settlements (BIS) reporting banks (not located in the emerging-market country) vis-à-vis the emerging market country, as reported in the BIS Consolidated Banking Statistics.[25] Large multinational banks often provide cross-border loans in foreign currency to households and firms. I include the log of *cross-border bank loans* in foreign currency as a control because it could be correlated with the presence of large multinational banks.[26] It is worthwhile to note, however, that cross-border lending is direct lending of banks to nonaffiliated entities in a foreign country.

Walter (2013) argues that large privately held foreign currency debt explains credible commitments of governments in emerging Europe to low

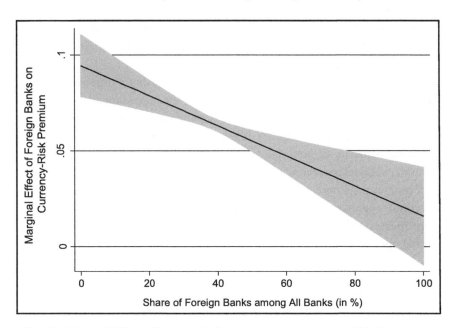

Fig. 3.1. Marginal Effect of Foreign Bank Ownership on Currency-Risk Premium

inflation and fixed exchange-rate regimes. This would represent a different causal path than the one proposed in this book. In other words, private debt in foreign currency rather than foreign bank ownership would be a pathway to monetary stability.[27] A considerable amount of loans in Swiss francs to domestic households was recorded in some countries of emerging Europe. Loans in Swiss francs to households (secured by mortgages) represented more than 30 percent of all loans in Hungary and 17 percent in Poland. Yet it is also important to note that Swiss franc loans in these countries have been extended not only by foreign banks but equally by large and small domestic banks (Brown, Peter, and Wehrmüller 2009). Model 5 shows that, as expected, large cross-border loan exposures increase interest rate differentials.[28] But the coefficient on multinational banks remains negative and statistically significant, with much the same magnitude as in previous specifications. I discuss in detail foreign currency lending—both cross-border lending and lending by foreign bank affiliates—before and during the 2008 global crisis in chapter 6.

To provide a graphical representation of my findings, figure 3.1 shows the marginal effects of increasing average foreign bank ownership on currency risk (at the means of the other variables in model 1). It demonstrates that the predicted probability of reduced interest rate differentials rises with the increase in foreign bank presence.

I further establish the effect of foreign banks using a different dependent variable. Table 3.3 presents the results of the regression analysis using inflation differentials (*residuals*) as the dependent variable. The results for the foreign bank penetration are as before: the larger the presence of multinational banks in the host country's financial system, the more credible the country's monetary regime is. The coefficient for multinational banks is significant, at the 5 percent level across all specifications. As expected, capital account openness is associated with lower inflation differentials. Trade openness, on the other hand, has the opposite sign as expected: greater trade openness seems to be associated with greater inflation differentials.

TABLE 3.3. Foreign Banks and Inflation Differentials

	(1)	(2)	(3)
Constant	0.361	1.634	1.598
	(0.845)	(1.074)	(1.067)
Multinational Banks	−0.011**	−0.012**	−0.010**
	(0.004)	(0.005)	(0.005)
Trade Openness	0.011***	0.011**	0.013***
	(0.004)	(0.004)	(0.004)
Capital Account Openness	−0.178***	−0.202***	−0.163**
	(0.057)	(0.067)	(0.066)
Government Expenditure (log)	0.073	−0.521	−0.596*
	(0.272)	(0.346)	(0.344)
Banking System Development	−0.040	0.244**	0.060
	(0.105)	(0.118)	(0.118)
Checks (log)	−0.113	−0.031	0.017
	(0.117)	(0.135)	(0.136)
Political Instability	−0.033	−0.025	−0.053
	(0.130)	(0.147)	(0.147)
Central Bank Independence		−0.198	0.041
		(0.420)	(0.417)
Hard Peg		−0.622*	
		(0.336)	
Soft Peg		−0.522***	
		(0.161)	
Inflation Targeting			−0.596***
			(0.170)
N	822	541	541

Note: Dependent variable is inflation differentials. This table reports the results of fixed effects regression. All models include fixed effects for year.

Standard errors are in parentheses. * Significant at 10%; ** significant at 5%; and *** significant at 1%.

One plausible explanation is that openness to trade may increase the susceptibility of a country to foreign shocks, such as high oil prices, which are associated with higher domestic price inflation.

Columns 2 and 3 in table 3.3 show that there is a little support for the notion that an autonomous central bank, an alternative variable associated with credibility concerns, has an impact on inflation differentials. The estimated coefficient of central bank independence does not attain statistical significance. Monetary regimes are considered to be a credible commitment in their own right: the coefficient estimates for hard and soft pegs and for inflation targeting are negative and significant. This suggests that these monetary regimes help reduce inflation differentials. It is notable that checks and political instability stand as insignificant predictors of inflation differentials. The coefficient on government expenditures is mostly insignificant too. Banking system development is significantly related to inflation differentials only in the specification that includes pegs, but it has the opposite sign as expected.

The principal results reported above are robust. The strongest and most consistent result is that financial integration through multinational banks delivers credibility for monetary policy commitments of governments. I conducted numerous robustness checks and my results appear to be robust (see table 3.A1 in the appendix to this chapter). Beyond the set of core variables, I included a country's *current account balance* as a share of GDP (model 1).[29] It is plausible to assume that current account deficits, driven by a fall in public and private savings, are the underlying macroeconomic source of reduced interest rates. Capital inflows may be also correlated with increased global bank presence, and controlling for the balance of payments should address this concern.[30] The coefficient on current account balance is not statistically different from zero but the significance of my key variable is not affected. I further control for *European Union* accession that I model with the aid of a dummy variable that takes a value of 1 for the year when a country joins the EU and thereafter (model 2). I ask whether and to what extent the process of EU accession influences the effect of foreign bank presence on interest rate differentials. The EU variable (lags of) is not significant at conventional levels, but the coefficient of multinational banks remains negative and statistically significant at the 1 percent level. I also analyze whether my results change if I use foreign bank claims on local residents relative to domestic credit volumes (the latter are converted into U.S. dollars) as an alternative measure of foreign bank penetration, as in

Goldberg (2013) (model 3). This measure is based on credit provision reflecting the lending operations of branches and subsidiaries of multinational banks to the residents of emerging economies.[31] Across the two alternative measures of the presence of multinational banks, a consistent finding is that these banks are associated with a lower currency risk.

I conducted additional robustness checks that are not shown to conserve space.[32] I included the lagged dependent variable to account for the gradual buildup or loss of credibility. The other specification incorporates a dummy variable to control for the effects of currency crises, as in Schmukler and Servén (2002). Whereas the crisis dummy has a significant positive impact on the currency-risk premium, the coefficient on the multinational banks variable remains significant. The key point is that introducing these additional variables does not alter the main story: the presence of multinational banks remains associated with a low currency-risk premium. The model fits the data well when I split the sample into the precrisis and postcrisis period. The year of 2006 was used as the cutoff to avoid any interference from the 2008 global financial crisis. The results are in line with the full sample. The coefficient on multinational banks not only continues to be negative and significant, but becomes even slightly larger in the precrisis periods. Next, I re-estimate the model using panel-corrected standard errors as an alternative estimation method. I correct for serial autocorrelation in each country time series via first-order autocorrelation (AR1) term. This method of estimation does not alter the main results.

In sum, many versions of the empirical models were assessed, with multinational banks having consistent effects throughout, in line with my expectations. Greater penetration by foreign banks is associated with more credible monetary regimes in the host countries. It is important to note that when controlling for the type of monetary regime and central bank independence—alternative explanations—foreign bank presence still influences both interest rate and inflation differentials. Crucially, however, rival explanations did not yield consistent results. Taken together, my results are robust to alternative explanations and variable definitions, different model specifications, sample periods, and different estimation methods.

It might be the case that the specific characteristics of multinational banks (such as their health, size, business models) may be capturing some of the variation in credibility of monetary regimes across emerging markets. Additionally, because the statistical analysis stops in 2009, some important temporal dynamics during the recent global financial crisis are left out. In later chapters I discuss some of these considerations related to the functions of multinational banks in different localities and their activities during the recent global crisis.

Financial Reforms

I further investigate the causal claim that multinational banks exert a significant positive influence on the credibility of monetary regimes of host countries. Foreign bank ownership and other policies leading to lower risks of currency devaluation might also be due to financial reforms. It might be argued that governments have to reform their financial systems (for example, to improve the protection of creditor rights) prior to the entry of foreign banks. These financial reforms, rather than foreign bank ownership, might then cause the observed effect of multinational banks on currency risk. Thus this might result in a spurious correlation between foreign banks and interest rate differentials. Following Rose (2004), I include various leads and lags of the principal explanatory variable. For instance, if financial reforms are implemented three years prior to the entry of multinational banks and these reforms decrease the currency-risk premium, the coefficient on the third lead of the multinational bank variable should be significant. When I include three lags and three leads of the multinational bank variable together, neither the coefficients on leads nor the coefficients on lags are significant at conventional levels (model 1, table 3.4). This implies that the effect of foreign banks on a nation's currency risk materializes *after* rather than prior to their entry.

I also analyze more explicitly whether *financial reforms* alter the impact of foreign banks on the currency-risk premium by employing the Financial Reform Index, developed by Abiad, Detragiache, and Tressel (2008).[33] The index tracks reforms in the financial sector. It is normalized to be between 0 and 1, where higher scores represent a more reformed financial system. Arguably, if the influence of foreign banks is through their impact on the reforms in the banking sector at the onset of their entry, the effect should no longer be possible once reforms are directly controlled for in regressions. As model 2 in table 3.4 reveals, the coefficient on the financial reform index (lagged one period) is not significant at conventional levels, whereas the coefficient on the multinational bank variable retains its strong statistical significance at the 5 percent level.

Endogeneity

The results reported so far assumed foreign bank presence to be exogenous. But there is a possibility of reverse causation in the sense that a more credible monetary regime may be driving the entry of foreign banks into emerging markets and not the reverse. If endogeneity is a problem, fixed-effects estimations will yield inconsistent regression estimates. Reverse causality can be addressed partially by estimating the models with lagged independent variables. When I esti-

TABLE 3.4. Causality

	(1)	(2)
Constant	0.921***	0.091
	(0.265)	(0.257)
Multinational Banks		−0.001**
		(0.000)
Multinational Banks ($t + 1$)	−0.000	
	(0.001)	
Multinational Banks ($t + 2$)	0.000	
	(0.001)	
Multinational Banks ($t + 3$)	−0.001	
	(0.001)	
Multinational Banks ($t − 1$)	−0.000	
	(0.001)	
Multinational Banks ($t − 2$)	−0.000	
	(0.001)	
Multinational Banks ($t − 3$)	0.000	
	(0.001)	
GDP Per Capita (log)	−0.043	0.058*
	(0.031)	(0.030)
Growth	−0.004***	−0.005***
	(0.001)	(0.001)
Capital Account Openness	−0.002	−0.005
	(0.004)	(0.004)
Inflation	0.570***	0.569***
	(0.049)	(0.035)
Reserves (log)	−0.020***	0.024***
	(0.005)	(0.005)
Left Government	0.001	0.002
	(0.004)	(0.003)
Government Fractionalization	0.030***	0.030***
	(0.011)	(0.011)
Financial Reforms ($t − 1$)		0.000
		(0.002)
N	539	543

Note: Dependent variable is interest rate differentials. This table reports the results of fixed effects regression. All models include fixed effects for year.
    Standard errors are in parentheses. * Significant at 10%; ** significant at 5%; and *** significant at 1%.

mated models with lagged regressors, the results are undisturbed. This provides some evidence that reverse causality is not a paramount concern. Another way of addressing endogeneity concerns is through an instrumental variable approach. One of the preconditions for this method is that there is an instrument that is strongly correlated with the independent variable in the first stage (here, foreign bank ownership) but is not correlated with the outcome variable in the second stage (currency-risk premium). If the instrument is weak, instrumental variables estimation is not better than fixed-effects regressions.

I use the instruments that have been identified in the literature on global banking and depicted by senior executives at major European banks whom I interviewed. My identification strategy is based on the assumption that the instruments have no direct or indirect effect on currency risk. The first set of instruments captures information costs measured by observable proxies for cultural, legal, and economic proximity. The information costs associated with multinational banking are of two types: the costs of screening and monitoring borrowers and the costs to the banks' directors and shareholders associated with monitoring the affiliates' managers and loan officers in host countries (García-Herrero and Martínez Pería 2007, 1623). Following García-Herrero and Martínez Pería, I use the number of *Internet hosts* (per one hundred people) in each country as a measure of access to communication that can potentially reduce information and monitoring costs. Internet connections bridge physical distances, thus they may facilitate oversight of foreign affiliates' managers and projects and access to information from distant places. The data come from the World Bank's World Development Indicators.

It is generally assumed that cultural similarities lower information costs and thus should have a positive impact on foreign bank expansion. To measure cultural distance based on language, I use a dummy variable set equal to 1 if the official language in a host country is a *European language* (English, German, French, or Spanish), as in Buch (2003) and Detragiache, Tressel, and Gupta (2008). This variable captures cultural proximity to Western Europe and North America, where the largest multinational banks are headquartered. Data on languages spoken in emerging market countries come from Mayer and Zignago (2011).

The third instrument is the log of *population* as a measure of potential market size, following the identification strategy similar to Detragiache, Tressel, and Gupta (2008). The assumption behind the choice of this instrument is that multinational banks operating in many markets can better diversify country-specific risk than domestic banks can, which is particularly valuable in smaller countries. Moreover, multinational banks can acquire a "monopolistic advantage" in small markets by making a relatively small initial investment.[34] My interviews with bankers and recent empirical studies find that foreign banks perform better when they take a large share of the host market and share the official language with the host countries (Claessens and van Horen 2012). Data on population comes from the World Bank's World Development Indicators.

Finally, several studies use improvements in the conditions for the entry of foreign banks as an instrument for their presence (Jayaratne and Strahan 1996; Giannetti and Ongena 2009; Bruno and Hauswald 2014). Thus, I employ the Heritage Foundation's *Financial Freedom* Index, which measures the relative openness of a host country's banking system. The index takes into account the stringency of banking regulation, ease of entry, and restrictions on foreign banks opening branches or subsidiaries, among other factors. It takes values from 0 to 100, where higher values represent higher levels of banking sector openness and fewer regulatory restrictions. Restrictions on bank activities and regulations that influence foreign bank expansion are expected to have a negative effect on the entry of foreign banks.

Table 3.5 reports the results of the two-step generalized method of moments estimations (GMM) with heteroskedasticity-robust standard errors (clustered by country). In the first-stage estimations, all instruments are highly significant and the partial R^2 is above 20 percent. The F-statistic allows the rejection of the null hypothesis of weak instruments. In the second-stage regression, the Hansen J-statistic and the corresponding chi^2 p-value suggest that we cannot reject the null hypothesis of validity of the overidentifying restrictions when more than one instrument is used. I infer that together these tests provide strong evidence for the validity of the instruments. The regressions indicate that, for the most part, the results are similar whether we treat the multinational bank variable as endogenous or exogenous. While there are always questions about the suitability of instruments, I take these results as evidence that a substantial presence of foreign banks enhances the credibility of the host country's monetary regime (reduces the currency-risk premium).

Nonreputable Multinational Banks in Emerging Markets

As the theory suggests, international financial markets should react not only to the presence of multinational banks in general but also to the reputation of these banks. The entry of reputable multinational banks should be perceived as an indicator of the host government's intention to reform its banking system. A reputable multinational bank needs to protect its brand name, hence it is unlikely to behave opportunistically because a risky decision would affect its market share and thus its profits. Multinational banks from developed countries (France, Germany, the Netherlands, Spain, the United Kingdom, and the United States) with long banking histories and

TABLE 3.5. Instrumental Variable Regression

	(1)	(2)
Second Stage		
Constant	0.224***	0.331***
	(0.053)	(0.108)
Multinational Banks	−0.002***	−0.001***
	(0.000)	(0.000)
GDP Per Capita (log)	0.003	−0.004
	(0.004)	(0.010)
Growth	−0.006***	−0.005***
	(0.001)	(0.001)
Capital Account Openness	0.002	0.002
	(0.002)	(0.004)
Inflation	0.049***	0.040***
	(0.005)	(0.008)
Reserves (log)	−0.008***	−0.011***
	(0.002)	(0.004)
Left Government	0.004*	0.004
	(0.003)	(0.005)
Government Fractionalization	0.022**	0.021
	(0.010)	(0.018)
First Stage		
European Language	5.770***	
	(1.732)	
Population (log)	−12.479***	−13.405***
	(1.044)	(2.615)
Internet Hosts	2.971***	
	(0.492)	
Financial Freedom		0.424***
		(0.121)
Partial R^2	0.234	0.246
Hansen J statistic	5.551	3.178
(p-value)	(0.062)	(0.075)
F-statistic (excluded instruments)	91.46	28.60
N	796	789

Note: Dependent variable is interest rate differentials. The table reports the results of generalized method of moments estimations. The instruments are the European language dummy, the log of population, Internet hosts, and the Heritage Foundation Financial Reform Index.

Robust standard errors in parentheses. * Significant at 10%; ** significant at 5%; and *** significant at 1%.

high credit ratings assigned by the leading rating agencies dominate foreign bank investments (that is, north-south multinational banking). But as noted earlier, large emerging-market banks recently started expanding across borders into other emerging or developing countries.

I operationalize the prestige of multinational banks by drawing on the Claessens et al. (2008) coding of the south-south banks, defined as the multinational banks whose major shareholders come from another less developed country. To measure the market power of these less reputable banks, I use the count of south-south banks in the local banking system. The south-south banking has expanded in recent years but it still represents a small portion of global banking activities. Twenty-seven percent of all foreign banks located in developing countries are headquartered in another developing country, but this corresponds to only 5 percent of foreign assets (van Horen 2007). The earliest and the largest presence of south-south banks has been recorded in sub-Saharan Africa; it amounted to 19 percent of all banks in 2006 (Claessens et al. 2008, 17). It should be noted, however, that in some countries (for example Kyrgyzstan, El Salvador, and Malawi), south-south banks now constitute nearly half of all banks (Claessens et al. 2008, 18). A small number of emerging markets dominate south-south banking. The multinational banks headquartered in Panama, South Africa, and Brazil owned the greatest number of affiliates in other developing countries (28 percent of all south-south banks) in 2006 (Claessens et al. 2008, 20).

I argue that for the most part, when a south-south bank—a bank about which financial markets have mixed expectations—enters an emerging-market country, the credibility of monetary commitments of its government should not be enhanced substantially. Most of these banks have not encouraged financial and institutional reforms in the host countries that would warrant a substantial reduction in risk. South-south banks tend to be less risk-averse and invest in countries with lower income, weaker institutions, and a greater political risk than reputable Western banks (van Horen 2007). In other words, these banks invest in countries with similar investment and business environments, often in the same region. It is thus reasonable to assume that market reaction to the entry of these banks is not being conflated with pre-existing financial and institutional reforms in their host countries.

Table 3.6 reports the results of the analysis designed to check the impact of south-south banks (measured as their relative count of all banks) on interest rate differentials (see the appendix, table 3.A2 for the impact of south-

south banks on inflation differentials). Across the two dependent variables, the consistent finding is that the coefficient on the south-south banks does not attain statistical significance. This lends support to my prediction that the presence of south-south banks in emerging markets does not reduce interest or inflation differentials. Lower interest rate differentials are associated with hard pegs and independent central banks, but the adoption of inflation targeting does not decrease currency risk. The impact of control variables is similar to previous specifications.

Eastern Europe saw the greatest increase in south-south banking, 276 percent between 1995 and 2006 (Claessens et al. 2008, 15). Who is investing? The leading state-owned Russian banks that operate primarily in former Soviet republics. Some of Russia's largest public banks operating in East

TABLE 3.6. South-South Banks and Interest Rate Differentials

	(1)	(2)	(3)
Constant	1.016***	0.681*	0.587*
	(0.263)	(0.352)	(0.342)
South-South Banks	−0.001	−0.001	−0.001
	(0.001)	(0.001)	(0.001)
GDP Per Capita (log)	0.010	0.053	0.069*
	(0.032)	(0.041)	(0.040)
Growth	−0.007***	−0.008***	−0.008***
	(0.001)	(0.001)	(0.001)
Capital Account Openness	−0.009**	−0.006	−0.004
	(0.004)	(0.005)	(0.005)
Inflation (log)	0.031***	0.035***	0.035***
	(0.004)	(0.004)	(0.005)
Reserves (log)	−0.047***	−0.046***	−0.049***
	(0.007)	(0.010)	(0.010)
Left Government	0.001	0.006	0.006
	(0.004)	(0.005)	(0.005)
Government Fractionalization	0.029**	0.030**	0.027*
	(0.012)	(0.014)	(0.014)
Central Bank Independence		−0.064**	−0.063**
		(0.032)	(0.032)
Hard Peg		−0.041*	
		(0.021)	
Soft Peg		−0.002	
		(0.011)	
Inflation Targeting			−0.006
			(0.012)
N	583	418	418

Note: Dependent variable is interest rate differentials. This table reports the results of fixed effects regression. All models include fixed effects for year.

Standard errors are in parentheses. * Significant at 10%; ** significant at 5%; and *** significant at 1%.

European countries include Sberbank, with a market share of 21.8 percent of total East European assets; VTB, with 13.7 percent; and Gazprombank, with 5 percent (Raiffeisen Research 2012). In the next section I show, using the case study of Ukraine, that south-south banks do not significantly influence the credibility of monetary policy commitments of the country's government. Ukraine represents a mixed case involving the presence of both reputable and nonreputable banks. The following short account of the Ukrainian experience with international credibility building thus allows us to compare the positive role of reputable (Austrian) banks with nonreputable (Russian) banks.

The Quest for Credibility: Foreign Banks in Ukraine

Ukraine is an example of a country whose government has lacked international credibility due to its history of failed institutional reforms, hyperinflation, banking crises, and debt defaults throughout most of the postcommunist period. Leonid Kravchuk, Ukraine's first president, did not make a decisive break with the past; instead he continued in the Soviet-style economic micromanagement, and Leonid Kuchma, the country's second president, delayed stabilization and financial reforms (Stone 2002, 169). In November 1992, the government introduced a transitional currency, the coupon-karbovanets, to pursue a more inflationary monetary policy than was consistent with the membership in the ruble zone. The government used state-owned banks to direct credits to powerful agriculture and energy lobbies (Petryk 2006). The government was unable to commit to the requirements associated with a credible fixed exchange rate regime; instead it floated the national currency.

A consequence of inconsistent economic policies was one of the worst cases of hyperinflation in the former Soviet Union in 1993–94. Inflation, peaking at more than 10,000 percent, had devastating consequences for Ukraine's economy, with real output falling by more than 23 percent (Petryk 2006). Victor Yushchenko, who was appointed governor of the central bank in 1993, tightened monetary policy and set a narrow corridor for the exchange rate of the coupon-karbovanets against the U.S. dollar. The central bank also replaced the two-tiered exchange rate system, used to subsidize imports by state-owned enterprises, with a unified exchange rate. Eventually, during the monetary reform of 1996, the temporary currency was exchanged for the permanent currency, the hryvnia, at the rate of

100,000 to 1 (Stone 2002, 183). In order to stabilize the new currency, an exchange-rate-based stabilization program was adopted to assist the government in building credibility for low-inflation monetary objectives. The government officially claimed to pursue a fixed exchange rate regime between 1995 and 1997, but the peg lacked credibility because monetary policy remained the primary tool for the wealth redistribution.

Throughout most of the 1990s, Ukraine's banking sector was dominated by the so-called "pocket banks" or "agent banks," which were the extended financial departments of owner firms, frequently engaged in connected lending (Barisitz 2006). The population had little trust in domestic banks because of the losses it had to endure during the hyperinflation period (Barisitz 2006, 66). Bad macroeconomic and financial policies and distaste for reforms left the financial system fragile. As a consequence, Ukraine suffered the currency crisis in 1998 associated with massive capital outflows, abrupt 75 percent devaluation of the hryvnia, inflation, and severe banking problems. To make matters worse, with Ukraine suffering from increased credit risk shortly after the Ukrainian government defaulted on its foreign debt in 1998–2000, investors, lacking confidence in the government, started to sell Ukrainian Treasury bills (Barisitz 2006, 67). This precipitated a fiscal crisis, followed by a sharp increase in sovereign bond spreads, which peaked at 1,784 basis points in 2000.

The year 2000 marked a radical change in Ukraine's economy history. A new, reform government of Victor Yushchenko came to power with ambitious reform goals. It adopted the new Law on Banks and Banking Activity to strengthen the supervisory powers of the central bank and improve the regulatory standards for commercial banks. In spite of political opposition, the central bank liquidated the powerful state-owned bank, Bank Ukraina, which subsidized nonviable state-owned enterprises and the unreformed agricultural sector (Barisitz 2006). The central bank recommitted to the fixed monetary regime based on the U.S. dollar to stabilize inflationary expectations.

The Ukrainian case demonstrates, as Tschoegl (2003, 222) argued, that the positive effects of foreign bank presence can be constrained by their relatively small market share. The share of foreign banks increased from 4 percent in 1995 to 46 percent in 2009 (Claessens and van Horen 2014). Then the trend reversed with the 2008 global financial crisis when the share of foreign banks shrank from 37 percent to 16 percent between 2010 and 2013 (Raiffeisen Research 2014). The Yanukovych administration, hostile to foreign presence, imposed various restrictive business policies, which also contributed to the exodus of several large foreign banks (Skandinaviska Enskilda Banken, Société Générale, Erste Bank, and Swedbank) (Åslund 2015, 176). As table 3.7 illustrates, out of the Western banking groups, only Austrian Raiffeisen and UniCredit Bank Austria were among the major players in the Ukrainian banking system. Austrian banks were among the earliest to enter the Ukrainian market. ING Bank, Citibank Ukraine, and HVB Bank Ukraine ranked among the top twenty banks in the Ukraine's banking system (Barisitz 2006).

It should be recognized, however, that some benefits of the increased presence of reputable Austrian and other Western banks that started to move in the mid-2000s have been transferred to Ukraine. The index of banking sector reform developed by the European Bank for Reconstruction and Development (EBRD), measuring the soundness and regulatory quality of the banking system, has slightly improved in recent years. The ratio of nonperforming loans (loan repayment is past due ninety days or more) to total loans, another indicator of sound banking, declined from 34.6 percent in 1998 to 15.3 percent in 2010, but subsequently increased again and remains between 30 and 40 percent (Raiffeisen Research 2014).

The lack of credibility of the financial policies of the Ukrainian government can be linked to two factors. In addition to the relatively low overall presence of foreign banks, south-south banks, primarily headquarted in Russia, started to expand into the Ukrainian market. The major state-owned Russian banks—Sberbank, Alfa Bank, and VTB—are among the leading banks in Ukraine. Their market share further increased with the 2008 global crisis to 16 percent by September 2014 (Åslund 2015, 177). The share of private domestic banks directly linked to powerful business groups also in-

TABLE 3.7. Leading Banks in Ukraine

Bank Name	Market Share (end–2013) (% of total assets)	Parent Bank (Country)
PrivatBank	16.8	Ukraine (private)
Oshadbank	8.1	Ukraine (state-owned)
Ukreximbank	7.4	Ukraine (state-owned)
Delta Bank	4.3	Ukraine (private)
Raiffeisen Bank Aval	3.4	Raiffeisen Bank (Austria)
Ukrsotsbank	3.4	UniCredit Bank Austria (Austria)
Prominvestbank	3.1	Vnesheconombank (Russia)
Sberbank	2.7	Russia

Source: Fungáčová and Korhonen (2014, 11).

creased after the recent crisis, representing now over half of the banking sector assets (Fungáčová and Korhonen 2014, 6). As a consequence, the Ukrainian banking system remains on a weak footing. Related-party lending continues to be widespread, creditor rights and banking supervision are weak, bank risk management and loan practices are underdeveloped, and the opacity of the enterprise sector impedes banks' risk assessment. All of this indicates that the banking system is not resilient to systemic banking crises (Duenwald, Georguiev, and Schaechter 2005).

Indeed, at the height of the 2008 global credit crisis, devaluation and banking problems provoked a massive run on deposits, and banks incurred large losses. Prior to the crisis, domestic banks faced severe currency mismatches after borrowing for the short term in foreign currencies and providing loans in domestic currency, which was then sharply devalued (Åslund 2015). One-third of the biggest Ukrainian banks defaulted on interbank credit market and were consequently closed. The government provided bailouts or nationalized most medium-sized banks facing liquidity problems. By mid-2009, the costs of bank restructuring were estimated at 5 percent of GDP, but the total costs may have reached twice that level (Barisitz et al. 2010, 59). The Ukrainian parliament modified the 2009 budget law to allow government interference with the central bank's refinancing decisions and facilitated the monetization of the fiscal debt (Barisitz et al. 2010, 72).

The currency-risk premium first decreased from 40.0 percentage points in 1999 to 0.95 percentage points in 2005 before substantially increasing again. This was because the monetary policy of the government was not firmly anchored and reinforced by financial policies, leaving the country open to speculations based on rumors and herd instinct. The country-risk premium followed the same trend; after an eight-fold decline in the average sovereign bond spreads between 2000 and 2007, the spreads started to rise again. Repeated bailouts of domestic banks resulted in deteriorated fiscal accounts as the government deficit reached 11 percent and external debt peaked at 174 percent of GDP in 2009. In February 2009, Standard & Poor's downgraded Ukraine's long-term sovereign foreign currency rating to non-investment grade, suggesting that the country was "vulnerable to non-repayment" of its external debt. Taken together, both the statistical models and the Ukrainian case demonstrate that south-south banks neither bring reforms in the financial system nor significantly enhance the international credibility of a host country.

On the whole, however, the presence (albeit limited) of reputable Western banks has proven a source of strength for the Ukrainian banking market during the recent financial crisis. Since late 2008, the Ukrainian government has been unable to borrow on international capital markets, but in reaction to the crisis, Western parent banks injected the necessary capital to their subsidiaries, and direct credit lines from foreign banks were rolled over. Sustained support and commitment by the Western European, mainly Austrian, parent banks has been widely viewed as one of the most important stabilizing factors in the 2008 crisis (Barisitz and Lahnsteiner 2009). These banks remained committed to the Ukrainian market and took on risk in order to retain their reputation in the region in spite of the country's bad economic policies, politically unstable environment, and regulations protecting domestic banks.

Multinational Banks, Monetary Rules, and Country Risk

As we have seen, the presence of multinational banks reduced currency risk in emerging market economies. I test an additional aspect of the credibility theory: the presence of multinational banks can lower country risk directly in addition to its indirect effect through enhancing the credibility of monetary regimes. I also look for the effects of a monetary regime on country risk to determine whether a credible monetary regime influences the risk perception of international markets. In other words, I consider whether the credibility of monetary regime is priced into other assets, including long-term sovereign bonds.

The relationship between monetary regimes and country risk has long been considered an important policy issue, but it has hardly been explored empirically. Only a handful of empirical studies that shed some light on how the choice of monetary regime impacts a country's foreign borrowing exist. Some studies explore the impact of the adherence to the gold standard on the country-risk premium (that determines the cost of government borrowing). As explained earlier, Bordo and Rockoff (1996) find that countries that adhered to the gold standard were charged lower interest rates in the sovereign bond market before 1914. In contrast, Ferguson and Schularick (2012) demonstrate that adherence to the gold standard did not result in a reduction in risk premium for poor, peripheral countries facing a severe credibility deficit. Obstfeld and Taylor's (2003) study of the effect of the gold standard on borrowing spreads in the London bond market between the 1870s and the 1930s supports the prevailing view concerning the low credibility of the interwar gold standard. Empirical studies focusing on recent periods yield mixed results. Whereas Jahjah, Wei, and Yue (2013) show that governments in developing countries with less flexible exchange-rate regimes are charged higher interest rates in sovereign bond markets (and are less likely to issue sovereign bonds), Gumus (2011) finds the opposite.

I first investigate the effect of the adherence to hard pegs, soft pegs, and inflation targeting on country risk. Empirical studies have shown that both hard pegs (such as currency boards) and inflation-targeting regimes decrease inflation in emerging markets (Ghosh, Gulde, and Wolf 2002; Rose 2014; Mishkin and Schmidt-Hebbel 2007). Hard pegs are shown to enhance economic growth in these countries through lower interest rates and reduced exchange rate volatility translated into lower country risk. Inflation targeting in combination with exchange rate flexibility should induce market participants to hedge against foreign exchange risk that should translate into a positive impact on the country-risk premium (Fouejieu and Roger 2013, 8).

Then I test the proposition that a credible monetary regime confers a credibility bonus for an emerging country in the form of a reduced country-risk premium (lower sovereign bond yield spreads). Fouejieu and Roger (2013) find that inflation targeting reduces the country-risk premium not only through the adoption of this monetary regime but also through its actual performance in delivering low inflation. Therefore, I expect the choice of a monetary regime and its earned credibility to have a joint impact on interest rates on government bonds of emerging markets.

The country-risk premium is defined as the spread between the yield on a sovereign bond issued by an emerging-market government and the yield on the risk-free commonly traded securities (such as U.S. Treasury securities or German bunds). The spread is thus the premium that investors charge as a compensation for holding riskier investments, taking into account the general levels of market sentiment. Interest rates on these instruments are expressed in basis points, or hundredths of a percentage point. In the classical study by Edwards (1986), the sovereign bond spread (country-risk premium) is denoted as a function of the probability of default as perceived by the lender (p) and the risk-free world interest rate (i^*)

$$s = [\frac{p}{1-p}](1+i^*)$$

The primary measure of country risk in this book is J.P. Morgan's Emerging Market Bond Index (EMBI), which is a widely used emerging market sovereign debt benchmark.[35] The EMBI spreads measure the premium paid by an emerging market over a U.S. government bond with comparable maturity characteristics. The average spread on sovereign bonds across the sample is around 501 basis points (the standard deviation is 573).

Determinants of Country Risk

My empirical specifications include all standard variables used in previous studies of the determinants of country risk (see, e.g., Gumus 2011; Fouejieu and Roger 2013; Gray 2013; Jahjah, Wei, and Yue 2013; Ferguson and Schularick 2012; and Rojas-Suárez and Sotelo 2007). Higher GDP *growth* indicates long-term solvency and thus should decrease country risk. High *inflation* is a symptom of rising prices and a depreciated currency, thus a difficulty to service debt in the future. High inflation can result from monetization of the fiscal deficit and therefore signals bad economic policies. The intuition behind the inclusion of the *trade openness* variable is that in a closed economy, the government may have lower incentives to repay its debt because losses from sanctions following debt repudiation are smaller (Gumus 2011, 653).[36] Openness to trade may, on the other hand, increase the vulnerability of an economy to foreign shocks, such as large hikes in energy prices. A higher *external debt* as a share of GDP increases the probability that the country will be unable to service its foreign debt. The level of foreign exchange *reserves* as a share of GDP indicates a pool of hard currency to draw from to finance debt service payments in case of a sudden liquidity problem. All these variables come from the IMF's International Financial Statistics, the World Bank's World Development Indicators and the Global Development Finance databases.

To capture the effect of *institutional quality* (domestic political risk) on market risk perception, I collected the data from the International Country Risk Guide, as in Gray (2013). The database covers both political and social characteristics of a given country, including government stability, corruption, democratic accountability, and the quality of bureaucracy. Higher values indicate higher political quality and thus lower country risk.[37] Finally, I control for the U.S. financial market indicators by including the yields on

077077077077

the benchmark *10-year U.S. Treasury notes* as a proxy for international liquidity. More adverse international liquidity conditions and increased risk perception tend to increase bond spreads in emerging markets.[38]

Country Risk: Empirical Tests

The statistical results appear in table 3.8. The findings in this final analysis indicate that multinational banks are important factors in pricing sovereign debt. Starting with model 1, the results show that foreign bank penetration

TABLE 3.8. Foreign Banks, Monetary Regimes, and Country Risk

	(1)	(2)	(3)	(4)	(5)	(6)
Constant	9.255***	9.748***	9.278***	9.301***	5.034***	4.759***
	(0.571)	(0.671)	(0.585)	(0.571)	(0.427)	(0.809)
Multinational Banks	−0.013***	−0.012***	−0.013***	−0.013***	−0.007**	−0.007**
	(0.004)	(0.004)	(0.004)	(0.004)	(0.003)	(0.003)
Institutional Quality	−0.036***	−0.034***	−0.037***	−0.034***	−0.020***	−0.020***
	(0.005)	(0.005)	(0.005)	(0.005)	(0.004)	(0.005)
Growth	−0.011*	−0.012*	−0.011*	−0.011*	−0.063***	−0.065***
	(0.007)	(0.007)	(0.007)	(0.007)	(0.008)	(0.006)
Inflation	0.653**	0.688**	0.526*	0.649**		
	(0.277)	(0.277)	(0.282)	(0.276)		
Trade Openness	0.003	0.003	0.004	0.003	0.000	−0.001
	(0.002)	(0.002)	(0.003)	(0.002)	(0.001)	(0.001)
External Debt (log)	0.792***	0.783***	0.737***	0.807***	0.093	0.102
	(0.102)	(0.102)	(0.107)	(0.102)	(0.191)	(0.145)
Reserves (log)	−0.285***	−0.284***	−0.309***	−0.288***	−0.214***	−0.384***
	(0.065)	(0.065)	(0.066)	(0.065)	(0.073)	(0.078)
US 10-Year Treasury Note Yield	−0.084	−0.106*	−0.090	−0.104*	−0.233***	−0.290***
	(0.057)	(0.058)	(0.057)	(0.058)	(0.022)	(0.016)
Membership in IOs		−0.622				
		(0.445)				
Hard Peg			−0.224**			
			(0.110)			
Soft Peg			−0.012			
			(0.081)			
Inflation Targeting				−0.123		
				(0.083)		
Inflation Differential					0.060*	
					(0.035)	
Credible Inflation Targeting						−0.336***
						(0.085)
N	292	292	288	292	189	283

Note: Dependent variable is EMBI interest rate spreads. Specifications 1–4 report the results of fixed effects regression. Models 5 and 6 report the results from two-step dynamic system generalized methods of moments estimation and include a lagged dependent variable. All models include fixed effects for year.

Standard errors are in parentheses. * Significant at 10%; ** significant at 5%; and *** significant at 1%.

reduces the country-risk premium of the emerging market countries. On theoretical grounds, the entry of multinational banks may represent a "signaling effect" influencing forward-looking expectations of markets. But it may also reflect the impact of financial and institutional reforms accompanying the entry of multinational banks on the country-risk premium (Fouejieu and Roger 2013, 18).

Model 2 tests a rival explanation that financial markets are responsive to a country's membership in international organizations. In other words, joining an international organization should be associated with a reduced country risk. The membership in international organizations variable does not attain statistical significance, however. Therefore, the alternate hypothesis of changed risk perception as a result of international allegiances does not appear to be confirmed.

Models 3 and 4 take into account the impact of the type of monetary regime on country risk. Hard pegs, it seems, contribute to lower risk premium. Therefore, limiting exchange rate fluctuations pays off in terms of lower sovereign bond yield spreads. These results also indicate that the effect of hard pegs on country risk is not only related to the direct impact of this monetary regime on a country's inflation performance. In contrast, an inflation-targeting regime does not appear to be a significant determinant of government bond yield spreads. It is important to note that the coefficient on the multinational bank variable is consistently negative and statistically significant at the 1 percent level.

The control variables, for the most part, have the expected signs and are statistically significant. Higher domestic institutional quality (lower domestic political risk) leads to reduced country-risk premium. Economic growth and reserves-to-GDP ratio are also associated with a drop in sovereign bond spreads. In contrast, high external debt-to-GDP and high inflation increase government borrowing costs. Trade openness is not statistically significant at conventional levels. The U.S. Treasury securities variable reduces bond spreads but it has a significant effect on currency risk in only two specifications.

The second hypothesis is that a credible monetary regime should reduce the country-risk premium. This hypothesis is tested in model 5, in which dummies for monetary regimes are replaced with *inflation differentials*. In model 6, I replace the inflation targeting dummy with a proxy for *credible inflation targeting*, which is based on Fouejieu and Roger (2013).[39] A credible inflation-targeting regime is measured through the inflation volatility relative to the announced inflation target for each inflation targeting country. The higher the volatility of inflation around the target, the lower the credibility of the inflation-targeting regime is. The resulting index ranges between 0 (denoting that inflation target has no credibility) and 1 (denoting the complete credibility of inflation targeting).

As in prior studies (Fouejieu and Roger 2013; Ferguson and Schularick 2012), the results of models 5 and 6 are based on the dynamic system generalized-method-of-moments estimation (see Blundell and Bond 1998; Arellano and Bover 1995). This dynamic panel data estimation allows us to address the potential endogeneity of some regressors and the omitted variable bias by using internal instruments. As explained earlier, monetary regimes are not randomly distributed across countries. Furthermore, policy commitments of governments and institutional structures are critical for rendering them credible. It is thus important to recognize the endogeneity in the choice of monetary regimes. The dynamic system GMM also permits us to account for the persistence of country risk over time, whereas fixed-effects estimators with a lagged dependent variable lead to biased results. More generally, this estimator produces consistent parameter estimates for empirical samples characterized by short time dimension relative to the number of countries (that is, large cross-sectional dimension); hence it is appropriate here.

I examined the validity of the internal instruments and tested for the serial correlation of the error term. Tests for the absence of serial correlation yield the expected diagnostics: I find evidence for first-order but not for second-order serial correlation. The statistic of the Hansen J-test for overidentification indicates that the internal instruments appear to be valid. Models 5 and 6 show that the coefficients on inflation differentials and credible inflation targeting are negative and significant. This indicates the benefits of a credible monetary regime for a country's creditworthiness, above and beyond the independent effects of lower inflation or the type of monetary regime.

I checked the sensitivity of my findings by using two alternative dependent variables: I have compiled the data on ten-year government bond yields and three-year government bond spreads.[40] Furthermore, I estimated the specifications that included a dummy variable for countries that were not honoring their debt obligations, in other words, sovereign defaulters.[41]

Conclusion

The empirical analysis presented in this chapter confirms that international markets react to the presence of multinational banks in emerging economies. The chapter has demonstrated that, consistent with my credibility theory, international markets consider countries with a substantial foreign bank ownership less risky. Specifically, deep financial integration through the presence of multinational banks reduced currency- and country-risk across emerging markets. The second conclusion is that international markets do not perceive as less risky those countries whose banking systems are penetrated by banks headquartered in other emerging or developing countries. In this respect, this chapter shows that financial markets pay attention to the reputation of multinational banks. They are most responsive to the entry of reputable multinational banks headquartered in North America and Western Europe. They seem to react less if a multinational bank from a less developed country decides to establish its presence in a country at a similar level of economic and political development. In such cases, investors focus on more identifiable indicators about the country's economic performance and its monetary regime choices.

These findings hold true for more than eighty emerging-market countries over the past fifteen years. The main finding of this study stands against the principal rival explanations of the international reputations of nation-states in international markets. Whether an emerging market adopts a fixed monetary regime, grants independence to its central bank, or joins international organizations has no impact on the importance of the multinational bank presence. While these alternative credibility explanations cannot be excluded, the effects of central bank autonomy and monetary regime on currency and country risks are mixed. The positive impact of reputable multinational banks on the international credibility of emerging-market countries is not simply the outcome of domestic political and financial reforms that can be observed in macroeconomic fundamentals or in reform efforts. This chapter also provides a careful modeling of the potential selection bias associated with foreign banks seeking out those emerging countries that are less risky. My findings are robust to a wide range of alternative specifications and tests with no impact on the principal results: those pertaining to the foreign bank ownership.

The objective of this chapter was to provide large-N statistical evidence to demonstrate the generalizability of my principal theoretical prediction.

The statistical models in this chapter cannot tell us much about the dynamic implications and the precise mechanisms through which multinational banks affect international credibility outcomes. I leave more detailed analysis to subsequent case study chapters.

Appendix

TABLE 3.A1. Robustness Checks

	(1)	(2)	(3)
Constant	0.806***	0.873***	1.154
	(0.153)	(0.151)	(0.832)
Multinational Banks	−0.001***	−0.001***	−0.003*
	(0.000)	(0.000)	(0.002)
GDP Per Capita (log)	−0.033*	−0.042**	−0.042**
	(0.017)	(0.018)	(0.020)
Growth	−0.003***	−0.003***	−0.006***
	(0.000)	(0.000)	(0.001)
Capital Account Openness	−0.006**	−0.008***	−0.002
	(0.003)	(0.003)	(0.003)
Inflation	0.615***	0.585***	0.634***
	(0.028)	(0.028)	(0.029)
Reserves (log)	−0.021***	−0.020***	−0.016***
	(0.004)	(0.004)	(0.004)
Left Government	0.002	0.002	0.002
	(0.002)	(0.002)	(0.002)
Government Fractionalization	0.022***	0.016*	0.017*
	(0.008)	(0.008)	(0.009)
Current Account Balance	−0.000		
	(0.000)		
European Union		0.022	
		(0.016)	
European Union $(t-1)$		0.023	
		(0.021)	
European Union $(t-2)$		−0.021	
		(0.017)	
N	844	858	693

Note: Dependent variable is interest rate differentials. This table reports the results of fixed effects regression. All models include fixed effects for year.

Standard errors are in parentheses. * Significant at 10%, ** significant at 5%, and *** significant at 1%.

TABLE 3.A2. South-South Banks and Inflation Differentials

	(1)	(2)	(3)
Constant	0.659	1.431	1.448
	(0.764)	(0.940)	(0.963)
South-South Banks	−0.003	0.014	0.004
	(0.007)	(0.010)	(0.010)
Trade Openness	0.006**	0.005	0.004
	(0.003)	(0.003)	(0.004)
Capital Account Openness	−0.098	−0.176**	−0.153**
	(0.062)	(0.072)	(0.073)
Government Expenditure	0.093	−0.294	−0.374
	(0.256)	(0.305)	(0.312)
Banking System Development	−0.177*	0.079	−0.010
	(0.104)	(0.119)	(0.120)
Checks (log)	0.035	−0.068	0.000
	(0.121)	(0.150)	(0.154)
Political Instability	0.037	−0.034	−0.070
	(0.152)	(0.167)	(0.168)
Central Bank Independence		0.185	0.168
		(0.415)	(0.420)
Hard Peg		−0.772**	
		(0.354)	
Soft Peg		−0.566***	
		(0.169)	
Inflation Targeting			−0.455**
			(0.205)
N	581	402	402

Note: Dependent variable is inflation differentials. This table reports the results of random effects regression. All models include fixed effects for year.
Standard errors are in parentheses. * Significant at 10%; ** significant at 5%; and *** significant at 1%.

CHAPTER 4
Currency Boards and Foreign Bank Presence

The mechanisms by which foreign banks can influence the credibility of policies of host governments are not easily judged though simple quantitative indicators. This and the following chapter complement statistical findings about multinational banks as the external drivers of reputation by examining four country cases in greater depth. Comparative cases of four emerging European countries—Estonia, Bulgaria, the Czech Republic, and Poland—discussed in this and in the subsequent chapter rely on detailed examination of events and firsthand interviews to demonstrate the effects of the entry of multinational banks on currency-risk and country-risk perceptions. The cases contribute to a richer understanding of reputations by discussing the three channels through which foreign banks can make the policy commitments of the host nations credible: by increasing transparency in their financial systems, by contributing to local financial development and regulatory oversight, and by providing commitment and external funding in times of crisis. Foreign banks in these countries, as money doctors in Latin America from the 1890s to the present, provided outside expertise, transferred technology, management techniques, and institutions, and reduced information asymmetries in international markets.[1]

These four cases show that governments lacking reputation can more credibly commit to a chosen monetary regime when they liberate economic policies from the influence of incumbent banks. Credible exchange-rate-based stabilization programs, aiming at combating high inflation, require the political will to depoliticize the allocation of credit and create an independent banking sector. The directed credit that dominated the lending operations of state-owned banks was a major source of inflation and undermined the credibility of the Eastern European governments' monetary commitments. The presence of foreign banks contributed to a reduced government control and interference in the domestic financial sector and severed the links between banks and vested interests. I show that not only did the entry of multinational banks signal the governments' commitments to sound economic policies, but it also translated into the actual reform policies.

Although the governments of these four countries sought to establish the credibility of their monetary commitments by moving to a rigorous monetary regime (such as a currency board or inflation targeting) or by granting independence to their central banks (albeit at different points in their trajectory), that alone was not enough. It was only when multinational banks established their presence to certify the monetary rectitude of host governments and to promote reforms in the local banking systems that uncertainty in international markets was reduced.[2] Overall, these cases also suggest that the credibility of monetary policy in emerging economies can be more successfully established when all three of the following conditions are fulfilled: a rigorous monetary regime (currency board or inflation targeting), an independent central bank, and a substantial presence of reputable multinational banks. Soft pegs and managed currency tend to be associated with credit booms and fiscal excess. Increased international capital flows and speculative currency attacks render soft pegs less sustainable and successful in stabilizing inflation. Furthermore, the behavior in currency markets tends to be the mirror of what is happening in the sovereign debt markets.

All four emerging European countries examined in this book share a number of commonalities and legacies, which make them suitable candidates for comparison. They inherited a common set of economic distortions from communism, including repressed inflation in the form of a monetary overhang (excess savings due to controlled prices and rationed goods that represent high potential inflation),[3] large fiscal deficits and debts, weak trade and financial links with Western markets, nonconvertible currencies, and large black exchange rate market premium (the difference between the value of currency on the black market and its official exchange rate) (de Melo et al. 2001). The initial choices of their exchange rate regimes were part of stabilization packages. The standard instruments of monetary and fiscal stabilization required the transformation of a *monobank* that performed all banking functions (issuing money, acting as the state treasury, and being the only source of credit) to a two-tier banking system, which would allow the central bank to influence monetary creation by commercial banks through an interest rate policy. In the institutional vacuum after the collapse of communism, new institutions, including central banks, had to be created. Postcommunist central banks were new and had no experience in implementing an independent monetary policy. They lacked public and political support for market-based discipline that would signal their commitment to (costly) anti-inflationary policies.[4] The monobanks transferred assets to the newly created banks, which remained fully owned by the state. The financial systems of these emerging European countries were thus dominated by state-owned banks trying to achieve short-term profits by taking excessive risks, often in the form of high-risk lending to state-owned enterprises and assuming large open foreign exchange positions. High inflation and macroeconomic instability magnified the power and rents of incumbent banks and industrialists.

In spite of these similarities there is also observed variation in the approaches of these countries' governments to credibility building, which presents a series of puzzles. Why have the nations that started out in fairly similar conditions responded differently by implementing different macroeconomic and financial policies? What explains the differences in policymakers' perceptions on the need and value of international credibility? How have changes in these perceptions affected the opening of local banking sectors to foreign investors? I chose the four countries that capture a large range of cross-country variation in scale of foreign bank penetration. The cases also illustrate temporal elements of variation: the dynamics of foreign bank penetration over time so as to maximize the within-country variation in the principal explanatory variable. Finally, the chosen countries represent a wide range of economic conditions ranging from the disastrous economic crises in Bulgaria in the mid-1990s to the relative economic stability of Poland.

This chapter traces the trajectories of Estonia and Bulgaria, two specific cases involving currency board arrangements and the elevated presence of foreign banks from Sweden and Finland (Estonia) and Austria, Italy, and Greece (Bulgaria). Estonia and Bulgaria are different from each other in their approach to economic reforms but similar in terms of the general problems of communism that Eastern Europe experienced as a whole. Both countries embarked on economic reforms in the early 1990s without established reputations for sound policies. That said, the Estonian and Bulgarian governments had a different capacity to resist the pressures of incumbent interests, protect their central banks from political interference, and commit to banking-sector opening that brought in foreign owners.

Estonia could be used as the paradigmatic case of a newly independent nation in which the transformation of the financial system from state-owned to predominantly foreign-owned rendered the government's commitment to the currency board credible. Estonian political elites had a strong desire to build monetary policy credibility quickly after achieving national independence. A crucial precondition for the credibility of the currency board, adopted in 1992, was the political will to pursue sound monetary and fiscal policies and thus to resist demands from incumbent interest groups for credit and resource extraction. This goal was achieved by the radical withdrawal of the government from banking and by hard budget constraints but more importantly by the commitment to a radical exercise in banking-sector opening from the beginning of transition. The commitment of the Estonian government to a hard peg prohibited the newly established central bank from bailing out incumbent banks, which benefited from high inflation and exchange rate speculations prior to the monetary reform of 1992. The currency board also imposed fiscal discipline by prohibiting the government from borrowing from the central bank. It was only when the country attained a high level of foreign ownership of its banking system, however, that the credibility of the currency board was successfully anchored. The currency board has been successfully sustained over twenty years with changing presidents and parliaments, several bank failures, and the 2008 global financial crisis.

In contrast to the cumulative reform trajectory of Estonia, the financial crisis of 1996–97 divided Bulgaria's experience with economic reforms into two contrasting periods, both associated with different monetary regimes. Prior to the traumatic economic crisis, Bulgarian governments on both the left and the right proved unable to cut their ties with incumbent interest groups. The political choice of not letting foreign banks in and a flexible regime lacking credibility allowed the policy of high inflation to continue. State-owned banks were granting loans to enterprises on behalf of the government, and their losses were subsequently nationalized. In a generalized atmosphere of soft budget constraints, inflationary credit policies, and weak banking regulation, new private banks replicated the behavior of public banks. The influence of powerful incumbent interests capturing the government and the central bank resulted in repeated bank bailouts, monetization of the budget deficit, and sharp devaluations of the domestic currency. Only when the 1996 dramatic twin crisis (banking and currency) led to the collapse of one-third of the banks, hyperinflation, and a run on the currency did Bulgaria adopt a highly restrictive currency board. More importantly, as the financial crisis was primarily caused by the lack of credibility of financial policies, the crisis also triggered extensive banking-sector opening to foreign banks that introduced credible mechanisms for compliance with the currency board rules, whereas prior to their entry the government had proven unable to show that its monetary commitments were credible.

In short, foreign bank presence made the currency board arrangements credible in both countries examined in this chapter. These two countries represent different experiences with currency boards and banking-sector opening that offer empirical leverage on the question of credibility of monetary regimes. Before I proceed with examining evidence from case studies, I first offer a brief overview of the history and basic features of currency board arrangements.

Currency Boards

I begin with a short analysis of the foundations of currency board arrangements. As Jeffrey Sachs (quoted in Nash 1995) pointed out, "A currency board is a straitjacket on a central bank, an extreme discipline on extremely bad behavior." In the currency board, the authorities abandon autonomous monetary policy and replace it with an automatic mechanism that links money supply changes to the balance of payments. Domestic currency is issued only if it is fully backed by foreign exchange reserves. In the orthodox (pure) currency board, monetary policy is de facto transferred to a foreign central bank. In other words, the local central bank does not determine interest rates and is not allowed to finance government deficit or provide credit to banks. Under a modified currency board, however, the monetary authority can exert its function of a lender of last resort (i.e., it can provide rescue loans to banks to avoid a systemic banking crisis) from its excess foreign exchange reserves. Since the money supply is determined by foreign exchange reserves, the credibility of the currency board arrangement in the eyes of market participants is of paramount importance.

Currency boards are usually established by law to guarantee their independence from political interference.[5] Although currency boards are usually transitional arrangements to establish the initial credibility of a national currency, they may also serve as a more permanent type of monetary regime in very small open economies, in countries with a history of chronic and high inflation, and in countries with a history of speculative attacks and crises (Pautola and Backé 1998). Currency boards have often been introduced after severe financial or political crises to enhance the credibility of domestic currency or because of the lack of local expertise in monetary policy. In other words, governments adopt a currency board to establish the credibility of their central banks, stop inflation, and produce institutional reforms in fiscal policy.[6]

The first currency board was established in Mauritius in 1849. In the nineteenth century they were common in the British colonies, where more than seventy currency boards operated. Before World War II, some countries adopted currency boards, including Argentina (from 1902 to 1914) and Ireland, which operated a de facto currency board until the 1970s. After World War II, countries were reluctant to commit to a currency board because it meant a complete abandonment of their monetary sovereignty. After abandoning the nineteenth-century version of this monetary regime in 1974, Hong Kong reintroduced the first modern currency board in 1983. In 1991, Argentina adopted a currency board to halt hyperinflation, but the board collapsed in 2001. In the 1990s, several governments in emerging Europe introduced currency boards as a response to severe economic imbalances and political difficulties after the collapse of the socialist regime. As of 2013, the IMF classified the following (small) countries as pursuing currency boards: Antigua and Barbuda, Dominica, Grenada, St. Kitts and Nevis, St. Lucia, St. Vincent and the Grenadines, Djibouti, Hong Kong SAR, Bosnia and Herzegovina, Bulgaria, Brunei, and Darussalam. Estonia had pursued a currency board from 1992 to 2011, when it adopted the euro. Prior to joining the euro area in 2015, Lithuania pursued a currency board, which had been established in 1994. The adoption of a currency board was also considered in postconflict Liberia and Somalia, and in Russia and Ukraine.

The adoption of a currency board does not automatically lead to sound monetary policy and fiscal responsibility, however. The government may be tempted to put pressures on state-owned banks to provide loans to selected sectors or firms. It may therefore be reluctant to privatize these banks because they can serve as the "government lender of last resort" (Pautola and Backé 1998, 76). As Baliño and Enoch (1997) note, "a currency board cannot itself create credibility unless accompanied by firm supporting policies. Without such policies, credibility will remain low, which will undermine the sustainability of the currency board itself." Most countries that pursued currency boards have had a dominant foreign bank presence (Miller 2001, 67–68). But as noted earlier, the existing literature has yet to examine the impact of foreign banks on the credibility of currency boards. This book suggests that the credibility of currency boards is associated with transparent and sound financial policies, which in turn, hinge on the presence of multinational banks.

Estonia: A Fast Track to Credibility

Estonia emerged on the international scene in August 1991, when it broke away from the Soviet Union, with no reputation in international markets. It had a brief period of independent statehood from 1918 to 1949, but its democratic experience had been short-lived. Estonia spent fifty-one years under central planning. It was a fully developed communist state along the standard Soviet lines, with full nationalization of production and services, collectivization of agriculture, and five-year plans. Many predicted that Estonia would face a gloomy postauthoritarian future in the shadow of Russia, its powerful neighbor. The country's economic dependence on Russia made it risky to investors.[7]

Monetary chaos in the final years of the ruble zone—a currency union based on the Soviet ruble—due to Russia's mismanagement of the ruble, contributed to soaring inflation in post-Soviet Estonia. The result was a deep recession; the cumulative fall in real GDP was about 35 percent for the years 1991 to 1994 (Knöbl, Sutt, and Zavoico 2002, 9). The informal dollarization of the economy (dollars or other hard currency were used extensively in daily transactions, alongside the local currency) reached 60 percent in 1992 (Khoury and Wihlborg 2006). Because of low credibility and low levels of foreign exchange reserves, the government's only access to foreign financing was at the door of international financial institutions. A positive element in Estonia's story was that its debt burden was only 10 percent of GDP because Russia assumed all the Soviet-era debt, freeing other post-Soviet republics from past international obligations (Hanson 1995, 160). All things considered, the Estonian authorities sought to establish international credibility in a difficult economic situation following the collapse of communism and the Soviet empire.

The Politics of Monetary Reform

In January 1990, Edgar Savisaar, the first prime minister of independent Estonia,[8] undertook the first steps toward monetary reform when the Supreme Council (re)established the Bank of Estonia (Eesti Pank, BOE).[9] The single most important task was the introduction of a national currency considered a symbol of national identity.[10] The commitment to currency reform and an independent currency found expression in the formation of the Monetary Reform Committee, whose members (including the Estonian-born Swedish banker Rudolf Jakalas) were committed to market-based reforms and sought to isolate monetary policy from politics.[11] Its mandate was to implement monetary and banking sector reforms.[12]

The deterioration of economic conditions underlined the urgency of fast and coherent reforms. The post-Soviet shocks associated with price liberalization, the elimination of Soviet subsidies on imported raw materials, and the deliberate undervaluation of the new currency contributed to hyperinflation (Brown 1993, 494–95). By 1992, the annual inflation reached nearly 1,100 percent (Staehr 2004, 45). The Savisaar government, blamed for the bad economic situation and delays in economic reforms, fell in January 1992 and was replaced by a caretaker government led by Tiit Vähi, the former transportation minister.

It is unclear who was the first to seriously suggest the adoption of a currency board in Estonia. According to Prime Minister Laar, the initial idea came from Harvard Professor Jeffrey Sachs,[13] who arrived in Tallinn in April 1992, accompanied by his former student Ardo Hansson, an Estonian-born economist from the World Bank.[14] Swedish and American academics Lars Jonung, Steve Hanke, and Kurt Schuler were also instrumental in bringing this monetary arrangement about by proposing that Sweden would grant Estonia the needed initial reserves. To this end, the currency board would have three Swedish and two Estonian representatives, who would enjoy the exclusive right to issue the Estonian currency fully backed with gold and foreign exchange reserves (Hanke, Jonung, and Schuler 1992). Although the inclusion of a foreign central banker might have brought some credibility to this new monetary arrangement, this proposal did not find the support of the Estonian authorities because the BOE would have been removed from regulating the circulation of money (Kallas and Sorg 1994, 5).

At that point, the uncertainty surrounding the monetary reform trajectory in Estonia was high. In spite of the IMF disapproval of and discontent with the domestic political and financial community, Prime Minister Vähi introduced the Estonian kroon and the currency board arrangement in June 1992.[15] Estonia was the first country of the former Soviet Union to establish its own currency.[16] The kroon, perceived as a symbol of a break-away from Soviet influence, became the sole legal tender in June 1994. The new BOE governor, Siim Kallas, built his political capital around his role as "father of the national currency." Kallas favored the currency board regime because it was associated with the same transparency and credibility as the gold standard (in place from 1927 to 1933), under which Estonia achieved monetary stability (Knöbl, Sutt, and Zavoico 2002). Because the political and institutional landscape was largely unstable, he feared that if a flexible regime was chosen, constant disputes and political pressures would cause extra confusion and dual money circulation (the kroon along with the ruble) (Kallas 2002, 130). Instead, a currency board promised an immediate solution to the problem of resisting demands for credit from politicians and incumbent interest groups.

The Estonian currency board is a semiorthodox version of this monetary arrangement, although it was operated in an orthodox fashion (Khoury and Wihlborg 2006) (see table 4.A1 in the appendix to this chapter).[17] Under a currency board, the BOE is not permitted to finance a government deficit, engage in selling securities, or lend to banks. Therefore, it cannot assume the responsibilities of lender of last resort. Any change in the currency board requires a two-thirds parliamentary majority. The BOE reports only to the Parliament and is prohibited by law from devaluing the kroon; only the Parliament has this right.[18]

The German mark, endowed with credibility from the Bundesbank's commitment to price stability, was chosen as the anchor currency, even though Germany accounted for only 0.2 percent of Estonia's trade in 1991 (Sulling 2002, 472). The exchange rate between the kroon and the German mark was set at eight kroon to one German mark. To support the newly established currency regime, the BOE needed $120 million in foreign exchange reserves (Laar 2002, 120). At the time of the currency reform, only the gold restituted from the United Kingdom was available ($52 million). Thus the Estonian Supreme Council decided to commit the state forest (which could have been sold in the event of crisis), which had an estimated value of $150 million, to complement the reserves (Kallas and Sorg 1994). The currency board thus started with partial backing of the BOE liabilities.[19] The precariousness of the situation with reserves illustrates the great need for international capital to support a new monetary measure of containing inflation.

The adoption of the currency board did not buy immediate credibility for the Estonian government in the eyes of international investors. The new monetary regime initially lacked credibility both domestically and internationally. The currency board was adopted nearly unanimously only because its implications were not fully grasped. Banks and the opposition parties were convinced that even after the monetary reform, the central bank would continue to provide "cheap credit" to failing factories and collective farms (Laar 2002, 121–22). Former prime minister Mart Laar recalls reactions of banks and politicians when the currency board was adopted in the Parliament:

> Banks were furious! They missed the moment because they did not understand what exactly they supported. We did not say much about the currency board in the Parliament before its adoption. There was only one economist from the Agricultural Party who understood what the currency board was and its consequences, and he voted against it.[20]

Of course, domestic banks did not support the currency board arrangement because it required commitment from the government and the central bank to low inflation, stable exchange rates, and financial reforms that would reduce banks' rent-seeking opportunities. Neither the new currency nor the currency board had international backing from the IMF and the European Community.[21] The IMF urged the Estonian authorities to postpone monetary reform until they could accumulate foreign exchange reserves and build technical capabilities (Laar 2002, 114).[22] Stanley Fisher (1997, 17), then first deputy managing director of the IMF, revealed the doubts of the international financial community on the fifth anniversary of the Estonian kroon in 1997: "Many of those who heard about the intention to introduce the currency board in 1992 were doubtful that it could succeed." The Estonian authorities' quest for international credibility has been a driver of domestic economic and institutional reforms, as the following section shows.

"Just Do It" Reform Strategy

After the election in September 1992, the right-wing coalition government led by the Pro Patria Union (formed in 1991) declared its commitment to economic openness and a radical withdrawal of the state from the economy.

Prime Minister Mart Laar believed that economic openness, though politically unpopular, attracts the foreign investments necessary to foster competition, reconstruction, and growth.[23] Seeking to build the credibility of the new monetary regime, the Laar's government (1992–94) immediately liberalized current account transactions, while most capital controls were abolished by the end of 1994. The key elements of the economic reform program were a conservative fiscal policy, ultraliberal trade and investment policies, and a full-scale privatization to facilitate market-based price and wage adjustments (Kallas and Sorg 1994; Sulling 2002).[24] The reform strategy, summed up by the advertising slogan "Just do it," intended to signal the commitment to stringent reform measures in spite of the high economic and short-term social costs (Laar 2007, 3).

The Laar government was determined to cut ties with incumbent interests from the communist era, and so it committed to rapid property transformation with the goal of attracting foreign investors.[25] A legal framework for foreign direct investments, adopted only a few months after the country regained its independence, featured direct sales with the participation of foreign investors as the main method of asset divestitures. Sales of local banks and enterprises to foreign capital were also seen a way to replenish foreign exchange reserves indispensable to ensuring the sustainability of the currency board (Terk 2000, 19–40).

Although credibility considerations were paramount, external pressures from international institutions were not drivers of reform. The government refused the loan from the IMF to balance the budget because it decided to construct the future of Estonia on "the momentum for radical reforms, not loans" (Laar 2007, 4, 6).[26] Attracting foreign investments was seen as a superior alternative to borrowing from international institutions, which supposedly preserved economic backwardness. Ultimately, the entry of foreign investors enabled the government to break decisively with the communist reputation, turning Estonia into the "Hong Kong of Europe."[27]

In the subsequent section, I will show that although the Estonian government demonstrated anti-inflationary resolve in its monetary policy, implementing the financial sector policies needed to establish the credibility of the currency board has proven to be more difficult. Because of this, the government needed to enhance its political clout by getting the backing of reputable foreign banks with first-class technical expertise in international finance.

Experimenting with Banking Reforms

Banking was a lucrative business in the chaotic institutional and hyperinflationary environment before Estonia regained its monetary independence.
State-owned banks earned most of their profits from foreign currency speculations and short-term foreign trade arbitrage transactions between the
USSR and the West (Barisitz 2002, 85; Hanson 1995, 150). With lax or non-
existent banking supervision stemming mainly from confusion over who
was in charge of licensing policies (the BOE or Gosbank, the Soviet Union's
central bank), few restrictions and sanctions were placed on such speculations (Hanson 1995). On top of that, large state-owned enterprises, en-
riched by speculations in a weakly regulated environment, were able with
relatively little money to create their own banks or grab the branches of all
Soviet Union banks and exploit these banks' resources to finance their own
activities (Sõrg 1998, 170–72). Hyperinflation further reduced the real
value of the obligatory initial bank capital. Lax licensing requirements led
to a proliferation of many very small banks. By the end of 1992, forty-three
banks were registered (Fleming 2001).

Domestic banks were able to remain liquid in the face of large portfolios
of bad loans by using their large profits from foreign exchange trading or by
relending cheap central bank credits while exploiting high interest rate
spreads. But monetary reform unified the exchange rate and reduced buy-
sell spreads, which substantially reduced the foreign exchange revenues of
banks (Hanson 1995, 150). As inflation declined, borrowers' distress became manifest. This caused liquidity problems in several domestic banks,
ultimately leading to the first banking crisis in 1992–93.

The government warned that the planned 1993 budget did not have
enough money for bank bailouts (Hanson 1995, 151). Ultimately the BOE,
faithful to the policy of the "hard kroon," decided to liquidate Tartu Commercial Bank (the first private bank in Estonia) because its liquidity problems stemmed from losses on foreign exchange speculations. Once again,
the Estonian authorities acted against the IMF's advice to merge the three
banks with liquidity problems to avoid a systemic banking crisis, fearing
that the banks' shareholders and customers preserved links with organized
crime in Russia (Laar 2002, 188). The government was also concerned that
the IMF's solution would require more resources from the state budget.[28]
But a different approach was taken with respect to the other two banks, for
their liquidity problems were caused mainly by the frozen foreign currency

assets in Moscow. These banks were forcibly merged into a new bank, the North Estonian Bank, which was subsequently recapitalized by the central bank (Fleming 2001). According to Laar, bankers misjudged the BOE's resolve and promised that the government would go down in three weeks, but the government was determined not to "waste a single cent of state money on saving the banks."[29]

The BOE's approach to the bankers was succinctly summarized by the title of the article in the Estonian newspaper, *Rahva Haal:* "Commercial Banks, Kallas, Kroon: Who Is Stronger?" (Buyske 1997, 85). Although the currency board permitted well-defined bank rescues as long as the country's foreign exchange holdings stayed sufficiently high (which was the case), the BOE refrained from intervention (Hanson 1995, 152). As former prime minister Laar (2002, 184–85) explained:

> The former Communist party bosses considered it only fair to compensate the loss of their high status by taking up positions in banks, knowing at the same time absolutely nothing about banking. Very soon they started trying to go about their business in the banking world in the same way as they had in the Communist party, by cheating and lying, and taking all the benefits for themselves and their friends. . . . The bankers fell back on their earlier experiences . . . hoping that the new young government would give in to their demands as easily as previous governments. In this situation, even indecisiveness would have been a decision, one which would probably ultimately have led to the fall of the kroon.

The BOE's president showed equal determination in his rejection of the requests of incumbent managers for cheap credit:[30]

> Some industrial circles, often connected with the former Soviet nomenklatura, have tried to force the Bank of Estonia to issue more kroons without proper backing. . . . The Bank of Estonia will never yield to such pressure.

The objectives of price and currency stability justified the unequivocal position of the BOE not to help troubled banks. This was a politically bold step that showed the resolve of monetary authorities to discipline powerful bankers. Nor has the BOE yielded to calls by the Ministry of Justice to limit the independence of the central bank on the grounds that the existing law "turns some functions of executive power over to the BOE" (Staprans 1994, 9).[31]

After the 1992–93 banking crisis was resolved, the BOE established a licensing review and froze the issuance of new bank licenses in its effort to strengthen banking regulations.[32] This tough message, however, may have been diluted by the interim efforts of the BOE to save the largest bank, the Social Bank (representing 20 percent of total bank assets), which was the government's main fiscal agent financing the oil and metal trade (Fleming 2001, 92).[33] This episode shows that the BOE's supervisory and regulatory powers were still relatively weak. In order to further increase the BOE's supervision and enforcement powers, a new Credit Institutions Act was adopted in December 1994.

The currency board gained initial credibility by disciplining monetary policies and public finances. The Estonian authorities remained committed to a strict fiscal policy, and they reduced their fiscal deficit to mere 1.2 percent of GDP and public debt to 9 percent of GDP in 1995 (table 4.1). The credibility of the currency board was widely seen as the "sacred cow" in Estonian politics, whereas the commitment to fiscal discipline was an important precondition (Korhonen 2000). The kroon has become fully secured by gold and convertible foreign currencies (Buyske 1997, 92). But the currency board proved only partially successful in combating inflation, which was brought down to 89.8 percent in 1993 (Laar 2007, 5) but double-digit inflation rates were still recorded in 1995 (table 4.1).

Ultimately, the establishment of a credible monetary regime in a fragile political and economic situation after the collapse of communism was dependent on the regulatory and supervisory capacity of the BOE to limit the banks' creation of credit. In the first half of the 1990s, the Estonian supervisory authorities experienced difficulty in improving the transparency and soundness of the banking system and thus in curbing devaluation expecta-

TABLE 4.1. Macroeconomic Indicators for Estonia

	Inflation (annual %)	Total reserves (minus gold) in US$ million	Public finances as a % of GDP[a]	External debt as a % of exports	Public debt as a % of GDP[b]
1995	28.78	580	−1.2	24.3	9
2000	4.03	921	−0.6	62.9	5.1
2005	4.09	1,943	1.6	102.9	4.6
2009	−0.08	3,972	−1.7	185	7.1

Source: World Bank, World Development Indicators; European Bank for Reconstruction and Development, various Transition Reports.
[a]Cash surplus/deficit (% of GDP) is closest to the overall budget balance.
[b]Abbas et al. (2010).

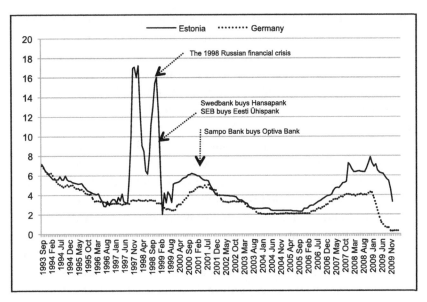

Fig. 4.1. Money Market Rates: Estonia and Germany (%)
Source: International Monetary Fund, *International Financial Statistics.*

tions. As a consequence, the country's risk perceptions by international markets continued to fluctuate and did not change dramatically in spite of the government's reform commitments. As figure 4.1 shows, short-term interest rate differentials with Germany remained positive, which implies an incomplete credibility of the Estonian monetary regime. Long-term government bonds yielded over 11 percent in 1997, demonstrating the relative riskiness of the Estonian government.[34] These developments clearly highlight the complexity and difficulty of building credibility for the monetary regime domestically.

Outsourcing Central Banking

The design of the currency board was based on the idea of opening the banking sector to foreign strategic investors to strengthen the financial system and assure access to international markets (Hanke, Jonung, and Schuler 1992). And whereas the Estonian government lifted restrictions on foreign bank entry right from the outset of transition intending to privatize state-owned banks and make them accessible to foreign investors, there was initially a lack of foreign interest. The government, in turn, did not have the financial resources to recapitalize domestic banks to make them more attractive (Sõrg1994). Admittedly, the government was also politically motivated to resist the influx of "dirty" Russian capital into the Estonian financial system. One manager of American Bank of the Baltics commented on the Estonian monetary authorities' licensing policy in 1992 in the following way: "If a big Western bank like NatWest were to apply, they wouldn't say no. But they would turn down one of the small, newfangled Russian banks."[35] In the end, a few foreign players bought shares in Estonian banks and held about 24 percent of total assets in mid-1990s (table 4.2).[36] Branches of two Finnish banks, Union Bank of Finland and KOP (merged into Merita bank in 1995), started to operate Estonia in 1994 but provided services mostly to Finnish clients.

How do we explain this initial lack of enthusiasm on the part of foreign banks for entering into the Estonian banking market? Nordic banks returned to an expansion strategy only in the second half of the 1990s because the banking crisis that hit Finland, Norway and Sweden in the early 1990s put severe strains on them.[37] Despite a slow pace in the early 1990s, the privatization of state-owned banks to foreign strategic investors was nearly completed by the end of the 1990s. The power of the incumbent banking community was decisively broken with bank privatizations to foreign *strategic* investors that had a profound impact on domestic groups and complex

TABLE 4.2. Transparency and Regulatory Quality of the Estonian Banking System

	Foreign bank assets as a % of total assets[a]	Nonperforming loans as a % of total gross loans[b]	Credit reporting institutions[c]	EBRD index of banking sector reforms[d]
1995	24	2.4	Private credit bureau	3.0
2000	98	1.0	Private credit bureau (est. 2001)	3.7
2005	99	0.2	Private credit bureau	4.0
2009	99	5.4	Private credit bureau	4.0

Source: Data for each column from the respective sources:
[a]Data from Claessens et al. (2008); Claessens and van Horen (2012).
[b]Data from World Bank, *World Development Indicators.* Data for 1995 from the EBRD *Transition Reports.*
[c]Data from World Bank, *Doing Business.*
[d]Data from European Bank for Reconstruction and Development, *Transition Reports,* various issues. The index measures reform progress in the following areas: liberalization of interest rates and the credit allocation process, volume of lending to the private sector, private ownership in the banking sector, degree of bank competition, bank solvency, and establishment of a framework for regulation and prudential supervision. The indicator can take values between 1 and 4.33, with 1 representing little or no progress and 4.33 corresponding to the full convergence of banking laws and regulations with the Bank for International Settlements' standards.

power relations. In 1994, the Swedish Swedbank acquired 33 percent in Hoiupank. When Hoiupank merged with Hansapank, Swedbank acquired a majority of shares in the largest Estonian bank, Hansapank, in September 1998.[38] With nearly 42 percent market share, Swedbank has become the most important player in the Estonian banking market (table 4.3). The history of Swedbank, the largest retail bank in Sweden, can be traced back as far as 1820 when the first Swedish savings bank was founded in Göteborg. The other major Swedish bank, Skandinaviska Enskilda Banken (SEB), established by A. O. Wallenberg in 1856, acquired a majority share in Eesti Ühispank, the second main banking giant in Estonia, in 1998. The acquisition of majority stakes in the two largest Estonian banks by the Swedish banks have strengthened the capital asset ratio and liquidity of these banks and facilitated their access to international markets (International Monetary Fund 1999, 33). The presence of foreign banks provided a valuable signal that acted as a "seal of approval" for good economic policies, which was particularly valuable under the unfavorable conditions that existed after the 1998 crisis. With the entry of Swedbank and SEB, money market rates dropped substantially from above 15 percent in November 1998 to only 2 percent in April 1999. The entry of these reputable foreign banks thus sent a credible signal to international markets about the inflationary resolve of the Estonian monetary authorities. Then, the Finnish Sampo group acquired a 58 percent stake in Estonia's third largest bank, Optiva Bank, in June 2000.

By 2005, large Nordic banks owned 99 percent of the market share in Estonia (table 4.2). How did the Estonian authorities manage to get away with such a dramatic change in the structure of ownership of the banking sector? When it came to the banking sector, the government enjoyed a high degree of autonomy. As a lobby, Estonian public and private bankers were

TABLE 4.3. Market Shares of Top Multinational Banks in Estonia, 2012

Bank Name	Assets held by a bank as a % of total banking assets	Parent Bank (Country)
Swedbank (Hansapank)	41.6	Swedbank (Sweden)
SEB Eesti Ühispank	19.3	Skandinaviska Enskilda Banken (SEB) (Sweden)
Sampo Pank (Danske Bank)	10.2	Danske Bank (Denmark)
Nordea Bank Finland	15.5	Nordea Bank (Sweden, Finland, Denmark, Norway)

Source: Raiffeisen Research (2012); Bank of Estonia (2013).

weak. The BOE's solutions to banking crises usually consisted of bank mergers, bankruptcies, and privatizations. Consequently, the number of banks was reduced from twenty-one in 1992 to five by the end of 1998. At the same time, the government's role in finance declined sharply. The European Bank for Reconstruction and Development (EBRD) reports that the share of assets of state-owned banks represented only 6.56 percent of total banking assets in 1996.

How important was the presence of foreign banks in enhancing the transparency and regulatory quality of Estonia's banking sector? The takeover of Estonian banks by Nordic banking groups was accompanied by substantial capital and liquidity injections and the development of a new regulatory framework to overhaul the banking system. The entry of Nordic banks also led to intensified competition, improved transparency, and risk management in the Estonian banking sector. Swedish banks pursued "a homogeneous business model, that in effect, extended uniform credit instruments, risk management tools, and credit strategies" throughout the Baltic region (Leven 2011, 184). The recommendation of foreign experts was followed when unified financial supervision (banking, insurance, and securities markets), modeled on Germany, was established in 2002 and taken over by the Estonian Financial Supervision Authority.[39] Furthermore, memoranda of understanding have been put in place between supervisory authorities of Estonia and the Nordic countries, facilitating information sharing among supervisors about the performance of Nordic parent banks and their subsidiaries (International Monetary Fund 2011). According to the IMF Report on the Observance of Standards and Codes, the quality of prudential regulation and supervision in Estonia in 2001 was considered to be comparable to that of the most developed countries, just a few years after the entry of Nordic banks (Ådahl 2002).

My theoretical predictions are borne out with remarkable consistency. The credibility of the currency board was enhanced by introducing foreign private agents to ensure the government's compliance with the rules of the monetary regime. In a way, both monetary policy and banking supervision in Estonia were "outsourced" to Nordic supervisors (Khoury and Wihlborg 2006). The dominance of foreign banks in the Estonian banking sector makes all banks subject to consolidated supervision by the Nordic supervisory authorities. For a hard peg to be credible, "the domestic banking sector has to be particularly solid in order to minimize the frequency of banking crises" (Edwards 2003, 56). Foreign banks helped to build confidence in the currency board by adding to the soundness of the Estonian banking sector and reducing its vulnerability to crises by increasing its transparency and regulatory oversight. Table 4.2 illustrates the two mechanisms through which foreign banks increase monetary policy credibility—transparency and regulatory quality of the local banking system—discussed in detail in chapter 2. The EBRD banking reform index demonstrates that Estonia's banking laws and regulations fully converged to BIS standards by 2005. Furthermore, Swedish regulators, drawing on lessons from their own banking crisis of 1991–93, were quick to respond to the 2008 global credit crisis through imposing higher capital standards (a core Tier 1 ratio of at least 12 percent of risk-weighted assets) on its four largest banks operating internationally. One of the standard measures of financial stability is the amount of nonperforming loans, which, as table 4.2 shows, decreased to nearly zero in 2005. The independence and credibility of the BOE, which has proven to be the locomotive of economic reforms, has been reinforced too (Grønn and Fredholm 2013, 7).[40]

Figures 4.1 and 4.2 present the evolution of Estonia's currency- and country-risk premiums graphically. Figure 4.1 shows a decrease in interest rate differentials between Estonia and Germany to nearly zero basis points (or negative), indicating that the currency board was perceived by markets as credible. The currency board's foreign exchange reserve amounted to 125 percent in May 1998 after the crisis-related temporary decline (Pautola and Backé 1998). The yields on long-term government bonds also decreased notably. The biggest jump downward—from 15.27 percent in December 1998 to 7.17 percent in February 2002—was recorded after the sale of the largest Estonian banks to the Nordic multinational banks was complete (figure 4.2). In sum, the positive effects of Nordic banks on the soundness and stability of the Estonian banking system increased the credibility of monetary commitments of Estonian authorities. The effectiveness of the BOE in solving credibility problems in financial policies was in the end dependent on the presence of foreign banks.

Nordic Banks as Lenders of Last Resort

In addition to improving transparency and the regulatory quality of the Estonian banking system, Nordic banks improved the credibility of the currency board by serving as lender of last resort. In 1998–99, Estonia experienced the second banking crises, caused mainly by the financial contagion

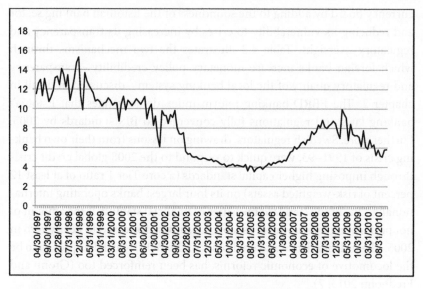

Fig. 4.2. Estonia Long-Term Government Bond Yields (%)
Source: Global Financial Data.

from Russia. Whereas the domestic monetary authorities had to resolve the banking problems during the first banking crisis in 1992–93, foreign banks assisted during the second (Sõrg and Uiboupin 2004). The aggregate market share (in term of assets) of four major Nordic banks—Swedbank, SEB, Nordea Bank, and Danske Bank—amounted to nearly 77 percent in 2012 (table 4.3). Swedish banks have the largest market share in Estonia, thus the lender of last resort function has been de facto assumed by the Swedish central bank (Berensmann 2002).[41] Just as Estonia is dependent on the health and business strategy of Swedish banks, the reputation of the parent banks also depends on the performance of their Baltic subsidiaries.[42] An important characteristic of the centralized business model pursued by the Nordic banking groups is that their subsidiaries in Estonia (and other Baltic countries) are, to a large extent, financed through parent bank funding (Grønn and Fredholm 2013).

While foreign bank presence reduced liquidity risks, it contributed to a credit boom, particularly in 2005–2007. Eighty percent of loans extended to primarily Estonian households were denominated in foreign currency. A well-capitalized Estonian banking sector, however, provided a buffer against deterioration in nonperforming loans; the capital adequacy ratio of 21 per-

cent was well above the required 10 percent (Brixiova, Vartia, and Wörgötter 2010, 63). Furthermore, during the 2008 financial crisis, Nordic parent
banks again assumed the role of lender of last resort to their Estonian subsidiaries. As the Swedish finance minister said, "We have declared to our
banks that they are supposed to behave responsibly—to perceive these Baltic countries as their home market" (Dougherty 2009). The "outsourced"
nature of supervision was exemplified by a direct precautionary swap line
obtained by Estonia from the Swedish central bank in March 2009 to meet
its liquidity needs and insure against a depositors' run on its banks (Ingves
2010). The Swedish government was aware that the situation in the Baltic
countries was important to the stability of the Swedish financial system, so
it contributed large sums to international efforts to help these countries, in
addition to helping Swedish banks (Dougherty 2009).

   In conjunction with lender-of-last-resort support provided by multinational banks, the right-leaning Estonian government led by Andrus Ansip
sought to prevent potential damage to the credibility of the currency board
by ruling out any exchange rate adjustment during the 2008 crisis (Raudla
and Kattel 2011, 176). Instead, it adopted the austerity-led internal devaluation strategy that involved extensive fiscal retrenchment. Why did the Estonian government sacrifice the goal of a monetary policy oriented toward
domestic objectives in order to save the hard peg? A widely held conviction
among Estonian political elites was that the fiscal austerity would signal a
deeper commitment to their policy promises to international creditors and
rating agencies (Raudla and Kattel 2011).[43] Estonia was hailed as a "poster
child" of fiscal discipline (Raudla and Kattel 2011, 164), recording a budget
deficit of only 1.7 percent of GDP in 2009 (table 4.1). Additionally, the Estonian authorities, together with home regulators of multinational banks,
acted jointly to demonstrate the credibility of the government's commitment
to sound financial policies via further regulatory and legislative reforms in
the banking sector. In 2010, the Nordic and Baltic central banks, governments, and financial supervisory authorities agreed on a cooperation agreement on cross-border financial stability and crisis management aimed at
preventing and resolving cross-border financial crises. Simultaneously, the
Nordic-Baltic Macro-Prudential Forum to coordinate macro-prudential
policy frameworks came into existence (see Grønn and Fredholm 2013).

   Overall, the 2008 crisis was a stress test for the currency board. The liquidity support from Nordic banks played a pivotal role in maintaining the
confidence of international markets in the monetary regime. It also pre-

vented the deterioration of the creditworthiness of the Estonian government, whose credit rating by Standard & Poor's was raised to A (from A–) in June 2010. As depicted in figure 4.1, the kroon came under heavy pressure and the currency-risk premium increased, peaking at 521 basis points in July 2009. But this was short-lived and interest rate differentials with Germany fell to 67 basis points by November 2010. Similarly, yields on Estonian long-term bonds topped nearly 10 percent in March 2009, but they dropped in half in mid-2010. And if the credibility of the currency board reflected the probability that the exchange rate would not be altered, the Estonian authorities succeeded. A credible currency board served as the pillar of stable economic policies until Estonia was invited to join the eurozone as of January 2011.

Bulgaria: The Imperatives of Crisis

Whereas the Estonian government embarked on the road to economic orthodoxy after gaining independence in 1991, the Bulgarian transition experiment represents a classic case of delayed stabilization. Delays in stabilization arise due to a "war of attrition" (Alesina and Drazen 1991) between societal groups with conflicting objectives concerning fiscal policy reforms involving the restrictions on the monetization of deficits. The consequence of purchasing debt with newly printed money is high inflation. The Bulgarian governments were unable to impose monetary and fiscal discipline on domestic groups until the traumatic 1996–97 economic crisis, when the new reformist government, trying to ramp up the credibility of its monetary commitments by moving to a currency board, wanted banking reform with the involvement of reputable foreign banks. The absence of a central bank to manage the currency board and regulate the domestic banking system threatened to undermine any attempt to build the credibility of the currency board arrangement.

Like Estonia, Bulgaria, which spent forty-three years under central planning, inherited the negative socioeconomic legacies of communism. Led by a hardline Stalinist, Todor Zhivkov, Bulgaria was perceived as the country closest to the Soviet Union, at least since the 1960s. Its industrial structure was the result of socialist industrialization oriented toward the Soviet markets, and more than 50 percent of its trade was with the Soviet Union.[44] The trade shock to the Bulgarian economy resulting from the disintegration of the communist bloc caused shortages of goods and raw materials and a loss of export markets (Dobrinsky 2000, 582–83). As a consequence, the cumulative fall in real GDP was 28 percent for the years 1989 to 1993. Although there were some early attempts at economic reforms from 1982 to 1986 to enhance the self-management of enterprises, Bulgaria started the postcommunist transition with a similar property rights structure and degree of *etatization* as Estonia.

Notwithstanding, establishing the confidence of international markets in the economy was even more critical to the Bulgarian case. In contrast to Estonia, the presence of a large stock of foreign-currency-denominated debt, inherited from the communist era, put Bulgaria on unsustainable debt path. This debt was composed primarily of loans from foreign banks to the Bulgarian government, subsequently recorded internally as foreign currency loans to state-owned enterprises (Caporale et al. 2002, 231). In Estonia, hyperinflation wiped out most loans extended by socialist banks. The majority of bad loans in Bulgaria, however, were denominated in foreign currency and thus were not swept by the initial high inflation and currency devaluation. In 1989, Bulgaria had a $10.1 billion in foreign debt (net of reserves) while its annual real GDP was only $15 billion. As a result, its debt service accounted for 63 percent of the country's export earnings (Pop-Eleches 2009, 219). Then, in March 1990, Bulgaria announced a unilateral moratorium on its foreign debt service. The level of dollarization amounted to 30 percent in 1991 (Baliño, Bennett, and Borensztein 1999). Due to its bad repayment record, the only access the government had to foreign financing was on an official level from international institutions. Bulgaria was excluded from international credit markets, unable to borrow abroad until July 1994, when the foreign debt was restructured in a Brady deal.

The Inconsistent Path to Economic Reforms

The inherently vulnerable macroeconomic context was further compounded by political instability and distributional conflicts. The absence of a strong opposition in 1989 led to a political victory of the former communists—the Bulgarian Socialist Party (BSP)—in the first free elections in June 1990.[45] The BSP was unable to implement any coherent set of economic reforms, and the prime minister, Alexander Lukanov, was forced by mass protests to resign (Koford 2000; Stone 2002). In the second elections in October 1991, the opposition, the Union of Democratic Forces (UDF), emerged victorious.[46] The UDF-led government of prime minister Filip Dimitrov (1991–92) was largely responsible for the implementation of the initial liberalization reforms. In February 1991, it also launched the stabilization program, attached to the one-year standby agreement with the IMF that envisaged, for example, reduction of the fiscal and current account deficits and the unification of the exchange rate (Dobrinsky 2000, 583).

Price liberalization, leading to high inflation that reached 474 percent at the end of 1991, was the point of departure for discussions on the choice of an exchange rate regime (Berlemann, Hristov, and Nenovsky 2002, 18). The architects of the Estonian currency board, Stephen Hanke and a team of U.S. economists, advised the Bulgarian authorities to adopt the same monetary regime with the currency pegged to a basket of goods rather than to a foreign currency. As in Estonia, the IMF was reluctant to support the currency board that would not be fully backed by foreign exchange reserves. In contrast to Estonia, a genuine political will to commit to monetary stabilization was missing in Bulgaria (Christov 1997, 140).

Why were the Bulgarian authorities reluctant to take the same step as Estonia in 1992 by adopting a currency board to stabilize inflationary expectations? Clearly, the initial choice of the currency regime was not simply a matter of insufficient international reserves, as was presented.[47] There are two possible explanations of this decision. First, a flexible regime allowed the central bank—Bulgarian National Bank (Blgarska Narodna Banka, BNB)—to continue its policy of high inflation and depreciated currency to support uncompetitive state-owned enterprises.[48] Second, a managed float was a desirable exchange rate regime arrangement for powerful bankers who favored inflation instead of price stability.[49] As we will see, prior to the 1996–97 crisis, no Bulgarian government was able to break the power of the domestic banking community by opening the banking sector to foreign competition, opting instead for repeated bank bailouts through the central bank's credits (Stone 2002, 213).

In the following sections I give evidence for the claim that in the pre-1996 environment of the subordinated central bank and the poorly regulated and supervised banking sector, consisting of domestic state-owned and politically connected private banks, the government did not establish the credibility of its monetary policies. Before 1995, the Bulgarian authorities restricted the entry of foreign banks, so that domestic banks, incapable of competing with large international banks, could flourish behind protective walls (Caporale et al. 2002). When it came to opening of the banking sector, state-owned banks became a powerful constituency keeping foreign competition out.[50] The BNB lacked the authority and the ability to conduct its monetary policies without interference from the government. Although the 1991 Law on the BNB granted substantial de jure independence to the central bank, in practice it was subordinate to the government's political guidance and captured by interest groups. Whereas in the early 1990s the BNB scored higher on the Cukierman, Webb, and Neyapti's (1992) index of legal independence than central banks in some industrial countries (e.g. Belgium in 1980–89), its actual independence was below the median (Christov 1997, 140).

The "Credit Millionaires"

During most of the communist period, all banking functions were the responsibility of the BNB, a *monobank*, created by a nationalization process in 1947 when all existing commercial banks were merged.[51] Alongside the BNB, only two other banks existed: the State Savings Bank (Darzhavna Spestovna Kasa, DSK), the only bank allowed to hold the accounts of individuals, and the Bulgarian Foreign Trade Bank, in charge of all foreign exchange operations for the country.[52]

Following the political changes of 1989, the banking system was transformed into a two-tier system consisting of the central bank and commercial banks. Sectoral banks and the existing fifty-nine branches of the BNB were transformed into autonomous banks (Caporale et al. 2002, 224). During their tenures, both the Dimitrov's administration and the technocratic Berov government (1992–94) attempted to consolidate, restructure, and privatize undercapitalized state-owned banks. A government-orchestrated merger of twenty-two former BNB branches resulted in the establishment of the United Bulgarian Bank (UBB). The final outcome of the consolidation was a concentrated banking structure, where the newly created three large state-owned banks—UBB, Expressbank, and Hebrosbank—gained the dominant position. By the end of the consolidation period (1992–95), the Bulgarian banking sector consisted of thirty-five banks, but state-owned banks preserved their privileged position (Berlemann, Hristov, and Nenovsky 2002, 22). Because of politics, not a single government bank was privatized by 1995 (Miller and Petranov 2001).

State-owned banks did not act like traditional banks but rather as government offices used to distribute political loans to loss-making state-owned enterprises.[53] Because state-owned banks served as the "cash cows" for the economy, it was difficult to build a political coalition behind bank privatization.[54] Kalin Hristov, deputy governor of the BNB, reflects:

> The Bulgarian governments on the left and right held the view that the domestic banks were the jewels of the economy. They did not want to sell these banks for nickels. . . . In the end, however, banks have proven to be rather fake jewels.[55]

At the same time, illegal and hidden privatization of banks took place in the sense of unregulated and illegal transfer of capital from state to private hands (Peev 2002). Although no legislative procedure for selling the shares of public banks existed, some banks increased their capital by issuing new shares and selling them to political insiders. Meanwhile, the BNB and DSK (the state savings bank) provided financial resources for these capital expansions (Dobrinsky 1994). The owners of new private banks used the regulatory vacuum to "decapitalize" state-owned banks and transfer the capital to their own banks, and then used bank funds to finance their personal activities (Peev 2002, 24).[56] At first sight, the expansion of the number of private banks might appear as increased banking competition. But in reality, a liberal licensing regime, low capital requirements, and weak banking regulation led to the proliferation of new private banks with political connections engaging in reckless lending.[57] Clearly, these new private banks acted like the Ponzi schemes.[58] Concurrent with the proliferation of private banks, powerful financial-industrial conglomerates (Multigrup, Orion, Olimp, Tron, and Euronergy) emerged during the Berov administration. The most influential among them created Group-13 (Peev 2002), whose most powerful member was Multigroup, with over 3,500 employees in more than fifty enterprises that included a bank, an insurance company, the country's most active stock exchange, and a sugar plant (Barnes 2007, 78).

Although the BNB had issued prudential regulations in a number of areas including bank licensing, bank liquidity, and capital adequacy, it repeatedly failed to enforce them (Christov 1997). Thus these so-called "credit millionaires"—which included government banks and enterprises, crony private banks and enterprises, and financial-industrial groups—were uniquely positioned to exploit their political connections to take over the banks, flout supervision laws, and siphon the assets from the most profitable state enterprises and put them into private hands (Koford 2000; Stone

2002).[59] They engaged in "the economy of transfer"[60] making spectacular profits by failing to service bank loans (Peev 2002).

A closer look reveals that the government and the bank managers followed a contract based on direct political instructions. Banks took an active part in this process by providing loans to enterprises, which did not intend to repay their debts, thus making these loans implicit subsidies.[61] Public and new private banks were dependent on personal relations with the BNB and the government, and they cultivated their lobbying activities.[62] Consequently, the level of bad loans soared and more than 74 percent of total bank loans were nonperforming by 1995 (Miller and Petranov 2001, 13). The Organization for Economic Cooperation and Development (OECD 1999, 32) reported that "[u]ntil 1996, commercial credit was expanded to the nonfinancial sector in Bulgaria to a degree that was unprecedented relative to any other European transition economy." While high inflation was wiping out some of the banks' bad loans, many of these loans were denominated in foreign currency, thus the inflation actually increased the debt burden of enterprises (Caporale et al. 2002).

The situation worsened further. The banks, overburdened with bad loans, were repeatedly refinanced by the BNB on a completely subjective and discretionary basis. The most striking example of these bailouts was a special program introduced by the Berov government in December 1993 that replaced enterprise debt with government bonds, the so-called ZUNK bonds (twenty-five-year government debt instruments) (Wyzan 1998, 8). Bonds were distributed as capital contributions to the banks, which could have exchanged these bonds for stakes in to-be-privatized state-owned enterprises at face value via debt-for-equity swaps and used them as collateral for central bank financing (Dobrinsky 1994, 2000).[63]

Evidently, the country lacked leaders who could precommit to bold reforms to gain international credibility. Bulgaria repeatedly defaulted on foreign currency bank debt in 1990–94 (Beers and Chambers 2006). Given the high probability of default, financial markets naturally required a higher interest rate on the sovereign debt to compensate for their increased risk. In the period from 1993 to 1995, short-interest rate differentials vis-à-vis Germany remained substantial, averaging over four thousand basis points, as figure 4.3 illustrates. Similarly, ten-year government bonds yielded over 50 percent over the same period, illustrating that markets were inclined to regard the country as being risky (figure 4.4). The next section takes a look on how the BNB repeatedly accommodated the fiscal needs of the government,

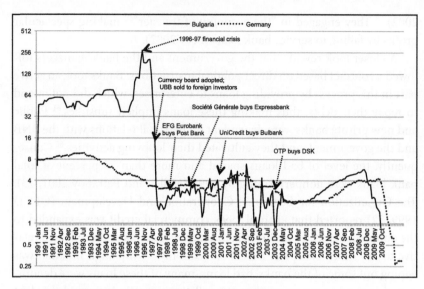

Fig. 4.3. Money Market Rates: Bulgaria and Germany (%)
Source: International Monetary Fund, *International Financial Statistics.*

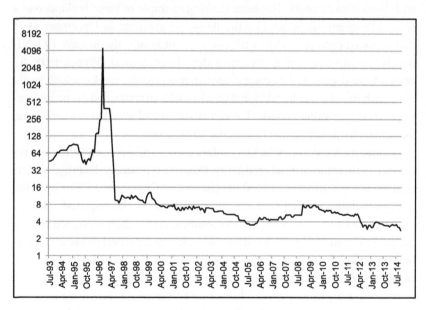

Fig. 4.4. Bulgaria Ten-Year Government Bond Yields (%)
Source: Global Financial Data.

an action that had deleterious consequences for the credibility of the central bank's price stability mandate.

The Bulgarian National Bank: The Lender of First Resort

The government was systematically trying to influence interest rate policy, requesting that the central bank adjust credit ceilings upwards for individual banks and provide credits to specific sectors (Christov 1997, 147). The Law on Budget that required the central bank to print money for unsecured credit to finance up to 50 percent of the annual budget deficit had particularly constrained the BNB autonomy (Nenovsky and Rizopoulos 2003; Christov 1997). So, while in 1992, 94 percent of the budget deficit was monetized, the direct BNB lending amounted to 121 percent of government borrowing in 1994 (Christov 1997, 143–44). The Ministry of Finance routinely took financing from the BNB via various channels, including direct loans and sales of government securities.[64] The resulting high level of monetization reflected a lack of fiscal discipline and redistribution of state resources through the banks (Ganev et al. 2001). This contrasts sharply with the commitment of the Estonian government to fiscal orthodoxy.

The government was not ready to grant the BNB more institutional and political independence. When faced with resistance to its demands to bail out banks, the government simply changed the BNB's management. A prominent example of this approach was when Emil Harsev, the deputy governor of the BNB in charge of banking regulation, was removed by a vote of Parliament in July 1993, an act that violated the provision of the central bank law (Christov 1997). The government subsequently amended the central bank law, allowing Parliament to terminate the term of the BNB's governor and deputy governors (by a 60 percent majority vote) for no specific reason.[65] In retrospect, the former deputy governor of the BNB, Tsvetan Manchev, observed, "It was much easier to change the governor of the central bank than to change the economic policies of the government."[66]

The main goal of the central bank, as defined in the 1991 Law on the BNB (Article 2), was "to maintain the internal and external stability of the national monetary unit." But as a former member of the BNB Managing Board, Lubomir Christov (1997, 40), explains, "Price and exchange rate stability [were] among the bank's objectives, but not first priority. . . . Concerns over liquidity problems of some large banks have too often taken precedence in monetary policy decisions." As a consequence, the de facto monetary policy of the central bank was accommodating, compromising the credibility of its commitment to low inflation (Dobrinsky 2000, 586). In other words, the BNB acted as the "lender of first resort" rather than a lender of last resort (Berlemann and Nenovsky 2004).

Inflation and Currency Speculations

Not only the central bank but also DSK, the bank with the biggest household deposit base, was active in refinancing other banks on the interbank market. The DSK was also one of the principal buyers of government securities, so it actually functioned like the central bank (Berlemann and Nenovsky 2004). The series of unconditional bailouts created a vicious circle. The problem with bad loans persisted because new bad credits continued to emerge, requiring increasing amounts of public money to be wastefully distributed in the system (Dobrinsky 2000, 588). The confidence of the public in the banking sector was a key factor in relative financial stability before 1995. Because of the absence of alternative investment options, most of the savings of the population was channeled to banks. They provided the basis for financing budget deficits and the activities of banks (Dobrinsky 2000, 590).

The entire economic environment was conducive to inflation, and as a consequence debilitating inflation persisted, although it was reduced from 80 percent in 1992 to 62 percent in 1995 (table 4.4). As Barro and Gordon (1983) highlighted in their influential article, excessively high inflation reflects a credibility problem in monetary policy. Banks profited from the inflationary environment by paying negative interest rates on deposits and earning positive interest rates on credits.[67] Given high inflation, real deposit rates were negative throughout 1991–93 but deposits were rising rapidly;

TABLE 4.4. Macroeconomic Indicators for Bulgaria

	Inflation (annual %)	Total reserves (minus gold) in US$ million	Public finances as a % of GDP[a]	External debt as a % of GDP	Public debt as a % of GDP[c]
1995	62.05	1,236[b]	−5.1	149.85	104.3
2000	10.32	3,155	−0.4	164.04	n.a.
2005	5.04	8,041	3.1	104.72	29.4
2009	2.75	17,127	−0.1	228.30	15.6

Source: World Bank, *World Development Indicators*; European Bank for Reconstruction and Development, *Transition Reports*.
[a]Cash surplus/deficit (% of GDP) is closest to the overall budget balance.
[b]484 in 1996.
[c]Abbas et al. (2010).

thus the outcome was an outflow of real income from depositors to banks (Dobrinsky 1994, 50).

In contrast to the Estonian central bank, the BNB did not have the political power to liquidate domestic banks when they became insolvent. It was difficult for the BNB to force bank closures because its banking supervision department was closely connected to the management circles of major state-owned enterprises and banks (Wyzan 1998, 31). As noted earlier, foreign banks, which could have had disciplined the inflationary behavior of the government and its cronies, were not authorized to enter the Bulgarian banking market. Not surprisingly, lacking credibility for sound policy, the BNB was gradually losing control over the rapidly growing money supply and its foreign exchange reserves were shrinking.

The central bank often acted as a "firefighter."[68] It was habitually attempting to pursue two mutually exclusive goals. On the one hand, it tried to maintain the stability of domestic currency by pursuing a monetary policy of high interest rates, but on the other, it provided bailouts to banks with liquidity problems. This put pressure on the exchange rate because the refinancing of banks added to the demand for foreign exchange. As a consequence, the BNB's interventions in international financial markets were inconsistent; at times it intervened in an often futile attempt to prevent the decline in the value of the national currency, the lev, but at other times it intervened in the opposite direction to build up foreign exchange reserves (Dobrinsky 2000, 596). But for the most part, the BNB had a problematic threefold mission. In addition to protecting the exchange rate and the banks, the BNB was obliged to finance a large part of the budget deficit. Even more shocking, though, was that the BNB coalesced with the government, state-owned enterprises, and banks in speculative operations related to exchange rate movements. In 1994, as Hristina Vucheva, former minister of economy and finance recalls, "every weekend there was an attack on the cash market, an agreement was reached among several banks and the exchange rate was changed in the direction of lev devaluation to ensure safe profits for the players. Then the BNB intervened, buying expensive dollars and so on and so forth till the next hit" (quoted in Nenovsky and Rizopoulos 2003, 935 n. 44).

Incumbent banks generated large profits from exchange rate fluctuations and currency depreciation. Georgy Ganev put it this way:

Banks were opportunistic, risk-taking, and speculating at the expense of tax payers. They took excessive risks in maintaining large credit exposures in foreign currencies that were not subject to any regulation . . . floating enabled the banks to earn rents from exchange rate manipulations. . . . There was a huge moral hazard problem in the banking sector.[69]

In short, the BNB was unable to build credibility as a monetary authority committed to price and currency stability. It adopted a full float initially, but in 1992 switched to a managed float and kept it until 1994. The inconsistency of the monetary regime became visible when the lev started to experience large swings, particularly from 1994 onward. The interest rate reductions triggered a sharp depreciation of the lev by 50 percent against the U.S. dollar in March 1994 (Wyzan 1998, 21). Depreciated currency boosted exports and contributed to a short-lived positive trade balance of $121 billion for the first time in fifteen years (Minassian 1998, 332–34). Still, this depreciation was gradually absorbed by rising inflation, which by the end of 1994 exceeded 120 percent. In 1995–96, the monetary regime approached a full float again due to substantial losses of foreign exchange reserves (table 4.4)

Concurrently, the majority (thirty-five of forty-four) of domestic banks began to experience financial difficulties in June 1994 (Vutcheva, quoted in Berlemann and Nenovsky 2004, 256). The BSP won a narrow majority in the ensuing elections in December 1994 and formed a government under a young reformer-communist Zhan Videnov as prime minister. The political influence and rent seeking of banks worsened further. The policy of soft budget constraints gave rise to reckless credit policies and the snowballing of a new wave of bad loans. Depositors, fearing that their foreign deposits would be confiscated by the government in order to meet its interest payments on the external debt due in July 1996, started to withdraw their deposits en masse.

Crisis and Critical Juncture (1996–97)

Table 4.5 illustrates the timeline of the 1996–97 financial crisis. The first wave of the crisis came from the banking system when the BNB put five insolvent commercial banks under conservatorship and suspended their operations in May 1996. To stop the panic among depositors, two parallel strategies were implemented (Ganev et al. 2001, 30; Berlemann, Hristov, and Nenovsky 2002, 29). First, the Parliament passed the Bank Deposit Guarantee Act, guaranteeing the repayment of individual deposits in full. Second, after a long period of debt monetization, the BNB started to pursue a restrictive policy toward banks by increasing minimum reserve requirements. Interest rates climbed to 300 percent in September 1996 (from 108 percent in May).

At this point, the high interest rate policy recommended by the IMF further intensified the crisis, causing bank failures and a sharp increase of government internal debt.[70] Altogether, fourteen banks (out of forty-six) were closed in 1996, representing 24 percent of the banking system's assets. The economic costs of the banking crisis were staggering—almost 42 percent of GDP—and the economy contracted rapidly (Tang, Zoli, and Klytchnikova 2000). The banking crisis was accompanied by a currency substitution; the share of foreign exchange in broad money (currency in circulation, short-term deposits in banks and money-market funds) went up from 27 percent in 1995 to 50 percent in 1996 (Ulgenerk and Zlaoui 2000, 7).

In the face of a severe crisis of confidence in government, no market participant was willing to buy government bonds. Minister of finance Dimitar Kostov invited primary dealers of banks and "begged" them to buy government securities.[71] Since banks did not show any interest, the government, fearing a moratorium on internal debt, forced the central bank to provide extensive monetary financing of the unsustainable fiscal deficit. Although the BNB initially resisted, it eventually ceded and granted to the

TABLE 4.5. Chronology of the Financial Crisis in Bulgaria, 1996–97

	Dates	Major Events
1995	4th quarter	Early warning signs: Foreign currency reserves begin to fall (after rising in 1994).
		First bank runs occur. BNB refinances banks as lender of last resort.
1996	1st quarter	Foreign currency reserves fall sharply.
	2nd quarter	BNB no longer intervenes in the foreign currency markets.
		Basic interest rate rises in several steps from 34% to 108% (annual rate). Lev depreciates by 100%.
	3rd quarter	Conservators appointed for 9 banks (bringing the total to 15). Basic interest rate is raised to 25% per month. More support given to the viable banks.
	4th quarter	Basic interest rate lowered to 15% per month to help banks.
		November: IMF recommends the establishment of a currency board.
		December: There are street demonstrations and the government resigns.
1997	1st quarter	Early February: Political crisis is resolved. An interim government is appointed.
		Negotiations between the IMF and the new interim government begin.
	2nd quarter	April: Agreement is reached with the IMF on new standby package.
		April: UDF wins majority in parliamentary elections.
	3rd quarter	July 1: Currency board established.

Source: Adapted from Beck, Miller, and Saad (2003, 7).

Ministry of Finance a loan of 115 billion lev that represented a full 7 percent of GDP in 1996 (Berlemann and Nenovsky 2004, 258). Clearly, the BNB was pursuing a dangerous policy mix of high interest rates combined with expansionary financing of the government debt.

Inevitably, the banking crisis led to a currency crisis that exemplified the third-generation model of crises highlighting moral hazard in the banking sector (Krugman 1998; Chang and Velasco 1998).[72] The lev depreciated by an alarming 590 percent in 1996. The central bank interventions in foreign exchange markets to defend the value of the lev had no lasting effect and only led to a dramatic decrease in foreign exchange reserves. External debt service increased from 3 percent of GDP in 1996 to over 14 percent in 1996, so the government was again on the verge of default (Nenovsky, Tochkov, and Turcu 2013, 16). These macroeconomic indicators illustrate the dramatic nature of the crisis and the abrupt movements of the lev exchange rate due to the distrust of foreign exchange markets. It is crucial to understand that, as Bordo and MacDonald (2012, 13) argued, "countries unprepared to have disciplined monetary policies will face a continual lack of credibility and repeated currency crises when such noncredibility becomes too large." As figure 4.3 shows, the short-term money market interest rates jumped to above 270 percent in October 1996. The lack of monetary credibility was also priced into long-term sovereign bonds, whose yields averaged 380 percent in 1996, peaking at 4,465 percent in October 1996) (figure 4.4).

IMF Urges Adoption of Currency Board

The IMF, which stepped in in May 1996, was deeply involved in shaping the Bulgarian economic stabilization plan after the crisis. Michael Deppler, director of the European Department of the IMF, urged the Bulgarian authorities to adopt a currency board.[73] The IMF considered a currency board to be the only potent tool to deal with the financial crisis because it promised a framework to discipline both monetary and fiscal policies.[74] The IMF, reluctant to trust the BSP government, publicly announced that further financing would be conditional upon the adoption of a currency board.[75] Without exchange rate stabilization in the form of a currency board, the IMF officials feared the government would not be able to resist the temptation of inflationary finance.[76] At the same time, the IMF insisted that a currency board needed to be supported by a vigorous commitment to banking-sector opening and privatization. This strategy would allow the government to cut off the rent-seeking banks and enterprises from the state and the BNB financing.[77]

Then the exchange rate collapsed in February 1997, and the lev depreciated by close to 3,000 percent in the first half of 1997 (Carlson and Valev 2001, 585). The currency collapse was accompanied by a 45-day period period of hyperinflation, which reached 243 percent in February 1997. The annual inflation for 1997 was 1,056 percent. The hyperinflation reduced the government's domestic debt to 2.5 percent in 1998 from its unsustainable levels in 1996, when interest payments represented 18 percent of GDP (Avramov 1999, 10–11). The social fabric of Bulgarian society began to unravel. The economic crisis was accompanied by a deep political crisis and forty days of street protests throughout the country. In the face of an imminent economic disaster, Prime Minister Videnov decided to establish a currency board arrangement; but even though this had become an unavoidable option,[78] the crisis brought down the Videnov government and destroyed the BSP's electoral base.[79] New parliamentary elections were held in April 1997, when the UDF won an overwhelming victory (52 percent of the popular vote and 57 percent of the seats). On July 1, 1997, the new UDF-led government of Ivan Kostov, who had served as finance minister in the previous short-lived UDF administration, officially adopted a currency board, modeled on the successful Estonian example. The lev was fixed at the exchange rate 1,000 lev per 1 German mark (see table 4.A1 in the appendix to this chapter).[80] The "money doctor" Steven Hanke, who was involved in the establishment of the Estonian currency board, became advisor to the Bulgarian president (Nenovsky and Rizopoulos 2003, 936). Foreign agents were also appointed to advise on and mediate bank privatization process.

In sum, the historical record, supported by both insiders' experiences and financial data, shows that the adoption of a rigorous monetary regime occurred only when the country was on the brink of economic collapse. How crucial was the IMF pressure in forcing a monetary regime change? To be sure, the IMF imposed conditionality must have strengthened the resolve of the Bulgarian policymakers to adopt a hard peg and open the banking sector. Establishing the currency board was also justified by the need to end practices that were impeding banking reforms (Wyzan 1998). The credibility of currency board required that the Bulgarian government grant independence to the central bank and limit money and credit creation to levels consistent with the sustainability of the currency board in the long run. After all, the insolvency of the banking system, burdened by large volumes of nonperforming loans, was at the heart of the crisis.

Foreign Banks and the Credibility of the Currency Board

According to Caporale et al. (2002, 236), the adoption of a currency board "brought about radical changes in the structure of the banking system, encouraging the entry of foreign banks," viewed now as the only means to improve the soundness of the financial system rather than as "unfair competition." When looked at from the perspective of a government with a complete lack of credibility, turning to reputable multinational banks makes sense. By encouraging foreign bank entry, the government was signaling its intentions of altering its behavior. From this perspective, the presence of foreign banks was considered to be critical for two reasons. First, foreign banks were seen as "instruments of system wide reform" that would limit the government's own power to use banks to support connected parties (Tschoegl 2005). Second, by allowing affiliates of foreign banks to enter the domestic market, the Bulgarian authorities were in effect importing a lender of last resort from Western parent banks (Ševič 2000, quoted in Koford and Tschoegl 2003).

To this end, the UDF government adopted an approach to bank privatization similar to the Estonian strategy, pursuing vigorously the sale of domestic banks to foreign strategic investors.[81] Table 4.6 shows the market shares of the top bank investors in Bulgaria. Bank privatization started in July 1997, shortly after the currency board was officially established, with the sale of United Bulgarian Bank, the nation's third largest bank, to the EBRD and US Oppenheimer and Company, later acquired by the National Bank of Greece. Then, in August 1998, the American Life Insurance Co., a subsidiary of American International Group Inc., and Greece's Consolidated Eurofinance Holdings bought Post Bank. The annual inflation fell from 2,040 percent in the first quarter of 1997 to 1 percent in 1998 (Lewis 2002, 141). The currency premium became slightly negative and hardly different from the money market interest rates of Germany in August 1997, one month after the first large state-owned bank was privatized to foreign investors (figure 4.3). This sharp initial decrease in risk can be attributable not only to the adoption of the currency board but also to opening the banking sector to foreign banks, which signaled to international markets the government's acceptance of policies consistent with a credible currency board.

In 1999, more big state-owned banks were sold. Expressbank-Varna was acquired by Société Générale, and Hebrosbank Plovdiv was acquired by an investment management company, the Regent Pacific Group. Hebrosbank was subsequently bought by Bank Austria Creditanstalt, a subsidiary of HypoVereinsBank Group, which also acquired Biochim Bank. A Bulgarian subsidiary of Austria based Raiffeisen Bank opened already in 1994. By the end of 1999 more than half of the thirty-five banks operating in Bulgaria were foreign.[82] With the sale of Bulbank, the largest state-owned bank with a 27 percent market share, to the Italian bank UniCredit, which took a 93 percent stake in 2000, a substantial part (45 percent) of banking assets were in foreign hands.[83] Importantly, privatization to foreign investors reduced the share of state-owned banks to less than 20 percent by 2000 (International Monetary Fund 2002). In 2002, the Greek EFG Eurobank acquired a 43 percent participation in Post Bank and subsequently increased its stake to 97 percent in 2004. Bank privatization ended with the privatization of DSK in 2003 by OTP, the largest Hungarian bank. While between 1993 and mid-1997, the foreign share of bank assets in Bulgaria increased from 0.1 percent to 4.9 percent, this share reached 71 percent in 2005, and grew further to nearly 80 percent by 2009 (table 4.7). Revenues from the privatization to foreigners doubled the amount of foreign exchange reserves. Foreign banks, with better access to best-practices in credit risk management, banking infrastructure, and capital, improved the management of the acquired banks (International Monetary Fund 2006, 578).

The changes in ownership structure were accompanied by several institutional changes in the financial system. The 1997 Law on the BNB substantially increased the independence of the central bank from the government. The BNB was prohibited from monetizing the government debt. Also, the Parliament passed a new law on commercial banks. These two new laws incorporated a tightening of banking regulation and supervision to en-

TABLE 4.6. Market Shares of Top Multinational Banks in Bulgaria, 2011–12

Bank Name	Assets held by a bank as a % of total banking assets	Parent Bank (Country)
UniCredit	15.1	UniCredit (Italy)
DSK Bank	13.7	OTP Bank Hungary (Hungary)
United Bulgarian Bank	9.7	National Bank of Greece (Greece)
Raiffeisenbank Bulgaria	9.0	Raiffeisen Bank (Austria)
Eurobank Bulgaria (Postbank)	7.9	EFG Eurobank (Greece)

Source: Raiffeisen Research (2012).

hance transparency and regulatory capacity of the banking system, so that its instability would not prevent monetary stabilization. Bank privatization to foreign strategic investors, combined with restrictions on the central bank lending to banks and to the government, weakened corruptive and rent-seeking networks. The new legal framework also strengthened the BNB's role in bank supervision.

A currency board reduces the risk of currency devaluation, but it increases the risk of bank failures because the central bank is restricted to act as lender of last resort; therefore the soundness of the financial system is particularly important in this type of exchange rate regime arrangement (Miller 2001, 68). Foreign banks delivered everything that had been hoped for on the financial soundness and stability front. They helped to increase the transparency in the financial system by developing credit-score evaluations and being instrumental in establishing credit bureaus (table 4.7). The number of firms and individuals listed by a public credit bureau reached 60 percent of adults in 2013, more than in France. The services of credit bureaus are accessible to all banks, providing them with information on repayment history, unpaid debt, and outstanding credit. As a result of privatization, the asset quality and capitalization of the banking sector significantly improved (International Monetary Fund 2002, 42); consequently, the nonperforming loans declined to 2.2 percent in 2005, indicating a significantly reduced credit risk (table 4.7).

To understand the improvements in the regulatory quality of the bank-

TABLE 4.7. Transparency and Regulatory Quality of the Bulgarian Banking System

	Foreign bank assets as a % of total assets[a]	Nonperforming loans as a % of total gross loans[b]	Credit reporting institutions[c]	EBRD index of banking sector reforms[d]
1995	1	12.5	No	2.0
2000	45	17.3	Public credit registry (est. 1998)	3.0
2005	71	2.2	Public credit registry and private credit bureau (est. 2004)	3.7
2009	79	6.4	Public credit registry and private credit bureau	3.7

Source: Data for each column from the respective sources:
[a]Data from Claessens et al. (2008); Claessens and van Horen (2012).
[b]Data from World Bank, *World Development Indicators*; data for 1995 from the EBRD *Transition Reports*.
[c]Data from World Bank, *Doing Business*.
[d]Data from EBRD *Transition Reports*, various issues.

ing system, we can use the EBRD index of banking reforms reported in table 4.7, which shows that the Bulgarian banking sector performed well. The European Central Bank (2006) praised the Bulgarian government for a sound fiscal policy and characterized its banking system as "well supervised, highly capitalized and profitable." Banking reforms since the 1996–97 crisis have improved "transparency and enhanced banks' decision-making process," and "the entry of foreign banks have played an important role in the development of the banking system (International Monetary Fund 2006). Foreign bank involvement improved the regulatory environment and had a disciplinary effect on the financial policies of the BNB, now freed from its obligation to refinance the banking sector. For instance, when two banks (Credit Bank and Bulgarian Universal Bank) suffered liquidity difficulties in 1999 and 2000, the BNB (as had its Estonian counterpart) did not bail them out and instead let these banks fail. The BNB took this approach even though it was allowed to serve as a limited lender of last resort to stabilize the banking system (Nenovsky and Hristov 2002).

The banking-sector opening to foreign banks via privatization became a cornerstone for the credibility of the Bulgarian currency board.[84] International financial markets perceived the Bulgarian government as being less risky, as reflected in a substantial drop in government bond spreads by 773 basis points between 1998 and 2004.[85] Yields on long-term sovereign bonds, averaging 386 percent in 1996, decreased to 7.6 percent in 2000, and then further to 3.49 percent in 2005 after the privatization of banks was completed (figure 4.4). In 2006, Moody's upgraded Bulgaria's long-term foreign currency rating from Ba1 to Baa3, becoming the last major credit rating agency to upgrade the country to investment-grade status. Confidence of the population in the lev has been gradually restored from near zero when almost the entire economy was dollarized (Miller 2001, 68). Surveys show that a large majority of the Bulgarians believe in the sustainability of the currency board (Valev and Carlson 2007). Indeed, the Bulgarian currency board survived the 1998 Russian crisis and the collapse of a currency board in Argentina.

Bulgaria also imported from abroad the function of lender of last resort. The effects of the 2010 European sovereign debt crisis were felt in Bulgaria because of large exposures of Greek and Austrian banking groups. In reaction to the credit boom (foreign loans accounted for more than 50 percent of total loans) the BNB adjusted reserve requirements of banks and imposed ceilings on credit growth. Yet like Estonia, Bulgaria did not have to tap rescue funding from the IMF to bolster confidence. The Greek parent banks remained committed to their affiliates in Bulgaria by providing them with liquidity (Anastasakis, Bastian, and Watson 2011). Many worried about the financial contagion from the Greek crisis through its banks, but experts agree that Greek subsidiaries in Bulgaria are financially sound, with healthy balance sheets and high liquidity levels, and are equipped with a better reputation than Bulgarian-owned banks (Higgins 2015). During another crisis episode in 2014, one of the largest Bulgarian banks, Corporate Commercial Bank, collapsed. However, the crisis did not spread to other banks and the subsidiaries of Western parent banks were not affected by deposit withdrawals. The Fitch credit rating agency assessed the banking sector in Bulgaria as "well-capitalized, liquid, and profitable" and decided to leave the country's rating unchanged.[86] Shortly afterward, the government was able to sell ten-year government bonds at interest rates of 2.95 percent, a record low for Bulgaria, while demand doubled the amount on sale (Ewing and Kantchev 2014).

Conclusion

The comparison of the different national trajectories in Bulgaria and Estonia reveals the importance of international banking integration as a necessary condition for credible monetary commitments. The banking-sector opening created an environment that favored outsiders and helped to dismantle domestic distributional coalitions. The story of banking-sector reforms driven by foreign banks and their persistent effect on policy credibility in these two countries is one of the most important narratives of financial globalization.

The history of the politics of economic reforms in Bulgaria and Estonia highlights the complexity of the influence of global banks as it relates to how and whether political leaders prioritize their need to establish an international reputation. In the closed-economy context in pre-1997 Bulgaria, the governments discounted the future costs of current opportunism that led to high inflation expectations and high borrowing costs in international markets. Political elites in Estonia, perceiving a greater need to build credibility with financial markets, committed to a model of development based on economic and financial openness right from the beginning of the post-communist transition.

Two criticisms of alternative theories of credibility raised in previous chapters are also borne in the context of these two cases. The first issue is that law alone does not prevent politically motivated capture of the central bank, especially in emerging markets, where the rule of law is weak and law enforcement inadequate. Based on its legal statutes, the position of the BNB in the international rankings of central bank independence before 1996 was significantly higher than its actual degree of independence. The competing argument based on the association with the European Union is not supported by the history of these two countries either. Both Estonia and Bulgaria joined the EU in May 2004 and January 2007, respectively; hence they had powerful external incentives to align with the policies of fixed exchange rate regimes in the single currency area. Although EU accession may have decreased the risk of both countries, international markets did not regard these two countries as being more credible when the European Commission in Brussels announced their official candidacy. Yields on ten-year government bonds dropped from 386 percent in 1996 to 12 percent in 1997 upon the entry of the first foreign banks, but only from 7.6 percent to 6.65 after 2000, when EU officially opened its negotiations with Bulgaria.

A theoretical view based on the weight of government partisanship is also a poor predictor of the credibility of monetary regimes. The Bulgarian case shows that it is difficult to sustain the view that prior to the crisis, the left party, the BSP, promoted ideas about redistribution, while the right party, the UDF, was willing to adopt liberal reform policies for the business constituencies or that the ideological orientation of parties would ameliorate the credibility problem of their policy announcements. The Bulgarian government, whether dominated by left or right, was unable to precommit itself to low inflation, sustainable fiscal positions, and banking reforms. Only the presence of foreign banks made government commitments credible. While there has been considerable continuity in both cases in terms of the communist pedigree of the political elites in the first years of the transition, the strong successor to the Communist Party did not survive in the political space of postcommunist Estonia.[87] Estonian politics has been dominated by centrist or center-right parties and conservative-liberal politicians. Even political parties belonging to the left of the Estonian political spectrum adopted pro-market-oriented economic policies.[88] The distinction between left-wing and right-wing parties concerns values rather than economic policies,[89] so the policy announcements of economic reform choices of the right did not necessarily solve information asymmetries in international markets.[90]

The monetary regimes of Estonia and Bulgaria have been success stories, and both countries experienced drops in risk shortly after they implemented banking reform programs. Currency boards in both countries enjoyed international credibility and a strong public support, being perceived as a pillar of successful monetary and exchange rate policies. While there have been occasional complaints and discussions about possible changes of hard pegs motivated by appreciation of their national currencies, no economic actor or politician seriously questioned the currency board policies. The 2008 financial crisis showed a jump in risk for these two countries, which had some basis in financial contagion. But neither Estonia nor Bulgaria received bailouts from the IMF. In sum, these cases clearly show that a currency board cannot itself create credibility unless it is accompanied by firm supporting policies, of which liberalization of the banking sector is of paramount importance. Assessing the predictions for a credible currency board, Vahur Kraft (2002, 18), the former governor of the BOE, proudly exclaimed, "Today I dare to recall ten years and say—it has been worth it to adhere to firm principles to have an open banking system."

Appendix

TABLE 4.A1. Main Characteristics of the Estonian and Bulgarian Currency Boards

	Bulgaria (est. July 1997)	Estonia (est. June 1992)
Previous exchange rate regime	Floating	Ruble standard
Access to convertibility at the monetary authorities	General public and banks	In principle, general public; in practice, only banks
Coverage of backing	100 percent of monetary base and government fiscal reserves	100 percent of monetary base
Power to change the exchange rate rule and backing rule	Devaluation needs to be done by an act of the Parliament	The BOE has the right to revalue the exchange rate; devaluation requires an act of Parliament
Lender of last resort	By the BNB, restricted to systemic and emergency situations; limited to the amount of foreign exchange in excess of backing requirement (i.e., reserves of the Banking Department)	By the BOE; restricted to systemic and emergency situations; limited to the amount of foreign exchange in excess of backing requirement (i.e., reserves of the Banking Department)
Reserve requirements	Yes	Yes
Treasury bills	No	No
Credit to government by the monetary authorities	Prohibited	Prohibited; BOE assets are kept separate from the state budget
Political commitment	Moderate (political unanimity with desultory voices advocating abandonment of the currency board)	Strong (full political unanimity)

Source: Adapted from Nenovsky, Hristov, and Mihaylov (2002, 12–13).

CHAPTER 5
Inflation Targeting and Foreign Bank Presence

In this chapter I illustrate the main theoretical predictions about the dynamics of credibility building for inflation-targeting regimes. Currency boards, examined in chapter 4, and floating with an inflation target are fairly different monetary regimes, providing a sharp contrast and comparison. This chapter reinforces the analysis by exploring the reputation dynamics in two countries that although they emerged from the communist regime without market institutions, they benefited from more favorable historical legacies than their postcommunist peers.[1] Yet favorable legacies of macroeconomic and currency stability during the precommunist era proved inadequate in establishing and preserving the credibility of their fixed exchange rate regimes in the first postcommunist decade. Both countries officially adopted inflation targeting as their monetary policy frameworks in the late 1990s. This chapter shows that the presence of foreign banks made inflation targeting easier to pursue, because monetary policy was less likely to be thrown off course by excessive credit creation and banking sector instability.

The Czech Republic, trying to avoid floating altogether for several years, was forced to shift to a flexible exchange rate regime in the late 1990s because the government's commitment to the currency peg lacked the necessary credibility as a result of chronic financial instability. The early history of banking in the independent Czech Republic was characterized by a reproduction of the financial hegemony of large public banks that, with bank-sponsored investment privatization funds (IPFs), became new sources of power. There was inconsistency between the government's liberal rhetoric and its continual interference with the economy. The involvement of the government in the banks generated incentives for moral hazard in the financial sector. Public banks acted as extended hands of the government and provided credits to domestic firms based more on political expediency

131

than on prudent credit risk policies. As a result, banks were permitted, if not encouraged, to discount the risk of default and repeat imprudent lending practices and short-term capital speculations that undermined the credibility of a fixed exchange rate regime, eventually leading to its collapse in 1997. At the heart of the political struggle was the conviction that Czech banks should be in domestic hands. Only the financial crisis helped to break the monopoly of the right-wing government and trigger full opening of the banking sector to foreign banks, which were essential for the credibility of a new monetary policy strategy based on inflation targeting.

From a bird's-eye view, there are some common features between the 1997 Czech currency turmoil and the 1996–97 Bulgarian crisis examined in the previous chapter, both associated with the fragility of the banking system. A common feature of these two cases was the presence of a financial channel that had fed on monetary policies. It was the predation of credit policies by governments, which caused financial instability and exchange rate devaluations. Notwithstanding, the central bank, with an excellent anti-inflation reputation and strong fiscal institutions in the Czech Republic to ensure that the budget deficits did not get out of control, contrasted sharply with the institutional setup in Bulgaria. Thus the Czech case is a particularly good example of the difficulties in achieving and maintaining a credible monetary regime originating from a nontransparent banking system and bad financial policies.

Unlike in the Czech Republic, Polish enterprises and banks were facing hard budget and credit constraints from the outset of transition. The government's approach was to let banks solve their bad loan problems with their debtors. Against the background of privatizing public banks and the entry of foreign banks, Polish banks were forced early on to compete with each other. The Polish government took a positive stance toward foreign investments in the banking sector initially but then backtracked temporarily before opening the banking sector to foreign buyouts again in 1997, when its need for international credibility began to rise. In contrast to the Czech case, the central bank in Poland had a firm domestic political mandate for its mission to support national competitiveness in addition to maintaining a stable price level. Thus the commitment to the fixed exchange rate regime lacked the necessary institutional support. The institutional changes related to central bank autonomy coincide with a substantial entry of foreign strategic investors into the Polish banking sector. Poland's experience also confirms the conviction that foreign banks are instrumental in successfully strengthening the banking sector and ensuring the ability to control credit. Foreign banks proved critical to the renewed confidence of international markets in the monetary commitments of the Polish government to the inflation-targeting regime.

This chapter demonstrates that the degree of banking integration creates room for both reputational destruction and recovery. I show how reputation changes when governments act contrary to their perceived type and how reputation can be restored. The Czech case, in particular, illustrates this point. Like its counterpart in Estonia, the Czech government undertook sweeping liberalization of trade and capital flows. But unlike those in Estonia, the Czech financial markets were exposed only to a limited degree of openness as the government resisted the acquisitive advances of foreign banks. The Czech right-wing cabinets were reluctant to dismantle the intricate web of financial-industrial links by opening the banking sector to foreign competition, which eventually eroded the initial credibility of the fixed regime and brought costly financial turmoil. The evolution of credibility in the Czech Republic resembles the Guidotti and Végh's (1999) dynamic political economy model of credibility. The adoption of a fixed exchange rate regime provides a sense of stability and initial (albeit conditional) credibility. But, as time goes by, the continuing real appreciation of domestic currency together with the inability to establish the political consensus on banking-sector reforms starts to destroy credibility and increase devaluation expectations.

I also illustrate that it matters *how* the presence of foreign banks is established. Emerging evidence demonstrates that a precondition for financial stability is the acquisition of major public banks by foreign strategic investors. In thinking about the advantage of this approach, one should understand that large government banks are usually politically well-connected with the ruling elite and are the main source of inflationary finance. In both countries, whereas foreign banks were granted licenses to establish their affiliates as *greenfield* investments (the creation of new foreign affiliates) from the start of the transition, restrictions were imposed on takeovers of large state-owned banks, which had a detrimental effect on financial stability and hence on the credibility of their monetary regimes.

This chapter provides a historical background and a narrative analysis of the currency policies in the Czech Republic and Poland, highlighting the significance of multinational banks in making them credible. This analysis is preceded by a discussion of the history and the main features of an inflation-targeting regime and of the necessary preconditions for adopting it.

Inflation Targeting

Over the past decade, many emerging markets moved toward either of the extreme monetary regimes: currency boards, discussed in the previous chapter, or inflation targeting as a complement to the flexible exchange rate regime. Inflation targeting was first introduced in New Zealand in 1990. It spread quickly, first to other developed countries in the early 1990s and since 1997 to developing and emerging-market economies. As of December 2012, thirty-four countries, most of them emerging markets, pursued inflation targeting (for example, Brazil, Colombia, Hungary, Korea, Romania, Turkey, Chile, Israel, Mexico, Slovakia, Poland, the Czech Republic) (International Monetary Fund 2013).

The main characteristics of an inflation-targeting regime include the announced numerical targets for inflation to be achieved during a specified time horizon (for example, 2 percent per year over the next two years) and high degree of transparency and accountability (Svensson 2010, 1). The central bank should provide regular public information about its monetary policy strategy and decisions. Mervyn King, governor of the Bank of England, underlines "credibility, predictability and transparency of decision-taking" as the key principles underlying inflation targeting.[2] This high degree of transparency is exceptional in light of the history of central banking. Conventionally, central banks have been secretive institutions and their policy goals and deliberations purposely opaque. And yet transparency helps reduce uncertainty about the future directions of monetary policy and helps manage private-sector expectations.

The credibility of an inflation-targeting regime refers to "the proximity of private-sector inflation expectations to the inflation target" (Svensson 2010, 3). In other words, a central bank enhances credibility when it establishes a good track record of achieving the annual inflation target. Advocates of inflation targeting argue that if credible, this monetary regime is a serious alternative to a hard peg for emerging markets seeking monetary stability because it anchors inflation expectations (Bernanke and Mishkin 1997, Svensson 1999, Mishkin 1999, King 2002). There are number of preconditions that must be met, however, if inflation targeting is to be successful. Inflation targeting requires institutional independence of the central bank, an institutional commitment to price stability as the primary goal of monetary policy, and a healthy financial system with sound banks (Mishkin 2004).

The impact of global banks on the credibility of inflation targeting has not received much attention. The objective of this chapter is to fill this gap by analyzing the experience of two inflation targeters from emerging Europe. I look specifically at the ways foreign banks improved the transparency and soundness of the financial systems of these countries. Ultimately, a high degree of transparency is considered to be of paramount importance for the credibility of an inflation-targeting regime (Svensson 2010).

The Czech Republic: National Capitalism

I begin my analysis with a consideration of legacies of the Czech Republic that gave it an advantage in establishing the confidence of financial markets in the chosen economic policies. The former Czechoslovakia was the only Eastern European country that experienced continuous democratic capitalism during the interwar period, and it had a history of successful economic policies and stable currency.[3] Along with the former East Germany, it had been the most industrially advanced country in the Soviet bloc.[4] The Czechoslovak communist governments were fiscally conservative, so the country enjoyed low domestic government debt (less than 1 percent of GDP), small external debt ($8 billion), virtually nonexistent inflation, and no shortages or parallel markets (see Soukup, Taci, and Matoušek 2004; Drábek 1995; Erbenová and Holub 2006). Yet some initial conditions were unfavorable. Much like in Estonia and Bulgaria, Czechoslovak trade was heavily concentrated on the communist bloc, reaching nearly 80 percent share of trade in the late 1980s. The fall of the Soviet Empire thus produced serious disruptions to the country's production, trade, and capital flows, resulting in 30 to 50 percent output loss in 1991–92 (Drábek 1995, 244). The proximity of Czechoslovakia to the German and Austrian markets, however, soon provided new markets for exporters.

The Origins of Czech Capitalism and Exchange Rate Policy

Following the "velvet revolution" of November 1989, the Civic Forum (Občanské forum)—the mass organization formed in 1989 by a group of prominent dissidents from Charter 77—decisively won the first free elections in June 1990, considered to be a referendum on the communist regime (Stroehlein 1999, 3).[5] Václav Klaus led a liberal minority within the

first Civic Forum government (December 1989–June 1992) as the Czechoslovak minister of finance.[6] Klaus proposed a liberal program of economic
reforms that was ratified by the Parliament in September 1990.[7] It became
the official *Scenario of Economic Reform* (referred to as the "Capitalist Man-
ifesto"), whose goals included price and foreign trade liberalization, macroeconomic stabilization, liberalization, and westward reorientation of foreign trade (Schwartz 2006, 130). The Czechoslovak reform program
introduced in 1991 was inspired by the earlier Balcerowicz "shock therapy"
reforms in Poland (examined later) but was less radical because it incorporated labor protection measures to maintain public support for the reforms.[8] Economic reform programs included rapid privatization through
the voucher scheme that would place a majority of shares in the hands of
the population.

Liberalization of prices resulted in a one-off increase in prices; the average
annual inflation rate jumped to 57 percent in 1991 (Holub and Tůma 2006).
Hence, the primary objective of the initial stabilization program was to contain inflationary pressures and achieve price stability (Drábek, Janáček, and
Tůma 1994, 238).[9] The political debate over the initial monetary regime cen-
tered on two alternative views. One, promoted by the IMF, focused on the
importance of stable nominal exchange rates, citing the examples of Poland
and Latin American countries. Proponents of the second view highlighted
the favorable historical legacies of Czechoslovakia that did not necessitate a
fixed exchange rate regime.[10] Ultimately, the fear of inflation, economic instability, and the desire to import credibility from the countries with reputable
central banks prevailed. Consequently, a fixed exchange rate regime was adopted in spite of insufficient foreign exchange reserves with which to defend
the exchange rate.[11] Yet the government did not make a binding public commitment to maintain the fixed exchange rate regime or a particular exchange
rate level (Hrnčíř 1999, 309). The exchange rate, fixed in a narrow band of
plus or minus 1.5 percent against a basket of currencies of five major trading
partners, served as a nominal anchor for low inflation expectations.[12]

Initially, Finance Minister Klaus did not favor a currency peg. He recalls, "I was horrified at the very beginning with the idea of having fixed
exchange rates. I remember at the same time that the IMF was shocked
when I suggested a flexible exchange rate regime" (Klaus 1993, 531). He
held strong reservations about a currency board arrangement, which he
viewed as a compensation for the lack of political responsibility or the inability of politicians to establish support for a "rational" economic policy

(Klaus 1993). Eventually, he realized that a peg was the only possible anchor and "the only fixed variable" in an economy in which other variables underwent changes and fluctuations (Klaus 1994, 174).[13] Clearly, Klaus (1997b, 144) also recognized that even though the Czechoslovak reform program was not designed by foreign experts, its endorsement by the IMF sent a positive signal to world markets.

The most contentious debate, however, concerned the level of fixity of the exchange rate. It reflected anxiety over the consequences of economic liberalization for domestic exporters and the objective of successfully reorienting the country's trade toward the West (Kutan and Brada 1998; Hrnčíř 1999; Dědek 2000). To this end, Klaus formulated the so-called "hypothesis of two transformation cushions," suggesting a substantial currency devaluation before trade liberalization (Klaus 1994, 176). As a result, the exchange rate was devalued in four successive rounds that took place in 1990 and 1991, altogether by more than 110 percent. It was finally pegged at 28 Czechoslovak koruna per 1 U.S. dollar. Clearly, a fixed exchange rate regime and undervalued currency favored domestic exporters who benefited from a competitive exchange rate and protection against exchange rate risk.[14] The 55 percent devaluation of October 1990 in particular was intended to protect banks with deteriorating loan portfolios (Hrnčíř 1999, 319). In hindsight it became clear that these devaluations were excessive; they contributed to inflation shocks and prevented the government from making a fixed exchange rate a credible anchor.[15] Gaining public confidence in the antiinflationary resolve of the Czech authorities was further complicated by the fact that according to the first postcommunist law on the central bank, the State Bank of Czechoslovakia (SBCS) remained subordinate to the government. Not until February 1992, when the new law was adopted, was the central bank endowed with independence.

By the time the next elections took place, the Civic Forum had split into several competing factions. Klaus founded the Civic Democratic Party (Občanská Demokratická Strana, ODS) from the most conservative faction of the Civic Forum. ODS decisively won the June 1992 elections, and Klaus became the prime minister of the Czech Republic.[16] The Klaus government (1992–1998) had great political freedom because the competition in the political system was weak, the opposition parties of the fragmented left were weak and ineffective, the powers of the president were restricted, the media were inexperienced, and the civil society was undermined (Vachudová 2001, 336–37).[17] The Czech bureaucracy during Klaus's tenure was highly centralized in the hands of the Ministry of Finance and Ministry of Privatization (McDermott 2004, 192).

After the dissolution of the Czechoslovak Federation on January 1, 1993, a monetary union between the newly independent Czech and Slovak Republics was created to mitigate the economic effects of the split. The Czechoslovak monetary union was planned to be maintained for at least six months, but market confidence in the political commitment to the common currency was low.[18] Consequently, the monetary union officially ceased to exist and the new independent currencies were introduced on February 8, 1993, less than six weeks after the breakup of Czechoslovakia![19] The Czech Republic continued to peg the currency, the Czech koruna, to the dollar (35 percent) and German mark (65 percent). The koruna fluctuated within a narrow band of plus or minus 0.5 percent. The need for international credibility of the Czech monetary regime began to rise.

To signal the government's preferences for price stability, the new central bank law further strengthened the political independence of the Czech National Bank (Česká národní banka, CNB), the successor of the SBCS (Soukup, Taci, and Matoušek 2004).[20] The CNB was made responsible for setting monetary policy (Article 2) and for proclaiming the exchange rate for the Czech currency vis-à-vis foreign currencies (Article 35) (Koch 1997, 7). The main goal of CNB, to ensure the stability of the national currency, was incorporated into the 1993 Constitution, thus making it difficult to change.

Inside the CNB there was a belief in the theory of "borrowed credibility" from a foreign central bank with an anti-inflationary reputation.[21] The CNB sought to build monetary policy credibility by pursuing an exchange-rate-based stabilization program that induced a swift transition to a regime of relatively low interest rates. Short-term interest rates declined to 13 percent in 1993 and again to 9 percent in 1994, closely following the German interest rates. The central bank's commitment to price stability quickly stabilized inflation, which fell to 9 percent in 1995 (table 5.1). The government budget was close to being balanced due to conservative fiscal policy, and external debt remained low (table 5.1). As the research on European macroeconomic policymaking suggests, countries with an independent central bank, a weak left, and less centralized labor unions focused historically on price stability (Straumann 2010). Right-wing governments view price stability as the most important policy goal; hence they are less concerned about the consequences of tight monetary policy for unemployment and less responsive to the demands of organized labor (Eichengreen 1992; Simmons 1994).

The macroeconomic policies of the Czech right-wing government, therefore, were largely consistent with theoretical expectations.

The Czech right-wing government's commitment to market reforms thus displayed all the ingredients for establishing the credibility of the fixed exchange rate regime as an anchor for inflation expectations. The government, however, diverged from free-market orthodoxy in designing banking reforms. It undertook fast and extensive capital account liberalizations in 1994–95, but restrictions on foreign investments in the banking sector were maintained (Árvai 2005, 9–10).[22] Klaus promoted a strategy for national development, the so-called "Czech way," appealing to an old tradition from the nineteenth century, when the development of the Czech state (within the Austro-Hungarian Empire) was pursued by promoting domestic businesses through domestic banks (Orenstein 1997, 9).[23] Klaus seemed to have remembered Lenin's dictum about banks being the "commanding heights" of the economy and was reluctant to let these institutions go and risk their coming under the control of foreign financiers (Stroehlein 1999, 13). As we will see below, the crucial factor that hurt the credibility of the peg was the financial instability that resulted from the preservation of an opaque domestic banking system.

Banking Socialism (1990–97)

The banking sector during the communist era comprised SBCS, which served as both the central bank and the institution for channeling commercial credit and providing services to state-owned enterprises and four specialized banks. These included the Czech Savings Bank (Česká Spořitelna,

TABLE 5.1. Macroeconomic Indicators for the Czech Republic

	Inflation (annual %)	Total reserves (minus gold) in US $ million	Public finances as a % of GDP[a]	External debt as a % of exports	Public debt as a % of GDP[c]
1995	9.17	13,843[b]	−0.9	61	14.6
2000	3.90	13,019	−3.3	60.3	18.5
2005	1.84	29,330	−3.4	51.8	29.7
2009	1.05	41,157	−5.7	75.3	34.3

Source: World Bank, World Development Indicators; European Bank for Reconstruction and Development, Transition Reports; International Monetary Fund, International Financial Statistics.
[a]Cash surplus/deficit (% of GDP) is closest to the overall budget balance.
[b]9,734 in 1997.
[c]Abbas et al. (2010).

CS), with a history dating back to 1825, taking deposits and extending credit to individuals; the Investment Bank, later the Investment and Postal Bank (Investiční a Poštovní Banka, IPB), established in 1948 to promote investments; the Czechoslovak Trade Bank (Československá Obchodní Banka, CSOB), established in 1965 to specialize in foreign exchange operations; and Živnostenská Banka (ZB), established in 1868 to conduct retail foreign currency operations for small firms. Banking reforms began on January 1, 1990, with the establishment of a two-tier banking system, liberalization of bank entry, and voucher privatization. The functions of SBCS on Czech territory were taken over by the Commercial Bank Prague (Komerční Banka Praha, KB).

The first banking legislation adopted in November 1989 was simply a modified product of the communist regime. The rules for establishing a new bank were very liberal, so firms were able to establish their own banks using bank loans (Mejstřík, Dvořáková, and Neprašová 2004, 23).[24] As a result, there were already twenty-three banks registered in December 1990 and the number jumped to fifty-seven by mid-1995 (Procházka 1996, 26). Most of these new private banks were small and undercapitalized. They offered high interest rates to attract deposits and engaged in questionable insider lending practices (Nollen, Kudrna, and Pazderník 2005, 368).

Domestic banks were practically the only source of enterprise finance because the voucher privatization (initiated in spring 1991) that placed the majority of shares in the hands of the population did not bring new capital to firms, capital markets were underdeveloped, and foreign investments were restricted (Kreuzbergova 2006).[25] The Klaus government envisaged keeping the "Big Four" state-owned banks—KB, CS, IPB, and CSOB—under state control so they could play an active role in the process of the transformation of industry by providing credit. Snyder and Kormendi (1997) argue that the government's decision against a privatization of KB, for instance, was motivated by the desire to preserve the channels to pursue credit allocation for politically vested clients.[26] The government was reluctant to sell majority shares of the big Czech banks, regarded as "family silver," to foreigners, fearing that these new foreign owners would be reluctant to lend to domestic firms.[27] As Klaus explained:

> The reason for the delay of big banks' privatization did not consist of ideological fears. It was a purely practical consideration that private banks will behave too prudently . . . and de facto not dip into the real economy. . . . It

is possible to be such a parasite . . . I was always very afraid that while attempting to follow their private interests, the loan channels would be blocked. (quoted in Nollen, Kudrna and Pazderník 2005, 366)

Instead of selling the Big Four to foreign investors, the government included minority shares of three of these banks in voucher privatization. The government retained control, as the single largest shareholder, with stakes ranging from 45 percent in CS to 95 percent in CSOB (Schwartz 2006, 209).[28] One of the principal motives behind the voucher privatization, initiated in spring 1991, was to build national capitalism by excluding foreign participation.[29] A particular resentment was felt toward Germans; Czechs feared the prospect of becoming low-wage subcontractors for German firms (Horowitz and Petráš 2003, 257). For many nomenklatura managers, voucher privatization was a protection against being taken over by foreign owners, who would likely replace them with Western managers (Schwartz 2006, 206). Privatization was thus characterized by an aversion to the sale of national property to foreign capital.

Voucher privatization resulted in a highly concentrated structure of control rights due to the emergence of IPFs controlled by large government banks and by emerging privately owned financial groups that accumulated their capital during the privatization (Rao and Hirsch 2003; Schwartz 2006).[30] Of the top IPFs, nine were founded and controlled by the major domestic banks, attracting vouchers to control nearly 30 percent of the shares of privatized firms (Appel 2004, 62). Competition in the banking sector was further restricted by the emergence of cross-ownership networks that formed when investment subsidiaries of banks acquired significant portions of shares (thus indirect control) not only in industrial firms but also in other banks. Contrary to its goals, the voucher privatization did not transfer property rights from the state to private hands; instead it created a "recombinant property" through IPFs (Stark and Bruszt 1998).[31]

In the end, the voucher privatization led to so-called *banking socialism*.[32] The Czech financial system remained dominated by the Big Four banks, which, because they were viewed as "the heart of the economy," remained in state hands.[33] In 1995, these banks accounted for 76 percent of all banking assets, 83 percent of deposits, and 80 percent of loans (Snyder and Kormendi 1997, 110). The cross-ownership structures provided the government with multiple channels to influence the policies of banks (Nollen, Kudrna, and Pazderník 2005, 366; Snyder and Kormendi 1997, 105). The government exercised its ownership rights through the National Property Fund, established to implement the privatization of state property. The National Property Fund placed its representatives on bank boards and exerted direct control over the banks' senior management. It could replace the management of banks, determine its dividends, define banks' strategic objectives, and intervene in credit policies. The outcome was a pervasive moral hazard arising from the role of the government in the financial sector.

Banks became an instrument of governmental policy. The government encouraged bank lending (and rolling over troubled loans) to prevent bankruptcy of insolvent firms and unemployment in return for the promise of bank bailouts and regulatory protection, including protection from foreign competition.[34] This policy helped the ODS-led governments to remain highly popular and to neutralize political opposition to economic reforms.[35] The Czech government and the banks' senior management followed an "implicit contract" based on public statements and personnel appointments rather than on direct political instructions. The contract focused on government objectives that involved subsidizing key political constituencies (Snyder and Kormendi 1997).

The second source of moral hazard stemmed from the dual role of banks as the owners and creditors of enterprises that reduced their incentives to apply prudent banking practices (Kreuzbergova 2006). Banks were tied to enterprises not only by large outstanding loans but also by credit relationships that often got turned into ownership ties through debt-equity swaps. In exchange for equity, the state-owned banks extended "privatization loans" to domestic entrepreneurs, providing them with financial resources for privatization of state-owned enterprises (Drábek, Janáček, and Tůma 1994, 169–70). As creditors, banks were expected to apply prudent credit criteria. But as owners, banks wanted to promote the competitiveness of firms and prevent their closures, thus they were intrinsically motivated to relax credit conditions (Nollen, Kudrna, and Pazdernik 2005, 370). If a borrower could not repay a loan, the bank would not initiate bankruptcy proceedings but instead would provide the so-called co-owner loan. At times, banks used their dual role to extract rents from healthy firms to bail out failing projects (Desai and Plocková 1997). So, as one Czech commentator pointed out, "the government did not privatize the banks but the borrowers privatized the money" of the banks (Havel 2004). The World Bank (1999) expressed concerns that a significant part of the privatization of enterprises was leveraged, generating firms with no capital because their shares were used as collateral for loans.

The Klaus government did not see free market policies and state interventions in the financial sector as mutually exclusive. The government's approach to regulation of markets derived from a belief in the laissez-faire doctrine (Schwartz 2006, 212–213). "Too big to fail" considerations united bankers and industrialists when lobbying state officials for subsidies, for loan forgiveness, and against strict financial regulation (Schwartz 2006, 249). Not surprisingly, the domestic regulatory framework with regard to insider lending, loan collateralization and classification stringency, and effective bankruptcy procedures was either weak or absent (Barth, Caprio, and Levine 2002).

How influential were the Czech public bankers vis-à-vis the state? Compared with their Estonian counterparts, they enjoyed substantial advantages in terms of structural and lobbying power.[36] The Klaus governing party, ODS, had close relationships with big public banks, whose managers were members of the former banking-industrial nomenklatura (Schwartz 2006).[37] They came from the socialist *monobank* and retained their positions until the late 1990s (Palda 1997, 89).[38] Klaus, himself a former banker with sixteen years of experience with the same bank, was not willing to sacrifice the interests of banks.

Overall, banking socialism generated incentives for moral hazard in the financial sector. The main symptoms were soft bank credit, the accumulation of bad loans, weak financial regulation, nontransparent transfers of ownership, and various forms of asset stripping in privatized enterprises (so-called tunneling). Eventually, this gravitated to financial instability and undermined the credibility of the fixed exchange rate regime. The behavior of short-term interest rate differentials with Germany suggests that after the initial decline in the currency-risk premium, it started to climb again in June 1994. Short-term interest rate differentials attained more than 950 basis points in December 1996 (figure 5.1). Under a fixed exchange rate regime, a rise in short-term interest rates indicates a lack of trust in the stability of the value of the currency.

The End of the Czech Miracle

The real exchange rate of the Czech currency appreciated by 30 to 40 percent between 1992 and 1997 (Horváth 1999, 285). Currency appreciation was primarily driven by massive inflows of short-term foreign capital encouraged by high interest rates.[39] The CNB, endowed with a high degree of autonomy, pursued a tight monetary policy of high interest rates in the pur-

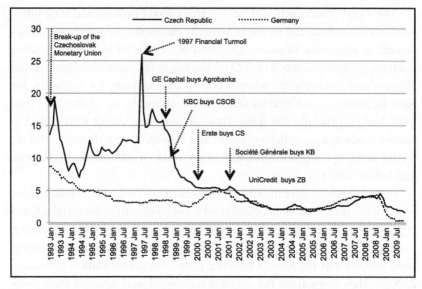

Fig. 5.1. Money Market Rates: The Czech Republic and Germany (%)
Source: International Monetary Fund, *International Financial Statistics*.

suit of price stability. Widened interest rate differentials against Germany (by two to three times) and the public commitment of the CNB to the peg encouraged strong inflows of foreign portfolio capital, reaching 17 percent of GDP in 1995 (Hallerberg and de Souza 2000, 22).

Foreign credits increased, too. The foreign borrowing of domestic banks amounted to 6 percent of GDP and 40 percent of total foreign debt in 1995 (Tůma 2006, 4). Banks were borrowing in international financial markets in foreign currencies to profit from lower foreign interest rates (without bearing exchange rate risk under a fixed exchange rate regime). Subsequently, banks provided foreign currency loans to domestic firms. As a consequence, they transformed a foreign exchange risk into a credit risk now borne by these firms. Confronted with large foreign currency liabilities, banks hedged them by off-balance sheet operations to avoid currency mismatches (Holub and Tůma 2006; Erbenova and Holub 2006).

In addition to speculative motives of banks seeking to exploit profitable investment opportunities, foreign borrowing was a source of credit to bank-controlled firms (Christensen 2004). The big Czech banks, in particular, worked toward consolidation of domestic firms so they could compete with the dominant European players in the traditional sectors of Czech exports, such as heavy engineering, transport equipment, and chemicals (Koleva and Vincensini 2002). The appreciating domestic currency was making these sectors internationally uncompetitive.

The soft credit policies and disregard for the principles of prudent banking led to the accumulation of large inter-enterprise debt that increased by 250 percent in 1991 and by 100 percent in 1992 (Rao and Hirsch 2003, 263). The bank loan portfolios were heavily concentrated among a few enterprises and industrial sectors, so foreclosing on the biggest borrowers would threaten the banks themselves. As table 5.2 shows, nonperforming loans soared, amounting to more than 40 percent of all loans in 1995. The CNB had to maintain high interest rate spreads between lending and borrowing rates (around a 6 percent range) to boost bank profits and their ability to build up their reserves (Desai 1995). But the creation of these artificial bank profits led to the emergence of small undercapitalized banks that continued to make risky loans (Brada and Kutan 1999, 6–7).

The CNB delivered everything that had been expected on the monetary policy front, but it was not able to perform its banking supervision tasks effectively. Its task was further hampered by its sharing of authority over financial markets with the government (Neumann and Egan 1999, 184). The central bank lacked clear authority over the large state-owned banks, since the regulation of banks was primarily the responsibility of the Ministry of Fi-

TABLE 5.2. Transparency and Regulatory Quality of the Czech Republic Banking System

	Foreign bank assets as a % of total assets[a]	Nonperforming loans as a % of total gross loans[b]	Credit reporting institutions[c]	EBRD index of banking sector reforms[d]
1995	49	40.4	No	3.0
2000	68	29.3	No	3.3
2005	83	3.9	Public credit registry and private credit bureau (est. in 2002)	4.0
2009	86	4.6	Public credit registry and private credit bureau	n.a.

Source: Data for each column from the respective sources:

[a]Claessens et al. (2008); Claessens and van Horen (2012).

[b]World Bank, *World Development Indicators*. Data for 1995 from the European Bank for Reconstruction and Development, *Transition Reports*.

[c]World Bank, *Doing Business*.

[d]European Bank for Reconstruction and Development, *Transition Reports*, various issues.

nance (McDermott 2007, 233).[40] When the CNB's banking supervision observed the first signs of banking problems in 1993, it stopped granting new banking licenses. It also implemented two assistance programs, the Consolidation Program I (1991–94) and Consolidation Program II (1995–96), to clean up the balance sheets of banks and to prevent the destabilization of the banking system. In the 1993–96 period, several small banks collapsed, and the CNB revoked the licenses of others. The government followed with a Stabilization Program in 1996 that involved acquiring bad-quality receivables from the small domestic banks by Česká finanční (an agency established by the Consolidation Bank, the state-owned "hospital" founded in 1991 to solve bad loan problems) (see Mejstřík, Dvořáková, and Neprašová 2004).

All of these programs were costly and had limited success; 22 percent of all bank loans remained uncollectible and bad loans accounted for more than 30 percent of total loans in 1996.[41] The exception was CSOB, which had only 8 percent of bad loans in its portfolio. CSOB had several domestic (Ministry of Finance, National Property Fund, and CNB) but also foreign institutional owners (including the EBRD and International Finance Corporation) that mutually controlled each other. Not surprisingly, the CSOB's management was less responsive to government pressures for enterprise financing.[42]

While the 1992 banking law allowed greenfield investments, foreign investors could not acquire controlling stakes in Czech banks. Among the first foreign-owned greenfield entrants in 1991 were Bank Austria Creditanstalt, BNP Paribas, and Citibank, but their market shares were very small (Mejstřík, Dvořáková, and Neprašová 2004). Commerzbank opened a branch in 1992. Then, at the end of 1993, the government applied a two-year moratorium on licensing of foreign banks to limit competition (Schwartz 1997). The official explanation was that domestic banks needed "breathing space" to consolidate and restructure (Konopielko 1999). By 1995, out of twenty-five banks, there were eleven foreign greenfield investments (De Haas and van Lelyveld 2006). Crucially though, no Czech state-owned bank was sold to a foreigner until 1998. I am arguing here that privatizing state-owned banks to foreign strategic investors would have helped to enforce financial discipline and strengthen the government's policy credibility by signaling to the market the compatibility of monetary and financial policies.

The 1997 Financial Turmoil

By and large, the early history of banking in the Czech Republic was dominated by two forces, state-owned banks and investment funds. The reckless behavior of these actors exacerbated credit risk and generated inflationary inertia. Inflation rates in mid-1990s may have been lower than in Poland or Bulgaria but still were too high in comparison with the German rates, indicating the low credibility of the peg. The CNB engaged in massive sterilizations of capital flows to prevent excessive real exchange rate appreciation associated with devaluation risk. There is some narrative evidence suggesting that the central bank as guardian of the value of the national currency was unsuccessful due to the "sterilization game" played by domestic banks (Christensen 2004). Banks borrowed cheaply abroad and invested in the high-yielding sterilization bonds issued by the CNB, making significant profits from these short-term speculations.

As a consequence, the CNB was forced to widen the exchange rate band to plus or minus 7.5 percent in February 1996. By then, the extent of the band widening and the timing of this notice, prior to parliamentary elections set for May 1996, further reduced the credibility of the government's commitments to the fixed exchange rate regime. Investor sentiment turned against the country, leading to (desirable) one-off outflow of short-term speculative capital.[43] The CNB simultaneously tightened monetary policy by raising interest rates and intervened vigorously to avoid currency devaluation. Banks, concerned about the adverse impact of the restrictive monetary policy on the financial position of their debtors, were pushing for a monetary easing (Geršl 2006). Klaus (2000, 13–14) blamed the CNB's monetary policy of high interest rates and minimum reserve requirements for the banking problems and indirectly for the financial turmoil:

> Our commercial banks, relatively weak and ill-equipped with capital, being . . . at the edge of their possibilities, were hit by these monetary restrictions to a greater extent than our central bank expected or realized afterwards. I would like to argue that right then we embarked on the financial crisis.

And yet, Klaus considered the long-sustained hard currency policy as a source of national pride and a strong koruna as a symbol of the successful policies of the ODS-led government.[44] The Czech government, inspired by the successful example of a credible fixed exchange rate regime in Austria, was overly optimistic about the resilience of its banking system. Of course, the Austrian model proved inappropriate because its financial system was much sounder than the Czech one.[45] It is worth emphasizing that the Czech banks negatively affected the credibility of the peg by channeling short-term capital flows into the economy, by speculating with the central bank's sterilization bonds, and by engaging in inflationary, politicized lending to connected parties. To make matters worse, the evidence indicates that some banks were betting against the koruna and publicly predicted its devaluation from the beginning of 1997, triggering a speculative currency attack (Šmídková et al. 1998; Horváth 1999).

In addition to worsening economic fundamentals, tensions inside the ruling coalition that began to intensify toward the end of 1996 were worrying investors, too. A closer look at the dynamics of the tense political environment before the crisis provides a better understanding of the complicated interaction between political and monetary authorities. The high degree of independence of the CNB became the source of particularly strong tensions. The personal tensions between Prime Minister Klaus and the CNB governor, Josef Tošovský, were apparent. Tošovský was committed to building the credibility of the central bank, a goal that was incompatible with Klaus's vision of the central bank supporting the objectives of economic reform.[46] During Tošovský's governorship (1993–97), the CNB had established itself as a conservative, independent institution that sought to "keep distance" from the banks.[47] Consequently, it found itself in frequent conflict with the Ministry of Finance. The government repeatedly criticized the central bank for being too autonomous and unwilling to coordinate monetary policy with other economic policies.

It is fair to conclude that intra-institutional tensions and financial instability were perceived as a growing risk among investors and market confidence in the Czech government fell. As figure 5.1 depicts, the credibility of the peg took a dip, as the Czech money market rates peaked at nearly 16 percent, five times as high as the German rates. In April 1997, the Czech government, worried about its international credibility, issued two packages of economic reform measures to tighten fiscal policy, ameliorate the banking regulation, and correct for the fiscal-monetary mismatch. But distrustful markets had grown wary of the empty promises of the government, which lost much credibility because it was unable to commit to financial reforms. The country risk premium soared; five-year government bonds yielded nearly 13 percent in May 1997 (figure 5.2).

Just a few weeks later, the first speculative attack on the Czech koruna came (table 5.3 illustrates the chronology of the 1997 financial crisis).[48] In the initial stages of the turmoil, the CNB tried to defend the currency peg by massive interventions and several interest rate hikes. The CNB administered a credit squeeze in defense of exchange rate parity in spite of the risk

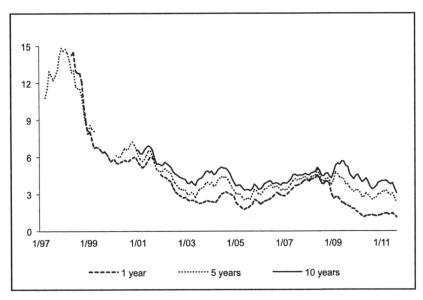

Fig. 5.2. Sovereign Bond Yields (% per annum) in the Czech Republic, 1997–2011
Source: Czech National Bank.

this move posed for domestic banks. In the game of confidence that lies behind financial turbulence, the Czech policymakers were unable to maintain the confidence of investors. The situation sharply escalated when the population, losing faith in the koruna, started massively converting it into foreign currencies. The Czech currency came under heavy pressure and expectations of devaluation increased. The central bank lost $2.5 billion of foreign exchange reserves during the crisis episode, which lasted less than two weeks (Šmídková et al. 1998). The CNB devalued the koruna by 10 percent and abandoned the peg on May 27, 1997.[49] It subsequently adopted a managed float. The financial markets were not convinced that the crisis was under control and the currency-risk premium peaked at over two thousand basis points in June 1997 before decreasing gradually.

According to the criteria stipulated by Bordo and Schwartz (1996, 438), the Czech financial turmoil constitutes a currency crisis, defined as "a market-based attack on the exchange value of a currency. It involves a break with earlier market judgment about the exchange value of a currency." But the Czech crisis was less conventional. It did not reflect a general deterioration in macroeconomic fundamentals, traditionally associated with currency crises. Inflation was relatively low and the central bank accumulated sufficient foreign reserves thanks to large capital inflows, and although the government's fiscal stance deteriorated, it was not excessive. By contrast, the banking sector was vulnerable.

Gaining Credibility for Inflation Targeting

After the painful learning experience with the failed peg, the CNB publicly announced a new monetary regime of inflation targeting combined with a flexible exchange rate regime in December 1997.[50] After the CNB officially proclaimed a float, it continued to systematically intervene in foreign exchange markets until 2002. In the initial period, the inflation target had been set at 5.5 to 6 percent. The CNB, seeking to increase its autonomy further, decided to switch to the new monetary regime without consulting with the collapsing government.[51] Šmídková and Hrnčíř (2003, 13) explain:

> A change to inflation targeting has an effect analogous to increasing the independence of central bank since it moves the central bank to the center

TABLE 5.3. Chronology of the 1997 Czech Currency Turmoil

Date	Event
February 11	Early warning signs: Czech koruna reaches its high above the central parity.
March 12	Prime Minister Klaus criticizes the restrictive monetary policy of the CNB.
March 25	Prime Minister Klaus rules out devaluation.
April 17	Government approves a stabilization package that strengthens the koruna. Prime Minister Klaus urges a loosening of monetary policy, again.
May 14	Koruna at its low, 3.88% in the devaluation band. The *Financial Times* publishes a negative survey for the Czech Republic. Opinion poll shows Prime Minister Klaus's ruling party popularity at all-time low.
May 15	The first speculative attack. Koruna fell sharply within the band to 5.25% below its central parity. CNB engages in unsterilized intervention, reflected in reserve losses and high interest rates.
May 16	CNB raises the Lombard rate (interest rate charged to other banks for very short loans against collateral) from 14% to 50%.
May 20	CNB limits access to the Lombard window. Overnight interbank rates rise to almost 100%.
May 22	The Czech koruna depreciates to 6.2% below parity and then recovers to 3–4% below parity. Overnight interest rates reach almost 200%. Public confidence weakens; residents start to exchange koruna into foreign currencies.
May 26	The CNB Governor in a joint press conference with prime minister announces that the ±7.5% target band will be replaced by managed float.

Source: Horváth (1999); Begg (1998).

of economic discussions. In this sense, formal independence of the central bank is fully realized. Specifically, the CNB announced inflation targets according to its own assessment.

The CNB was forced to act rapidly to reassure markets and build the credibility of the new monetary regime in the context of a weak banking sector. In some ways, the central bank was the only public institution in the country that had some credibility with the international financial community. The Klaus government was forced from power late in 1997 by the financial turmoil and a campaign finance scandal. As Vachudova (2001, 343) noted, "It emerged that money had flowed into the ODS party coffers in exchange for favors related to privatization and banking." In January 1998, the president dissolved the ODS-led government and appointed a new caretaker government on professional merits rather than political affiliation. Led by the former central bank governor, Tošovský, the new government started with the implementation of banking reforms that involved opening the sector to foreign investors.[52]

After the early parliamentary elections of June 1998, a single-party minority Social Democratic government led by Prime Minister Miloš Zeman (1998–2002) occupied all the ministerial posts (controlling 74 out of 200 seats in the Parliament) (Roberts 2003). The ideas of the new finance minister, Pavel Mertlík, about the banking system stood in sharp contrast with those of his predecessors. He pushed for the privatization of big public banks to foreign strategic investors and fought demands to pump government money into failing industrial conglomerates (Andrews 2001). The most urgent problem was how to maintain adequate capitalization levels in banks and avoid a general loss of public confidence in the banking system. Confronted with a postcrisis recession and severe solvency problems in the banking system, further aggravated by devaluation and interest rate hikes, the government assumed the responsibility for troubled banks. The task was finding new sources of fresh capital. To this end, the Social Democratic government began to actively promote foreign investments in banking through tax advantages and subsidies.[53]

The only case of a bank privatized to a foreign strategic investor prior to the financial turmoil was when the German BHF-BANK acquired a majority (40 percent) stake in ZB in 1992. Then, Bankgesellschaft Berlin took over BHF-BANK's stake (increasing its ownership to 85 percent) in 1998 but subsequently sold it to Italian UniCredit in 2002 (Tschoegl 2003). Foreign buyers introduced the "standards of Western banking culture" in ZB (Havel 2004, 179). The post-1997 bank privatization started with the tender for privatization advisors won by large U.S. investment banks, such as Merrill Lynch and Goldman Sachs, which represented a commitment of the Czech policymakers to transparency of the process. The invitation of foreign banks sent signals to the markets that deep flaws in the banking system would be addressed. To prevent the collapse of Agrobanka, the biggest private bank (controlled by Motoinvest, an aggressive brokerage firm), the CNB ordered the Big Four banks to extend a large credit line to the bank, and then sold its stakes to General Electric in June 1998.

Consequently, money market rates dropped from 15.55 to 10 percentage points between May and December 1998. This initial drop in currency risk could be credited to the signaling effect of the first major foreign bank acquisitions. After that the government sold a 65.7 percent stake in CSOB to Belgian KBC in June 1999, followed by the acquisition of a 52.10 percent stake in CS by Austrian Erste Bank in March 2000. In June 2001, Société Générale acquired 60 percent majority stake in KB after the huge state intervention to stabilize the bank's capital.[54] Foreign banks held a 68 percent market share by 2000, which further increased to nearly 86 percent by 2009 (table 5.2). Table 5.4 shows the market shares of the top multinational banks (in terms of assets) in the Czech banking system.

The privatization of IPB, the third largest Czech bank, might appear to be inconsistent with the argument of this book because its foreign owner engaged in risky behavior that led to the eventual failure of the bank. IPB became the dominant financial group with the most opaque ownership structure in the country. The bank was one of the leading sponsors of the ODS (Anderson 2006). In 1997, the Czech government sold its 46 percent

TABLE 5.4. Market Shares of Top Multinational Banks in the Czech Republic, 2011

Bank Name	Assets held by a bank as a % of total banking assets	Parent Bank (Country)
Česká spořitelna	17.8	Erste Bank (Austria)
Československá obchodní banka	17.6	KBC (Belgium)
Komerční banka	15.5	Société Générale (France)
Živnostenská banka	7.9	UniCredit (Italy, Austria)
Raiffeisen Bank	6.6	Raiffensen Bank (Austria)
Agrobanka	4.2	GE Capital (United States)
Commerzbank	2.0	Commerzbank (Germany)

Source: Raiffeisen Research (2012).

controlling stake to a foreign investor, Nomura Europe, the Japanese investment house. The Tošovsky government neither assumed bad loans at IPB prior to sale nor provided guarantees to the buyer. The bank had a weak portfolio but provided misleading information about its true financial situation to the banking supervisors. After the sale, the bank's asset quality deteriorated further. In June 2000, there was a run on the bank, which resulted in forced administration by the CNB. In the meantime, Nomura sold some of IPB's most profitable industrial assets (such as the world-renowned Pilsner Urquell). IPB was too big to fail, and so saving it became the priority for the Czech authorities. In its search for a bank savior, the government quickly sold IPB to CSOB, owned by the Belgian bank KBC. Since the costs of IPB's losses were high, the sale entailed cleaning the bank's balance sheet and obtaining the government's guarantees on deposits after the sale.[55] The forced takeover of IPB has been one of the costliest and the most controversial bank failures in emerging Europe.

This study's analytical framework can still be useful for understanding the IPB's case. It is worth repeating that the argument of this book emphasizes that emerging markets can borrow credibility from reputable multinational banks investing as *strategic* investors (involved in the business operations), not portfolio investors. First and foremost, Nomura bought IPB for its equity shareholdings and not for its banking business; hence it considered this acquisition a portfolio investment. The IPB shares were held by Saluka Investments, a Dutch-based special purpose vehicle. Nomura did not engage in IPB restructuring. It also resisted the pressures of the supervisory authorities for recapitalization when the problems in the bank became apparent. Second, Nomura is an investment bank and lacks expertise in conventional commercial banking activities. Finally, Nomura was a minority holder of the IPB and thus did not have control over IPB's lending decisions, which were kept firmly in the hands of the incumbent Czech management. So Nomura did not exercise real control of the IPB's management and did not properly supervise its local representatives (Čulík 2000).

Overall, the entry of foreign strategic investors was associated with massive improvements in the Czech banking sector, notably its transparency and regulatory quality, the channels of influence that my theory identifies. HVB Bank, together with GE Capital and other foreign banks, founded a private credit bureau in 2002 (De Haas and Naaborg 2006) that induced a radical improvement in credit analysis at local banks, not least because they had been unable to rely on the information sharing among creditors (table 5.2). An information-sharing system reduced information asymmetries and enhanced transparency in the financial system. For instance, hidden bank losses had to be recorded in the accounting books and new information disclosure requirements were adopted (Havel 2004, 195). The 2002 Provision on Credit Risk Management, Asset Classifications and Provisioning required banks to have internal audit policies. With the entry of new foreign strategic investors, many banks underwent major internal reorganizations that resulted in improved risk-management procedures (International Monetary Fund 2002). As bank risk taking was reduced, banking sector stability and resilience was strengthened. Foreign parent banks provided sufficient funds to cover the capital requirements of their Czech subsidiaries. Thus, following the completion of bank privatization, capital adequacy ratios were at satisfactory levels of around 12 percent and the quality of bank lending improved, with the ratio of nonperforming loans in banks' portfolios declining from 40 percent in 1995 to just 3.9 percent in 2005 (table 5.2). The progress in banking and regulatory reforms as measured by the EBRD transition indicator shows significant improvements and full compliance with international and supervisory standards by 2005 (table 5.2). In 2003, the CNB signed memoranda of understanding with foreign supervisory counterparts in Austria, Germany, Belgium, France, and the State of New York for exchange of information and supervisory cooperation. The entry of foreign banks was also instrumental in the development of the interbank foreign exchange market, providing an "important stabilizing element" into the management of exchange risks (Ötker-Robe et al. 2007, 27).

Foreign bank presence put an end to the country's banking troubles, so the CNB could have focused on its primary mandate for monetary stability. The CNB's policy of high interest rates to attain inflation targets motivated politicians to pursue legislative efforts, albeit unsuccessful, to limit CNB's independence in 1999 and 2000 (Geršl 2006).[56] Through its low inflation performance, the CNB maintained an anti-inflation reputation equivalent to that of the Bundesbank.[57] By 2003, inflation had fallen to just 0.11 percent. As the inflation targeting gained in credibility, the inflation differential with Germany disappeared and remained that way. In an inflation-targeting regime, the central bank's gains in credibility come from evaluating the role inflation targets play in the formation of expectations. Just how successful the CNB was in establishing the credibility of the inflation-targeting regime is depicted in figure 5.3, which compares inflation expectations of forecast-

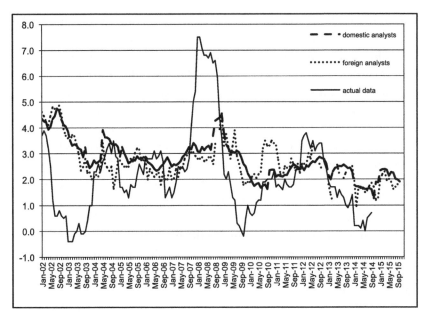

Fig. 5.3. Inflation Expectations and Actual Annual Consumer Price Inflation in the Czech Republic (%)
Source: Czech National Bank.

ers from financial institutions (domestic and foreign) with the actual inflation performance.

The evident example of the influence of foreign bank presence was the evolution of money market rates, which decreased from 16 percent in 1997 to 5.17 percent in 2001 when the privatization of major public banks to reputable foreign strategic investors was completed. As demonstrated in Figures 5.1 and 5.2, rapid convergence of money market rates and significant drops in sovereign bond yields and a decline in long-term interest rate differentials with the German levels indicates significant gains in the credibility of the inflation-targeting regime (Matousek and Taci 2003). For most of the period after its adoption, the Czech inflation-targeting regime has been credible. Money market interest rate differentials relative to the German mark (and then to the euro) converged to zero.

The currency-risk premium increased slightly during the 2008 global crisis, but this increase was short-lived. Crucially, however, the Czech Republic did not experience an unsustainable credit boom or asset bubble except for short-lived exchange rate volatility during the peak of the crisis

(Åslund 2011a). Multinational banks played a stabilizing role during the crisis; the credit expansion of multinational banks (26 percent) was significantly higher than that of domestic banks (0.6 percent) in the 2007–09 period (Dietrich, Knedlik, and Lindner 2011, 426). But, owing to "healthy capital and liquidity buffers" and "limited exposure to foreign currency risk," subsidiaries of foreign banks operating in the Czech Republic did not require emergency liquidity assistance (International Monetary Fund 2010, 36). As a consequence, the damage to the country's credibility was minimal. Yields on ten-year government bonds increased from 3.27 percent in September 2005 to 5.66 percent in June 2009 but then dramatically decreased to slightly above 2 percent in September 2010 (figure 5.2). What was the secret of the Czech success? To be sure, the CNB, committed to price stability, was an important consideration in the international confidence game. But we can safely say that foreign banks crucially enhanced the credibility of inflation targeting by bringing transparency and stability to the Czech banking sector.

Poland: Stop-and-Go Reputation-Building Process

Compared to the Czech Republic, less favorable economic legacies of communism made the task of establishing international credibility more difficult in Poland. In the 1970s, the Polish communist leadership used external loans to finance consumption and the military efforts of the Soviet bloc. The resulting large foreign debt stood at $41 billion, or about 58 percent of GDP. In 1981, the Polish government stopped servicing its foreign debt, an act of defiance that sent negative signals to the international financial community. Furthermore, the inconclusive economic reforms in the 1982–88 period resulted in deep macroeconomic imbalances. As part of these reform efforts, the communist governments increased enterprise autonomy, which was associated with strong wage growth. They also pursued a loose credit policy and an accommodating monetary policy involving monetization of the budget deficit by the central bank. All these policies led to inflationary pressures. As a consequence, Poland in the final years of the 1980s was plagued by hyperinflation, colossal budget deficits, and unserviceable external debt.[58]

It is not surprising that the Polish government encountered difficulties in establishing the credibility of its monetary commitments. There are two plausible explanations for these difficulties. The first is related to the lack of a transparent and sound domestic financial system due to a stop-and-go process of opening the banking sector. The second difficulty stemmed from not fulfilling the institutional prerequisites to contain inflation, mainly because the central bank was unable to conduct monetary policy independently of the government needs.

The Balcerowicz Plan

The landslide victory of Solidarity in (partially) free elections in June 1989 marked the start of political and economic reforms in Poland. The first Solidarity-led government that emerged in September 1989 inherited a half-dismantled command economy hovering on the verge of hyperinflation, which stood at 3,000 percent in the last five months of 1989 (Gomulka 1995, 323). Prime Minister Tadeusz Mazowiecki and his team of technocrats led by the finance minister, Leszek Balcerowicz,[59] launched a radical reform program known as a "shock therapy."[60] Balcerowicz, the architect of this program (also known as the "Balcerowicz Plan"), maintained that the initial transition period, which he referred to as the "period of extraordinary politics," provided a window of opportunity for policymakers to push for decisive reforms.[61] The key components of the reform program were the removal of all price controls, fiscal and monetary austerity, currency convertibility, trade liberalization, and massive and rapid privatization. The program was an expression of the government's willingness to cut its ties with the past.

The communist status quo was destroyed and new interest groups were not in place yet, so the government operated under conditions of minimal political friction, albeit only for a few months (Kaminski 2001, 323).[62] Reforms quickly gained the political support of the government and the Parliament. Lech Wałęsa, who won the presidential election in 1990, also supported the policies of Mazowiecki's government notwithstanding his pre-election rhetoric (Stone 2002, 95). Initially, the shock therapy program had negative effects on the economy, which contracted by 7.6 percent in 1991.[63] The political backlash against orthodox reforms contributed to the collapse of the Mazowiecki government (August 1989–January 1991), which was replaced by another right-of-center Solidarity government led by Jan Krzysztof Bielecki (January–December 1991) promising a "controlled liberalism" version of the transition. The subsequent government led by Jan Olszewski (December 1991–May 1992) also came to power by opposing shock therapy while promising low interest rates and government assistance to farmers and industries. Paradoxically, neither Bielecki's nor Olszewski's governments devised a transformation program that would differ markedly from the Balcerowicz Plan. The next Solidarity cabinet of Hanna Suchocka (July 1992–April 1993) appeared to follow the economic orthodoxy too (King and Sznajder 2006; Stone 2002).

Fighting Hyperinflation

One of the principal goals of Polish reformers was to combat hyperinflation. As Balcerowicz put it, "Inflation was like a spreading inferno, which had to be quenched, or at least contained, in order to make it possible to change the economic system" (Balcerowicz, quoted in Stone 2002, 91). Fear and doubts about ending hyperinflation and the lack of anti-inflationary credibility of the Polish monetary authorities brought a quick political consensus within the government about the need to peg the national currency, the Polish zloty.[64] But the political debate over the level of the exchange rate was more complex and contentious. The proposals were ranging from 5,000 zloty per one U.S. dollar to 28,000 zloty per one U.S. dollar (Kowalski and Stawarska 1999, 356). In the end, the exchange rate was fixed at 9,500 zloty per one U.S. dollar (after a 46 percent upfront devaluation) in January 1990.[65] As in the Czech Republic, the prevailing view on the initial devaluation was that the exchange rate would give the export industry a competitive advantage. The deliberate undervaluation was also intended to help the accumulation of foreign exchange reserves needed to adhere to the fixed exchange rate regime (Wellisz 1997, 159).

A high external debt, which placed a significant and increasingly worrisome burden on public finances, and low foreign exchange reserves gave the government a strong desire to improve the country's credibility. The government needed to obtain the support of the international financial community for the rescheduling and reduction of its foreign debt. It also needed to gain international credibility for its economic reforms and to secure new credits (Gomulka 1995, 320; Kaminski 2001, 312–15). The international financial institutions and foreign advisors played a critical role in advising and providing multilateral support, which created the initial credibility for Polish economic and institutional reforms. Behind the Balcerowicz reform program was a tightly knit group of foreign advisors that included then Harvard professor Jeffrey Sachs, who had successfully convinced the Solidarity parliamentarians of the necessity of rapidly combating hyperinflation and had advocated for a reduction of Polish debt on the international scene.[66]

A number of authors have argued that the IMF can provide credibility to reform programs. During the negations of December 1989, the IMF insisted on the adoption of a fixed exchange rate regime to anchor inflation expectations.[67] The Polish negotiators agreed to pursue a fixed regime for at least three months but did not make any commitment beyond that. Stanislaw Gomulka (1995), one of the negotiators and advisors to Balcerowicz, maintained that although the Polish stabilization program resembled a typical IMF package in its logic and main features, it was locally conceived and designed by the Balcerowicz team and *only* then approved by the IMF. He further claimed that reforms implemented by the Polish government were more ambitious than the reform steps suggested by the IMF.[68]

Whatever their exact arguments, the need to "anchor" the national currency but at the same time preserve room for readjustment explains why the Polish authorities adopted a limited-horizon commitment to a fixed exchange rate regime (Wellisz 1997, 158). The insufficient levels of foreign exchange reserves at the time the peg was adopted made the zloty vulnerable to speculative attacks. To reassure the markets, the Bank for International Settlements granted a loan of $215 million as a reserve supplement. In addition, the G-24 governments created a $1 billion Zloty Stabilization Fund to underpin the confidence in the fixed exchange rate.

The peg to the U.S. dollar, adopted as part of the initial economic stabilization program, exposed it to changes in the value of the U.S. dollar at a time when Polish trade with European countries increased. The government thus devalued the zloty 14 percent against the U.S. dollar in May 1991 and pegged it to a basket of five currencies.[69] But persistently high inflation differentials, reflecting the lack of credibility of the fixed exchange rate regime, led to a quick appreciation of the zloty, which resulted in a sharp increase in imports and put pressure on the competitiveness of domestic exporters. Consequently, a large current account deficit emerged. The soft peg policy opened the central bank of Poland to pressures for devaluation from exporters (Kowalski and Stawarska 1999, 356).[70] As the subsequent sections will show, the adoption of a fixed exchange rate regime was not enough to convince markets about the government's monetary rectitude without the reassuring influence of global banks that would safeguard the stability of the banking system.

A Blueprint for Banking Reform

Unlike in the Czech Republic, banking reforms in Poland, initiated in 1988–89, included opening the banking sector (Polanski 2002, 107). Two pieces of legislation, the act on the central bank and the Banking Act, modeled on German legislation, laid the foundation for the establishment of a two-tier banking structure. The new legislation allowed the transformation of nine regional agencies of the central bank—the National Bank of Poland (Narodowy Bank Polski, NBP)—into independent state-owned banks, while the NBP assumed the role of a classical central bank. Nine state-owned banks, created from the *voivodship* and former branches of the NBP, included Wielkopolski Bank Kredytowy (WBK) in Poznań, Bank Śląski in Katowice, Bank Przemysłowo-Handlowy (BPH) in Kraków, Bank Gdański (BG) in Gdańsk, Pomorski Bank Kredytowy (PBKS) in Szczecin, Bank Depozytowo-Kredytowy (BDK) in Lublin, Bank Zachodni (BZ) in Wrocław, Powszechny Bank Gospodarczy (PBG) in Lódz, and Powszechny Bank Kredytowy (PBK) in Warsaw. Several specialized banks existed alongside these: Bank Handlowy w Warsawie S.A. (BH), serving as the foreign trade bank; Bank Polska Kasa Opieki S.A. (Bank Pekao), handling foreign currency transactions of individuals; and Powszechna Kasa Oszczędności Bank Polski (PKO BP), a savings bank.[71]

In addition, the government liberalized the "third" tier of the banking system, the system of cooperative banks, which were permitted to leave the Bank Gospodarki Żywnościowej S.A. (BGZ), a national umbrella bank for local cooperative banks financing agriculture and the food industry. The 1989 Banking Act further permitted the establishment of new banks organized as joint-stock companies with the participation of both Polish and foreign banks. Like in the other three transition countries treated in this study, licensing policy was initially very liberal. The NBP issued forty-two licenses in 1990 alone (Polanski 1997, 66). Taking advantage of the liberal entry rules, state-owned enterprises and local governments established "crony" private banks, which were generously extending credits to privileged groups of customers.[72]

The inflationary environment of the early 1990s guaranteed banks' profits from high interest rate spreads. Real interest rates remained negative while spreads between lending and deposit rates amounted to 7 and 9 percentage points in 1992 and 1993 respectively, according to the OECD estimates (Montes-Negret and Papi 1996, 20). High interest rate differentials encouraged banks to speculate with Treasury bills and the NBP's steriliza-tion bonds.[73] Polish banks were not keen supporters of anti-inflationary policies, but as a lobbying group they were relatively weak.[74]

The combination of rapidly rising interest rates, appreciating currency, and suppression of subsidies, in addition to the collapse of Soviet markets, aggravated the situation of Polish exporters and contributed to a dramatic increase in the share of bad loans in banks' portfolios (Polanski 1997, 74). In mid-1991, bad loans represented 17 percent of total credits and were concentrated in credit portfolios of the nine large public banks (42 percent) (Gomulka 1993). Although for the most part these bad loans resulted from the political allocation of credit during communism, the legacy of bank-enterprise links led to a continuous flow of credit. As a consequence, the Polish banking system experienced a mini-crisis that culminated in the bankruptcy of several banks in 1993 (Polanski 1994, 34).

The monetary authorities, attempting to contain expansive credit poli-cies and reduce the capacity of banks to create money, implemented a pol-icy of high interest rates (103 percent in 1990, 53 percent in 1991, and 39 percent in 1992) and reserve requirements of 30 percent on deposits (Po-lanski 1997). The tightening of monetary policy was only sufficient to par-tially reassure foreign exchange markets but not sufficient to curb inflation. A policy of fixed exchange rates brought a sharp reduction in inflation from 1,096 percent to 249 percent in 1990 (Gomulka 1995, 323). After that, how-ever, the inflation rate declined slowly, from 60 percent in 1991 to 44 per-cent in 1992 and 38 percent in 1993 (Gomulka 1995, 323). As table 5.5 shows, inflation was still over 28 percent in 1995.

Overall, then, the persistence of high inflation and interest rate differen-tials suggest that the fixed exchange rate regime was not perceived to be

TABLE 5.5. Macroeconomic Indicators for Poland

	Inflation (annual %)	Total reserves (minus gold) in US$ million	Public finances as a % of GDP[a]	External debt as a % of exports	Public debt as a % of GDP[b]
1995	28.07	14,774	−1.9	147	47.7
2000	10.06	26,562	−3.0	160	36.8
2005	2.11	40,864	−5.1	118	47.1
2009	3.83	75,923	−7	165.9	50.9

Source: World Bank, *World Development Indicators*; International Monetary Fund, *International Financial Sta-tistics*; European Bank for Reconstruction and Development, *Transition Reports*.
[a]Cash surplus/deficit (% of GDP) is closest to the overall budget balance.
[b]Abbas et al. (2010).

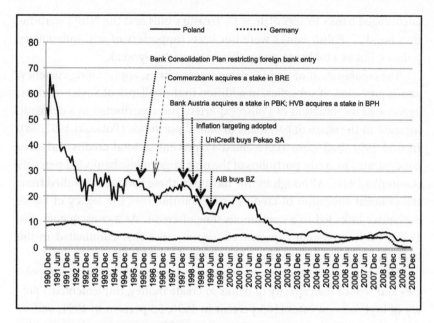

Fig. 5.4. Money Market Rates: Poland and Germany (%)
Source: International Monetary Fund, *International Financial Statistics*.

credible. At the end of 1993, Poland still exhibited a sizeable currency-risk premium, as measured by the interest rate differentials with Germany, amounting to 19 percentage points (or 1,900 basis points), as figure 5.4 illustrates graphically. The fragility of the Polish banking system was one of the key factors that increased the international markets' perception of risk.

Bank-Led Restructuring

Faced with a weak banking system and weak domestic institutional framework, the Polish government changed its approach from establishing new banks to restructuring and privatization of state-owned banks. The World Bank recommended a standard procedure for cleaning up bad loan portfolios, applied previously in Spain and some Latin American countries, which envisaged the transfer of bad loans from banks to so-called "bank hospitals." But the Stefan Kawalec, former deputy minister of finance, was skeptical about the ability of a centralized, government-run restructuring agency to resist political pressures.[75] As we have seen in the Czech case, the centralized approach to bad loan problems proved unsuccessful in changing the rent-seeking behavior of incumbent banks.

In the end, Poland adopted a bank-led "decentralized" approach to restructuring. The focal point was the 1993 Law on Financial Restructuring of Enterprises and Banks, according to which banks themselves were expected to solve the problem of nonperforming loans. Banks and enterprises were encouraged to reach a conciliatory agreement, which could take one of the following forms: rescheduling claims, debt/equity swaps and loan write-offs, bankruptcy, liquidation, or sale of claims. Unlike in the Czech Republic and Bulgaria, where the governments engaged in multiple bank recapitalizations, the Polish government recapitalized state-owned banks only once.[76] In the words of Andrzej Bratkowski, former chief economist at Bank Pekao:

> Moral hazard was contained because the government publicly announced that after the first stage of recapitalization, nobody could expect a bailout. Polish banks were thus in a weak position to lobby. They preferred to cooperate with foreign banks.[77]

Banks learned how to deal with financial risks, and consequently bad loan problems have not re-emerged in the banks involved in the restructuring program. More importantly, a bank-led restructuring plan, unique among countries of Eastern Europe, linked bad-debt workouts directly to bank privatization.[78] The Balcerowicz team preferred to restructure and consolidate banks prior to their privatization to maximize budget revenues from bank sale and to promote stock market development (Mortimer 1995; Abarbanell and Bonin 1997). As Kawalec and Kluza (2003, 7) remark, "the banks retained capital adequacy and were profitable. They did not need further infusions of capital by the government and ultimately were sold to strategic investors with high premiums to their book values." In other words, the restructuring program and the commitment of the government to privatize public banks successfully changed the behavior of domestic banks (Polanski 1994, 38). Because the government made it clear that it would not be "paternalistic," bank managers realized that if they wanted to survive, they should not engage in imprudent credit policies and excessive risk taking.[79]

Unlike the Czech government that favored domestic over foreign capital, the involvement of foreign financiers in Polish privatization was welcome. There was a political will to privatize banks quickly, with a privileged position reserved for foreign investors.[80] Another major distinction in the Polish approach was that the Polish regulatory authorities, successfully learning from foreign advisors, were able to limit bank speculations and prevent cross-ownership of banks and industries. To this end, tight prudential regulations of banks' foreign exchange positions had already been introduced in 1993 before capital flows were liberalized.

Experimenting with Banking Sector Opening

The Polish government has sought to create a favorable environment for foreign direct investments in banking, expecting to reap credibility gains by signaling to markets its commitment to sound financial policies. The 1989 Banking Act legalized the operations of foreign banks in Poland. Believing that foreigners could increase the banking competition necessary to transform and modernize Polish banks, the government encouraged greenfield investments in the banking sector (Epstein 2008). But some restrictions on foreign capital were retained. If a foreign bank wanted to obtain a license, at least one member of the bank's managing board had to have Polish citizenship. As a consequence, in the early 1990s, the dominant investment strategies of foreign banks were greenfield investments or the establishment of new banks with Polish partners. The Austrian Raiffeisen Bank and Creditanstalt and American Citibank and GE Capital were among the first foreign banks that established greenfield operations in Poland in the period from 1991 to 1992.

The Economic Committee of the Council of Ministers adopted the bank privatization program in 1991. The Polish government was convinced that due to a lack of sufficient domestic capital, the privatization of banks could not take place without foreign investors. The objective was to find a foreign strategic investor for each public bank, with some important qualifications: foreign participation in individual Polish banks would be limited to 30 percent of total shares, and the Ministry of Finance would retain 30 percent of the shares, with voting rights limited to strategic decisions (Szymkiewicz 2001).[81] Technical assistance in the process of restructuring and privatization was provided by a consortium of Polish and foreign consulting firms. Western donor countries (of which the United States was the largest contributor) allocated $600 million from the Bank Privatization Fund to recapitalize banks to make them more appealing to potential buyers. The U.S. Treasury played a key role in establishing this fund in 1992 originally to support the fixed exchange rate regime (the Zloty Stabilization Fund) (Mortimer 1995, 96). The condition for disbursements of funds for recapitalization of a bank was its privatization (Abarbanell and Bonin 1997, 32). Through the provision of information and financial resources, foreign advisors made the policy commitments of the Polish government to banking reforms more transparent and easier to control and thus more credible.

The government chose the two best banks, in terms of the quality of their portfolios and management, to spearhead the bank privatization. The privatization of WBK started in June 1991. Due to the initial lack of interest of foreign strategic investors, the government decided to sell 29 percent of the bank shares to the EBRD to provide a counterbalance to the state's influence in the bank governance (Bonin 1993, 111–12). The second transaction was an agreement with the Dutch ING, which acquired 26 percent of the shares in Bank Śląski in 1993 (at present ING has a majority 87.77 percent stake). By the end of 1995, two additional public banks were privatized. Irish Allied Bank acquired a 16.3 percent stake in WBK (increasing its ownership to 60 percent by 1997) and the EBRD bought 26.4 percent of shares in BPH (Bonin and Leven 1996). As we can see, in most of these cases, foreign banks acquired only minority stakes in privatized local banks. What was needed were foreign strategic investments in banking.

In spite of the prevailing government incentives, multinational banks were initially reluctant to commit to future investment in Polish banking sector mainly due to "the country's difficult situation with debt reduction."[82] The agreement with the Paris club creditors, signed in 1991, reduced debt by 50 percent, but the agreement with the London Club, reducing outstanding debt by 45 percent, was not reached until 1994 (Polanski 2002; Angresano 1996). 1994 constituted the starting point for the expansion of foreign banks. According to the EBRD Banking Survey, foreign banks controlled only 3.4 percent of Poland's banking sector assets in 1994. This share increased to 10 percent in 1995 (table 5.6). At the same time, the number of bank licenses issued to new banks fell from sixteen in 1991 to five in 1992 and to only one each in 1993 and 1994 (Polanski 1997, 66). Between 1992 and 1996, only twenty new licenses were granted (Szymkiewicz 2001, 56). To be sure, this temporary freeze on granting new licenses also affected operations of foreign banks. From 1992 to early 1995, the NBP refused to grant banking licenses directly to foreign banks unless they invested in problematic Polish banks (Polanski 1997, 68).

In the September 1993 elections, the Polish electorate voted Solidarity (that had disintegrated into several factions) out of power after a wave of protests. The former Communist Party—the Democratic Left Alliance (SLD)—controlling sixty-six seats, formed a government coalition with the former communist satellite Polish Peasant Party (PSL). The approach of the SLD-led government to the banking system stood in sharp contrast with those of its predecessors. In July 1995, the SLD-affiliated minister of finance, Grzegorz Kolodko, announced the Bank Consolidation Plan, which envisaged putting off bank privatization and instead consolidating state-owned banks into two groups around Bank Handlowy and Pekao SA. By postponing privatization, the government intended to create a Polish-owned internationally competitive banking conglomerate, arguing that Polish banks were too small to survive the invasion of foreign banks (Epstein 2008). The strategy was thus to facilitate bank acquisitions by domestic buyers to preserve the government's informal role in bank management and credit allocation. As a result, the banking system remained weak and burdened with nonperforming loans amounting to over 23 percent in 1995 (table 5.6). This discontinuity in opening the banking sector reinforced the risk aversion of the international community. After a temporary decline, the currency-risk premium increased again, averaging over 2,100 basis points.

Central Bank (In)Dependence

The second reason behind the lack of market confidence in the anti-inflationary resolve of the Polish central bank, in addition to financial insta-

TABLE 5.6. Transparency and Regulatory Quality of the Polish Banking System

	Foreign bank assets as % of total assets[a]	Non-performing loans as a % of total gross loans[b]	Credit reporting institutions[c]	EBRD index of banking sector reforms[d]
1995	10	23.9	No	3.0
2000	62	15.5	No	3.3
2005	76	11	Private credit bureau (est. in 2001)	3.7
2009	68	7.9	Private credit bureau	3.7

Source: Data for each column from the respective sources:
[a]Claessens et al. (2008), Claessens and van Horen (2012).
[b]World Bank, World Development Indicators; data for 1995 from the EBRD Transition Reports.
[c]World Bank, Doing Business.
[d]EBRD Transition Reports, various issues.

bility, was its lack of autonomy from the government. The NBP did not enjoy the same degree of independence from the government as its Czech and Estonian counterparts did (Cukierman, Miller, and Neyapti 2002). The Ministry of Finance and Ministry of Foreign Relations influenced the NBP's exchange rate and monetary policies, and so did Parliament. Although the 1989 Act on the NBP stipulated that the governor of the NBP would be nominated by the president and confirmed by the Sejm (the lower house of Parliament), the annual monetary program of the central bank still required direct parliamentary approval. As a consequence, Parliament had preserved a significant role in the conduct of monetary policy and in overseeing the NBP's activities (Kochanowicz, Kozarzewski, and Woodward 2005, 49).

The NBP, being committed to competitiveness-conscious monetary policies, sought to strike a balance between price stability and the objectives of government economic policy. It is evident that the NBP, frequently lowering interest rates, pursued only a mildly restrictive monetary policy (Kowalski and Stawarska 1999, 362). The first NBP presidents—Hana Gronkiewicz-Waltz and Grzegorz Wojtowicz—were too weak politically and too reluctant to apply drastic monetary measures.[83] The government repeatedly pushed the NBP to lower interest rates to boost Polish exports and to grant access to cheap credit to selected economic sectors. In addition to resorting to discretionary methods in monetary policy, the NBP engaged in inflationary financing of budget deficits, even though it was prohibited by law to finance more than 2 percent of the annual state budget expenditures. In 1992, the central bank began to acquire short-term Treasury bills and eventually became the main financier of the growing government deficit. The NBP financed a large share of the fiscal deficit, 80 percent in 1991, 52 percent in 1992, and 65 percent in 1993.[84] Not surprisingly, the monetization of the fiscal deficit by the NBP acted as the "motor of inflation" (Wellisz 1997).

Similarly, the decisions on exchange rate policy and financial liberalization were much more involved than in the Czech Republic and Estonia because several parties participated in the decision-making process. The Polish legislation stipulated that exchange rate policy was to be determined by the Council of Ministers upon a proposal from the president of the NBP in consultation with the minister of finance and the minister of foreign relations. Yet the final decision in the exchange rate policy area rested with the Council of Ministers (Koch 1997, 7). The ambiguity of the law on the NBP lent itself to be interpreted as the right of the government to veto the central bank's decisions.[85] The decision making on exchange rates was further complicated by the need to find a compromise among the conflicting views of these three institutions. The NBP focused on price stability, the Ministry of Foreign Relations favored a weak currency to facilitate exports, and the Ministry of Finance was caught between the two.

The SLD-led government attempted to further limit the independence of the NBP. Kolodko, finance minister in the left-wing Polish government, criticized the central bank for its anti-inflation "crusade" and called for an interest rate reduction on numerous occasions. Furthermore, the SLD-PSL coalition submitted a legislative proposal to establish a council responsible for monetary policy, whose members would be appointed by the government and the Sejm (three members each) and by the Polish Union of Banks (two members). The president of the NBP would be appointed by the prime minister instead of the president, thus making this appointment subject to greater political oversight.[86]

Although not stated in official documents, the narrative evidence suggests that policymakers assumed from the beginning that crawling peg (the currency is adjusted periodically in small amounts) might follow the rigid peg when the exchange rate started to substantially appreciate (Gomulka 1995, 336). In October 1991, the government introduced a compromise solution in the form a pre-announced crawling peg to a basket with occasional step devaluations. The crawling peg allowed for limited exchange rate flexibility, so the exchange rate continued to be a nominal anchor for disinflation policy, but at the same time, the rate of crawl was to ensure a competitive exchange rate (Koch 1997). Then in May 1995, a crawling band was introduced. The zloty was allowed to fluctuate within a band of plus or minus 7 percent (for the evolution of monetary regimes in Poland, see also table 5.A1 in the appendix to this chapter).

In sum, the objective of the exchange rate policy in the first half of the 1990s was to achieve a compromise between low inflation and an exchange rate set at a competitive level.[87] Yet the goal of national competitiveness was hard to reconcile with monetary stability. Once the accelerating inflation was brought under control, the Polish authorities gave low priority to further reductions in inflation; instead they tried to improve the competitiveness of the domestic trading sectors (Burdekin, Nelson, and Willett 1999). Soft pegs pursued to promote national competitiveness were an "inflationary *perpetum mobile*" and reduced the NBP's control over money supply and inflation.[88]

Foreign Banks to the Rescue

To make the victory over inflation durable, the government had to secure a lasting change in inflationary expectations. Under pressure from the IMF and other international institutions, in 1996 the government dropped the plan for bank consolidation and strengthening of domestic ownership and resumed fast-track privatization with foreign capital (Epstein 2008).[89] When the Cimoszewicz SLD-led administration took office in February 1996, it launched a new ambitious plan to privatize ten state-owned banks between 1997 and 2000. Privatization strategy focused on a search for foreign strategic investors to ensure financial stability and increase the quality of governance. Although this plan was only partially implemented due to the government's defeat in the elections of October 1997, the following right-wing government of Jerzy Buzek (October 1997–October 2001) accelerated the sale of public banks to foreign investors. As foreign-owned banks started to dominate the Polish financial system, banking competition intensified. Surprisingly, local banks themselves had become active in introducing foreign capital. They understood that it was better to adapt to competition from Western banks than to build on the former communist networks.[90]

As figures 5.4 and 5.5 graphically illustrate, opening the banking sector triggered positive market perceptions of risk. Markets were already pricing in the announcement, rallying strongly in anticipation of the entry of foreign banks. The government announcement of privatization involving foreign strategic investors helped to decrease uncertainty over its commitment to reforms in the banking sector. Investors perceived the new policy of opening the banking sector and increasing central bank independence as a commitment to price stability and fiscal prudence. The country-risk premium as measured by the sovereign bond yield spreads plunged from 390 basis points in 1995 to 140 basis points in 1997 (figure 5.5).[91] The evolution of the currency-risk premium confirms this impression; the money market interest rate differentials were reduced to about half of their levels by the end of 1998 (figure 5.4).

Whereas foreign banks entered through greenfield investments or by acquiring minority stakes early on, later they ended up taking over Polish banks (brownfield investments). In 1996, Commerzbank acquired a 33 percent stake in BRE (bringing its ownership to 72.16 percent by 2003). In 1998, Bayerische Hypo-und Vereinsbank acquired 36.72 percent in BPH, and Bank Austria bought a 15 percent stake in PBK (bringing its stake to

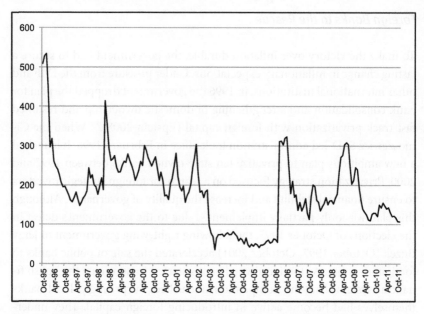

Fig. 5.5. EMBI and Poland Ten-Year Government Bond Yield Spreads (basis points, monthly)
Source: Global Financial Data.

43.5 percent in 1999 and to 57.13 percent in 2000). The most important was the sale of Bank Pekao, the second largest Polish bank (with 20 percent of total assets) to the Italian UniCredit and Allianz AG, which acquired a majority (52 percent) stake in August 1999 (figure 5.4). This was the first time a major Polish bank was sold to foreign strategic investors. Between January 1998 and September 1999, following the privatization of Bank Pekao, money market rates decreased from 26 percent to 14 percent. In 1999 this was followed by the acquisition of 80 percent majority holding of BZ by the Irish AIB European Investment Limited (BNP 2001). Whereas in 1996, out of thirty-nine banks operating in Poland, there were ten greenfield foreign banks and no foreign takeover; in 2000, out of thirty-eight banks, there were thirteen foreign greenfields and ten takeovers of Polish banks by foreign strategic investors (De Haas and van Lelyveld 2006).[92] Market shares of multinational banks increased from 10 percent in 1995, to 62 percent in 2000, and to 76 percent in 2005 (table 5.6). In 2011, Santander Group acquired a 70 percent share in Bank Zachodni WBK (the outcome of the 2000 merger between WBK and BZ), Poland's third largest bank by profits and by

number of branches. The year 2011 also saw a merger between Bank Handlowy w Warsawie and Citibank. Table 5.7 lists the top multinational bank
investors in the Polish banking system in 2011.

In addition to the launch of an ambitious bank privatization program,
the year 1997 also marked the beginning of a steady increase in the authority of the central bank, which culminated in the new NBP Act, introduced
in the 1997 Polish Constitution (Cukierman, Miller, and Neyapti 2002). The
Constitution granted the NBP "responsibility for the value of Polish currency," as well as "the exclusive right . . . to formulate and implement monetary policy (Article 227, paragraph 1). In 1998, a new NBP decision-
making body, a ten-person Monetary Policy Council modeled on the
Banque de France, was established to depolitize monetary policymaking
(Polanski 1998, 22). The new central bank charter has also eliminated the
obligation of direct lending by the NBP to the government to reduce the
inflationary effects of fiscal policy (Cukierman, Miller, and Neyapti 2002).

Long Road to Inflation Targeting

In search of ways to anchor inflation expectations and insulate monetary
policy from the vagaries of the political process, the new Monetary Policy
Council of the NBP publicly announced the adoption of the inflation-
targeting regime in September 1998, setting a short-term inflation target at

TABLE 5.7. Market Shares of Top Multinational Banks in Poland, 2011

Bank Name	Assets held by a bank as a % of total banking assets	Parent Bank (Country)
Powszechna Kasa Oszczędności Bank Polski (PKO BP)	13.8	PKO BP (Poland)
Bank Pekao SA	10.6	UniCredit Bank Austria (Italy, Austria)
Bank Rozwoju Eksportu S.A. (BRE)	7.2	Commerzbank (Germany)
Bank Śląski (BSK)	5.0	The ING Group (Nether-lands)
Bank Zachodni Wielkopolski Bank Kredytowy (WBK)	4.3	Santander (Spain)
Raiffeisen Polbank	4.2	Raiffensen Bank (Austria)
Bank Millennium	3.7	Banco Comercial Português (Portugal)
Citibank Bank Handlowy	3.1	Citibank (United States)
Kredyt Bank	3.0	Santander (Spain)

Source: Raiffeisen Research (2012).

the level of 8 to 8.5 percent.[93] Then, in September 1999, the central bank set the medium-term inflation target at a level below 4 percent by the end of 2003, while allowing the Polish zloty to move within a plus and minus 15 percent band (widened several times thereafter). At that point, a crawling peg was still maintained, cloaking monetary policy in considerable ambiguity. Although inflation targeting was in the hands of the NBP, the exchange rate remained codetermined by the central bank and the Council of Ministers. A pure float, an important precondition for the efficiency of the new monetary regime, was finally adopted in April 2000, preceded by abandoning sterilized foreign exchange interventions in mid-1998 (Pruski and Szpunar 2005). Inflation targeting combined with a full float left much less room for a government maneuver because the exchange rate policy ceased to be a policy parameter. Like in the Czech Republic, an inflation target is announced and adopted by the central bank, allowing it to assume the responsibility for monetary policy (Krzak and Ettl 1999). The institutional independence of the NBP imported a significant degree of credibility to monetary policy (Łyziak, Mackiewicz, and Stanislawska 2007, 71).[94]

It was widely perceived that the inflation-targeting regime, replacing the currency peg as the policy disciplinary anchor, provided an effective tool to combat inflation. But the Polish government could adhere to the inflation-targeting regime only after ensuring the soundness and transparency of its banking system with the help of reputable multinational banks. Under the influence of foreign banks, a private credit bureau was established in 2001 to increase transparency, share information about the quality of potential borrowers, and simplify lending. The substantial foreign bank entry coincides with the establishment of information-sharing mechanisms because the Western banks were familiar with the benefits of credit bureaus from their home countries. Information sharing among banks disciplined borrowers who knew that a loan default would tarnish their reputation and make it more difficult to get new credit. Not surprisingly, credit risk and bad loans decreased from nearly 24 percent in 1995 to slightly over 11 percent in 2005 (table 5.6). Foreign banks further tightened lending standards. For instance, UniCredit, the main player in the Polish banking market, adopted "a Pan-European bank strategy of forming one integrated bank across national borders which maintained tight lending standards" (Leven 2011, 184). Foreign banks enhanced the soundness and stability of the Polish banking system because they considered their investments strategic and long-term (Leven 2011, 184).

The EBRD index measuring the quality of banking regulation and supervision attests a score on a par with advanced emerging European countries (table 5.6). The 1997 Banking Act entrusted banking supervision tasks to the Banking Supervision Commission, which is organizationally independent of the central bank. Although this solution could have potentially made banking supervision vulnerable to political influence, foreign banks, supervised by their home country supervisors, monitor local supervisory authorities. Poland also saw a substantial change in financial regulation (for instance, banks were required to measure credit risk and to cover it by specific provisions).

The new policy stance of containing inflation increased the credibility of the monetary commitments. Consequently, the annual average inflation rate fell from 11.8 percent in 1998 to 1.9 percent in 2002, reaching the level observed in developed countries (Pruski and Szpunar 2005). Because the actual inflation was below the target, the NBP further lowered the inflation target to the current plus or minus 2.5 percent. The average inflation was 2.75 percent between 2004 and 2010 (Łyziak 2013). Gains in the credibility of inflation targeting are obvious when evaluating the target deviation, which was small, of an average only 0.25 percent.

In summary, the evidence discussed in this section indicates that one of the factors that undermined the effectiveness of the NBP in building the credibility of monetary policy in the 1990s was its obligations to support government economic objectives and purchase government debt. An additional factor was the temporary restrictions on foreign bank entry that sent negative signals to international markets about the soundness of the financial system and suggested potential bailouts. Only bank privatization to foreign strategic investors successfully reduced the problem of asymmetric information in financial markets about the monetary policy preferences of the Polish government. The government's motivation to privatize state-owned banks to reputable multinational banks was clear and specific: maintenance of price stability, a key to international credibility of a monetary regime, requires the ability to control credit.

Survey-based measures of inflation expectations formed by the financial sector and the public reveal that the inflation targeting achieved a high degree of credibility, which made the victory over inflation durable (Łyziak 2014) (See also figure 5.6). With this notable increase in the credibility of the central bank and the monetary regime, the country risk measured by sovereign bond spreads also substantially declined by nearly 300 basis

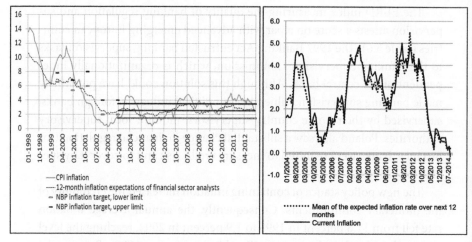

Fig. 5.6. Inflation Expectations in Poland, 1998–2014 (%): (a) Inflation Expectations and the NBP Inflation Target; (b) Twelve-Month Inflation Expectations and the Actual Inflation

Source: Łyziak (2013, 15), National Bank of Poland.

points between 1995 and 2003 to 91 basis points (figure 5.5). Furthermore, Fitch Ratings, one of the "Big Three" rating agencies, rewarded the government by upgrading its credit rating from A– to A+ in 1998.

The 2008 global credit crisis was the first time the behavior of multinational banks had been tested since the substantial wave of foreign investments in Poland. Whereas most countries in emerging Europe may have temporarily lost the confidence of financial markets during this crisis, the spreads on Polish sovereign bonds were only slightly affected; the EMBI spreads increased by mere one hundred points. The zloty depreciated by 35 percent but then quickly appreciated between February and September 2009 by 19 percent, demonstrating confidence of currency traders in the Polish currency (Leven 2011). In addition to the credible monetary regime anchoring inflation expectations, Poland did not overextend itself with mortgages, which represented only 10 percent of the country's GDP in 2008 (as compared to 18 percent in the Czech Republic and 70 percent in the United States) and there was practically no subprime lending (Leven 2011, 185). The indicators of banking sector stability—capital adequacy and nonperforming loans (accounting for only 4.5 percent of all loans in July 2009)—remained relatively stable (Leven 2011, 185). Again, a telling example is the prudent lending behavior of UniCredit, whose strategy to issue mortgages only in zlotys buffered 30 percent of all Polish mortgages from short-term currency depreciation and in so doing helped to prevent capital outflows and the erosion of credibility (Leven 2011, 185). Besides, foreign parent banks provided liquidity to their subsidiaries in reaction to the crisis. Ultimately, the Polish banking system, dominated by foreign players, remains sound; "by international standards, the loans extended to customers are backed by plenty of equity, meaning the banks have buffers to weather a medium-sized storm."[95]

Conclusion

Evidence from the Czech Republic and Poland coheres with the theory advanced in this book: only the successful strengthening of the legal framework and increased transparency in local banking systems through foreign banks ensured the credibility of the chosen monetary regimes. A successful financial reform and privatization with the participation of foreign strategic investors weakened the political influence of incumbent public banks, as the outsider financiers brought with them more competition and stronger bank regulatory and supervisory institutions.

All factors taken together, in the Czech Republic the lack of credibility of the fixed exchange rate regime was primarily because regulatory institutions lacked the skills to reign over large state-owned banks taking on excessive risk and control domestic credit expansion. The reform approach of the right-wing governments aimed at promoting a domestic class of entrepreneurs through the voucher method of divestiture of state assets. The central bank failed to persuade its government to impose hard budget constraints on domestic banks. Inevitably, the outcome was the devastating financial turmoil in 1997 that forced the central bank to drop formal promises to maintain a fixed regime that had persisted for sixty-two consecutive months, surviving the split of Czechoslovakia and the dissolution of its common currency.

The history of Polish exchange rate policymaking is punctuated by four turning points evolving from fixed exchange rate regime (1990–91), through crawling-peg (1991–95) and crawling band (1995–99), to a floating regime. The currency realignments, associated with the adoption of less rigid fixed exchange rate regimes, indicate that monetary policy faced a confidence crisis inasmuch as a credible monetary regime was dependent on the capacity of the government to rule out any exchange rate adjustment.

An additional obstacle was the lack of institutional independence of the central bank of Poland. This reinforced inflationary pressures caused by the monetization of budget deficits and the policy of low interest rates to promote the competitiveness of domestic industries. The BNP abandoned a hard peg after the first sixteen months and pursued various soft pegs until 2000, at which point it gradually adopted a combination of inflation targeting and exchange rate flexibility. There is no question that the preference for the involvement of foreign strategic investors in bank privatization was driven by the need of the Polish government to build the credibility of the monetary regime of inflation targeting.

The criticism of central bank independence raised in chapter 2 is also borne in the context of the Czech history. The Czech case demonstrates that central bank independence is not a sufficient condition for a credible monetary regime if a domestic banking system is closed and remains the source of wealth accumulation for the politically connected elite. The CNB enjoyed a high degree of independence from the government to pursue monetary policy focused on price stability. But the Klaus government was committed to certain ideologies and policies that often conflicted with those of the central bank, resulting in a monetary policy–fiscal policy mismatch. By contrast, the history of the politics of Polish central banking suggests that central bank autonomy is an important institutional condition for solving credibility problem. Measures of central bank independence based on central bank statutes reveal insufficient independence of the Polish central bank throughout the 1990s. The BNP shared the authority over exchange rate policy with the government, which compromised its independence. A credible monetary regime requires a "fiscal dominance," as Mishkin (2004) notes. If monetary authorities are required to purchase government debt, they compromise the credibility of monetary commitments.

In cross-national comparative terms, there are also some reasons to doubt the validity of the arguments regarding the importance of international organizations in signaling credible commitments. The role of the IMF in Czechoslovakia and its successor state, the Czech Republic, in reputation building was limited; the government introduced many reform program elements before signing the standby agreements. Klaus was notoriously known for his negative attitude toward foreign advisors and international institutions. He accused international financial institutions of focusing on "catalyzing loans for big multinationals" and claimed that these institutions were of no use because of the uniqueness of the reform process in individual countries (Klaus 1997b, 144). His party also regularly attacked the EU for imposing excessive infringements on national sovereignty; his party instead promoted nationalist policies and anti-foreign investment sentiment (Roberts 2003). When placed in comparative perspective, Poland has always been considered to be "the best student in class . . . and in the end one of the few examples of success of the IMF" (Belka, quoted in King and Sznajder 2006, 768). The Polish government was more dependent on international assistance because of high levels of indebtedness. The IMF conditionality must have surely strengthened the resolve of the Polish policymakers and provided credibility to its initial exchange-rate-based stabilization program. Yet at the same time, the Polish authorities shared some aversion to a fixed exchange rate regime and allowed for devaluation.

These cases illustrate, contrary to the expectations of the literature on political parties (Hibbs 1977), that right-wing parties are not less inflation-averse than left-wing parties. The Klaus right-wing government refrained from imposing strict banking regulation and provided guarantees for bad loans and bailouts using foreign exchange reserves in return for the banks' support of industries and employment. These policies generated inflation. The political-economic history of Polish exchange rate policies highlights the ways in which the preferences of the policymakers—on both the right and left—for competitive valuation of the currency have competed with the objective of price stability. Exchange rate policy in Poland was an integral part of a national strategy of export-stimulated economic growth. As a consequence, the right-wing governments did not manage to convey the credibility of their commitments to currency stability. Ideology thus rings hollow as a guide to the financial markets.

Were the left or right governments acting on behalf of domestic bankers? Surprisingly, the evidence supports the hypothesis that the Polish left had close links with former communist managers in state-owned banks (and enterprises) who were the only people with business experience at the outset of transition because the anticommunist opposition movement consisted of dissident intellectuals.[96] SLD was supported by industrialists and bankers who emerged from the nomenklatura privatizations under the last communist government, and it essentially continued with the business-friendly policies of the first postcommunist governments (Stone 2002, 111). In contrast, maintaining the dominance of the right-wing ODS in Czech politics came to depend on the support of large state-owned banks. Domestic banks were the beneficiaries of successive right-wing governments prior to 1997 (Horowitz and Petráš 2003).

Appendix

TABLE 5.A1. The Evolution of Monetary Regimes in the Czech Republic and Poland, 1990–2000

Czech Republic	Poland
The initial choice of a nominal anchor was a peg to US dollar/German mark combination (after a cumulative devaluation of 95%).	*January 1, 1990*: After a devaluation of zloty by 42%, exchange rate fixed to US dollar (1 US dollar = 9,500 zloty) as a part of an exchange-rate-based stabilization program.
January 1991: A peg to a currency basket: US dollar (31.34%), German mark (45.52%), Austrian schilling (12.25%), Swiss franc (6.55%), and British pound (4.24%).	*May 16, 1991*: Devaluation by 17%. Exchange rate fixed to a currency basket (45% US dollar, 35% German mark, 10% British pound, 5% French franc, 5% Swiss franc.
January 1992: Change in basket composition: 36.15% German mark, 49.07% US dollar, 8.07% Austrian schilling, 2.92% French franc, 3.79% Swiss franc.	*October 14, 1991*: Crawling peg to the currency basket with occasional step devaluations (monthly devaluations initially set at 1.8%; from 1996 at 1%).
February 1993: Split of the Czechoslovak currency. The Czech koruna introduced. No change in basket composition or band width.	*January 1, 1995*: Redenomination (1 new zloty equal to 10,000 old zlotys).
May 1993: A peg to a basket (65% German mark, 35% US dollar) in ± 0.5 band from the central parity.	*March 6, 1995*: Exchange rate band was widened to ±2%.
February 18, 1996: The band was broadened to ± 7.5%.	*May 16, 1995*: Crawling band ±7%, crawling rate 1.2%.
May 15, 1997: The koruna was devalued by 10%.	*October 28, 1998*: Crawling band was widened to ±12.5%.
May 16, 1997: managed float (with German mark and later euro as reference currency) was adopted.	*January 1, 1999*: Change in currency basket: 55% euro, 45% US dollar.
January 1, 1998: Inflation targeting officially adopted.	*March 25, 1999*: Monthly rate of crawl reduced to 0.3%. Exchange rate band widened to ±15%.
	January 1999: Inflation targeting officially adopted.
	June 7, 1999: National Bank of Poland is not obliged to perform transactions with commercial banks during fixing.
	April 12, 2000: Inflation targeting with a floating exchange rate regime adopted.

Source: Czech National Bank; National Bank of Poland.

CHAPTER 6

Reputation in Crisis

The previous chapters tested the main prediction of my credibility theory: that the presence of reputable multinational banks makes host countries more credible in the eyes of financial market participants. This chapter investigates how multinational banks behaved during financial booms and busts in both their host and home countries, and consequently whether countries' reputations changed during bad times. I look at the 2001 financial crisis in Argentina, the most prominent recent example of financial crises in emerging markets, accompanied by public outrage against foreign banks. I also examine the 2008 global financial crisis, which by any measure qualifies as the most severe crisis in the history of the global economy since the Great Depression in the 1930s. I recognize that these are two very different financial crises. The task of this chapter is not to compare and contrast the nature of these crises, but to assess the behavior of multinational banks during the hard times in home or host countries. This chapter thus sheds light on the behavior of foreign banks in the face of adverse conditions.

The previous case study chapters focused primarily on the first two mechanisms through which foreign banks affect the reputation of host countries. These involved the contribution of foreign banks to transparency and soundness of financial systems in host countries. This chapter will take snapshots of dynamics of the two crises that shed light on the third mechanism, which involves the transfer of the role of lender of last resort from the local central bank to the foreign parent bank. Examining the role of multinational banks as crisis lenders and crisis managers in host countries is an important component of the central argument. The chapter also shows the conditions under which multinational banks are likely to cut and run instead of supporting their foreign affiliates. Thus the task of this chapter is to explore the limits and downsides of global banking.

Chapter 3 demonstrated that, consistent with my theory, foreign bank presence can enhance monetary credibility. This result was shown to hold true for more than eighty emerging markets over the past fifteen years. After providing evidence to support my theory on the cases from emerging Europe in chapters 4 and 5, I turn my attention to assessments of foreign bank presence in Latin America and Asia in this chapter. Emerging Europe and Latin America include countries with among the highest levels of foreign bank ownership. A look at the countries with high levels of foreign bank presence affords an opportunity to examine how these banks affect market perception of risks of these countries, holding the level of banking integration constant. In contrast, foreign bank presence in emerging Asia has been small. This cross-regional comparison maximizes the variation in banking integration by looking at regions with very high global bank presence (emerging Europe),[1] medium (Latin America), and low (Asia). Overall, two crisis episodes examined in this chapter offer significant variation in the degree and forms of banking integration and policy credibility across countries and regions.

The first part of the chapter examines the 2001 Argentine crisis that resulted in a collapse of the currency board regime. This crisis is already well-studied, but I wish to revisit it to explain the effects of foreign bank presence prior, during, and after the crisis. Argentina, plagued by numerous episodes of fiscal mismanagement, debasement of the national currency, forty years of high inflation, and two years of hyperinflation, adopted the currency board in 1991, which was a turning point in its monetary and financial history. Argentina has also become one of the first countries in Latin America with a relatively large presence of foreign banks. Multinational banks encouraged reforms that increased transparency and the regulatory quality of the Argentine banking system, the two important components of the theory of credibility proposed here. Foreign banks stood behind their affiliates during the 1994 Mexican peso crisis. Yet some multinational banks failed to act as lender of last resort to their subsidiaries during the 2001 crisis; instead they chose to retrench and exit the Argentine financial market. There are three reasons why this happened. The first explanation has to do with the politically motivated "asymmetric pesification"—forced conversion of dollar-denominated bank assets into pesos at a less-than-market rate—introduced by the Argentine government, which antagonized foreign banks, who viewed it as the violation of property rights. The second explanation highlights the importance of the business models pursued by multinational banks. Spanish banks, which dominated the Argentine banking sector, followed a decentralized model in running their international ac-tivities. In this model, foreign bank subsidiaries enjoyed a significant degree of financial autonomy from their parent banks; they were thus adversely affected by the Argentine crisis. Lastly, the influence of multinational banks on policy credibility was constrained because large public banks remained dominant players in the Argentine banking sector.

The 2008 global financial turmoil is examined in the second part of the chapter. This crisis, originating in developed countries of North America and Western Europe—home markets of reputable multinational banks—raised questions about the implications of the activities of these banks for financial stability and the international credibility of emerging-market countries. How does a foreign bank's parent cope with subsidiary distress when the parent bank itself faces challenges? Although multinational banks may have temporarily transferred bad reputations, they were instrumental in reassuring financial markets during the crisis. I show that foreign banks remained the key to macroeconomic stability in emerging markets in times of crisis. There were, however, differences in the channels of transmissions and in the intensity of the propagation of the crisis across emerging market regions. How can we explain these differences? One explanation suggested here is tied to whether countries are investment or funding locations for global banks (i.e., foreign bank presence or direct cross-border lending). Other explanations highlight the differences in the business models that multinational banks use to expand abroad. One could argue further that emerging Europe, where the stabilizing impact of foreign banks is rein-forced by European integration, represents a special case. Finally, this chap-ter also examines the reverse: What happens to risk perceptions of those developed countries that are the homes of multinational banks, particularly the ones with large cross-border exposures and international portfolios? Not many scholars have addressed this question. And yet a high degree of financial integration with emerging markets through their systemically im-portant banks made their home countries vulnerable.

The Argentine Financial Crisis of 2001

The argument in this book suggests that foreign banks should be a stabiliz-ing force for host countries by acting as the international lender of last re-sort. The Argentine case helps us better understand how and why foreign banks behave when a crisis hits a host country and the implications of their behavior for the risk perceptions of international markets.

When Carlos Menem was elected president in 1989, Argentina was in the throes of hyperinflation after unsuccessful reforms by the centrist Alfonsín government (Pop-Eleches 2009, 266). Inflation rose above 2,000 percent in 1990 (Mishkin 2006, 106). In April 1991, economy minister Domingo Cavallo launched the ambitious Convertibility Plan. Its centerpiece was a currency board with the objective of establishing the credibility of anti-inflationary monetary policy. De La Torre et al. (2003, 47) characterize the intended effect of the currency board on Argentinean society as a one-way nonreversible path forward, similar to the way "Hernon Cortes' decision to burn the ships represented a decisive turning point for his crew." The establishment of the currency board in Argentina, a large and diversified economy, was an experiment (Marshall 2008, 352).

As in the Estonian case, the key feature of Argentina's currency board was that the central bank could not expand the money supply (often referred to as "printing money") because it was legally bound to guarantee full convertibility of the Argentine peso into U.S. dollars on one-to-one basis. The U.S. dollar was granted the status of legal tender alongside the peso. The Congress approved a new central bank charter in September 1992, which equipped the Argentine central bank (Banco Central de la República Argentina, BCRA) with independence (as when it was originally established in 1936) (Calomiris and Powell 2001). The new charter restricted central bank financing of government deficits and lengthened the governor's term of office, and the BCRA was charged only with the objective of price stability (Maxfield 1997, 63).

The Argentine currency board played an important role in containing inflationary pressures and restoring the confidence of international investors (Pop-Eleches 2009, 268). Inflation decreased from 2,300 percent in 1990 to below 5 percent in 1994 (Mishkin 2006, 108). The fall in inflation was accompanied by strong economic growth, 10.6 percent in 1991, 9.6 percent in 1992, and 5.8 percent in both 1993 and 1994 (Woodruff 2005, 21). The Convertibility Plan became the principal component of the "social contract" (De La Torre et al. 2003, 47). It was hoped that it would become an institutional anchor that would bring fiscal responsibility and a sound banking system to underpin the credibility of the currency board.[2]

The fiscal constraint imposed by the currency board restricted the ability of the central bank to act as the lender of last resort. To compensate for restrictions on the BCRA's lender-of-last-resort powers, the Argentine authorities were fully aware of the need to build a resilient banking system that would be less vulnerable to speculative attacks.[3] The government implemented a series of measures to strengthen the banking system. The first was banking-sector liberalization following the decades of severe financial repression. In addition, the government initiated extensive financial regulatory reforms. To this end, the BCRA was granted considerable autonomy in the area of banking regulation, and the Superintendency of Financial and Exchange Institutions, responsible for banking supervision, was reestablished as a semiautonomous unit within the central bank (Calomiris and Powell 2001, 154). These reform efforts proved successful. Because of the consensus among policymakers that risk taking by banks should be reined in, in 1993 the BCRA removed the deposit insurance and established the new rules, signaling to banks that their insolvency would be followed by liquidation without any use of fiscal resources (Schumacher 2000, 260). Furthermore, in 1994 the authorities set minimum capital requirements at 14 percent of risk-weighted assets, well above the 8 percent minimum set by the international banking standards in the Basel Accord (Calomiris and Powell 2001, 154).

Yet in spite of these regulatory improvements, the Mexican peso crisis of December 1994 (also known as the Tequila Crisis) initiated a run on the Argentine currency, signaling that financial markets had limited confidence in the ability of the Argentine government to maintain the currency board.[4] The central bank lost some 30 percent ($5 billion) of international reserves (Calomiris and Powell 2001, 159). As figure 6.1 illustrates graphically, the Tequila Crisis triggered an increase of the currency-risk premium (measured as the difference between the one-month peso and dollar local deposit rates) by 382 basis points (Schmukler and Servén 2002, 371).

The expectations that the Argentine peso could be also devalued were rising and were further augmented by the upcoming presidential elections in May 1995. Generally, political uncertainty, associated with elections in emerging markets, tend to have significant effects on risk premium. The EMBI spreads, measuring the riskiness of Argentine sovereign assets, jumped to 1,800 basis points in March 1995 (figure 6.2). But Menem's reelection indicated popular support for his economic reform program (Pop-Eleches 2009), and market sentiment started to improve.

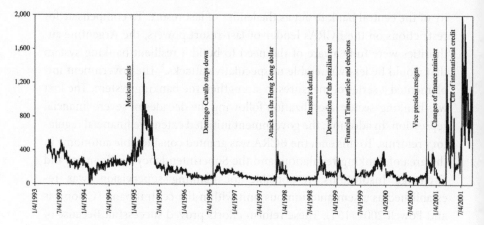

Fig. 6.1. Currency-Risk Premium from Argentina's Time Deposit Rates
Source: Reprinted from Schmukler and Servén (2002, 371). Copyright (2016), with permission from Elsevier.

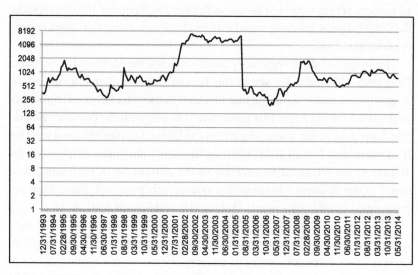

Fig. 6.2. EMBI and Argentina Government Bond Yield Spreads, 1993–2014 (basis points)
Source: Global Financial Data.

Foreign Banks and Banking Reforms after the Tequila Crisis

The Tequila Crisis also severely tested the banking system, which experienced an outflow of 18.4 percent of bank deposits ($8 billion) between December 1994 and May 1995 (Calomiris and Powell 2001, 159). But the bank run was not an episode of random withdrawals. Instead, as Schumacher (2000) explains, informed depositors rushed to pull out their savings in U.S. dollars from domestic banks and place them with foreign banks. Depositors took this step because they believed that foreign banks were better able to withstand the crisis. They could not rely on the net worth of the domestic banks to provide a buffer against losses on deposits. Depositors thus clearly engaged in a "flight to quality." The secret of foreign banks' success was stronger and less volatile loan growth, better loan loss provisioning, and higher loan recovery rates compared to local banks (Dages, Goldberg, and Kinney 2000; Crystal, Dages, and Goldberg 2001).

As a consequence, the solvency of domestic banks was severely affected. As in Estonia in the early 1990s, the political commitment of the Argentine authorities to low inflation and a sound banking system limited the possibility of large bank bailouts. Thus, as their Estonian counterparts had, they chose to close insolvent banks to reduce the moral hazard in the banking sector. In December 1995, out of 137 private banks, 9 failed and more than 20 were forced to merge (Schumacher 2000, 261). The government further consolidated the banking system, reducing the number of banks from 166 in 1994 to 89 in 2000 (De La Torre et al. 2003, 84). But the banking sector remained fragile and prone to external shocks. Whereas the removal of restrictions on foreign capital and capital repatriation resulted in an increase in the number of foreign banks, their market share was less than 20 percent through 1995 (Crystal, Dages, and Goldberg 2001, 34). The banking system remained controlled by domestic, mostly state-owned, banks dependent on foreign financing (Marshall 2008, 351).[5]

The country's investment law has provided for equal treatment of both foreign and domestic banks since 1957, but prior to 1994 foreign banks were allowed to enter only on the condition of reciprocity (Martinez-Diaz 2009, 192).[6] The Tequila Crisis marked a turning point in the development of the Argentine financial system, bringing about policies of a more extensive opening of the banking sector and the privatization of public banks. In the BCRA, the dominant view was that an increased presence of foreign banks was needed to bolster the soundness of the domestic banking system.

In other words, the credibility of financial policies in the eyes of international market participants would be enhanced by importing financial stability from abroad. From the point of view of Argentine authorities, foreign bank ownership also offered an ideal solution to the problem of access to credit in international markets during financial crises because multinational banks do not face significant credit rationing. Multinational banks operating in several countries have easier access to funding in foreign exchange, especially in times of crisis. Therefore they could be counted on to recapitalize the local banking system, reduce the credit crunch, and prevent a systemic banking crisis. Because the currency board prevented the BCRA from assuming the role of lender of last resort, foreign banks were ideally positioned to fulfill this role (Marshall 2008).

As expected, foreign parent banks stood behind their affiliates during the Tequila Crisis and afterwards were assigned an important role in recapitalizing the Argentine banking system (Crystal, Dages, and Goldberg 2001; Dages, Goldberg, and Kinney 2000). Moreover, ambitious reforms in the banking sector in the second half of the 1990s resulted in its consolidation and internationalization. Consequently, in addition to the U.S.-based global banks Citibank and Bank of Boston, which established their presence in Argentina in 1914 and 1917 respectively, ABN AMRO of the Netherlands and the British bank Lloyds entered Argentina's banking system. Then, between 1996 and 1998, Banco Santander of Spain, HSBC of Great Britain, and Scotiabank (formerly Bank of Nova Scotia) of Canada acquired Argentina's banks.[7] In 1999, Spain's Banco Bilbao Vizcaya (BBV) acquired the Argentine bank Argentaria to become BBVA. By late 1990s, Banco Santander Central Hispano and BBVA together held a 39 percent market share in Argentina's banking sector.[8] The sale of weak private banks, privatization of public banks, and the recapitalization of the remaining banks resulted in a significant increase in foreign bank presence from 24 percent of all banks in 1996 to 37 percent in 2000, as table 6.1 shows. By 1999, foreign banks accounted for 40 percent of all banking deposits (Peek and Rosengren 2000). The number of foreign bank branches increased from 391 in 1994 to 1,863 in 2000 (De La Torre et al. 2003, 94).

Extensive opening of the banking sector was accompanied and underpinned by the efforts of the BCRA, led by its president Roque Fernández, to strengthen its regulatory and supervisory framework. Forging partnerships with foreign banks put the government in a much stronger position to craft the regulatory and accounting rules that would establish the confidence in the banking system. The outcome was an innovative regulatory and supervisory regime called BASIC: *bonos* (bonds), *auditoria* (auditing), *supervisión consolidada* (consolidated supervision), *información* (information), and *calificadoras de riesgo* (risk rating). The BASIC regime consisted of several elements including the enhanced quality and dissemination of information (for instance, banks were required to submit financial reports according to standards comparable to those in the U.S.); mandatory audits of banks; consolidated supervision of financial conglomerates; risk-based capital requirements of 11.5 percent (more stringent than the international standards); and the introduction of the credit rating scheme requiring each bank to have an annual rating of its credit risk from authorized rating agencies (Calomiris and Powell 2001; Peek and Rosengren 2000; Mishkin 2006).

Foreign bank presence effectively reduced the clientelistic system of cross-subsidization of industries through public banks (Guillén and Tschoegl 2000). By 1999, both public registry and private credit bureaus operated in the country. Foreign banks, in their effort to bypass their need for local knowledge, started to use credit scoring approaches that allowed them to increase their lending in provinces outside of Buenos Aires (Clarke, Crivelli, and Cull 2005). Increased market discipline through greater transparency and information sharing was a way to reduce the risky behavior of banks. The acquisition of Argentina's banks by reputable multinational banks caused the ratio of nonperforming loans to decrease to 5.3 percent in 1998 (table 6.1). It is also worth noting that reputable foreign banks strengthened liquidity and the solvency buffers of the banking sector to withstand the shocks (De La Torre et al. 2003, 51). Moreover, the central bank established a contingent credit line with international banks, which was a partial substitute for a limited lender of last resort function (Del Ne-

TABLE 6.1. The Financial System in Argentina, 1996–2002

	Foreign banks as a % of all banks[a]	Nonperforming loans as a % of total gross loans[b]	Financial Reform Index[c]
1996	24.0	n.a.	0.81
1998	32.0	5.3	0.81
2000	37.0	16.0	0.76
2002	34.0	18.1	0.67

Source: Data for each column from the respective sources:

[a]Claessens and van Horen (2014).

[b]Federal Reserve Bank of St. Louis; https://research.stlouisfed.org/fred2/.

[c]Abiad, Detragiache, and Tressel (2008). The Financial Reform Index ranges from 0 to 3 (fully liberalized = 3; partially liberalized = 2; partially repressed = 1; fully repressed = 0).

gro and Kay 2002, 11–12). Foreign parent banks publicly committed to re-capitalize their local affiliates in case of financial turbulences (Marshall 2008, 352–53).

Overall, the entry of foreign banks strengthened the Argentine banking system, whose soundness was being praised by almost everybody. The 1998 World Bank study rated the Argentine regulatory system among the top three emerging markets (on par with Hong Kong, behind Singapore, but ahead of Chile) (Calomiris and Powell 2001, 148). A leading Wall Street investment bank, Salomon Smith Barney, in its report from November 2001 stated, "We believe systemic risk in the [Argentine] banking system … is low, as 43% of its equity is controlled by foreigners" (quoted in Del Negro and Kay 2002, 23). These optimistic expectations were based on the rationale that given the size and financial resources of a large multinational bank, a crisis in a country like Argentina with the economic size of Connecticut could be easily solved by such a bank (Del Negro and Kay 2002, 1). Others highlighted that the Argentine banking system has become "the crown jewel of convertibility-induced reform" (De La Torre et al. 2003, 50). The most pronounced changes in the foreign participation in the banking sector reflected the efforts to build a shock-resistant banking sector necessary for the credibility of the currency board (De La Torre et al. 2003). The Argentine authorities could thus claim success. Always being an "Achilles' heel for Argentina," the financial sector in the second half of the 1990s contributed to the "long-run credibility of fiscal, monetary, and regulatory policy," as Calomiris and Powell (2001, 176) convincingly argued.

The increase in foreign bank presence in Argentina coincides with the enhancement of the credibility of the currency board. In the period from 1996 to 1998, "the currency board was feted internationally as a great success" (Bleaney 2004, 701). The currency board enjoyed relatively high credibility; the currency risk premium decreased after the Mexican crisis, averaging around 124 basis points (Schmukler and Servén 2002) (figure 6.1). Inflation fell below the U.S. rate in 1996 and remained low throughout the 1990s (Khoury and Wihlborg 2006). Interest spread volatility was also low and Argentine interest rates closely followed U.S. interest rates (Rivera-Batiz and Sy 2013, 823).

This era in Argentine's economic history illustrates that foreign banks were instrumental in securing the credibility of the currency board by increasing the transparency and soundness of the Argentine banking sector as well as acting as lenders of last resort during the Tequila Crisis. The credibility of the currency board was reflected in big drops in market perception of political risk: the EMBI spreads peaked at 934 basis points in 1995, and then fell to 290 basis points in 1997, notably decreasing the costs of capital for Argentina's government (figure 6.2). Despite these positive developments, the currency board eventually collapsed. What went wrong?

The Collapse of the Currency Board in 2001

The credibility of the currency board took a hit in the aftermath of the 1998 Russian sovereign default and the 1999 Brazilian financial crisis associated with sudden stops of capital flows that exacerbated the vulnerabilities of the Convertibility Plan. The currency risk, which reflected the risk of a nominal devaluation of the peso, increased from around 10 basis points in March 2001 to 600 basis points in late April 2001 (Mishkin 2006, 118–20). Given the interrelatedness of the currency-risk premium and sovereign bond yield spreads, the rates on Argentine sovereign bonds increased from below 300 basis points above U.S. Treasuries in August 1997 to over 1,000 basis points above them in August 1998, and crossed the 2,000 points frontier in July 2001, demonstrating doubts of international financial markets about the sustainability of the currency board (figure 6.2). The remarkable institutional and legal foundations for the credibility of the currency board reduced but could not remove the perception of exchange rate risk by the markets. During good times, the peso premium was very low, but in times of financial turbulence it sharply increased, reflecting the anxiety in financial markets.

In December 2001, the government defaulted on $155 billion of foreign debt, the largest sovereign default in its history (Feldstein 2002). On January 2, 2002, interim president Eduardo Duhalde announced the abandonment of the currency board. The peso was devalued to 1.4 pesos to the U.S. dollar four days later, and its value continued to decline rapidly. In less than two months, the peso slumped to almost 4.0 to the U.S. dollar, so it was subsequently allowed to float (Marshall 2008, 358). The Argentine economy was at the brink of collapse.

Much ink has been spilled over the causes of the 2001 crisis. Scholars identified various ingredients of the crisis.[9] One explanation highlights the high levels of financial dollarization (residents hold foreign currency denominated deposits and loans) as the key factor (De La Torre et al. 2003; Mishkin 2006). Ironically, the credible monetary regime encouraged financial dollarization that made Argentina vulnerable to an exchange rate shock. Private credit denominated in dollars increased to over 60 percent and credit to the public sector to over 90 percent (Mishkin 2006, 112). In spite of a major strengthening of financial regulation, the Argentine authorities did not introduce any special provisions for loans denominated in foreign currency. They followed the Basel international banking standards, which did not focus on currency risk because they had been created primarily for banks in developed countries, not exposed to high currency risks due to their ability to borrow in domestic currency (Mishkin 2006, 113).

Another view is expressed by Hanke (2002), who claims that the BCRA violated the rules of the currency board by pursuing a "super-activist" monetary policy. Domingo Cavallo, the architect of the Convertibility Plan, was again appointed by President Fernando de la Rúa (who took power in December 1999) as economy minister in March 2001. Upon taking office, Cavallo replaced central bank governor Pedro Pou, widely considered as a guardian of monetary stability and sound banking system, with a subservient successor. One of the first assignments of the new governor, Roque Maccarone, was the amendment of the BCRA Charter, which removed limitations on the central bank's ability to provide liquidity to the economy. The central bank, stripped of its autonomy, engaged in discretionary monetary policy and damaged the confidence in the currency board (Mishkin 2006, 117–21).

Yet another set of explanations of the proximate causes of the 2001 crisis focuses on insufficient fiscal stringency, which led to unsustainable debt. As De La Torre et al. (2003, 79) argue, "no matter how credible, a currency board (or dollarization) per se does not create fiscal discipline." The dramatic decline in inflation required a government commitment to reducing fiscal deficits, which was a difficult matter. Due to the fiscal relationships between provinces with control of a large share of public spending and the federal government responsible for raising the revenues, Argentina has traditionally run a fiscal deficit (Mishkin 2006, 114–15). Real exchange rate overvaluation has also been blamed for the collapse of the exchange rate regime. The credible currency board attracted large capital inflows that signaled a vote of confidence of financial markets but also contributed to the sharp real appreciation of the peso. The competitiveness of Argentine sectors exposed to trade deteriorated, and a big current account deficit emerged (Bleaney 2004, 702). As a consequence, instead of earning the foreign exchange from exports to pay the interests on its foreign debt, the government had to borrow to make these payments. By late 2001, its foreign debt reached 50 percent of GDP (including $30 billion due in 2002) (Feldstein 2002). Most of this debt was owned by the central and provincial governments since the currency board made it easier to borrow foreign funds. When the government was unable to place debt in the sovereign debt market, it decided to tap the money in the banks by forcing them to buy more government bonds. Financial markets were concerned about debt dynamics. Bond investors, compensating for the higher probability of default, started to charge higher interest rates on the Argentine debt, which entailed a substantial financial cost for the government. Eventually, the country entered a "growth-debt trap" when the spiraling spreads between the interest rates on Argentine sovereign debt and U.S. Treasury debt signaled that a default was likely (Mishkin 2006, 116).

The objective here is not to adjudicate among these different explanations of the currency board's collapse. For my argument this debate is not central. Instead, the question is what explains the "incomplete credibility" of the currency board given that it was underpinned by foreign bank presence and a resilient banking system? I argue here that the reform of the banking sector in Argentina was not complete. Privatization of public banks was less than full; the transfer of control of two large public banks holding 27 percent of banking system deposits in 1999—Banco de la Nación (owned by the federal government) and Banco de la Provincia de Buenos Aires (the largest province in Argentina)—met with political resistance (Calomiris and Powell 2001, 170). As a consequence, the indigenous banking elite remained an influential domestic constituency. Collaborative relations between domestic bankers and the government in designing the crisis solutions increasingly frustrated foreign bankers and facilitated their withdrawal, the issue explored in the next section.

Why Did Foreign Banks Cut and Run?

It should be noted at the outset that it was not a sudden stop in lending by foreign banks that precipitated the 2001 crisis but rather domestic deposit runs on Argentina's banks (Roubini and Setser 2004, 68). But some multinational banks reduced their presence during the crisis. Citibank announced a capital increase at its branch operations but sold its subsidiary, Bansud. Italian banking titan Intesa-Banca Commerciale Italiana sold its subsidiary Banque Sudameris. In May 2002, Crédit Agricole of France cut its losses by letting the Argentine government take over its subsidiaries Bersa, Banco Bisel, and Banco del Suquia (Cerutti, Dell'Ariccia, and Martínez Pería 2007). Similarly, the foreign shareholders of Scotiabank were unwilling to recapitalize its insolvent subsidiary Scotiabank Quilmes and turned it over to the Argentine government for rescue.[10] The management of Banco Río, the second largest private bank controlled by the Spanish banking behemoth Santander, publicly declared that it would not provide liquidity. Shortly thereafter, Spanish president José María Aznar declared that Spanish banks and businesses were not obliged to stay in Argentina given the host country's prospects (Marshall 2008, 361).

This raises an interesting question: Why did foreign banks cut and run? Without further explanation, this behavior of foreign banks may appear at odds with the basic assumptions of the theory put forward in this book. I have argued that foreign banks are pivotal in maintaining market confidence in the host financial system by acting as the lender of last resort. There are at least two possible explanations for why multinational banks abstained from providing liquidity to their affiliates and scaled back their operations in Argentina: asymmetric pesification and the bank business models.

Asymmetric Pesification

It is useful to start the discussion with the disastrous consequences of the 2001 currency crisis and the subsequent default for the Argentine banking system. Between January and November 2001, the banking system lost 22 percent of its deposits. In November 2001, the government persuaded the banks to voluntarily swap government bonds for illiquid government liabilities, which caused large deposit withdrawals. This was followed by a freeze on cash withdrawals from bank accounts to 250 pesos per month (*corralito*). This measure was soon accompanied by a freeze on deposits (*corralón*) to prevent a systemic bank run.

Prior to the crisis, foreign banks cooperated with many leading domestic firms from the industrial, financial, and energy sectors in the "group of eight," which was a forum for consultation and support for President Menem's policies (Woodruff 2005, 26).[11] But the freeezes led to an intense power struggle between foreign banks and the Argentine government (which has been studied in detail by Marshall 2008). The government was promoting the interests of domestic banks. In January 2002, the government started to seize and investigate the central offices of the largest foreign banks, accusing them of illegally sequestering and withdrawing funds from Argentina in the months prior to the crisis.

In mid-January 2002, a group of foreign banks led by the HSBC's president of operations in Argentina, Emilio Cárdenas, suggested a plan according to which the government would pursue a dollarization after the devaluation of the peso. Dollarization would involve the adoption of the dollar as legal tender. In return, foreign parent banks promised to stand ready to fully recapitalize their affiliates in Argentina. Together with the financial support from the IMF, the recapitalization would have been allowed to lift the *corralito* and end the banking crisis. But the plan also included a stick: if the government did not accept these conditions, foreign parent banks would not commit to providing liquidity to the banking system. The "dollarization" camp, consisting of foreign banks represented by the Asociación de Bancos de la Argentina, was backed by the IMF and factions of the federal government supporting former President Menem, the management of the BCRA, and the judiciary branch. The opposing "pesification" block, the Asociación de Bancos Públicos y Privados de la República Argentina, was formed exclusively by domestic banks and some key members of the federal government.[12]

Because public outrage turned against foreign banks and dollarization was perceived as support for former president Menem, the government resorted to confiscatory "asymmetric pesification," which meant a forcible conversion of domestic dollar debt into peso debt in February 2002 (De La Torre et al. 2003, 86). What might account for this choice? The literature suggests that the logic of politics may be largely responsible. Whereas debt denominated in dollars was converted into debt denominated in pesos at a one-to-one rate, bank deposits were converted at a higher rate to restore public confidence. Banks perceived this decision as a violation of their property rights. They obtained one peso per dollar of loans but had to pay 1.4 pesos per dollar of deposits (Mishkin 2006, 123–24) and therefore suffered huge losses. The asymmetric pesification represented a tax on bank capital and a transfer of funds to depositors (Tschoegl 2005). This measure affected primarily foreign banks because they held a substantial share of bank deposits.[13]

Multinational banks were unable to challenge the actions of the Argentine government in court. Therefore, they responded by reducing their presence in Argentina (Del Negro and Kay 2002). Multinational banks have this "limited liability" because they need to protect themselves from the expropriation of their assets by foreign governments. International markets viewed these actions negatively and exacted a substantial risk premium on Argentine sovereign bonds. The EMBI spreads jumped to above 5,000 basis points in March 2002 before peaking at 7,074 basis points in June 2002, as figure 6.2 demonstrates.[14]

Multinational Banks' Business Models

The second factor explaining the behavior of some multinational banks during the 2001 crisis highlights the importance of the banks' business models. Two-thirds of foreign banks operating in Argentina were headquartered in Western Europe (mainly in Spain) and one-third in the United States and Canada (Crystal, Dages, and Goldberg 2001, 34). Spanish banks have entered the Argentine market via acquisitions of local banks meant to operate in the mass retail market. This contrasted with the strategies of the U.S. banks, Bank of Boston and Citibank, which traditionally focused on a smaller, upper-income market and preferred to accompany multinational enterprises expanding abroad.

The Spanish parent banks have kept their new investments in Argentina as subsidiaries, rather than branches (Guillén and Tschoegl 2000, 76). The Spanish regulators treated subsidiaries as separate legal entities from the parents. More importantly, Spanish multinational banks operated a "decentralized" business model, in which subsidiaries raise funds autonomously in each host country instead of relying on cross-border intrabank funding and parental support (McCauley, McGuire, and von Peter 2010). In decentralized models, subsidiaries enjoy significant independence in liquidity management and are thus less vulnerable to problems in the home economy. But because decision making and funding takes place locally, subsidiaries are vulnerable to the problems of their host countries. The fact that subsidiaries of Spanish and other multinational banks operating in Argentina relied on their own capitalization proved a major constraint during the 2001 crisis. As the crisis unraveled, foreign subsidiaries had portfolios just as vulnerable to the default of the Argentine government as domestic banks had (Del Negro and Kay 2002, 13). In the end, however, the major Spanish banks did not leave, perhaps due to historical (colonial) links.[15]

The 2008 Global Financial Crisis

The 2008 global credit crisis helps gain insight on a different aspect of the theory: the implications of foreign bank presence in home-grown crises as compared to host-grown ones examined in the previous section. A particular feature of the recent global crisis was that it originated in the United States and swiftly turned to Western Europe. Thus the crisis began in developed countries, where most multinational banks are headquartered. This raised concerns about foreign banks spreading the crisis from developed countries to emerging markets through the lending channel. As the financial health of multinational banks deteriorated, pressures on their capital positions and the need to deleverage their balance sheets (to remove impaired assets to reduce indebtedness) mounted. These developments raised concerns about foreign banks' local lending and cross-border capital flows with potentially disruptive consequences for host countries. Credit booms and large current account deficits tend to be associated with banking crises and currency collapses. Not surprisingly, following the collapse of Lehman Brothers in September 2008, pressures on exchange rates of emerging markets increased substantially (Backé et al. 2010, 55). Consequently, the crisis sparked a debate on the question of whether foreign banks would be "shock transmitters" or "shock absorbers" (Winkler 2014).[16]

When assessing the implications of global banks, it is necessary to differentiate between cross-border lending of these banks and their presence as strategic investors in the emerging markets' banking systems. As briefly discussed in the previous section, it is also important to assess the implications of different business models of multinational banks that determine financial independence and funding sources granted to affiliates operating in emerging markets. Detailed information about these aspects of global banking makes it possible to take a closer look at the alternate ways global banks could potentially impact risks of host countries in times of financial turmoil. If we combine the findings of this section with those of the preceding one, the following picture emerges: Foreign banks have a solid track record of acting as stabilizers and lenders of last resort in times of crises, helping to maintain policy credibility of host countries with global market players.

Cross-Border versus Foreign Affiliate Lending

Global banks can extend credit to firms or households abroad directly from their headquarters or indirectly via foreign affiliates (subsidiaries or branches). Therefore, a distinction has to be made between cross-border and local lending of multinational banks. A greater reliance on cross-border bank lending, usually funded in international markets and denominated in foreign currencies, increases the exposure of global banks to international

interbank conditions. Cross-border lending in foreign currency increases
financial stress and exchange rate risks. By contrast, foreign bank affiliates
operating locally lend mostly in local currencies. This lending is much more
stable than the former type (García-Herrero and Martínez Pería 2007; Kamil and Rai 2010). The local presence of foreign banks reduces information
asymmetries and makes lending easier during crises. Indeed, most scholars
agree that the extent of contagion after the failure of Lehman Brothers was
lower when lending was conducted through local affiliates as compared to
cross-border bank lending (Kamil and Rai 2013; Cerutti and Claessens
2014; Cetorelli and Goldberg 2011).

In 2008, 70 percent of foreign bank lending to emerging markets was
through local affiliates (Kamil and Rai 2013). By the end of 2013, cross-
border lending declined by 23 percent below its precrisis peak, but local affiliates of multinational banks continued to expand credit even amid the financial crisis (their lending decreased by only 5 percent) (Cerutti and
Claessens 2014). But a relatively high share of cross-border bank loans (50
percent) made emerging Europe more vulnerable to sharp swings in capital
flows than was Latin America, where 60 percent of foreign bank lending was
denominated in local currency (Kamil and Rai 2013, 9; Kamil and Rai
2010).[17] In emerging Europe, foreign banks contributed to a rapid expansion
of credit by granting loans denominated in euros, Swiss francs, and Scandinavian kroner. At the end of 2007, the share of foreign-currency-denominated
loans was particularly high in Bulgaria (64 percent), Estonia (75 percent),
Latvia (81 percent), Lithuania (64 percent), Romania (66 percent) and Hungary (62 percent) (as compared to 55 percent in Germany).[18] High shares of
credit in foreign currencies made these countries vulnerable to currency depreciation. It should be noted, however, that foreign funding in other countries in emerging Europe with financial systems dominated by foreign banks
(for example, the Czech Republic, Slovakia, Albania, Macedonia, Montene-
gro) represented less than 20 percent of banking assets (Impavido, Rudolph,
and Ruggerone 2013, 38; Dietrich, Knedlik, and Lindner 2011, 422).

It is difficult to establish exactly the reasons for this excessive foreign
currency lending of global banks to emerging Europe. According to bankers, local regulators in emerging Europe sought to develop a mortgage market, but the domestic deposit base was limited and local capital markets,
where banks can raise funds to lend on to their customers, were underdeveloped. Foreign currency was thus the only viable option.[19] Lower inflation in the eurozone and Switzerland meant that loans denominated in

Swiss francs or euros carried lower interest rates than loans in local currencies. Relatively low exchange rate volatility (coupled with the prospect of the euro adoption) may have also provided the incentives for foreign banks to lend in foreign currency to some emerging European countries (International Monetary Fund 2011).

Nonetheless, most scholars agree that although the increase in bank credit in emerging Europe prior to 2008 was rapid, the amount of loans remained comparatively small as a share of GDP. Furthermore, a large portion of the loans provided by foreign banks to customers in emerging Europe were long-term and could not be easily recalled (Allen et al. 2011, 4). Regardless of the motives behind the credit boom, loans from foreign banks stimulated domestic consumption and economic growth in emerging Europe. None of the emerging European countries had high leverage, subprime mortgages, or collateralized debt obligations (Åslund 2011a, 378).

Is foreign bank lending less (or more) stable compared to lending by domestic banks? It is likely to be more stable because foreign parent banks remain committed to their subsidiaries when they get into financial difficulties. This type of support is not available to domestic banks. Indeed, lending by foreign bank subsidiaries during the global crisis was found to be more stable in countries where foreign banks dominate the financial system (Claessens and van Horen 2014) as the subsequent section shows.

Centralized and Decentralized Business Models

The additional factor that made a crucial difference between emerging Europe and Latin America in the probability of contagion during the 2008 crisis appears to be rooted in different funding models and expansion strategies adopted by multinational banks. The parent bank can transfer funds from subsidiaries when liquidity problems emerge in the home country. But this internal redistribution will be limited by the business model that determines the relationship between foreign affiliates relative to the parent bank. As I briefly explained earlier, in a decentralized model of multinational banking, the parent bank leaves their foreign subsidiaries the autonomy to raise funds to finance their activities in host countries, while in a centralized business model the funds are pooled at affiliates and redistributed around the multinational banking group (McCauley, McGuire, and von Peter 2012). A decentralized model reduces contagion risks to the parent bank when a host country experiences the crisis, but it heightens the risks to the subsidiaries. The case of Argentina illustrates this particularly well. By the same token, a decentralized model reduces the potential contagion effects to the subsidiary when a home country is confronted with the crisis. Moreover, the evidence indicates that a stand-alone subsidiary, facing stricter market discipline and reduced funding dependence on the parent bank, can over time become better-equipped to manage financial distress (International Monetary Fund 2011, 9). An important distinction between centralized and decentralized models relates to the extent to which loans provided by foreign subsidiaries are locally funded.

Research shows that the differences in multinational banks' funding models influenced the resilience of host countries during the recent global turmoil. The extent of transmission of external shocks was higher when lending was via capital transfers from parent banks or wholesale funding through international markets. By contrast, reliance on local deposits limited the potential destabilizing effects resulting from financial difficulties of the parent banks (Claessens et al. 2010; De Haas and van Lelyveld 2014). Multinational banks that pursued a decentralized business model and relied more on local funding (for example, Spanish and UK banks), were less affected by the disruptions to the international markets than those operating in a centralized funding model (for example Swiss, German, and Austrian banks) (McCauley, McGuire, and von Peter 2012) (figure 6.3). Most multinational banking groups active in emerging Europe pursue the centralized business models, whereas the decentralized model is more common for banking groups operating in Latin America. Foreign bank lending in Latin America was thus primarily dependent on the health of subsidiaries funded through local deposits, whereas a deterioration of the parent banks' financial soundness mattered more for emerging Europe due to dependence of foreign subsidiaries on intrabank funding (Cull and Martínez Péria 2012). Not surprisingly, Latin American countries, where foreign bank affiliates were funded mainly through domestic deposits, remained resilient during the crisis.[20]

Austrian Banks in Emerging Europe

Foreign banks in emerging Europe range from global banks (Deutsche Bank, HSBC, BNP Paribas, the Royal Bank of Scotland, and Crédit Agricole) to smaller, specialized groups (the Dutch Home Credit or the Austrian Hypo-Bank Burgenland) (Impavido, Rudolph, and Ruggerone 2013). Aus-

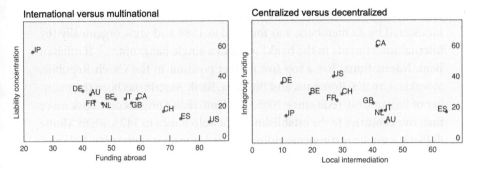

Fig. 6.3. Business Models of Global Banks: (a) Cross-Border Lending vs. Foreign Affiliate Lending; (b) Intragroup Funding vs. Local Deposits
Liability concentration: Herfindahl index of all foreign liabilities (cross-border and local) by office location (in %). Funding abroad: Percentage of foreign liabilities by offices outside the home country. Intragroup funding: Interoffice liabilities as a percentage of all foreign liabilities. Local intermediation (in %).
Source: Reprinted from McCauley, McGuire, and von Peter (2012: 13). Copyright (2016), with permission from Elsevier.

trian, Dutch, Belgian, German, and French banks active in emerging Europe pursue a centralized funding model in their business operations.[21] Swedish banks (Swedbank, Skandinaviska Enskilda Banken, and Nordea) that dominate the Baltic banking systems equally apply a highly centralized approach to funding.

Austrian banks, with sixty-three subsidiaries in eighteen countries, are the biggest players in emerging Europe. As table 6.2 shows, emerging Europe is particularly important for the subsidiaries of three Austrian banking groups, Erste Group, Raiffeisen Bank International, and UniCredit Bank Austria (Raiffeisen Research 2012). Austrian banks had started to expand into emerging Europe in the mid-1980s mainly to provide services to the Austrian firms operating in the region, but from the early 1990s they began to establish subsidiaries, initially as greenfield operations (Boss et al. 2007). Then in the mid-1990s they accelerated their expansion and changed their initial business strategy of organic growth to growth through acquisition, that is, by buying majority stakes in large state owned banks in emerging Europe.

The leading Austrian banks have a good reputation built on a long history of global operations. Erste Group was founded in 1819 as the first Austrian savings bank and grew through "acquisitive" growth (buying other banks).[22] Erste is the largest bank in Slovakia, the Czech Republic, and Romania. The first Austrian Raiffeisen banking cooperative, owned and administered by its members, was founded in 1886 and grew organically (by internal investments in the bank) without a single bankruptcy.[23] Raiffeisen Bank International has a top five market position in the Czech Republic, Slovakia, Croatia, Romania, and Bulgaria. Bank Austria has been the member of Italian UniCredit since 2005. The UniCredit's origins date back more than five centuries to the establishment of Rolo Banca in 1473, when Monte di Pietá, a public institute providing secured loans, was created in Bologna. More recently, UniCredit is the result of the merger of nine of Italy's largest banks and the subsequent combination with German HypoVereinsbank and Italian Capitalia Group. Bank Austria was created in 1855 by the merger of Austria's leading traditional banks. It acts currently as subholding company of UniCredit banking groups in charge of overseeing the group's activities in emerging Europe. The acquisition of Polish Bank Pekao initiated the expansion of UniCredit in markets of Eastern Europe. UniCredit is the largest bank by asset share in Croatia and Bulgaria.

TABLE 6.2. Top Multinational Banks in Emerging Europe

Bank	Total assets in central and eastern Europe (consolidated, billions of euros) in 2011[a]	Total assets in east central and southeastern Europe in 2010[b]	Share of assets of subsidiaries in central and eastern Europe as % of group assets in 2011	Home Country
UniCredit Group (Italy)	116.3	20.4	12.5	Austria (UniCredit Bank Austria)
Raiffeisen Bank	84.8	14.7	57.7	Austria
Erste Group	84.0	18.3	40.0	Austria
Société Générale	73.7	12.4	6.5	France
KBC Group	55.0	7.0	17.1	Belgium
Intesa Sanpaolo	40.6	9.6	6.4	Italy
Commerzbank	26.4	3.1	4.0	Germany
Santander[c]	24.4	1.8	1.9	Spain
Swedbank	17.1	2.0	8.2	Sweden

Source: Raiffeisen Research (2012).

[a]This list excludes Országos Takarék Pénztár (OTP) with a total of 35.9 billion euros, mostly in Hungary. It also excludes the Slovenian Nova Ljubljaska Banka with a total of 17.3 billion euros, of which the government owns 45 percent.

[b]Poland, the Czech Republic, Slovakia, Hungary, Slovenia, Latvia, Lithuania, Estonia, Romania, Bulgaria, Croatia, Serbia, Macedonia, Bosnia and Herzegovina, Albania, and Kosovo.

[c]Spain's Santander has for the first time entered the top ten of foreign banking groups in Eastern Europe after acquiring a majority stake in Polish Kredyt Bank in 2011.

When the 2008 crisis erupted in emerging Europe, the Austrian government approved a €100 billion rescue package (36 percent of GDP), composed of both capital support measures and guarantees to banks (without voting rights) (International Monetary Fund 2011, 21).[24] The recapitalization measures were pre-emptive to maintain funding to subsidiaries of Austrian banks in emerging Europe because Erste and Raiffeisen were still profitable at that time. Furthermore, in 2012 the Austrian central bank and the Financial Market Authority introduced new supervisory measures for large internationally active Austrian banks to strengthen standards on bank risk management and lending in foreign currencies.

Spanish Banks in Emerging Latin America

Spanish, American, and British multinational banks hold the largest market shares in emerging Latin America, while Canadian banks account for the largest market share in the Caribbean. As table 6.3 shows, the two largest Spanish banks—Banco Santander and Banco Bilbao Vizcaya Argentaria (BBVA)—are the biggest players. They belong to the group of the most reputable global banks. Banco Santander, the largest family-led (Boitín family) Spanish bank, was founded in 1857. In addition to commercial banking, it was entrusted with issuing notes until 1874. Initially, Banco Santander specialized in the Spanish-American trade. In the 1950s, it established representative offices in Mexico City and London. It continued in its international expansion into Latin America in the 1970s, trying to acquire majority control of local banks. Banco Central Hispano resulted from a merger between Banco Central (established in 1919) and the financially distressed Banco Hispano-Americano. It subsequently merged with Santander in 1999, forming a Banco Santander Central Hispano, which became the biggest multinational bank in the Latin American region.[25] Banco Bilbao Vizcaya is the outcome of a merger between Banco de Bilbao (founded in 1857) and Banco de Vizcaya (founded in 1901). In 1999, BBVA was formed from a merger of Banco Bilbao Vizcaya and Argentaria; the latter was a major player in Latin American pensions and investment funds. BBVA expanded into Latin America, originally aiming at minority stakes in local banks.

Spanish multinational banks operate a decentralized business model characterized by financial independence of their affiliates with regards to capital, liquidity, and funding. The choice of this model was partly due to harsh lessons learned from the decades of financial crises in Latin America in the 1980s and 1990s. In the early 2000s, the Spanish central bank issued a regulatory framework stipulating the new criteria with regards to transparency of global banking groups' structures and financial autonomy of subsidiaries. In this framework, each subsidiary is responsible for its own funding and liquidity management, while intragroup operations are limited to exceptional circumstances at market prices (BIS 2010, 12). Simultaneously, Latin American governments promoted the independence of foreign subsidiaries by developing the supply of long-term finance through pension reforms and other policies that spurred the development of local debt and equity markets. Latin American subsidiaries of Spanish banking groups have proven resilient during the 2008 crisis primarily because of their limited exposure to subprime assets and low reliance on short-term financing and funding through international markets. Foreign subsidiaries operating in Latin America have been able to rely on more stable and long-term local sources of funding, including deposits, bonds, and securities (Impavido, Rudolph, and Ruggerone 2013). Using a bank-level dataset on more than

TABLE 6.3. Major Multinational Banks in Emerging Latin America

Multinational Bank	Bank's Assets[a]		Countries of Operation	Home Country
	In $100M	As % of total banking assets		
Santander	4,246	37.0	Brazil, Mexico, Chile, Argentina, Colombia, Venezuela, Uruguay	Spain
BBVA	1,647	14.3	Mexico, Chile, Argentina, Colombia, Venezuela, Panama, Peru, Uruguay	Spain
HSBC	1,602	14.0	Brazil, Mexico, Chile, Argentina, Colombia, Panama, Peru, Uruguay, El Salvador, Costa Rica, Honduras	United Kingdom
Citigroup	1,456	12.7	Brazil, Mexico, Argentina, Colombia, Venezuela, Panama, Peru, Uruguay, El Salvador, Guatemala	United States
Scotiabank	466	4.1	Mexico, Chile, Panama, Peru, El Salvador, Costa Rica, Dominican Republic	Canada
Deutsche Bank	324	2.8	Brazil, Mexico, Chile	Germany
Itaú	114	1.0	Argentina, Colombia, Uruguay	Brazil

Source: Adapted from the European Commission for Latin America and the Caribbean (2012, 119).
[a]As of June 2011.

five hundred banks, Galindo, Izquierdo, and Rojas-Suárez (2010) find that Spanish banks in Latin American countries behaved like their domestic counterparts (but with foreign capital) during the recent crisis. They neither reduced lending nor increased interest rates more than their domestic counterparts.[26]

All factors taken together, the discussion leads to the following conclusion. As the crisis unfolded in developed countries and the health of parent banks deteriorated, foreign affiliates of multinational banks in emerging Europe were more affected and transmitted the external shocks to a greater extent than those operating in Latin America or other regions. Multinational banks maintained their commitment to host countries, as would be expected on the basis of historical patterns.[27]

Multinational Banks and Investor Risk of Home Countries

Has the relative deterioration in the health of multinational banks during the 2008 crisis had an impact on the sovereign risks of the countries in which these banks are headquartered? The exposures of Western European banks to the U.S. subprime market, and later to the 2010 sovereign debt crisis in the eurozone, have not only raised doubts about the credibility and sustainability of the single currency but put pressures on the banks holding bonds of distressed members. Spreads of the major multinational banks increased due to their large regional exposures and the reliance of their subsidiaries for funding from their parents. Consequently, a deterioration in market perceptions of fiscal risks related to bank bailouts had a negative (albeit temporary) effect on sovereign bond yield spreads of home countries too (International Monetary Fund 2011).

By 2008, international claims of Austrian banks operating in emerging Europe resulting from cross-border foreign currency lending amounted to 35 percent of Austria's GDP (or to 70 percent if lending in local currencies by Austrian subsidiaries is included) (Mitra, Selowsky, and Zalduendo 2010, 99–100). The data reported in table 6.4 show that high exposures of Austrian multinational banks to emerging Europe, combined with significant reliance of subsidiaries on parental support, were reflected in relatively high prices of credit default spreads (insurance contracts offering protection against the default of a government or a bank). Therefore, the fiscal risk associated with the lender-of-last-resort obligations of the Austrian authorities to their banks increased (International Monetary Fund 2011, 28). But table 6.4 also shows that credit default swap spreads decreased to normal levels relatively quickly. In fact, the Austrian banks even continued their international expansion after 2009. Raiffeisen bought a Polish Polbank, a branch of Greek EFG Eurobank, and Erste increased its ownership stake in its Romanian subsidiary (International Monetary Fund 2011, 15). But to protect the country's AAA credit rating, the Austrian authorities instructed their banks to boost capital reserves and limit cross-border lending (Wagstyl and Buckley 2011).

Spanish multinational banks were in a good financial position. They did not have to resort to transfers from their parents or to government liquidity support (BIS 2010). Consequently, Spanish banks weathered the crisis better and their credit default swap spreads were even marginally lower than that of Spanish sovereign credit default swap spreads (table 6.4). The largest Spanish banks also continued their international expansion after the 2008 crisis; for example, Banco Santander expanded in Poland and BBVA in Turkey.

Foreign Banks Remain Committed

In the remainder of this section, I provide further evidence for the claim that by acting as lenders of last resort during the 2008 global crisis, foreign banks prevented the reputational damage of host countries. The evidence suggests that a stable flow of intragroup funds between the parent bank and its foreign subsidiaries in emerging European countries was the principal factor in reducing the vulnerability of these countries to sudden stops of capital flows during the 2008 financial crisis (European Bank for Reconstruction and De-

TABLE 6.4. Multinational Banks and Home Country Credit Default Swaps, 2007–11

	Credit Default Swaps (spreads in basis points)	
	Pre-Lehman to Lehman Peak (8/1/2007–3/2/2009)	Sovereign Debt Crisis (6/1/2010–10/3/2011)
Multinational Bank		
Santander	124	112
BBVA	123	88
Erste Group	369	175
Raiffeisen Bank International	299	79
Home Country		
Spain	139	131
Austria	253	102

Source: Adapted from International Monetary Fund (2011, 28).

velopment 2009; Berglof et al. 2010; De Haas and van Lelyveld 2014; Vogel and Winkler 2012; Herrmann and Mihaljek 2013; Claessens and van Horen 2014).[28] Mindful of the reputational risk and the damage to their long-term business plans, Western European parent banks supplied their subsidiaries in emerging Europe liquidity and attenuated bank-lending outflows in the post-Lehman period (Berglof et al. 2010). In view of this fact, it is difficult to establish support for the common view that subsidiaries are more subject to abandonment by parent banks than are branches.

Whereas multinational banks pledged their commitments since the onset of the crisis, these commitments were not binding because there was no formal policy framework in place to ensure their credibility. Why didn't foreign banks cut and run, repatriating capital and assets to their home markets and abandon their subsidiaries? This puzzle is particularly pronounced in emerging Europe. Some scholars credit the specific type of financial integration, while others underline the importance of the Vienna Initiative, a voluntary rollover agreement to mitigate the sudden capital outflows.

"Home Market"
Western European multinational banks have pursued a long-term commitment strategy in their emerging European hosts (Bonin 2010), perceiving them as an extension of their home markets or as "second home markets" (Winkler 2009; Epstein 2014).The presence of foreign banks through privatization and control of large state-owned banks in emerging Europe resulted in the so-called "hybrid banks," characterized by the long-term commitment to their host countries to develop reputational capital (Bonin 2010). In this model, it is more difficult for a foreign parent bank to abandon its subsidiary without damaging its reputation and affecting negatively its long-term business potential in the region.

Because many countries in emerging Europe exhibit geographic and political proximity to the EU, multinational banks headquartered in the EU member states consider emerging European countries as part of the single European financial market (Gardó and Martin 2010, 5). This was particularly true of Austrian banks, which, driven by historical and cultural ties to the former Austro-Hungarian Empire, were interested in developing long-term relationships with their neighboring countries from emerging Europe.[29] Besides Austrian banks, Nordic banks remained equally committed to their foreign subsidiaries in the Baltic countries, motivated by large equity stakes in the Baltic region and the reputational costs of a disorderly exit (BIS 2010, 10–11). For example, in 2008, Parex bank, the second largest domestically owned Latvian bank, experienced a deposit run, which turned into a run on currency that fueled devaluation expectations. The Swedish and Danish central banks opened a swap line of €500 million to bridge the IMF stand-by loan, demonstrating the commitment of the Nordic countries to Latvia's stabilization. Nordic banks operating in Latvia absorbed substantial losses but none of them left (Åslund 2011b).

The case of Hungary appears, at first sight, to be at odds with the theory put forward in this book. The government of Victor Orbán and his center-right Fidesz Party, which won the 2010 parliamentary elections, introduced several "financial nationalist" policies to reduce the influence of foreign banks (Johnson and Barnes 2014). These policy measures included hiking taxes on banks, discouraging and converting foreign currency loans and permitting mortgage holders to repay their foreign currency balances at fixed, below-market exchange rates. But in spite of these unsavory policies of the Hungarian government that entailed high costs for foreign banks, these banks stayed put. Also, the financial policies of the Hungarian authorities remained rigorous. Foreign parent banks increased the capital of their Hungarian subsidiaries after 2009, which mitigated the risks arising from the high rate of short-term foreign funding (Lahnsteiner 2011). Not surprisingly, bond markets' punishment of the government policies in the form of higher borrowing costs was "small, short lived and ineffective" (Johnson and Barnes 2014, 556).

The Vienna Initiative

The second conventional interpretation of the commitment of parent banks to their subsidiaries in emerging Europe focuses on the role of the Vienna Initiative. This initiative, launched in February 2009, represented a public-private partnership bringing together multinational banks, host and home countries' ministers of finance and central bankers, the European Commission, and the international financial institutions (the EBRD, the European Investment Bank, the IMF, and the World Bank). Multinational banks participating in this agreement were promised financial support in return for their commitments to maintain exposures and to recapitalize their subsidiaries in five emerging European countries (Latvia, Hungary, Romania, Serbia, and Bosnia-Herzegovina). As part of the Vienna Initiative, seventeen major multinational banks entered into voluntary agreements that were not legally binding.[30]

Multinational banks committed not only to rolling over the existing lines of credit but also to providing subsidiaries in emerging Europe with additional capital. Furthermore, home country authorities promised to make bailout money available to parent banks, without restrictions. Simultaneously, the international financial institutions launched a Joint International Financial Institution Action Plan, making available more than €33 billion in crisis-related support for banking systems in emerging Europe. De Haas et al. (2012) find that the banks taking part in the Vienna Initiative increased their credit supply more than other multinational banks, proving that the agreement worked. In sum, in this account, the Vienna Initiative, backed by the IMF-led bailouts which stabilized the balance sheets of global banks, rather than the sheer presence of these banks, explain their commitment to emerging Europe.

Epstein (2014) and Grittersová (2014b) cast doubt on the indispensability of the Vienna Initiative as the external constraint (combined with outside assistance) on multinational banks' commitments by portraying the agreement as a derivative of the investment strategies of these banks. Austrian banks were instrumental in bringing forth the Vienna agreement. In November 2008, the chief executive of Austria's Raiffeisen Bank, Herbert Stepic, gathered top executives of five major European banks (Erste of Austria, UniCredit and Intesa both of Italy, Société Générale of France, and KBC of Belgium) to coordinate efforts to lobby for government support for emerging Europe. Subsequently, the major European banks sent a letter to the European Commission, the EBRD, and the European Investment Bank calling for a prompt and coordinated response. These efforts culminated in a meeting in Vienna, convened by the Austrian Finance Ministry, which laid the ground for the Vienna Initiative (De Haas et al. 2012).

Managers at multinational banks signed the agreement because they wanted to address the prisoner dilemma situation not among themselves but among other participants in international markets.[31] The thinking went that if one bank exited the region, a panic might ensue. The bankers' goal was to send a strong signal to the markets that they would stand behind their subsidiaries and that emerging Europe was not vulnerable to bank failures and economic collapse. This would in turn help banks to prevent a decline of asset values and alleviate funding problems. It should be underlined, however, that these two analytical approaches to explaining foreign banks' commitment can be reconciled once the selection bias problem is recognized: those banks with the greatest regional exposures (with affiliates in several countries), and thus facing the greatest difficulties, had the greatest incentive to self-select into the Vienna agreement to restore the confidence in emerging Europe and their profitability (Epstein 2014).

Although initially preoccupied with crisis management, the Vienna Initiative has subsequently moved to postcrisis governance (Pistor 2012). The concerns about excessive and disorderly deleveraging of foreign banks in emerging Europe due to the Greek and the eurozone crisis, accompanied by pressures from European regulators, motivated the EBRD to call for a renewed effort to keep banks involved in the region. Vienna Initiative 2.0 was launched in March 2012. Its goals and resources were more modest, but long-term. International financial institutions did not pledge a definitive monetary amount; instead they proclaimed that they "stand ready" to support foreign bank subsidiaries in emerging Europe if necessary (Buckley 2012). The main objective of Vienna 2.0 is to achieve better coordination between home and host financial sector regulators and supervisors and to contain negative spillovers from the eurozone crisis onto emerging Europe (De Haas et al. 2012).

Summarizing the analysis above, we can conclude that, contrary to initial expectations, foreign banks did not amplify the 2008 crisis in emerging markets, which holds true even when many Western (particularly European) parent banks experienced substantial losses and faced severe liquidity shortages. Thanks to the recapitalization of their subsidiaries, foreign parent banks directly ensured the financial stability of emerging European countries, and thus prevented the deterioration of their policy credibility, as I will show next.

Reputation amidst Uncertainty

The financial panic that erupted in emerging market countries after the bankruptcy of Lehman Brothers also reflected some fundamental weaknesses of their economies. Those in emerging Europe were running large current account deficits and experiencing excessive credit expansion and real estate booms. Paradoxically, as these economies became more financially integrated through Western banks and their monetary regimes became more credible, incentives to borrow in foreign currency increased because the nominal interest rates of euro loans were still slightly below rates on local currency loans (Darvas 2011).[32]

In the literature on financial crises, rapid credit growth is one of the best predictors of currency crises and collapses of fixed exchange rate regimes, particularly if financial development is characterized by large capital inflows that are vulnerable to sudden stops or capital flow reversals (Calvo 1998).[33] On the face of it, a strict application of the theory of credit booms and busts would imply that countries in emerging Europe in particular should have experienced runs on banks, systemic banking crises, and large currency devaluations. This is clearly at odds with the evidence. A few banking crises that occurred in Latvia, Ukraine, Slovenia, and Kazakhstan involved domestic banks only (Laeven and Valencia 2013). The extent of foreign currency lending in some emerging European countries increased the risk aversion of markets and induced depreciation pressures and exchange rate volatility, but currency markets stabilized shortly thereafter. Against the background of strongly appreciating currencies prior to the crisis and a negative sentiment of international markets during the crisis, no single country in emerging Europe with a fixed exchange rate regime has devalued its currency or changed its monetary regime. No country's currency has slumped in spite of calls for devaluation by some prominent economists (Åslund 2011a, 379).[34] Neither Eastern European (except for Hungary) nor Latin American countries had to drastically increase interest rates to defend their monetary regimes during the crisis (Backé et al. 2010, 59). Even though volatility of interest rates and foreign exchange risk premiums temporarily increased, partially reflecting a general aversion of financial markets, monetary regimes in emerging countries have remained "stable and unchanged" during and after the 2008 crisis (Rose 2014). Historically, by contrast, countries usually changed their monetary regimes during crises (Rose 2014). For instance, Russia and Argentina were forced to drastically devalue their currencies during the 1998 and 2001 crises, respectively.

Given these foreseeable consequences, it is important to understand why the inevitable devaluations and currency collapses did not happen. It is important to grasp the significance of the engagement with multinational banks in order to comprehend the crisis and its implications for the monetary credibility of emerging markets. I demonstrate here that one of the major factors influencing the market confidence in emerging economies during the 2008 global crisis was the international lender-of-last-resort support provided by multinational banks. This meant that the funds available to maintain the credibility of monetary regimes in emerging markets were not limited to those of local central banks but also included those provided by foreign parent banks. This provides a clear endorsement of my credibility theory.

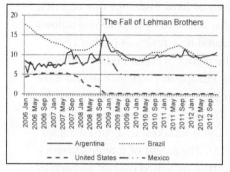
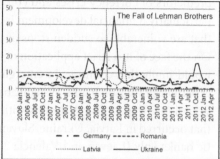

Fig. 6.4. Money Market Rates (2006–2012) (%): (a) Emerging Latin America; (b) Emerging Europe

Source: International Monetary Fund, *International Financial Statistics.*

Figure 6.4 (a) and (b) shows money market rates in selected countries in emerging Europe and Latin America, including those that have been badly affected by the recent crisis. Overall, the behavior of short-term interest rates in the emerging markets closely integrated via multinational banks (Mexico, Romania, Latvia) suggest that their monetary regimes remained relatively credible through much of the crisis period. Admittedly, short-term credibility took a hit late 2008 and early 2009, but it recovered relatively quickly. Peculiarly, between the outset of the crisis and the collapse of Lehman Brothers, when financial markets were characterized by the reduced risk appetite, currencies of some emerging markets, notably those of the Czech Republic and Poland, started to appreciate substantially vis-à-vis the euro. One explanation is grounded in the "safe haven" hypothesis, according to which, because of the high credibility of the monetary regimes of these countries, financial markets considered the Czech koruna and Polish zloty a safe haven (Crespo-Cuaresma, Geršl, and Slačík 2010). This explanation highlights that whereas banks in developed countries held toxic assets associated with subprime mortgages, foreign banks in emerging markets engaged in more traditional banking activities. Consequently, direct holding of subprime securities was negligible in the latter group of countries.

In the same vein, a closer look at the evolution of the country-risk premium, as reflected in sovereign bond yield spreads, reveals upward movements consistent with the overall market volatility (figure 6.5a and b). The peak of the crisis seems to coincide with the spikes in risk, but this is amid the worst financial crisis since the Great Depression. There is also a percep-

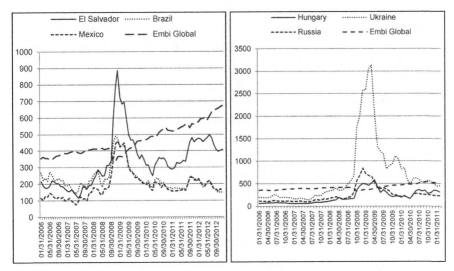

Fig. 6.5. EMBI Spreads (2006–2012) (basis points): (a) Emerging Latin America; (b) Emerging Europe
Source: Global Financial Data.

tible change in risk for some countries in emerging Europe at the time of the European sovereign debt crisis. Overall, however, policymakers in emerging markets with high degree of banking integration successfully maintained policy credibility in the face of particularly adverse conditions.

Yet it would be wrong to conclude that foreign banks would under all circumstances transfer good reputation. It seems perfectly consistent with the argument of this book that if multilateral banks are heavily affected by the crisis, they could transfer bad reputations too. Healthy parent banks continue to provide financial support to their subsidiaries, but fragile parent banks might fail to provide such support. Some weak parent banks repatriated funds from their subsidiaries to the headquarters during the 2008 crisis (for instance, subsidiaries in Russia and in the Czech Republic acted as creditors of their parent banks in Italy and France) (De Haas and van Lelyveld 2014, 334).

A Tale of Two Crises

Owing to large capital inflows that fueled asset price booms, excessive current account deficits, and foreign currency exposures, commentators compared the

2008 crisis in emerging Europe with the 1997–98 Asian currency crises. Just how important these similarities are is depicted in table 6.5. To illustrate, for the Asian crisis countries, the average credit growth of the three most affected countries was 114 percent in 1996 and for the three emerging European countries it was 75 percent in 2007. From a comparative perspective, however, there were notable differences between the crises in these two regions.

The first difference has to do with financial sector vulnerabilities (as measured by the number of nonperforming loans) that were much smaller in emerging Europe than in East Asia (table 6.5). The exception is Ukraine, whose financial system remains on a much weaker footing. Latvia and Ukraine, with banking sectors most severely hit by the 2008 crisis, required

TABLE 6.5. The 1997 Asian Crisis and the 2008 Global Crisis in Emerging Europe

Eastern Europe	2007	2008	2009
Foreign banks as a percent of total banks			
Hungary	93.0	93.0	92.0
Latvia	57.0	62.0	62.0
Ukraine	39.0	44.0	46.0
Domestic credit as a percent of GDP			
Hungary	75.7	80.9	81.4
Latvia	89.5	89.4	94.3
Ukraine	61.1	95.0	103.7
Bank nonperforming loans as a percent of total gross loans			
Hungary	2.3	3.0	6.7
Latvia	0.8	2.1	14.3
Ukraine	48.1	3.9	13.7
Asia	1996	1997	1998
Foreign banks as a percent of total banks			
Indonesia	26.0	26.0	27.0
Malaysia	25.0	25.0	24.0
Thailand	5.0	0.0	6.0
Domestic credit as a percent of GDP			
Indonesia	54.0	59.6	59.9
Malaysia	142.4	163.4	162.1
Thailand	146.4	177.6	176.7
Bank nonperforming loans as a percent of total gross loans[a]			
Indonesia	48.6	32.9	34.4
Malaysia	18.6	16.6	15.4
Thailand	42.9	38.6	17.7

Source: Claessens and van Horen (2014); World Bank, *World Development Indicators*; Federal Reserve Bank of St. Louis, https://research.stlouisfed.org/fred2/
[a]Data reported for 1998, 1999, and 2000 due to the unavailability of data for earlier years.

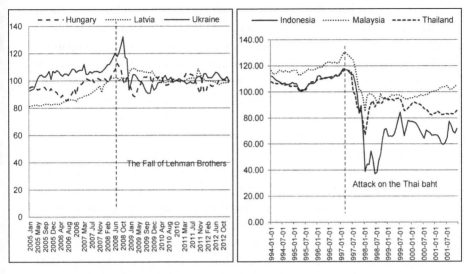

Fig. 6.6. Real Effective Exchange Rate (Index 2010=100): (a) Emerging Europe
(2005–2012); (b) Emerging Asia (1994–2001)

Source: International Monetary Fund, *International Financial Statistics*; Bank for International Settlements.

liquidity support of 6.75 and 7.50 percent of GDP, respectively. This remains
well below the liquidity support extended to Indonesia and Malaysia (17 percent and 22 percent of GDP, respectively) during the Asian crisis (European
Bank for Reconstruction and Development 2009, 12). With the exception of
Ukraine and Russia, where foreign bank presence was limited, the Eastern
European currencies depreciated between 3 percent and 15 percent between
2007 and 2010 (International Monetary Fund 2011; Åslund 2011a, 379). In
Asia, the decline in the real effective exchange rates ranged from 19 percent
for the Philippines to 40 percent for Indonesia (Truman 2013, 4). Figure 6.6
(a) and (b) illustrate these exchange rate movements graphically. Capital outflows from emerging Europe were much less pronounced, averaging 1 percent of GDP in late 2008 to early 2009, whereas the worst quarters of the
Asian crisis were associated with outflows of capital amounting to 4.5 percent
of GDP (European Bank for Reconstruction and Development 2009, 12).

Can foreign control of the banking sector explain the differences in the
magnitude of these two crises, not just their incidence? Winkler's (2009)
explanation of cross-regional differences focuses on information asymmetries. He argues that foreign parent banks enjoyed an information advan-

tage vis-à-vis other external creditors with regards to the solvencies of their affiliates in emerging Europe. In contrast, Asian banks engaged in short-term borrowing from global banks on the basis of an *arm's length* relationship (through international capital markets) prior to the 1997 crisis. Global banks, as external creditors, neither possessed good information about the long-term solvency of Asian banks nor did they invest in acquiring such knowledge, given that their loans were mostly short-term. When facing the risk, external creditors would recall their loans, triggering the panic and capital outflows in Asia.

Hence, the main reason why emerging Europe fared better than emerging Asia appears once more to be the substantial presence of multinational banks. Chapters 4 and 5 demonstrated that foreign strategic owners restructured local banks and improved the soundness and stability of the banking systems of the countries in emerging Europe. "Introducing foreign-owned banks . . . broke the symbiotic link between government and state enterprises and newly privatized enterprises. Foreign bank ownership helped harden budget constraints and attain macroeconomic stability," Mitra, Selowsky, and Zalduendo (2010, 11) note. As a consequence, the banking sector fragility—measured by credit quality and banking sector capitalization—which is typical for emerging markets, was reduced. Because of foreign bank presence, Moody's long-term foreign exchange deposit ratings and bank stock valuations also improved, signaling positive sentiment of international markets about banking sectors of emerging European countries (Herrmann and Mihajlek 2013).

Conclusion

This chapter shows that reputable multinational banks behaved as my credibility theory predicts during the crises originating in their home countries as well as those emanating from host countries. The comparative analysis of countries in emerging Europe, Latin America, and Asia suggests that the variation in the intensity and responses to the various crises can be traced back to differences in the level of foreign bank presence. Empirical evidence of behavioral responses of foreign banks in Argentina during the Tequila Crisis suggests that foreign bank presence exerted a stabilizing impact on the local banking system. The 2008 global financial crisis reduced opportunities for international operations of multinational banks and tested their commitments to emerging markets. Reputable Western banks were concerned about damage to their reputation and the implications for their market shares if they withdrew capital and liquidity. And while facing even more severe pressures during the eurozone crisis than in the post-Lehman period, they have not pulled out of emerging markets. The crisis also highlighted the importance of multinational banks' business models and funding structures for financial stability.

It seems clear that the resilience of emerging markets in the 2008 global financial crisis can be linked to financial integration through multinational banking groups. Nonetheless, it should be recognized that the specialty of emerging Europe is the "political and institutional integration with Western Europe," as Berglöf et al. (2010, 2) argue. Integration of emerging European countries within the European banking system has surely played a supporting role in ensuring stable support and commitment from parent banks to their affiliates, compared to other regions (Lahnsteiner 2011). The actions of foreign banks were reinforced by actions of home country fiscal authorities and the European Central Bank that provided support for the parent banks via equity injections, loans, guarantees, and liquidity (Winkler 2014).

Notwithstanding, the European Commission, particularly its Directorate-General for Competition, initially required that bailouts be accompanied by a commitment of banks to sell assets abroad and reduce risks in their portfolios, thus reinforcing incentives of Western banks to withdraw from emerging Europe (Epstein 2014).[35] European bailout packages were nationally oriented. In order to receive the liquidity, banks were expected to service their domestic markets.[36] The European Commission was further concerned that Western bank bailouts could distort the Single European Market by conferring advantages on banks receiving liquidity.

More generally, the likelihood of a systemic banking crisis appears to be lower in emerging markets that lowered entry barriers to foreign banks (Barth, Caprio, and Levine 2002). In many instances, foreign banks have been also invited to resolve the crisis by rehabilitating problematic banks and reforming the host countries' banking systems. Besides Argentina discussed in this chapter, examples include Mexico, Brazil, and Venezuela after the 1995 Tequila Crisis; Indonesia, South Korea, Philippines, and Thailand after the 1997 Asian crises; and Colombia after the 1980s debt crisis (Martinez-Diaz 2009).

CHAPTER 7

Conclusion

The need to establish policy credibility is acute in most emerging and developing countries, whether as a result of histories of high inflation and failed economic policies, or an absence of credible institutions, or because they are newcomers to the international stage. In writing this book, I have sought to demonstrate that countries with little reputational track record can import credibility from abroad through financial integration with multinational banks. The theory in this book builds upon and extends the existing scholarship on sources of credibility in international relations. Whereas the existing theories focus on good governance and sound domestic institutions or multilateral organizations, I add a new element, reputable global private banks. I suggest that the credibility of governments of emerging markets rests on a transfer of good reputation from reputable global banks that can send credible signals to international markets in both good and bad times.

I start with the theoretical framework for *why* multinational banks are solutions to credibility problems of emerging markets in chapter 2. I posit that in countries where information is scarce and unreliable, markets pay attention to the signals and events—such as foreign bank entry—that can be easily interpreted. In my theory of credibility, however, the presence of multinational banks not only generates expectations about a government's policy commitments but also gives assurances to markets that the proclaimed policies will be carried out. I argue that reputable multinational banks can send credible signals to markets because they are unlikely to behave opportunistically for a risky behavior that would affect their brand name, reputation, and profits.

My theory also generates concrete predictions about *how* multinational banks enhance the credibility of monetary commitments of emerging-market governments. Policymakers in these countries need to anchor inflation expectations, demonstrate the transparency of monetary and financial policies, and establish the credibility of their domestic institutions. Drawing on theories of global banking, I argue that the presence of reputable foreign banks signals to international financial markets the transparency and soundness of local financial systems, allowing better monitoring of monetary and financial policies. The presence of foreign banks also involves the transfer of the status of lender of last resort function from local central banks to foreign bank parents. The effects of multinational banks on credibility vary depending on their reputation and the level of financial integration (market share of multinational banks).

The quantitative and qualitative evidence presented in the book confirms that international markets react to foreign bank presence in emerging nations. Chapter 3 provides the broadest test of theory by analyzing data for more than eighty emerging-market countries from the mid-1990s to 2009. The findings of this statistical analysis suggest that the currency risk was lower in countries with a substantial presence of foreign banks in their financial systems because they offered a more predictable environment. This relationship is robust across numerous specifications and estimation techniques. I find that foreign bank presence matters above and beyond alternative explanations that depict reputation formation as being a result of autonomous central banks or membership in international organizations. Thus, the evidence not only fits my credibility theory, but it also challenges alternative accounts of international credibility building. This chapter also suggests that markets are not indifferent to the reputation of multinational banks. Specifically, I explore the effect of south-south banks, depicted as banks from other developing countries investing in their peers, on changes in market perceptions. Quantitative evidence complemented by a case study of Ukraine suggests that financial integration with less reputable multinational banks does not reduce risk for host countries. Finally, I investigate the implications of foreign bank presence and credible monetary regimes for country risk. The results show that multinational banks can affect the country risk of host countries indirectly through the positive effects conferred by credible monetary regimes on the pricing of sovereign debt. But this chapter offers evidence that foreign bank presence also has significant, direct positive effects on the country risk of host countries.

These statistical patterns are confirmed by the case evidence. Chapter 4 examined the dynamics of credibility building for currency boards in

Estonia and Bulgaria. Chapter 5 looked at the effects of foreign bank presence on the credibility of inflation-targeting regimes in the Czech Republic and Poland. Taken together, these four case studies demonstrate that banking sector opening and financial integration involving a greater participation of multinational banks helped policymakers to commit to sound financial policies and abide by their monetary policy targets. Emerging Europe, where the rates of growth of foreign bank ownership and the credibility deficit after the fall of communism in 1989 have been particularly striking, provides a particularly good opportunity to test my theory of reputation. An advantage to examining the credibility of monetary policy in emerging European states is that it limits variation pertaining to regional characteristics. It allows us to exploit quasi-experimental conditions under which these countries, unwinding years of communism, would choose new economic and political institutions and build their reputations from scratch. Furthermore, political integration with the EU, complementing financial integration, distinguishes emerging Europe from other emerging markets.

Chapter 6 looked at the challenges of banking globalization. That chapter studied the 2001 financial crisis in Argentina, the crisis that erupted in the emerging market country hosting Spanish and American banks. I next turned to the 2008 global credit crisis that originated in developed countries of North America and Western Europe, where most multinational banks are headquartered. These crises offered us an opportunity to study the behavior of foreign banks as international lenders of last resort to host countries in times of crisis. Additionally, the chapter looked at the effects of different business models pursued by multinational banks—centralized and decentralized—on their capacity to fulfill the lender-of-last resort function. The data from emerging Europe, Latin America, and Asia presented in chapter 6 suggests that multinational banks articulated a reputational rationale for providing liquidity to their foreign affiliates that equally limited damage to the reputations of the host countries.

The breadth and depth of these empirical tests, across time and space, give credence to my main theoretical prediction. There are certainly other factors that may affect the reputation of countries suffering a credibility deficit on the international stage. Still, this book makes a case for paying attention to reputable multinational banks as enhancers of policy credibility of emerging market governments.

Implications

The theory and evidence presented here have important ramifications for literature on the political consequences of financial globalization. This book offers a more encompassing account of how financial globalization influences policy choices. Most studies tend to cluster the entry of global banks with other components of financial reform or with international capital mobility, and the result has been to obscure the particular implications of banking globalization for less developed countries. While capital account liberalization may be the most visible element of financial globalization, its significance cannot be fully assessed apart from banking sector opening because banks have a broad economic impact and can mobilize a wide range of political actors and interest groups. My argument does not seek to defend financial globalization that is motivated by simplistic free-market ideology. Instead, I identify new, specific mechanisms through which the globalization of banking improves outcomes in emerging markets. I demonstrate that global banks can provide substantial benefits to emerging countries by improving regulatory quality and fostering financial stability by acting like private lenders of last resort. These benefits contrast with the conventional focus of the literature on financial globalization on international risk sharing and efficient international allocation of capital.

The study of multinational bank expansion provides us with a window into some of the most intense political struggles that lie at the heart of financial globalization. This book could inform important policy discussions on banking sector globalization. Why do national governments let foreign banks in? Opening the banking system to foreign capital is a sensitive issue, as it involves ceding to foreigners control over a sector traditionally considered strategic to national economic development. In many postcolonial countries, foreign banks are viewed as representing the economic interests of their shareholders and large multinational corporations from former colonizers at the expense of domestic clients (Andrews 2005). Besides economic nationalism, governments have also used economic arguments in favor of maintaining domestic control over banks. Governments adopted state-led developmental models (such as import-substitution industrialization in Latin America) that required state ownership of banks and directed credit to priority sectors.[1] The underlying assumption has been that domestic banks—embedded in the country's business, political, and social networks—are more susceptible to moral suasion of the government to lend to domestic rather than to foreign enterprises, the latter being considered insensitive to national goals. Also, domestic banks tend to establish longer-term relationships with local industries and provide them with more consistent financing. Barriers to foreign bank entry were relaxed first in developed countries in the 1970s. Then, during the 1990s, many transition and developing countries opened their banking sectors to foreign capital.

This book has investigated the *effects* of the entry of foreign banks, and so fully explaining banking sector opening is not the intention of this book. But the case study evidence presented here confirms some arguments explaining banking sector liberalization identified in the prior literature.[2] One argument is that external factors, such as international institutions and large global banks, applied a mix of structural power and political pressures to coerce governments into dismantling regulatory barriers in finance (Martinez-Diaz 2009). The role of external pressures varies considerably in emerging Europe. International financial institutions seemed to have an important influence on the decision of the Polish socialist government to resume the sales of banks to foreign investors in 1996 after it tried to postpone it. By contrast, while the conditions of the IMF programs in Bulgaria included opening the banking sector, successive Bulgarian governments fell behind those conditions. The IMF, in its effort to encourage the reduction of barriers to foreign entry into the banking sector, has often been considered by borrowing countries to represent the interests of foreign creditors (Nenovsky and Rizopoulos 2003, 918). Similarly, despite strong EU pressures, the Slovenian government was reluctant to sell its state-owned banks to foreigners. The assets of foreign banks accounted for only 21 percent of the Slovenian banking sector in 2004. Thus, in spite of international pressures, governments in emerging Europe appear to have enjoyed considerable room for maneuvering in financial reform policies.

Another important lesson that can be drawn from these empirical observations from emerging Europe is that banking crises can be critical triggers of banking sector liberalization. This finding is in line with Martinez-Diaz (2009), who identifies the banking crisis as a "critical juncture" in financial sector policies in Mexico, Brazil, South Korea, and Indonesia. The crises have large and visible fiscal effects and undermine the credibility of incumbent constituencies. Banking crises are usually associated with massive redistributions from taxpayers to the banks. For instance, the fiscal costs of the banking crises in the 1990s ranged from 7 to 42 percent of the output for the central European countries and between 0.1 and 18 percent in the post-Soviet republics (Tang et al. 2000). Furthermore, countries in crisis are often in greater need of international capital. Hence governments may be inclined to open their banking sectors to foreigners, partially to prevent the use of public funds for bailouts of domestic banks (Andrews 2005, 15). A closer look at economic reform trajectories of Bulgaria and the Czech Republic illustrates this argument. In both countries, severe banking and currency crises in the second half of the 1990s led to shifts in the relative power of domestic groups in a society that strengthened liberalizers at the expense of protectionist interests.[3]

The argument that deep economic crises facilitate the implementation of market-oriented reforms is not a new idea in the literature on the political economy of reforms (Haggard and Kaufman 1995; Pop-Eleches 2009).[4] The copious literature on the political economy of postcommunist transitions established that initial economic crises in Eastern European countries after the collapse of communism was necessary, if not always sufficient, to trigger decisive policy changes (Abdelal 2001; Orenstein 2001; Appel 2004; Frye 2010; Bohle and Greskovits 2012). Cases studies in chapters 4 and 5 lead to the belief that the salience of different crises and national consensus on reforms depend crucially upon domestic political dynamics. Estonian policymakers were determined to quickly establish the credibility of currency board. They opened the banking sector to foreign banks in their effort to keep incumbent banks and firms in check to curb inflation and eliminate a major source of fiscal indiscipline. Estonian nationalism thus manifested itself in liberal financial reforms. By contrast, populist and nationalist agendas of the pre-1997 center-right governments in the Czech Republic included the objective to create national champions by preventing the control of domestic financial institutions by foreigners. Economic nationalism in emerging Europe thus appears to be compatible with both protectionist policies and liberal economic reforms. The case studies in this book also demonstrate that distributional concerns can create strong incentives for policymakers to pursue "partial reforms" (Hellman 1998; McKinnon 1991) in response to pressures from incumbent groups, such as state-owned banks, that are detrimental in the long run.

In addition to domestic-international linkages, this book also highlights the relationship between the public and private sectors. The evidence presented here shows that in the presence of government protection, state-owned banks have often been supporters of discretionary monetary policies because they benefited from high inflation, which eased the burden of bad loans in bank portfolios and allowed banks to pay negative interest rates on deposits. Prior studies in international political economy posit banks as a homogeneous societal group that is uniformly conservative, inflation-averse, and supportive of monetary convergence.[5] A subset of the literature looks specifically at the dichotomy of large versus small banks, suggesting that large banks favor monetary convergence associated with a greater number of banking transactions (Cohen 1993; Hefeker 1997). Others argue that banks' preferences in monetary policy are conditioned by the character of national financial systems and bank-industry ties (Henning 1994). This literature, however, does not make explicit predictions about how the type of ownership might affect banks' preferences and behavior.

The arguments in this book speak to the literature on international development. This book sheds light on the processes of building fundamental market institutions in countries experiencing radical economic and political changes. The Arab Spring has created opportunities for reforms and institution building in countries that are in need of lessons from postcommunist countries so as not to repeat their mistakes. Evidence in this book shows the value of banking globalization for the development of financial systems and monetary stability in less-developed countries. The advice this book would give to policymakers is that if domestic institutions that guarantee financial transparency and regulatory oversight are weak, they may be imported from abroad, through banking integration with reputable global banks. I demonstrate that foreign bankers fundamentally changed ideas about the role of banks and led hands-on efforts to develop modern tools of commercial banking in emerging markets.

The theory presented here also has powerful ramifications for the research on global banking. The existing research has focused on the implications of foreign banks in three areas: resource allocation, efficiency, and degree of competition in the banking sector (Claessens, Demirgüç-Kunt, and Huizinga 2001; Gelos and Roldos 2004; Micco, Panizza, and Yañez 2007); financial development and banking sector stability (De Haas and van Lelyveld 2006; Detragiache and Gupta 2006); and finally, domestic credit creation and access to finance for small, informationally opaque borrowers (Mian 2006; Dages, Goldberg, and Kinney 2000; Detragiache, Tressel, and Gupta 2008, Clarke, Cull, and Martínez Pería 2006). The literature on global banking remains silent on how foreign banks might affect market perceptions of credibility of host governments and their policies. This book demonstrates that multinational banks can herald significant benefits for their host countries in the form of currency (and country) risk well beyond those that are identified by the literature on global banking.

This research is distinctive from other works in the field not only in terms of its theoretical orientation but also empirical coverage. Studies of the reputational effects of financial globalization in transition and emerging-market countries remain modest. At the same time, even though this book focuses on the credibility that reputable foreign banks can give to emerging-market governments, the basic argument can be also extended to advanced democracies to some extent. The findings of this book have particular relevance for several eurozone members, notably Greece, Ireland, and Spain, struggling to rebuild their credibility in international markets after the protracted crisis. Prior to the 2008 crisis, credibility spillovers from monetary policy to sovereign risk led to massive capital inflows to Greece and other eurozone countries that were catching up; this was seen as "as part of a well-functioning monetary union" (Gros and Alcidi 2013, 3). The sudden stop of capital inflows into the peripheral eurozone countries triggered banking and sovereign debt crises that ended the abundant international funding to their governments following their accession into the eurozone. The eurozone crisis, starting in 2010 and continuing thereafter in Greece, provided an unwelcome lesson for the EU that it is institutionally unable to deal with asymmetric shocks (affecting individual member countries differently) within the monetary union. Most banking in the eurozone countries is done by domestic banks, and penetration by foreign banks is low. Thus, when their domestic banks were badly hit by the crisis (for example, Spanish banks by the housing crisis), the affected eurozone countries had to rely solely on "public shock absorbers" such as the European Financial Stability Fund, the European Central Bank, or the IMF (Winkler 2014).

This contrasts with emerging European countries with a substantial foreign bank penetration, where much of the cross-border flows were channeled toward an internal capital market within the same bank, and thus "the incentive for the foreign lenders to withdraw, instead of internalizing losses" in times of crisis was substantially reduced (Gros and Alcidi 2013). Private foreign banks, benefiting from unimpaired access to international financial markets, reduced the vulnerability of emerging European countries to sudden stops of capital (Vogel and Winkler 2012; Gros and Alcidi 2013). Thus, global banks with an affiliate presence in emerging markets have implications for the macroeconomic policy trilemma, which postulates that in financially open economies, the cost of a fixed regime and monetary unions is the loss of monetary autonomy needed to stabilize business cycles. As Goldberg (2013) argues, if a presence of global banks means more stability in the supply of flows of capital in host markets, it can weaken the monetary trilemma.

Extensions

This analysis provides us with a better understanding of the benefits of sound banking and financial stability for monetary credibility. Financial stability, however, is a public good and thus has a distributional consequence. Future research could explore in more detail the distributional consequences of the post-2008 international regulatory harmonization aimed at global financial stability within and among countries. Global regulatory harmonization in banking is necessary to prevent harmful cross-border competition and regulatory arbitrage, but it may provide greater benefits for some societal groups (global banks) and some countries (large countries). Schoenmaker (2013) proposes the "financial trilemma," which takes into consideration the financial stability implications of global banking. The financial trilemma states that a stable financial system, global banking, and national banking supervision are not compatible. The major challenge for an international financial system is how to reconcile the mismatch between financial institutions that operate on a global scale and nationally based financial authorities.

It might be also fruitful to explore the trade-offs between voters and global capital. Research has shown that the relationship between voters and global portfolio investors is complex: if governments respond to voters' demands, they may lose access to cheap foreign funds. Alternatively, governments may pay a high price come election time if they satisfy preferences of international markets (Campello 2015). What remains less clear is how voters perceive reforms in the financial sector involving the entry of global banks. Sales to foreign banks carry political risks that governments have "sold out" (Caprio et al. 2004). Surprisingly, though, the presence of foreign banks has been fairly uncontroversial in most emerging European states. As Juhan Parts, Estonia's former economy minister (quoted in Caprio et al. 2004) remarks, "there are no worries here about losing independence or economic power." The Russian occupation of the Baltic countries for much of the twentieth century makes the presence of Nordic banks seem benign (Dougherty 2009). Foreign banks are important agents and highly trusted institutions in many emerging European nations, where some citizens trust them even more than their public institutions.[6] These banks have become the symbolic anchors not just of the financial system but of whole emerging Europe societies. But the global financial crisis, which illustrated once again the hazard of unfettered global finance, may have increased the attractiveness of economic nationalism and nationalist parties and leaders. Blaming economic hardship on global banks that have taken deposits but have been unwilling to make loans has been a tempting slogan for populist politicians. The electoral victory of Victor Orbán and his party running on a nationalist-populist platform is a prime example.

The goal of this book is to illuminate the complex interactions between multinational banks and national policymaking that characterize the process of financial globalization. The urge to build reputation becomes more constraining to the governments as financial globalization advances and countries become more dependent on mobile financial capital. Ultimately, this work reveals the importance of market confidence in a world of mobile capital.

NOTES

Chapter 1

1. Harrison (1948). I thank Shaun Bowler for suggesting this quote.
2. Marco Rubio, "Ukraine Needs a Lifeline—Now," *Wall Street Journal*, May 6, 2014.
3. To date, few works focus exclusively on the credibility of monetary regimes, making this area grossly understudied. A few notable exceptions include Eichengreen (1992), Svensson (1994), Bordo and Rockoff (1996), Schmukler and Servén (2002), Valev and Carlson (2007), and Bordo and MacDonald (2012).
4. The volume of trade in foreign-exchange markets is enormous and is fast growing. The daily global value of foreign-exchange trading had increased from about $600 billion in April 1989 to $4 trillion in April 2010 (Krugman, Obstfeld, and Melitz 2015, 46).
5. For excellent overviews of the history of the international monetary system, see, e.g., Bordo (2003) and Eichengreen (2008).
6. In some cases, these currency crises triggered banking crises, and in others banking crises led to currency crises. Since banking and currency crisis occur together, the ensuing crises are also called the "twin crises." See Kaminsky and Reinhart (1999).
7. I thank Lawrence Broz for this suggestion.
8. For the historical role of money doctors, see Drake (1994) and Flandreau (2003a).
9. The importance of fiscal policies for exchange rate policies has been underscored by Rose (2011) among others.
10. A different strand of research on transparency suggests that democratic governments collect and release accurate data on the state of the economy to ensure their accountability (Gelos and Wei 2005; Hollyer, Rosendorff, and Vreeland 2011).
11. I am thankful to anonymous reviewer for this interesting observation.
12. The Financial Stability Board is an international body that seeks to promote financial market regulation at the international level.
13. For the list of all global systemically important banks, see Financial Stability Board, "2015 Update of List of Global Systemically Important Banks," November 3,

2015,   http://www.fsb.org/wp-content/uploads/2015-update-of-list-of-global-sys temically-important-banks-G-SIBs.pdf

14. I thank an anonymous reviewer for this comment.

15. See, e.g., Kindleberger and Aliber (2005).

16. I thank Peter Katzenstein for this idea.

17. According to the so-called hollowing-out hypothesis that emerged after the emerging-market crises in the 1990s, countries are expected to abandon the middle ground of exchange rate regimes and pursue either hard pegs of free floats (Eichengreen 1994; Obstfeld and Rogof 1995; Fisher 2001).

18. The existence of capital controls, however, can create a wedge between domestic- and foreign-currency interest rates (Mitchener and Weidenmier 2009).

19. See Klein and Shambaugh (2010) and Levy-Yeyati, Sturzenegger, and Reggio (2010) for recent reviews of the choice and consequences of exchange rate regimes. Grittersová (2014a) surveys research on the exchange rate policies of transition countries.

20. It is worth noting that neither theory nor country experiences provide support for the concept that any exchange rate regime has unambiguous advantages in terms of its impact on long-term macroeconomic performance. See, e.g., Ghosh, Gulde, and Wolf (2002), Klein and Shambaugh (2010), and Rose (2011).

21. The "traditional" theory on optimum currency areas stipulates the circumstances under which it is optimal for a country to surrender its monetary autonomy (Mundell 1961; McKinnon 1963; Kennen 1969; Frankel 1995). The potential benefits of a fixed regime increase as the level of trade and financial integration between two countries increases, but they decrease in the face of asymmetries in exposure to external shocks and when shock absorbers such as labor mobility or fiscal transfers are absent.

22. Rose (2000) finds that countries that share a common currency or have irrevocably fixed exchange rates trade more than three times more among themselves than they do with countries with separate currencies.

23. Friedman (1953) provided a famous argument for the merits of flexible exchange rates.

24. Frieden (1991, 2015) put forward the widely cited sectoral model of exchange rate regime choice, according to which exporters and other groups heavily involved in international trade and investments should favor fixed exchange rate regimes because currency volatility may negatively influence their cross-border business activities. For excellent reviews of the scholarship on the politics of exchange rate policy, see Broz and Frieden (2001) and Bernhard, Broz, and Clark (2003).

25. On the legacies of communism, see Hanson (1995), Bunce (2003), and Hanson and Ekiert (2003).

26. In the monetary realm, most countries of Eastern Europe started the postcommunist transition with nonconvertible currencies and large black exchange rate premiums, which are considered to be indicators that devaluation may occur (de Melo et al. 2001, 8).

27. For the development of financial systems in Eastern European countries see

Johnson (2000), Berglöf and Bolton (2002), McDermott (2007), Denizer, Desai, and Gueorguiev (2006). On how a transnational central banking community guided the transformation of postcommunist central banks see Johnson (2016).

Chapter 2

1. See Grubel's (1977) seminal adaptation of the theory of multinational corporations to the study of multinational banking.
2. Multinational banking is distinguished from international banking. The latter does not require a physical offshore presence (branches and subsidiaries). International banks serve foreign markets through cross-border banking flows.
3. Chapter 6 goes into detail about the implications of business models for the lender-of-last-resort functions of parent banks.
4. For the history of multinational banking, see, e.g., Jones (1993, 2012) and Schoenmaker (2013).
5. German banks, in their "fight for financial supremacy" (Einzig 1931, 26–48), were particularly aggressive in imitating the British model of overseas banking in South America, in southern and eastern Europe, and in the Near East (Battilossi 2006, 363). In another example, 70 percent of foreign branches of French banks were concentrated in peripheral Europe and the Near East (Battilossi 2006, 367).
6. A senior official at Société Générale was forthcoming about the profitability of investments in Eastern European banking sectors: "The acquisition of the Czech Komerční banka was the most successful investment of the banking group." Chief economist at Société Générale, interview with the author, December 20, 2013, Paris.
7. Chief economist at Société Générale, interview with the author, December 20, 2013, Paris.
8. A standard definition in the empirical literature states that a bank is considered to be foreign owned if foreigners own 50 percent or more of its shares.
9. Only eleven countries had no foreign bank in 2009: Cuba, Ethiopia, Haiti, Iceland, Iran, Libya, Oman, Qatar, Saudi Arabia, Sri Lanka, and Yemen (Claessens and van Horen 2012).
10. For the link between foreign investments in banking and the internationalization of nonfinancial firms, see Grosse and Goldberg (1991) and Buch (2000).
11. For cross-border banking in Europe, see Allen et al. (2011).
12. For reviews of the literature on monetary policy credibility see, e.g., Blackburn and Christensen (1989) and Cottarelli and Giannini (1997).
13. I recognize that many factors could influence how governments perceive the costs and benefits of inflation stabilization, including the political strength of incumbents and interest groups and the time horizons of policymakers. Although the sources of preferences of governments are interesting in their own right, they are not the focus of this book.
14. Edwards (2005), analyzing the role of foreign advisors in the stabilization program in Chile in the mid-1950s, argues that although advisors of the Klein-Saks

Mission provided initial credibility to the Chilean program of inflation stabilization, this was not enough to ensure the program's success because the Chilean congress reneged on its promise to reduce fiscal imbalances.

15. Monetary models that incorporate uncertainty are based on the work of Kreps and Wilson (1982) and Milgrom and Roberts (1982).

16. Likewise, in situations of default and debt settlement in sovereign debt markets, lenders' knowledge about government preferences is often incomplete at the time a loan is made (Tomz 2007, 11).

17. Blackburn and Christensen (1989, 2) identify additional constraints on credibility building that may be pertinent for emerging markets. First are the technological constraints, which are a function of the unreliability of national statistics and forecasts. The second group includes administrative and political constraints associated with the ability of a government to carry through with necessary legislation and the government's vulnerability to political pressures.

18. Political instability often leads governments to discount the future (Stasavage and Guillaume 2002). Edwards (1996) shows that countries with frequent changes of government tend to renege on fixed-exchange-rate regimes more frequently.

19. According to one influential argument (Tornell and Velasco 2000), however, fixed exchange rate regimes can instigate a lax fiscal policy that can eventually lead to a costly collapse of the peg. In contrast, under floats, fiscal indiscipline can be revealed sooner.

20. Examples of exchange-rate-based stabilizations from hyperinflation over the past two decades include Argentina, Bolivia, Israel, Mexico, and several Eastern European countries.

21. On the incomplete credibility of fixed exchange rate regimes, see also Drazen and Masson (1994), Obstfeld (1997), and Irwin (2004).

22. The rising power of organized labor and universal suffrage forced central banks to be concerned about employment and output consequences of rigid monetary policies that were essential for maintaining the convertibility of gold after World War I (Eichengreen 1992; Simmons 1994).

23. Empirical research on exchange-rate-based stabilization programs shows a rapid decrease in inflation from high to moderate levels but a slow disinflation after that. See Bruno (1993), Calvo and Végh (1994).

24. As an alternative, countries may pursue money-based stabilization programs when the anchor of stabilization is the money supply or interest rates.

25. My analysis does not focus on why a government chooses to adopt an exchange rate anchor in its inflation stabilization program or on the distributional consequences of such programs. I do not explore the costs and benefits of stabilization programs for societal groups or how a government overcomes the opposition of entrenched interest groups. Governments often choose to adopt an exchange rate peg even when it involves high political costs (such as a reduced ability to respond to external shocks) (Canavan and Tommasi 1997).

26. For the dynamic political economy models of the credibility of disinflation programs, see Guidotti and Végh (1999).

27. I draw inspiration from and build upon studies of external sources of policy credibility. See Drake (1994), Dhonte (1997), Cottarelli and Giannini (1997), Edwards (2003), Flandreau (2003b), Gros (2003), and Flandreau and Flores (2009, 2012).

28. Drazen and Masson (1994) make a useful distinction between a policymaker's credibility and the credibility of its policies. Even if the type of policymaker is not in doubt, policymakers are sometimes forced to renege on their monetary commitments due to economic factors (e.g., if the unemployment rate dramatically increases). As a consequence, international markets do not automatically reward policymakers "tying their own hands" by fixing the exchange rate because the sustainability of their policy commitments depends on a country's political and economic conditions and prospects.

29. Credibility here is more in the spirit of Dornbusch's (1991) model, in which the credibility of the fixed exchange rate is conditional on a level of foreign exchange reserves sufficient to prevent a balance-of-payments crisis. Here the government devalues its currency and reneges on its monetary commitments because of the exhaustion of its reserves rather than because the benefits of doing so outweigh the costs. This contrasts with Barro and Gordon's (1983) time-inconsistency model.

30. This contrasts with earlier literature that focused predominantly on monetary and fiscal coordination. See Persson and Tabellini (2000) for a review.

31. The goals of financial stability and monetary stability may be in conflict. On the one hand, bailouts to banks to avoid banking crises may compromise the goal of maintaining price stability. On the other hand, through the level of interest rates, monetary policy influences the incentives for banks to take risks (i.e., low interest rates may create incentives for short-term loans in foreign currencies) and thus financial stability (Alesina and Stella 2010, 1025).

32. Credit reporting institutions can be classed as public or private. A public credit registry is established and managed by a central bank or a bank supervisor. All supervised financial institutions are required to participate in the public credit registry and to exchange credit information on borrowers. In contrast, private credit bureaus are created by banks and are voluntarily supported by their members. Public and private credit reporting systems play complementary roles.

33. The entry of U.S. banks into Mexico led to improvements in banking supervision and accounting standards there through the emergence of accounting and auditing firms and credit bureaus (Levine 2001). Similarly, the Belgian KBC and the Swedish Skandinaviska Enskilda Banken helped develop credit-evaluation systems based on financial statements in their Eastern European subsidiaries, and the Austrian Erste and Raiffeisen, the Belgian KBC, the Swedish Sampobank, and Skandinaviska Enskilda Banken created credit-scoring systems for small firms that were trying to obtain credit from their subsidiaries in emerging Europe (De Haas and Naaborg 2006).

34. Information sharing is particularly important in countries with weak company laws and creditors' rights because lax accounting and disclosure standards increase the cost of screening potential clients and poor legal protection makes loan contracts difficult to enforce (Brown, Jappelli, and Pagano 2009).

35. Associate director at Standard & Poor's, interview with the author, December 20, 2014, Paris, France.

36. Regulatory and supervisory policies that influence sound banking include restrictions on bank activities and on the mixing of banking and commerce, regulations on domestic and foreign bank entry, capital adequacy standards, a deposit insurance system, a stringent loan classification system, and actions for resolving the problems of troubled banks. See Barth, Caprio, and Levine (2002). The 2008 crisis brought the recognition that banking regulation cannot be based solely on the soundness of individual banks (a microprudential policy). Macroprudential regulation and supervision, which requires regulators to consider systemic risk associated with the activities of individual banks, is equally important for reducing the risk of financial instability. But there is still confusion about what constitutes macroprudential regulation and its institutional framework and a lack of agreement about the scope of financial regulation. For recent reviews, see Claessens (2014) and Freixas, Laeven, and Peydró (2015).

37. Rousseau and Sylla (2003) identify five components of a good financial system: sound public finance and debt management; stable money; a variety of banks, some with domestic and others with international orientations; a central bank to act as a lender of last resort and to manage international financial relations; and a well-functioning securities market. For the link between financial system development and exchange rate policies, see Bordo and Flandreau (2003), Domaç and Martínez Pería (2003), and Aghion et al. (2009).

38. Home country regulations that are applicable to a bank holding company affect the operations of its subsidiaries located in foreign countries (Cardenas, Graf, and O'Dogherty 2003). Furthermore, because foreign subsidiaries operate in riskier economic environments, they usually face higher capital and reserve requirements than branches do (Cerutti, Dell'Ariccia, and Martínez Pería 2007, 1675).

39. Banking supervision may depend on whether the foreign entry is accomplished through branches or subsidiaries. A branch is an integral part of the foreign group and is not a stand-alone alone entity and is thus subject to the home country's supervisory authorities. A subsidiary is a separate entity from its parent bank. According to the Basel Concordat of 1975, host- and parent-country supervisory authorities are jointly responsible for the supervision and solvency of subsidiaries. Although in theory branches and subsidiaries involve a different parent-bank responsibility and liquidity assistance, in practice the difference between them is often blurred. For a discussion of branches versus subsidiaries, see Tschoegl (2003) and Cerutti, Dell'Ariccia, and Martínez Pería (2007).

40. According to political theories, governments own banks so they can finance politically desirable projects without having to take into account the economic viability of those projects in exchange for votes, political contributions, and bribes. The empirical literature in finance demonstrates that widespread state ownership of banks is associated with high volumes of bad loans, poor protection of property rights, and financial instability. See Shleifer and Vishny (1998); La Porta, Lopez-de-Silanes, and Shleifer (2002); Sapienza (2002); Caprio et al. (2004); Andrews (2005); and Grittersová (2009).

41. Drazen and Masson (1994) suggest that, contrary to conventional wisdom, devaluation in the face of shocks can paradoxically improve policy credibility. If the government does not devalue its currency when the economy deteriorates, expectations that it will do so in the following period increase.

42. The theory of "lender of last resort" was first developed by Henry Thorton in 1802 and later refined by Walter Bagehot (1873). According to the famous Bagehot principle, the lender of last resort should "lend freely at a high rate against good collateral." For a recent review of the literature on the lender of last resort, see Goodhart and Illing (2002).

43. Note that this list includes global banks and banks whose international operations are less sizeable.

44. The effect of the democratic advantage on credibility in sovereign debt markets has been well-documented. Representative political institutions in democracies that limit executive discretion have been shown to improve a nation's access to credit and to lower risk premiums (North and Weingast 1989; Schultz and Weingast 2003; Stasavage 2007, 2011). On the links between democratic institutions and sovereign credit ratings, see Butler and Fauver (2006), Biglaiser and Staats (2012), and Beaulieu, Cox, and Saiegh (2012).

45. Nenovsky and Mihaylova (2007) argue that in Bulgaria (and in several other Eastern European countries), inflation has served as a major tool for redistributing debt from debtors (crony banks and enterprises) to creditors (the population) through the central bank. Debtors with debt in domestic currency benefited from high inflation because it reduced the real cost of servicing their debt. In contrast, inflation depreciated the savings of the population, the main creditor.

46. For instance, within the European Monetary System, countries such as Italy and Spain suffered from decreased competitiveness because their rates of inflation were higher than that of Germany, the anchor country, but they were unable to devalue their currencies. This undermined and led to the eventual collapse of this monetary arrangement. See De Grauwe (1994) and Knot, Sturm, and De Haan (1998).

47. Scholars also found evidence that the IMF has given preferential treatment to its geopolitical allies and important trading partners of its largest shareholders. See, e.g., Thacker (1999).

Chapter 3

1. The forward discount is another method of measuring the currency risk (Schmukler and Servén 2002). Unfortunately, consistent cross-country data with adequate time coverage do not exist.

2. In addition to interest rate targets, the credibility of the counterinflation reputation of national monetary authorities can be assessed by focusing on monetary targets or exchange rate targets (Weber 1991).

3. Data on foreign bank ownership are available only on annual basis. Thus, I am unable to conduct statistical tests employing high-frequency (for example, monthly or weekly) interest rates. In the case studies in subsequent chapters, I use monthly data.

4. Linda Goldberg generously provided the data on short-term interest rates.

5. The uncovered interest rate parity holds for countries with lower per capita income, higher inflation uncertainty, and lower credit ratings.

6. See also Schmukler and Servén (2002) and Mitchener and Weidenmier (2009).

7. It appears that the forward premium is equal to interest rate differentials in tranquil periods. Interest rate parity breaks down only during the financial turmoil (Rivera-Batiz and Sy 2013, 826).

8. A common problem underlying this approach is that interest differentials reflect both the expected inflation differentials and the default risk (a higher risk of default on a debt instrument means that investors will demand a higher interest rate in compensation). To cope with this problem, I use money market rates that are very short-term and on which the default risk is minimal. I am thankful to Barry Eichengreen for this remark.

9. It should be noted, however, that interest rate levels depend on the structure and development of the financial system (how competitive it is) and on inflation expectations. I thank Barry Eichengreen for this remark.

10. The Balassa-Samuelson effect means that in less-developed countries, as productivity and wages in the traded goods sector increase, so too do wages in the nontradable sectors, putting pressures on the national price level.

11. I thank Barry Eichengreen for this suggestion.

12. This measure is appropriate if the number of domestic and foreign banks determines the competition in the banking sector. Domestic banks may want to adjust their interest rates on loans and other activities to prevent foreign banks from capturing a large market share. See Claessens, Demirgüç-Kunt, and Huizinga (2001, 895–97). Prominent scholars in international banking have used this measure; see, for example, Goldberg (2013).

13. Almost half of the foreign banks in the region come from the United Kingdom, France, and South Africa (Claessens et al. 2008, 10).

14. Calvo and Reinhart (2002) show that many countries that officially claim to run floats actually intervene frequently in their foreign exchange markets to reduce exchange-rate volatility, even though the monetary authorities in these countries have no official commitment to maintaining parity. These authors dubbed this behavior as "fear of floating." On the other hand, Levy-Yeyati and Sturzenegger (2005) suggest that countries that frequently adjust the central parity can make an officially fixed regime resemble a flexible one, thus manifesting a "fear of pegging" behavior.

15. I focus on the country's de facto exchange rate regime as an endogenously determined variable.

16. Ilzetzki, Reinhart, and Rogoff (2008) have created a separate category for countries whose monthly inflation rate is above 40 percent; they classify such exchange rate regimes as "freely falling." Following standard practice, I discard the observations of free-falling and dual-market regimes because no secondary classification is available.

17. Data generously provided by Cristina Bodea and Raymond Hicks.

18. Axel Dreher generously shared this data.

19. See Eichengreen, Rose, and Wyplosz (1995), Frankel and Rose (1996), and Kaminsky, Lizondo and Reinhart (1998) for the factors that undermine the credibility of monetary regimes.

20. Regressions using the log of inflation rate yield similar results.

21. In the robustness checks, I also examined the impact of transparency in the political system in engendering low inflation expectations. I use the POLITY2 score from the Polity IV database, which combines the scores on the democracy and autocracy indices into an aggregate regime indicator. The index of democracy ranges from –10 (most autocratic) to +10 (consolidated democracy). The specifications that include the democracy variable (not reported here) yield nearly identical results. See http://www.systemicpeace.org/polity/polity4.htm

22. I ran the Breusch-Pagan Lagrange multiplier test to decide between using a simple OLS regression model or a random effects model. There is evidence of significant difference across countries, which implies that the data cannot be pooled.

23. The estimates obtained from the specifications that include monetary regimes may be plagued by the problem of regime selection. The decision about what type of monetary regime to implement may be made endogenously. The impact of monetary regimes should be thus interpreted cautiously. Following Rose (2014), I estimated (but not reported) the instrumental variable regression using the log of population and POLITY 2 from the Polity IV database as instruments.

24. As a robustness check, I use Goldberg's (2013) definition of soft pegs, where exchange rate bands are between plus or minus 2 percent and plus and minus 5 percent. I repeated the empirical analysis using several alternative definitions and groupings of exchange rate regimes. The main findings remained unchanged. The results are available upon request.

25. I thank Linda Goldberg for graciously sharing the data with me.

26. I thank an anonymous reviewer for pointing this out. I also controlled for external debt as a share of GDP because countries that are financially weak or are at the mercy of international capital markets tend to be more responsive to changes in the interest rates in base countries (Shambaugh 2004). The results are available upon request.

27. There are some important differences between Walter's (2013) analysis and mine. Walter seeks to explain the variation in governments' adjustment strategies, including decisions to adjust economic policies in response to economic distress and the type of adjustment they choose (internal or external devaluation). In contrast, I seek to explain the credibility of monetary policies. The continuous commitment of four governments in emerging Europe that Walter examined—Estonia, Latvia, Lithuania, and Bulgaria—to exchange rate stability during the 2008 crisis is not surprising when it is viewed through the lens of my argument. Levels of foreign bank participation were high in three countries with currency boards: the share of banking sector assets held by foreign banks was 99 percent in Estonia, 93 percent in Lithuania, and 92 percent in Bulgaria (Claessens and van Horen 2014). It is worthwhile to note that my theory explains both the incentive for governments to remain

committed to hard pegs (that is, to refrain from devaluing currency) and their ability to sustain these monetary arrangements. In my framework, multinational banks have proven instrumental in reassuring financial markets of the credibility of monetary commitments of emerging European governments by remaining committed to these economies and by providing the necessary capital to their affiliates. In doing so, foreign parent banks limited the size of sudden stops of capital that could have jeopardized the stability of monetary regimes of their hosts. Walter (2013, 189, note 7) acknowledges the benefits of the coordinated and continued commitment and support of Nordic parent banks to their subsidiaries in the Baltic states.

28. Credit growth is an important predictor of financial crises (Schularick and Taylor 2012).

29. Data comes from the IMF's World Economic Outlook.

30. I thank an anonymous reviewer for these suggestions.

31. Another measure of the presence of multinational banks is the share of banking assets foreign banks hold in each country. Claessens and van Horen (2014), however, report the share of total banking assets held by foreign banks only from 2004. Van Horen explained that asset data is missing for many banks prior to 2004. Also many banks switched to a different accounting system in 2004. In any case, the quality of data on ownership shares before 2004 is dubious because too many banks have not provided balance sheet information and asset data is missing for these banks. Neeltje van Horen, senior economist at the Research Department of De Nederlandsche Bank (and coauthor of the database on foreign banks used in this book), e-mail correspondence with author, August 22, 2015.

32. The results of these robustness checks are available upon request.

33. The database of financial reforms covers ninety-one countries over the period from 1973 to 2005. It addresses seven dimensions of financial policy: credit controls and reserve requirements, interest rate controls, barriers to entry for domestic and foreign banks, state ownership in the banking sector, restrictions on capital accounts, prudential banking regulation and supervision, and securities markets policies.

34. Chief economist at Société Générale, interview with the author, December 20, 2013, Paris.

35. Data generously provided by Ugo Panizza.

36. I do not include the fiscal balance because it may be influenced by sovereign bond spreads and thus may be an endogenous variable (Rojas-Suárez and Sotelo 2007).

37. I thank Benjamin Graham for sharing the International Country Risk Guide data with me.

38. As a robustness check (not reported here), I added the Volatility Index (VIX) of the Chicago Board Options Exchange measuring the implied volatility from option contracts on the S&P 100 as a control for global risk aversion.

39. I thank Armand Fouejieu and Scott Roger for sharing their data with me.

40. The data on ten-year government bond yields come from the Global Financial Database. See https://www.globalfinancialdata.com. I obtained the data on three-year government bond spreads from Julia Gray.

41. The results of these robustness checks are not reported here but are available upon request.

Chapter 4

1. For the role of foreign economic advisers in Latin America, see Drake (1994).

2. The key element of banking sector reforms in emerging Europe has been the divestiture of state assets in the banking sector through privatization to foreign strategic investors instead of simple openness to foreign greenfield banks.

3. Price liberalization at the outset of transition resulted in high inflation, but the worst hyperinflation in the early 1990s—57,000 percent per annum in Georgia—was driven by war finance.

4. For the initial economic conditions in Eastern Europe after the collapse of communism, see De Melo et al. (2001) and Fisher and Sahay (2000).

5. My discussion of the history and functioning of currency boards draws on Williamson (1995), Hanke (2002), and Valev and Carlson (2007).

6. Ghosh, Gulde, and Wolf (2002) find that inflation differentials are lower in currency board systems than in other types of monetary regimes.

7. In the second half of the 1980s, only 2 to 3 percent of Estonia's exports went outside the Soviet Union (Kukk 1997, 262).

8. Savisaar was the leader of the Popular Front, an opposition mass movement with sixty thousand members that was established in 1988. It was to fulfill the program of economic self-management (the Isemajandav Eesti, known as IME, was the Estonian word for miracle) that was designed to move Estonia away from the Soviet Union. See Terk (2000), Kallas and Sôrg (1994), and Knöbl, Sutt, and Zavoico (2002).

9. The BOE was founded in February 1919 when Estonia first gained its independence, but it was closed in June 1941 after the Soviet Union annexed the country.

10. For the role of economic nationalism in monetary reforms in Estonia and other Baltic states, see Abdelal (2001).

11. Mart Laar, prime minister of Estonia (1992–1994, 1999–2002), interview with the author, July 19, 2007, Tallinn, Estonia.

12. The BOE was granted extensive powers in economic reforms. It had the authority to "determine the time of monetary reform, [and] what to do with the Estonian financial system, taxes, debt, securities, pensions, wages, fines, foreign trade and with the USSR armed forces [in Estonia]" (Buyske 1997, 82).

13. Mart Laar, prime minister of Estonia (1992–1994, 1999–2002), interview with the author, July 19, 2007, Tallinn, Estonia.

14. Hansson later advised prime ministers Vähi and Laar (Feldmann and Sally 2002).

15. The Foreign Currency Act, the Currency Act, and the Act on the Security of the Estonian Kroon entered into force and established the Estonian currency as the sole legal tender and the principles of the currency board arrangement. See http://www.eestipank.ee/en/eesti-pank/history-eesti-pank

16. An alternative proposal, inspired by the experience of 1918, was that the Finnish currency be used alongside the Estonian one (Laar 2002, 109).

17. Ulo Kaasik, deputy governor of the BOE, interview with the author, July 18, 2008, Tallinn, Estonia.

18. For a comparison of experiences with currency boards in Estonia, Lithuania, and Bulgaria, see Berensmann (2002) and Nenovsky, Hristov, and Mihaylov (2002).

19. But full backing of the BOE liabilities was achieved within a month following further gold restitution from Sweden and the Bank of International Settlements ($45 million) (Knöbl, Sutt, and Zavoico 2002, 14 note 30). Before the occupation in 1940, Estonia had more than 11 tons of gold abroad: 4.8 tons in the United Kingdom, 2.9 tons in Sweden, and 3.3 tons in Switzerland in the Bank for International Settlements (Kallas and Sörg 1994, 8-9).

20. Mart Laar, prime minister of Estonia (1992-1994, 1999-2002), interview with the author, July 19, 2007, Tallinn, Estonia.

21. Although the IMF's Memorandum of Financial and Economic Policies from April 1992 suggested a freely floating regime, the IMF eventually issued the last-minute statement of support one day before the currency was introduced. See "Joint Statement by the Government of Estonia and the IMF on Currency Reform," IMF News Brief 92/16, 19 June 1992, reproduced in Knöbl, Sutt, and Zavoico (2002, 23).

22. Hannson and Sachs (1992) argue that the IMF was concerned that Estonia was not ready to introduce its national currency.

23. Mart Laar, prime minister of Estonia (1992-1994, 1999-2002), interview with the author, July 19, 2007, Tallinn, Estonia.

24. On trade liberalization in Estonia, see Feldmann and Sally (2002).

25. In its efforts to disassociate itself from Russia and communism, Laar's government publicly proclaimed a "housecleaning" campaign that successfully used radical economic reforms to break up the pre-independence nomenklatura coalition of state and party bureaucrats and managers of state-owned banks and enterprises (Steen and Ruus 2002, 237).

26. The government also introduced a flat income tax of 26 percent and eliminated state subsidies in order to limit redistribution policies and balance the budget.

27. Yet the Estonian government did not provide selective incentives (e.g., tax holidays) for specific foreign investors and did not implement an activist industrial policy (Feldmann and Sally 2002).

28. Mart Laar, prime minister of Estonia (1992-1994, 1999-2002), interview with the author, July 19, 2007, Tallinn, Estonia.

29. Ibid.

30. Argeo Ideon, "Estonia: Monetary Reform, Hard Style," Siim Kallas, president of the Bank of Estonia, interview in *The Baltic Review* 1, no. 3 (1993): 40-41.

31. In 1993, the government attempted to unify the budgets of the government and the central bank. The likely outcome would have been that any surplus in the BOE's budget would have been available to the government, which would have severely restricted central bank independence (Sörg 1994, 10).

32. A condition for the renewal of banking licenses was that a bank had to have a minimum of ECU 5 million equity capital. In 1993, new prudential requirements were established, including capital adequacy ratio of 8 percent, liquidity ratio of 30 percent, and the maximum loan to a client not exceeding 50 percent of the bank's equity (Sõrg 1998, 173–74).

33. The root cause of the bank's problems was connected lending to small shell enterprises. The bank's owners were distributing large loans among themselves at very low interest rates (Laar 2002, 193; Sõrg 1998, 174).

34. The yield of a bond is the annual income of a bond as a percentage of its market price. Investors demand higher yields from more risky borrowers.

35. *Euromoney*, June 1993, 164.

36. The American Bank of the Baltics was granted a license in 1992 and INKO Baltic Bank, a subsidiary of the Ukrainian bank, was granted one in 1994 (Sorg and Uiboupin 2004, 266).

37. Loan losses reached 6 percent of total loans in Norway in 1991, 4.7 percent in Finland in 1992, and 7 percent in Sweden in 1992. It is worth noting that Swedish authorities also hired foreign (mainly U.S.) investment bankers to help them address the banking crisis in the 1990s (Ingves et al. 2009, 8).

38. In the years after the first banking crisis, Estonian banks began to expand their activities into Russia, Ukraine, and other Baltic states, where interest rates and profitability were higher. Hansapank was the most successful. It established an extensive network of subsidiaries and acquired a control of 25 percent of the banking assets of Baltic countries (Ådahl 2002). Western foreign banks were still not interested in entering those markets.

39. Chairman of the Management Board of the Estonian Financial Supervision Authority, interview with the author, July 17, 2007, Tallinn.

40. The independence of the BOE was already high in 1993 (0.73), but it increased to 0.88 in 2003 (where 1 stands for the highest level of independence) (Arnone et al. 2007; Cukierman, Miller, and Neyapti 2002).

41. Ulo Kaasik, deputy governor of the BOE, interview with the author, July 18, 2008, Tallinn, Estonia.

42. Ådahl (2002) points to the "too small to fail" problem. Because Estonian banks are small compared to their parent banks, they pose a relatively small threat to financial stability in Nordic countries. The Nordic supervisory authorities may thus have weak incentives to assume responsibility for supervising the systemic risks in the Estonian banking sector. This increases the need for Estonian supervisory authorities to keep track of the financial strength of parent banks.

43. The Estonian authorities deeply resented the involvement of international financial institutions in domestic politics. After all, they had adopted the currency board against the IMF's advice. As Prime Minister Laar said, "If we do not cut the budget, Estonia would become the 'serf' of the IMF" (quoted in Raudla and Kattel 2011, 175).

44. Senior researcher at the Institute of Economics of the Bulgarian Academy of Sciences, interview with the author, June 27, 2007, Sofia, Bulgaria.

45. The political change in Bulgaria began in November 1989, when communist leader Todor Zivkov was ousted in a palace coup after ruling for eighteen years. The Communist Party, which was renamed the BSP, secured an absolute majority of 211 of 400 seats in the 1990 elections (Vachudova 2005, 42).

46. The UDF, which merged historic social democratic and Christian democratic parties, ecological movements, a trade union, and religious and human rights groups, announced its existence in November 1989. In the 1991 election, it won 110 seats (Vachudova 2005, 40).

47. Lena Roussenova, member of the Governing Council of the BNB, interview with the author, June 22, 2007, Sofia, Bulgaria.

48. Kalin Hristov, deputy governor of the BNB, interview with the author, June 21 and 27, 2007, Sofia, Bulgaria.

49. Former deputy governor of the BNB, interview with the author, June 26 and July 2, 2007, Sofia, Bulgaria.

50. Former deputy governor of the BNB and chairman of the currency board, interview with the author, June 28, 2007, Sofia, Bulgaria.

51. The BNB was established in 1897. Its first governor was an official at the Ministry of Finance in Russia. The BNB was not able to adhere to the gold standard because it lacked sufficient gold reserves and its war finance policies were inflationary. On the history of the BNB, see Avramov (1999).

52. In the late 1980s, the government established sector-specific banks (owned by sectoral ministries, the largest enterprises in their sectors, and the BNB) that could only lend to particular sectors. For example, Biohim Bank provided credit exclusively to the chemical industry. See Miller and Petranov (2000) and Barnes (2007).

53. Former member of the Managing Board of the BNB, interview with the author, June 24, 2007, Sofia, Bulgaria.

54. Lubomir Christov, chief economist and member of the Managing Board of the BNB (1991–1994), interview with the author, June 29, 2007, Sofia, Bulgaria.

55. Kalin Hristov, deputy governor of the BNB, interview with the author, June 21 and 27, 2007, Sofia, Bulgaria.

56. For instance, the infamous businessman Valentin Mollow used money from DSK to create his own First Private Bank, then took a loan from this new bank to establish another private bank, Mollow Commercial Bank (Barnes 2007, 78–82).

57. In 1991, the capital requirement for licensing a commercial bank was $500,000 and there were no regulatory prerequisites concerning the origins of the funds (Vincelette 2001).

58. Kalin Hristov, deputy governor of the BNB, interview with the author, June 21 and 27, 2007, Sofia, Bulgaria.

59. The patron of Multigroup was former prime minister Andrei Lukanov. The group later developed ties with the Berov government, which was nicknamed the "Multigroup government" (Barnes 2007).

60. Economist at the United Bulgarian Bank and a former official in the Banking Supervision Department of the BNB, interview with the author, June 25, 2007, Sofia, Bulgaria; financial journalist at the *Capital Weekly*, interview with the author, June 25, 2007, Sofia, Bulgaria.

61. Senior economist and researcher at the Center for Liberal Studies, interview with the author, June 29, 2007, Sofia, Bulgaria.

62. Lubomir Christov, chief economist and Member of the Managing Board of the BNB (1991–1994), interview with the author, June 29, 2007, Sofia, Bulgaria.

63. As an illustration, under the so-called Bulbank scheme, the Ministry of Finance paid Bulbank (a legal successor of the Bulgarian Foreign Trade Bank) $200 million for ZUNK bonds with a face value of $400 million.

64. Because of its role in bank refinancing, the BNB was often called the Ministry of Banking. Economist at the United Bulgarian Bank and a former official in the Banking Supervision Department of the BNB, interview with the author, June 25, 2007, Sofia, Bulgaria.

65. At times the BNB tried to push back against the government's attempts to infringe on its independence. For instance, in mid-1992, when the Ministry of Finance stopped paying interest on government debt, the BNB imposed a temporary halt on extending transfers of funds to the government, provoking an intense institutional conflict. However, the dispute was eventually settled to the detriment of the independence of the BNB. See Christov (1997).

66. Former deputy government of the BNB, interview with the author, June 26 and July 2, 2007, Sofia, Bulgaria.

67. Nikolay Nenovsky, member of the Governing Council of the BNB (2002–2008), interview with the author, June 26, 2007, Sofia, Bulgaria.

68. Lubomir Christov, chief economist and Member of the Managing Board of the BNB (1991–1994), interview with the author, June 29, 2007, Sofia, Bulgaria.

69. Senior economist and researcher at the Center for Liberal Studies, June 29, 2007, Sofia, Bulgaria. See also Dobrinsky (2000, 585).

70. Former BNB deputy governor Harsev harshly criticized the IMF's policy of high interest rates. For him, interest rate increases did not work because economic actors anticipated inflation and incorporated calculations adjusted to higher inflation when they priced their products. Former deputy governor of the BNB, interview with the author, July 2, 2007, Sofia, Bulgaria.

71. Lena Roussenova, member of the Governing Council of the BNB, June 22, 2007, Sofia, Bulgaria.

72. In contrast to the 1997 Asian financial crisis, the Bulgarian crisis was a closed-economy crisis. Capital outflows were very small (about $240 million) because there were no substantial capital inflows (Berlemann and Nenovsky 2004, 261). On the Bulgarian financial crisis see Dobrinsky (2000) and Berlemann, Hristov and Nenovsky (2002); on the banking crisis, see Ignatiev (2005).

73. The IMF first launched the idea of a currency board in 1994, but the timing was not right because of upcoming elections. Former member of the Managing Board of the BNB, interview with the author, June 24, 2007, Sofia, Bulgaria.

74. IMF managing director Stanley Fisher was initially critical of a currency board, but the successful experience of Estonia gradually convinced IMF representatives that a hard peg is an efficient stabilization tool (Stone 2002, 224).

75. Lena Roussenova, member of the Governing Council of the BNB, interview with the author, June 22, 2007, Sofia, Bulgaria.

76. The Bulgarian currency board, the strategy of banking sector opening, and the program of fiscal reforms were designed by the Charles Enoch, deputy director of the IMF's Monetary and Financial Systems Department. Former deputy governor of the BNB, interview with the author, June 26 and July 2, 2007, Sofia, Bulgaria.

77. See IMF, A Paper on Bulgaria's Request for a Stand-by Arrangement, EBS/96/116, July 5, 1996; and IMF, A Paper on the Request of the Government of Bulgaria for a Stand-By-Arrangement and Request for Purchase under the Compensatory and Contingency Financing Facility, EBS/97/53, April 3, 1997. In author's possession.

78. Initially, there was a considerable opposition to the currency-board-based program on all sides of the political spectrum and within the BNB, mostly on sovereignty grounds. Former deputy governor of the BNB and chairman of the currency board, interview with the author, June 28, 2007, Sofia, Bulgaria; former member of the Managing Board of the BNB, interview with the author, June 24, 2007, Sofia, Bulgaria.

79. Stefan Sofiyanski (UDF), the mayor of Sofia, led a nonpartisan caretaker government.

80. After the euro was introduced, the exchange rate was fixed at 1 euro=1.96 lev.

81. In 1994, only two branches of foreign banks operated in Bulgaria: Greek Xios Bank and the Dutch ING Bank. The BNP-Dresdner Bank (Germany) and the Ionian Bank (UK) opened branches in 1995.

82. See Caporale et al. (2002) on banking reforms in Bulgaria and Koford and Tschoegl (2003) on the history of foreign banks in Bulgaria.

83. The management of Bulbank fought the government's efforts to privatize the bank. In response, the government initially promised bank managers 2 to 3 percent of bank shares in exchange for their support for privatization, but then it sold most shares to UniCredit. Senior economist and researcher at the Center for Liberal Studies, interview with the author, June 29, 2007, Sofia, Bulgaria.

84. Former deputy governor of the BNB, interview with the author, June 26 and July 2, 2007, Sofia, Bulgaria.

85. Data comes from the *Global Financial Data*. See https://www.globalfinancialdata.com

86. https://www.fitchratings.com/site/pressrelease?id=838115&origin=home

87. The Communist Party's successor, the Estonian Left, made only a brief appearance in Parliament after the 1999 elections. The Center Party, led by Savisar, offered a leftist alternative to the losers of the transition. Professor of political science at the University of Tartu, interview with the author, July 20, 2007, Tallinn, Estonia.

88. The Coalition Party of the first prime minister, Tiit Vähi, in alliance with the Agrarian Rural People's Union, won again in 1995. Vähi admitted that while he favored a German-style "social market economy, in the end, he supported right-wing policies." See "Estonia: Success Punished," *Economist*, March 11, 1995, 51.

89. Professor of international finance at Tallinn University of Technology and research supervisor at the BOE, interview with the author, July 16, 2007, Tallinn, Estonia.

90. Perhaps the perception that Russia and the large russophone population constituted an external threat acted to unify Estonian elites about the need to conduct liberal reforms and cut ties with Soviet interest groups (Frane, Tomšič, and Kristan 2008; Abdelal 2001).

Chapter 5

1. Polish bonds were issued on the Dutch market for the first time in 1776 (Tomz 2007, 45). Both countries paid their debts for all but the final years of the 1930s (Tomz 2007, 102, 183).

2. The Stamp Memorial Lecture, London School of Economics, October 9, 2012. See http://www.lse.ac.uk/publicEvents/events/2012/10/20121009t1830vLSE.aspx

3. Czechoslovakia had four free elections during the First Republic (in 1920, 1925, 1929, and 1935) and a semifree election in 1946. See Korbel (1977) for the history of Czechoslovakia from its creation in 1918.

4. In 1938, the average GDP per capita income of $380 in Czechoslovakia was comparable to that of $400 in Austria (Dyba and Švejnar 1995, 22).

5. Václav Havel, a famous dissident playwright and the leader of the Civic Forum, became president.

6. Václav Klaus espoused a "Friedmanite-von Hayakian" free-market vision and Thatcherite policies (Saxonberg 1999, 401).

7. For the initial economic reforms, see Meaney (1997), Adam (1993), Orenstein (2001), Schwartz (2006), and Appel (2004).

8. Former director of the Department for Financial Policies, Ministry of Finance, interview with the author, June 15, 2006, Prague, Czech Republic. See also Orenstein (2001).

9. According to the Scenario of Economic Reform (a blueprint for a road to a market economy), "Macroeconomic priority in the process of transformation is the blocking of inflation and this priority must to a reasonable extent override all other foundations of macroeconomic aims-economic growth, employment, and the balance of payments" (cited in Schwartz 2006, 130).

10. Miroslav Hrnčíř, former advisor to the governor of the CNB, interview with the author, June 7, 2006, Prague, Czech Republic.

11. Former advisor to the vice-governor of the CNB, interview with the author, June 9 and 13, 2006, Prague, Czech Republic.

12. See table 5.A1 in the appendix to this chapter for the evolution of exchange rate arrangements in the Czech Republic.

13. Initially, following the example of the Bundesbank, the Czechoslovak central bank experimented (unsuccessfully) with monetary targeting. Zdeněk Tůma, governor of the CNB (2000–2010), interview with the author, June 15, 2006, Prague, Czech Republic.

14. Professor of economics at Charles University and a former vice-governor of the CNB, interview with the author, June 10 and 12, 2006, Prague, Czech Republic;

Miroslav Hrnčíř, former advisor to the governor of the CNB, interview with the author, June 7, 2006, Prague, Czech Republic.

15. Pavel Mertlík, minister of finance (1999–2001) and chief economist in Raiffeisenbank, Prague (2001–2012), interview with the author, June 16, 2006, Prague, Czech Republic. See also Drábek (1995).

16. After the ODS formed a coalition with another post–Civic Forum party, the Civic Democratic Alliance (ODA), and with the Christian Democratic bloc (KDU-CSL), it controlled 53 percent (105 of 200) seats until the 1996 elections (Vachudova 2005).

17. The Czech Communist Party was thrown from power in 1989 and remained loyal to its communist ideology. The historic Social Democratic Party (CSSD) was re-established in 1990, but it did not gain political strength until the second half of the decade. See Vachudova (2005).

18. Currency traders feared devaluation and stopped trading the Czechoslovak currency around mid-January 1993. Foreign exchange reserves declined substantially to only $0.5 billion in the period from November 1992 to January 1993.

19. For the Czechoslovak monetary union, see Fidrmuc, Horváth, and Fidrmuc (1999).

20. Act No. 6/1993 on CNB stipulated that the governor and other members of the Bank Board could be appointed and dismissed only by the president of the Republic. Cukierman's index shows that the newly created CNB was equipped with a high degree of independence (Cukierman, Miller, and Neyapti 2002).

21. Professor of economics at Charles University and a former vice-governor of the CNB, interview with the author, June 10 and 12, 2006, Prague, Czech Republic.

22. The government's reluctance to allow the entry of foreign investors has historical origins. In 1919, after the collapse of the Austro-Hungarian empire, Czechoslovakia introduced a Nostrification Law that required joint-stock companies to transfer their headquarters from Vienna to the newly established territory of Czechoslovakia where they had their firms (Tschoegl 2003, 48).

23. Teichova (quoted in Rao and Hirsch 2003, 260 note 3) notes that during the interwar period, "numerous industrial companies clustered around big banks, tied to them either by credits or direct investment. In this way, large joint-stock banks threw a net of relationships of various degrees of dependency over almost all branches of production in the country." For instance, nationality-based credit unions financed various agricultural development projects and the Czech grand bourgeoisie developed new heavy industries, such as Škoda Works in Plzeň, with strong links with the Czech banks, which became a powerful national symbol (Teichova, quoted in Orenstein 2001, 77). For the "Czech way" of national development, see Myant (2003).

24. The minimum basic capital required for establishing a new bank was only fifty million Czechoslovak koruna ($1.8 million at the 1990 exchange rate).

25. In the voucher privatization, all citizens over the age of eighteen could buy a book of one thousand voucher points for a fee of one thousand Czechoslovak koruna (equivalent to $35), or about the average weekly wage in 1992. The voucher

holders could use these vouchers to acquire shares in the largest state-owned enterprises in a public auction.

26. For the privatization of KB, see also Dlouhý (2004).

27. Tomáš Ježek, minister of privatization (1990–1992) and president of the National Property Fund (1992–1994), interview with the author, June 20, 2006, Prague, Czech Republic.

28. The government retained a majority of controlling stakes in forty "strategic enterprises" (in the banking, mining, energy, and insurance sectors) (Kreuzbergova 2006; Palda 1997).

29. The voucher method was also motivated by its speed, the lack of domestic capital, and the government's intention to create the first (but not the last) domestic owners of capital. Oldřich Dedĕk, interview with the author, June 10 and 12, 2006, Prague.

30. Regulation concerning the establishment and functioning of IPFs was lacking until the adoption of the Law on Investment Funds and Companies in April 1992, which was inadequate and was not properly enforced. As a result, more than 450 IPFs and 44 pension funds obtained a license from the Federal Ministry of Finance initially.

31. Some commentators argued that a system of cross-holdings among banks and industries was close to a German model of capitalism. In contrast to the German banks, however, the Czech banks neither shaped the long-term investment decisions of the enterprises they controlled nor forced them to restructure (Neumann and Egan 1999).

32. For the excellent treatment of banking socialism, see Kreuzbergova (2006).

33. Miroslav Hrnčíř, former advisor to the governor of the CNB, interview with the author, June 7, 2006, Prague, Czech Republic.

34. Former advisor to the vice-governor of the CNB, interview with the author, June 9 and 13, 2006, Prague, Czech Republic.

35. Director of the Macroeconomic Research at the Czechoslovak Commercial Bank, interview with the author, June 16, 2006, Prague, Czech Republic.

36. Minister of Trade and Industry, interview with the author, June 9, 2006, Prague, Czech Republic.

37. Senior official of the Czech Banking Association, interview with the author, June 20, 2006, Prague, Czech Republic.

38. A telling example is a former senior executive in SBCS, Richard Salzmann, who was appointed in 1991 as chief executive officer of KB. He was also the first chairman of the Prague Stock Exchange, which was clearly a conflict of interest. Salzman was a prominent member of ODS (Schwartz 2006, 245).

39. The Czech government completed the liberalization of capital movements by adopting the Foreign Exchange Law that came into effect just before the accession of the Czech Republic into the OECD in December 1995.

40. For instance, the Ministry of Finance blocked the CNB's efforts to impose a more stringent classification on nonperforming loans (Pazdernik, quoted in McDermott 2007, 236).

41. The Structural Change Indicators of the EBRD.

42. Pavel Mertlík, minister of finance (1999–2001) and chief economist in Raiffeisenbank, Prague (2001–2012), interview with the author, June 16, 2006, Prague, Czech Republic.

43. Miroslav Hrnčíř, former advisor to the governor of the CNB, interview with the author, June 7, 2006, Prague, Czech Republic.

44. Professor of economics at Charles University and a former vice-governor of the CNB, interview with the author, June 10 and 12, 2006, Prague, Czech Republic; former minister of finance, interview with the author, June 14, 2006, Prague, Czech Republic.

45. Miroslav Hrnčíř, former advisor to the governor of the CNB, interview with the author, June 7, 2006, Prague, Czech Republic.

46. Former minister of finance, interview with the author, June 14, 2006, Prague, Czech Republic.

47. Former director of the Department for Financial Policies, Ministry of Finance, interview with the author, June 15, 2006, Prague, Czech Republic.

48. For the 1997 Czech financial crisis, see Dědek (2000), Šmídková et al. (1998), Begg (1998), and Horváth (1999).

49. The CNB chose to devalue the koruna just before the elections, although it was apparently able to defend the peg (Horváth 1999, 288).

50. The Czech Republic was a pioneer of direct inflation targeting in Eastern Europe. It followed the examples of Finland, Sweden, and the United Kingdom, which implemented this monetary strategy after the 1992–93 crises in the European Monetary System. Miroslav Hrnčíř, former advisor to the governor of the CNB, interview with the author, June 7, 2006, Prague, Czech Republic.

51. The government expressed serious reservations about inflation targeting because involved a costly disinflationary policy (Klaus 2000, 20).

52. See Resolution No. 732 of November 19, 1997.

53. Pavel Mertlík, minister of finance (1999–2001) and chief economist in RaiffeisenBank, Prague (2001–2012), interview with the author, June 16, 2006, Prague, Czech Republic.

54. For the privatization of the major Czech banks, see Havel (2004) and Dlouhý (2004).

55. For a history of the privatization of IPB, see Wagner and Iakova (2001) and Karnitschnig (2000). This author also actively participated in the debates over the IPB privatization during her advisory assignment at the Directorate-General Competition of the European Commission in Brussels.

56. The amendment to the CNB Act that the ODS proposed suggested that monetary policy decisions be made in consultation with the government and political parties, which should have more power in appointing the governor and board members of the central bank. But this proposition failed after strong criticism from the IMF and the European Union (Jonas and Mishkin 2007).

57. The aggregate index for measuring central bank independence, which Arnone et al. (2007) developed, was 0.88 for the CNB at the end of 2003, the same as for the Bundesbank.

58. For the origins of the elevated external debt and inflation in the 1980s see Polanski (1991, 1994), Kochanowicz, Kozarzewski, and Woodward (2005), and Kaminski (2001).

59. Mazowiecki was searching for a "Polish Erhard," a reference to Ludwig Erhard, the author of West Germany's "economic miracle." It was Waldemar Kuczynski, the chief advisor to Mazowiecki, who "invented" Balcerowicz and launched his extraordinary political career. Former chief advisor to Tadeusz Mazowiecki and Jerzy Buzek, and a former minister of privatization, interview with the author, July 17, 2006.

60. See the Government's Memorandum on Economic Policy from January 1990.

61. For Balcerowicz (1995, 264–66), "major discontinuities, i.e. liberalization from external dependence and political liberalization produce a special state of mass psychology and a corresponding state of political system," which result in an unusually high level of acceptance of radical reform measures.

62. The accommodative communist regime allowed strong and well-organized societal interests (such as farmers' associations) to form. A negotiated exit mode from communism also provided an opportunity for these interest groups to entrench themselves. And yet, contrary to expectations, they have not been able to "politicize" the state (Grzymala-Busse 2002).

63. This drop in output was moderate and short-lived compared with that of other Eastern European states. Poland was the first Eastern European country that had exceeded its pretransition level of output by 1995 (Kochanowicz, Kozarzewski, and Woodward 2005, 45).

64. Cofounder of the Center for Social and Economic Research in Warsaw and former member of the Monetary Policy Council of the NBP, interview with the author, July 3, 2006, Warsaw, Poland.

65. The Polish zloty was initially pegged to the U.S. dollar instead of the German mark because of the high level of dollarization Poland inherited from the communist regime. Dollar accounts of Polish households were higher than the central bank's foreign exchange reserves.

66. In its October issue, the *New York Times* even referred to the Polish reform plan as "the Sachs Plan" (Kochanowicz, Kozarzewski, and Woodward 2005, 39–41). For Sachs's views on the Polish transition, see Sachs (1993). The "Balcerowicz Team" also included IMF economist David Lipton and foreign advisors of Polish origin, the so-called Polonia academics (Stanislaw Gomulka, Jacek Rostowski, and Stanislaw Wellisz).

67. The IMF also advised the government to publicly announce that it was committed to maintaining a peg for a period of at least twelve months to establish the initial credibility of its monetary policies.

68. Former advisor to Balcerowicz and reader in economics at the London School of Economics, interview with the author, July 13, 2006, Warsaw, Poland.

69. See table 5.A1 in the appendix to this chapter for the evolution of the exchange-rate system in Poland.

70. Stefan Kawalec, vice-minister of finance (1991–1994) and chief advisor to Balcerowicz (1989–1991), interview with the author, July 16, 2006, Warsaw, Poland. Polish authorities limited their export promotion policy to foreign-exchange interventions and capital controls, thus avoiding a proactive industrial policy in the interventionist sense, which would have negative fiscal consequences (Campbell 2001, 506). Two industries were particularly affected by currency appreciation: the shipyard industry, the entire production of which was designated for exports, and the coal industry, which was struggling with unsuccessful restructuring programs.

71. The list of the largest nineteen banks also included Bank Rozwoju Eksportu S.A. (BRE), which was established in 1986 as an export development bank. For the evolution of the Polish banking sector, see Bonin and Leven (2001) and Abarbanell and Bonin (1997).

72. Former senior official of the Association of Polish Banks, interview with the author, July 16, 2006, Warsaw, Poland. See also Polanski (1997).

73. Stefan Kawalec, vice-minister of finance (1991–1994) and chief advisor to Balcerowicz (1989–1991), interview with the author, July 16, 2006, Warsaw, Poland.

74. Andrzej Topiński, governor of the NBP (1991–1992), chairman of PKO BP (1994–1999), chairman of the Polish Bank Association (2000–2003), chief economist at Credit Information Bureau (2007–2010), interview with the author, July 17, 2006, Warsaw, Poland.

75. Stefan Kawalec, vice-minister of finance (1991–1994) and chief advisor to Balcerowicz (1989–1991), interview with the author, July 16, 2006, Warsaw, Poland.

76. The "lead" bank took responsibility for monitoring the agreement and for resolving the debt problems of its major clients in return for one-time bank recapitalization with interest-bearing fifteen-year "restructuring" government bonds. The program also imposed a formal ban on granting new loans to firms with doubtful or uncollectible loans.

77. Andrzej Bratkowski, member of the Monetary Policy Council of the NBP, deputy president of the NBP (2001–2004), and chief economist at Bank Pekao (2004–2008), interview with the author, July 17, 2006, Warsaw, Poland.

78. This analysis of the Polish bank–led restructuring program draws on McDermott (2007) and Kawalec and Kluza (2003).

79. Former advisor to president of the NBP and a professor of economics at Warsaw School of Economics, interview with the author, July 11, 2006, Warsaw, Poland.

80. Member of the Management Board of the NBP and former chief economist at Citibank Handlowy, interview with the author, July 14, 2006, Warsaw, Poland.

81. The government's intention was to attract capital from several countries to prevent the domination of German capital. Former member of the Monetary Policy Council of the NBP, interview with the author, July 11, 2006, Warsaw, Poland.

82. Stefan Kawalec, vice-minister of finance (1991–1994) and chief advisor to Balcerowicz (1989–1991), interview with the author, July 16, 2006, Warsaw, Poland.

83. Andrzej Bratkowski, member of the Monetary Policy Council of the NBP, deputy president of the NBP (2001–2004), and chief economist at Bank Pekao (2004–2008), interview with the author, July 17, 2006, Warsaw, Poland.

84. My discussion of the NBP's financing of budget deficits is based on Polanski (1994).

85. Cofounder of the Center for Social and Economic Research in Warsaw and former member of the Monetary Policy Council of the NBP, interview with the author, July 3, 2006, Warsaw, Poland.

86. Grzegorz Kolodko, minister of finance (1994–1997, 2002–2003), interview with the author, July 2 and 5, 2006, Warsaw, Poland. For political conflicts between the NBP and the government, see Huterski, Nicholls, and Wisniewski (2004).

87. Former chairman of the Polish Financial Supervision Authority and a former deputy governor of the NBP, interview with the author, July 12, 2006, Warsaw, Poland.

88. Cofounder of the Center for Social and Economic Research in Warsaw and former member of the Monetary Policy Council of the NBP, interview with the author, July 3, 2006, Warsaw, Poland.

89. Polish authorities adopted a cautious timetable for the liberalization of the capital account. They did not remove short-term restrictions on capital flows until 2002. These regulations thus fell short of the requirements for OECD membership at the time of Poland's accession into this organization in 1996 (Árvai 2005).

90. Researcher at the Institute of Philosophy and Sociology, Polish Academy of Sciences, interview with the author, July 4, 2006, Warsaw, Poland.

91. The contagion effects from the 1998 Russian financial crisis were reflected in a temporary increase of EMBI spreads to 201 basis points (Backé 1999).

92. Raiffeisen Bank acquired a 70 percent majority share in Polbank, a greenfield investment of the Greek EFG Eurobank, in April 2012.

93. Polish economists Jacek Rostowski and Andrzej Bratkowski (who became the deputy president of NPB) popularized, as an alternative way to dampen inflation, the idea of unilateral euroization (i.e., unilateral adoption of the euro), which is conceptually similar to a hard peg. But this idea did not find support among the domestic political elite and was strongly opposed by the European Commission. The European Commission viewed unilateral euroization as a way to circumvent the stages foreseen by the Maastricht Treaty for the adoption of the euro. See Bratkowski and Rostowski (2002).

94. At the end of 2003, the index of NBP independence was equivalent to that of the Bundesbank (0.88) (Arnone et al. 2007).

95. "Lucky Lenders: A Healthy Economy and Modern Offerings Have Boosted Polands' Banks," *Economist*, August 23, 2014.

96. Andrzej Bratkowski, member of the Monetary Policy Council of the NBP, deputy president of the NBP (2001–2004), and chief economist at Bank Pekao (2004–2008), interview with the author, July 17, 2006, Warsaw, Poland.

Chapter 6

1. Building on the varieties of capitalism approach, Nölke and Vliegenthart (2009) argue that some emerging European countries are "dependent market econ-

omies" because of the importance of foreign capital in their financial sectors. See also Bohle and Greskovits (2012).

2. The banking system was a significant source of fiscal pressures; bailouts and deposit insurance had created losses to the central bank of $14.6 billion during the preceding decade (Fernandez 1990, cited in Schumacher 2000, 260).

3. In the period from 1980 to 1992, forty-eight banks were closed (Calomiris and Powell 2001).

4. The Tequila Crisis was sparked by the Mexican government's sudden devaluation of the peso against the U.S. dollar in December 1994. The peso depreciated by 50 percent and Mexico experienced both a currency crisis and a banking crisis. See Mishkin (2006).

5. The importance of public banks in the Argentine banking system dates back to the nineteenth century (Guillén and Tschoegl 2000).

6. The liberal banking regime was cemented through a bilateral investment treaty between the United States and Argentina in 1994 (Martinez-Diaz 2009, 192).

7. For an excellent analysis of the development of the Argentine financial system, see Calomiris and Powell (2001).

8. Guillén and Tschoegl (2000, 2008) examine why and how Spanish banks expanded in Latin America.

9. For the 2001 crisis in Argentina, see Mishkin (2006), Bleaney (2004), and De la Torre et al. (2003), among others.

10. Nonetheless, Scotiabank made a voluntary payment of twenty cents on the dollar to holders of medium-term notes and other debt instruments of its subsidiary, Scotiabank Quilmes. It also gave severance pay to the five hundred employees who lost their jobs (Tschoegl 2005).

11. In the aftermath of Brazil's devaluation, the Group of Eight stopped functioning, however. Domestic firms, a construction industry association, and some agriculture producers formed a coalition called "grupo productivo" around the Argentine Industrial Union (Woodruff 2005, 27).

12. This discussion draws on Marshall (2008).

13. The government also expropriated the assets from the utilities, which foreign investors had privatized. It converted utility rates, which were denominated in dollars, into the sharply depreciated pesos on a one-to-one basis and then froze these assets (Mishkin 2006, 124).

14. The 2003 elections led to the victory of the traditional left wing of the Peronist Party under the leadership of Nestor Kishner, whose government adopted a hard negotiating line during the debt renegotiation process with international creditors in the period from 2003 to 2005 (Pop-Eleches 2009, 269). The government decided to pay only twenty-five to thirty cents on the dollar of the face value of government bonds owned by foreign creditors, which were valued at nearly $90 billion (Mishkin 2006, 124). As a consequence, market sentiment did not begin to improve until 2006, when bond spreads compressed from 1,833 to 343 basis points.

15. In 2013, Banco Santander Rio and BBVA Banco Frances, subsidiaries of Spanish banks, were among the top five banks in Argentina; they held $10,881 and

$ 9,143 million assets, respectively, according to the *Banker*. http://www.thebanker. com/World/Americas/Argentina/The-top-five-banks-in-Argentina?ct=true

16. The analysis here centers mostly on the first phase of the 2008 global financial crisis. The second phase, which began with the crisis in Greece at the end of 2009 and was followed by a sovereign debt crisis in the eurozone, is not the principal focus of this chapter.

17. Nevertheless, some cross-national differences are noticeable. While more than 50 percent of all foreign loans were denominated in local currency in Brazil, Mexico, and Venezuela, this share was less than 20 percent in the dollarized economies of Uruguay, the Dominican Republic, and Bolivia (Kamil and Rai 2013, 9).

18. For a criticism of the lending behavior of foreign banks in emerging Europe during the crisis, see, for example, Popov and Udell (2012).

19. Senior executive of Raiffeisen Bank International, interview with the author, July 24, 2012, Vienna.

20. See Backé et al. (2010), Cull and Martínez-Pería (2012); Galindo, Izquierdo, and Rojas-Suárez (2010); Kamil and Rai (2010) for a comparative analysis of global banking in Latin America and other emerging markets during the 2008 crisis.

21. The exposures of German banks are concentrated in Hungary, Belgian banks in the Czech Republic, and Dutch and American banks in Poland.

22. Senior executive of Erste Bank, interview with the author, July 24, 2012, Vienna.

23. The historical information on these banks was taken from their official websites.

24. The bailout package included €15 billion of capital infusions, €75 billion in state guarantees to ensure liquidity, and €10 billion as additional deposit insurance coverage (Winkler and Haiss 2010).

25. For the history of Santander, see Guillén and Tschoegl (2008).

26. Foreign subsidiaries of U.S. multinational banks pursue a centralized business model (Bank of International Settlements 2010). The U.S. banks operating in Latin America did not reduce credit growth during the recent crisis because they received substantial financial support from the U.S. government (Choi, Martínez Pería, and Gutierrez 2013, 14).

27. Foreign banks neither abandoned the Malaysian market after the 1997 financial crisis nor pulled back from Argentina, Brazil, and Mexico during the crises of the 1990s. Instead, they took the opportunity to become firmly implanted in these countries (Detragiache and Gupta 2006; Peek and Rosengren 2000).

28. Vogel and Winkler (2012) find that the stabilizing effect of foreign banks on cross-border flows was equally pronounced in sub-Saharan Africa. They suggest that Western banks with a long-standing presence in Africa that dated back to colonial times may have created stronger bonds with their subsidiaries in Africa than with their former colonies in Latin America, where colonial times ended earlier.

29. Senior executive of Raiffeisen Bank International, interview with the author, July 24, 2012, Vienna.

30. Alpha Bank, Bayerische Landesbank, Erste Group, Eurobank EFG, Hype

Alpe-Adria, ING, Intesa San Paolo, KBC Group, National Bank of Greece, Nordea Bank, OTP, Piraeus Bank, Raiffeisen Bank International, Skandinaviska Enskilda Banken, Société Générale, Swedbank, UniCredit, and Volsbank signed commitment letters pledging to maintain their exposure and keep their affiliates adequately capitalized.

31. Senior executive of Raiffeisen Bank International, interview with the author, July 24, 2012, Vienna.

32. According to the Austrian central bankers, the type of exchange rate regime did not play an important role in credit booms. Head of the Foreign Research Division of the Oesterreichische Nationalbank, interview with the author, Vienna, July 24, 2012.

33. For recent reviews of the scholarship on financial crises, see, for instance, Claessens and Kose (2013); and Reinhart and Rogoff (2009). Classical references are Minsky (1975) and Kindleberger and Aliber (2005).

34. Paul Krugman began the October 31, 2008 entry on his blog with the headline "Eastern Europe 2008 = Southeast Asia 1997," drawing attention to high foreign currency loan exposures in emerging Europe. See http://krugman.blogs.ny times.com/2008/10/31/eastern-europe-2008-southeast-asia-1997/?_r=0. In a VOX column from June 22, 2009, titled "Is Latvia the new Argentina?" Eduardo Levy Yeyati suggested that Latvia should leave its currency peg and opt for a contained devaluation, drawing an analogy between Argentina in 2001 and Latvia in 2009.

35. For instance, the European Commission required that Bayern LB, the German public bank, sell the Hungarian MKB in exchange for approving state aid.

36. For example, French multinational banks that benefited from government assistance pledged to increase domestic lending by 3 to 4 percent annually (Cerutti and Claessens 2014, 5).

Chapter 7

1. The proponents of the classic "development" view on the role of the state in finance, originated by Gerschenkron (1962), extol the virtues of government ownership of banks in stimulating economic growth in "late developers," denoted as countries where economic institutions are not sufficiently developed for private banks to play a development role. In an extremely backward nineteenth-century Russia, it was the state that fulfilled the functions of banks and financed industrialization. In a more recent "social view" on government participation in finance (Stiglitz 1994), governments create state-owned banks to maximize broader social objectives by allocating funds to projects with high social returns and to less privileged sectors and groups (such as small- and medium-sized enterprises, agriculture, and education).

2. See Pauly (1988) for the politics of banking-sector opening in industrialized countries, and Loriaux et al. (1997) and Martinez-Diaz (2009) for doing so in transition and developing countries.

3. Yet another set of arguments explains the relaxation of regulatory barriers in

the banking sector as the outcome of a shift in policymakers' ideas about the merits of protectionism (Martinez-Diaz 2009).

4. For economic reforms in postcommunist Eastern Europe, see also Murphy, Shleifer, and Vishny (1992); Roland (2000); and Beck and Laeven (2006).

5. See Posen (1993), Goodman (1992), and Kirshner (2007).

6. "Eastern Europe: Who's Next?" *Economist*, October 23, 2008.

BIBLIOGRAPHY

Abarbanell, Jeffery S., and John P. Bonin. 1997. "Bank Privatization in Poland: The Case of Bank Slaski." *Journal of Comparative Economics* 25 (1): 31–61.

Abbas, S. M. Ali, Nazim Belhocine, Asmaa El-Ganainy, and Mark Horton. 2010. "A Historical Public Debt Database." IMF Working Paper 10/245. International Monetary Fund, Washington, DC.

Abdelal, Rawi. 2001. *National Purpose in the World Economy: Post-Soviet States in Comparative Perspective.* Ithaca: Cornell University Press.

Abiad, Abdul, Enrica Detragiache, and Thierry Tressel. 2008. "A New Database of Financial Reforms." IMF Working Paper 08/266. International Monetary Fund, Washington, DC.

Ådahl, Martin. 2002. "The Internationalization of Baltic Banking (1998–2002)." *Focus on Transition* 2/2005: 107–31.

Adam, Jan. 1993. "Transformation to a Market Economy in the Former Czechoslovakia." *Europe-Asia Studies* 45 (4): 627–45.

Aghion, Philippe, Philippe Bacchetta, Romain Rancière, and Kenneth Rogoff. 2009. "Exchange Rate Volatility and Productivity Growth: The Role of Financial Development." *Journal of Monetary Economics* 56 (4): 494–513.

Alesina, Alberto, and Robert Barro. 2002. "Currency Unions." *Quarterly Journal of Economics* 117 (2): 409–36.

Alesina, Alberto, and Allan Drazen. 1991. "Why Are Stabilizations Delayed?" *American Economic Review* 81 (5): 1170–88.

Alesina Alberto, and Andrea Stella. 2010. "The Politics of Monetary Policy." In *Handbook of Monetary Economics*, edited by Benjamin M. Friedman and Michael Woodford. Amsterdam: Elsevier.

Alesina, Alberto, and Lawrence Summers. 1993. "Central Bank Independence and Macroeconomic Performance." *Journal of Money, Credit, and Banking* 25 (2): 157–62.

Alesina, Alberto, and Alexander Wagner. 2006. "Choosing (and Reneging on) Exchange Rate Regimes." *Journal of the European Economic Association* 4 (4): 770–99.

Allen, Franklin, Thorsten Beck, Elena Carleti, Philip R. Lane, Dirk Schoenmaker, and Wolf Wagner. 2011. *Cross-Border Banking in Europe: Implications for Fi-*

nancial Stability and Macroeconomic Policies. London: Centre for Economic Policy Research.

Alper, C. Emre, Oya Pinar Ardic, and Salih Fendoglu. 2009. "The Economics of the Uncovered Interest Parity Condition for Emerging Markets." *Journal of Economic Surveys* 23 (1): 115–38.

Anastasakis, O., J. Bastian, and M. Watson, eds. 2011. *From Crisis to Recovery: Sustainable Growth in South East Europe.* Oxford: SEESOX.

Anderson, Robert. 2006. "Light at the End of the Tunnel over Czech IPB Fiasco." *The Banker*, September 4.

Andrews, Edmund L. 2001. "Czech Resigns after Failure of Efforts to Privatize." *New York Times*, April 11.

Andrews, Michael A. 2005. "State-Owned Banks, Stability, Privatization, and Growth: Practical Policy Decisions in a World without Empirical Proof." IMF Working Paper 05/10. IMF, Washington, DC.

Andrianova, Svetlana, Panicos Demetriades, and Anja Shortland. 2008. "Government Ownership of Banks, Institutions and Financial Development." *Journal of Development Economics* 85: 218–52.

Angresano, James. 1996. "Poland after the Shock." *Comparative Economic Studies* 38 (2/3): 87–101.

Appel, Hilary. 2004. *A New Capitalist Order: Privatization and Ideology in Russia and Eastern Europe.* Pittsburgh: University of Pittsburgh Press.

Arellano, Manuel, and Olympia Bover. 1995. "Another Look at the Instrumental Variable Estimation of Error-Components Models." *Journal of Econometrics* 68 (1): 29–51.

Arnone, Marco, Bernard Laurens, Jean-François Segalotto, and Martin Sommer. 2007. "Central Bank Autonomy: Lessons from Global Trends." IMF Working Paper 07/88. IMF, Washington, DC.

Árvai, Zsófia. 2005. "Capital Account Liberalization, Capital Flow Patterns, and Policy Responses in the EU's New Member States." IMF Working Paper 05/213. IMF, Washington, DC.

Åslund, Anders. 2011a. "Exchange Rate Policy and the Central and East European Financial Crisis." *Eurasian Geography and Economics* 52 (3): 375–89.

Åslund, Anders. 2011b. *How Latvia Came through the Financial Crisis.* Washington, DC: Peterson Institute for International Economics.

Åslund, Anders. 2015. *Ukraine: What Went Wrong and How to Fix It.* Washington, DC: Peterson Institute for International Economics.

Avramov, Roumen, ed. 1999. *120 Years Bulgarian National Bank, 1879—1999: An Annotated Chronology.* Sofia: Bulgarian National Bank.

Backé, Peter. 1999. "Exchange Rate Regimes in Central and Eastern Europe: A Brief Review of Recent Changes, Current Issues and Future Challenges." *Focus on Transition* 2: 47–67.

Backé, Peter, Sonsoles Gallego, Sándor Gardó, Reiner Martin, Luis Molina, José Maria Serena. 2010. "How Did the Global Financial Crisis Affect the CESEE Region and Latin America?—A Comparative Analysis." *Focus on European Economic Integration* Q1/10: 49–66.

Backus, David, and John Driffill. 1985. "Inflation and Reputation." *American Economic Review* 75: 530–38.

Bagehot, Walter. 1873. *Lombard Street*. London: H. S. King.

Bailey, W., and Y. Peter Chung. 1995. "Exchange Rate Fluctuations, Political Risk, and Stock Returns: Some Evidence from an Emerging Market." *Journal of Financial and Quantitative Analysis* 30 (4): 541–61.

Balcerowicz, Leszek. 1995. *Socialism, Capitalism and Transformation*. Budapest: Central European University Press.

Baliño, Tomás, Adam Bennett, and Eduardo Borensztein. 1999. "Monetary Policy in Dollarized Economies." IMF Occasional Paper 171.

Baliño, Tomás J. T., and Charles Enoch. 1997. *Currency Board Arrangements: Issues and Experiences*. Washington, DC: International Monetary Fund.

Bank for International Settlements (BIS). 2010. *Funding Patterns and Liquidity Management of Internationally Active Banks*. Cgfs Papers No. 39. Basel, Switzerland.

Barisitz, Stephan. 2002. "The Emergence of Market-Oriented Banking Systems in Estonia, Latvia and Lithuania (1988–1997)." *Focus on Transition* 2: 84–106.

Barisitz, Stephan. 2006. "Booming, But Risky: The Ukrainian Banking Sector: Hot Spot for Foreign Strategic Investors." *Financial Stability Report* 12: 64–78. Oesterreichische Nationalbank, Vienna.

Barisitz, Stephan, Hans Holzhacker, Olena Lytvyn, and Lyaziza Sabyrova. 2010. "Crisis Response Policies in Russia, Ukraine, Kazakhstan and Belarus: Stock Taking and Comparative Assessment." *Focus on European Economic Integration* Q4/10. Oesterreichische Nationalbank, Vienna.

Barisitz, Stephan, and Mathias Lahnsteiner. 2009. "Investor Commitment Tested by Deep Crisis: Banking Development in Ukraine." *Financial Stability Report* 18 (December). Oesterreichische Nationalbank, Vienna.

Barnes, Andrew. 2007. "Extricating the State: The Move to Competitive Capture in Post-Communist Bulgaria." *Europe-Asia Studies* 59 (1): 71–95.

Barro, Robert J., and David B. Gordon. 1983. "A Positive Theory of Monetary Policy in a Natural Rate Model." *Journal of Political Economy* 91 (4): 589–610.

Barth James R., Gerard Caprio Jr., and Ross Levine. 2002. "Bank Regulation and Supervision: What Works Best?" NBER Working Paper 9323. National Bureau of Economic Research, Cambridge, MA.

Barth, James R., Chen Lin, Ping Lin, and Frank M. Song. 2009. "Corruption in Bank Lending to Firms: Cross-Country Micro Evidence on the Beneficial Role of Competition and Information Sharing." *Journal of Financial Economics* 91 (3): 361–88.

Battilossi, Stefano. 2006. "The Determinants of Multinational Banking During the First Globalisation 1880–1914." *European Review of Economic History* 10: 361–88.

Bearce, David H. 2003. "Societal Preferences, Partisan Agents, and Monetary Policy Outcomes." *International Organization* 57 (2): 373–410.

Bearce, David H. 2007. *Monetary Divergence: Domestic Policy Autonomy in the Post-Bretton Woods Era*. Ann Arbor: University of Michigan Press.

Beaulieu, Emily, Gary W. Cox, and Sebastian M. Saiegh. 2012. "Sovereign Debt and Regime Type: Re-Considering the Democratic Advantage." *International Organization* 66 (4): 709–38.

Beck, Stacie, Jeffrey B. Miller, and Mohsen Saad. 2003. "Inflation and the Bulgarian Currency Board." Discussion Paper 31/2003. Bulgarian National Bank: Sofia.

Beck, Thorsten, George Clarke, Alberto Groff, Philip Keefer, and Patrick Walsh. 2001. "New Tools in Comparative Political Economy: The Database of Political Institutions." *World Bank Economic Review* 15 (1): 165–76.

Beck, Thorsten, Asli Demirgüç-Kunt and Ross Levine. 2000. "A New Database on Financial Development and Structure." *World Bank Economic Review* 14: 597–605.

Beck, Thorsten, and Luc Laeven. 2006. "Institution Building and Growth in Transition Economies." *Journal of Economic Growth* 11 (2): 157–86.

Beers, David T., and John D. Chambers. 2006. "Sovereign Defaults: At 26-Year Low, To Show Little Change in 1997." Standard & Poor's Global Credit Portal, September 8.

Begg, David. 1998. "Pegging Out: Lessons from the Czech Exchange Rate Crisis." *Journal of Comparative Economics* 26 (4): 669–90.

Berensmann, Katrin. 2002. *Currency Boards: A Monetary and Exchange Rate Policy Solution for Transition Countries?* Baden-Baden: Nomos Verlagsgesellschaft.

Berglof, Erik, and Patrick Bolton. 2002. "The Great Divide and Beyond: Financial Architecture in Transition." *Journal of Economic Perspectives* 16 (1): 77–100.

Berglof, Erik, Yevgeniya Korniyenko, Alexander Plekhanov, and Jeromin Zettelmeyer. 2010. "Understanding the Crisis in Emerging Europe." *Public Policy Review* 6 (6): 985–1008.

Berlemann, Michael, Kalin Hristov, and Nikolay Nenovsky. 2002. "Lending of Last Resort, Moral Hazard and Twin Crises: Lessons from the Bulgarian Financial Crisis 1996/1997." William Davidson Institute Working Paper No. 464.

Berlemann, Michael, and Nikolay Nenovsky. 2004. "Lending of First versus Lending of Last Resort: The Bulgarian Financial Crisis of 1996/97." *Comparative Economic Studies* 46 (2): 245–71.

Bernanke, Ben, and Frederic Mishkin. 1997. "Inflation Targeting: A New Framework for Monetary Policy?" *Journal of Economic Perspectives* 11 (2): 97–116.

Bernhard, William, J. Lawrence Broz, and William Roberts Clark. 2003. *The Political Economy of Monetary Institutions.* Cambridge, MA: MIT Press.

Biglaiser, Glen, and Joseph L. Staats. 2012. "Finding the 'Democratic Advantage' in Sovereign Bond Ratings: The Importance of Strong Courts, Property Rights Protection, and the Rule of Law." *International Organization* 66 (3): 515–35.

Blackburn, Keith, and Michael Christensen. 1989. "Monetary Policy and Policy Credibility: Theories and Evidence." *Journal of Economic Literature* 27 (1): 1–45.

Bleaney, Michael. 2004. "Argentina's Currency Board Collapse: Weak Policy or Bad Luck?" *World Economy* 27 (5): 699–714.

Bleaney, Michael, Hock-Ann Lee, and Timothy Lloyd. 2013. "Testing the Trilemma: Exchange Rate Regimes, Capital Mobility, and Monetary Independence." *Oxford Economic Papers* 65 (4): 876–97.

Blundell, Richard, and Stephen Bond. 1998. "Initial Conditions and Moment Restrictions in Dynamic Panel Data Models." *Journal of Econometrics* 87 (1): 115–43.

Bodea, Cristina, and Raymond Hicks. 2015. "Price Stability and Central Bank Independence: Discipline, Credibility, and Democratic Institutions." *International Organization* 69 (1): 35–61.

Bohle, Dorothee, and Béla Greskovits. 2012. *Capitalist Diversity on Europe's Periphery*. Ithaca: Cornell University Press

Bonin, John P. 1993. "On the Way to Privatizing Commercial Banks: Poland and Hungary Take Different Roads." *Comparative Economic Studies* 35 (4): 103–19.

Bonin, John P. 2010. "From Reputation amidst Uncertainty to Commitment under Stress: More Than a Decade of Foreign-Owned Banking in Transition Economies." *Comparative Economic Studies* 52 (4): 465–94.

Bonin, John P., and Bozena Leven. 1996. "Polish Bank Consolidation and Foreign Competition: Creating a Market-Oriented Banking Sector." *Journal of Comparative Economics* 23 (1): 57–72.

Bonin, John P., and Bozena Leven. 2001. "Can State-Owned Banks Promote Enterprise Restructuring? Evidence from One Polish Bank's Experience." *Post-Communist Economies* 13 (4): 431–43.

Bordo, Michael D. 2003. "Exchange Rate Regime Choice in Historical Perspective." NBER Working Paper 9654. National Bureau of Economic Research, Cambridge, MA.

Bordo, Michael, and Marc Flandreau. 2003. "Core, Periphery, Exchange Rate Regime and Globalization." In *Globalization in Historical Perspective*, edited by Alan Taylor, Jeffrey Williamson, and Michael Bordo, 417–68. Chicago: University of Chicago Press.

Bordo, Michael D., and Ronald Macdonald, eds. 2012. *Credibility and the International Monetary Regime: A Historical Perspective*. Cambridge: Cambridge University Press.

Bordo, Michael D., and Hugh Rockoff. 1996. "The Gold Standard as a 'Good Housekeeping Seal of Approval.'" *Journal of Economic History* 56 (2): 389–428.

Bordo, Michael D., and Anna J. Schwartz. 1996. "Why Clashes between Internal and External Stability End in Currency Crises, 1797–1994." *Open Economies Review* 7 (Suppl. 1): 437–68.

Boss, Michael, Gerald Krenn, Claus Puhr, and Markus Schwaiger. 2007. "Stress Testing the Exposure of Austrian Banks in Central and Eastern Europe." *Financial Stability Report* 13: 115–34. Oesterreichische Nationalbank, Vienna.

Brada, Josef C., and Ali M. Kutan. 1999. "The End of Moderate Inflation in Three Transition Economies?" Working Paper 1993–003A. Federal Reserve Bank of St. Louis. https://research.stlouisfed.org/wp/1999/99-003.pdf. Accessed May 21, 2016.

Brandao-Marques, Luis, Gaston Gelos, and Natalia Melgar. 2013. "Country Transparency and the Global Transmission of Financial Shocks." IMF Working Paper 13/156. IMF, Washington, DC.

Bratkowski, Andrzej, and Jacek Rostowski. 2002. "The EU Attitude to Unilateral

Euroization: Misunderstandings, Real Concerns and Sub-Optimal Admission Criteria." *Economics of Transition* 10 (2): 445–68.

Brealey, Richard A., and Evi C. Kaplanis. 1996. "The Determination of Foreign Banking Location." *Journal of International Money and Finance* 15 (4): 577–97.

Brixiova, Zuzana, Laura Vartia, and Andreas Wörgötter. 2010. "Capital Flows and the Boom-Bust Cycle: The Case of Estonia." *Economic Systems* 34 (1): 55–72.

Brown, Martin, and Ralph De Haas. 2012. Foreign Currency Lending in Emerging Europe: Bank-Level Evidence. *Economic Policy* 27 (69): 59–98.

Brown, Martin, Tullio Jappelli, and Marco Pagano. 2009. "Information Sharing and Credit: Firm-Level Evidence from Transition Countries." *Journal of Financial Intermediation* 18 (2): 151–72.

Brown, Martin, Marcel Peter, and Simon Wehrmüller. 2009. "Swiss Franc Lending in Europe." Unpublished policy paper, Swiss National Bank. http://www.snb. ch/n/mmr/reference/sem_2008_09_22_background/source/ sem_2008_09_22_background.n.pdf. Accessed May 22, 2016.

Brown, William S. 1993. "Economic Transition in Estonia." *Journal of Economic Issues* 27 (2): 493–503.

Broz, J. Lawrence. 2002. "Political System Transparency and Monetary Commitment Regimes." *International Organization* 56 (4): 861–87.

Broz, J. Lawrence, and Jeffry A. Frieden. 2001. "The Political Economy of International Monetary Relations." *Annual Review of Political Science* 4 (1): 317–43.

Bruno, Michael. 1993. *Crisis, Stabilization and Economic Reform: Therapy by Consensus.* Oxford: Oxford University Press.

Bruno, Valentina, and Robert Hauswald. 2014. "The Real Effect of Foreign Banks." *Review of Finance* 18 (5): 1683–1716.

Buch, Claudia. 2000. "Why Do Banks Go Abroad—Evidence from German Data." *Markets, Institutions and Instruments* 9 (1): 33–67.

Buch, Claudia. 2003. "Information or Regulation: What Drives the International Activities of Commercial Banks?" *Journal of Money, Credit, and Banking* 35: 851–69.

Buckley, Neil. 2012. "Prospects Depend on Western Support." *Financial Times* (Special Report), May 18.

Bunce, Valerie. 2003. "Rethinking Recent Democratization: Lessons from Postcommunist Experience." *World Politics* 55 (2): 176–92.

Burdekin, Richard C. K., Heidi Nelson, and Thomas D. Willett. 1999. "Central European Exchange Rate Policy and Inflation." In *Exchange-Rate Policies for Emerging Market Economies,* edited by Clas G. Wihlborg, Richard J. Sweeney, and Thomas D. Willett. Boulder: Westview Press.

Butler, Alexander W., and Larry Fauver. 2006. "Institutional Environment and Sovereign Credit Ratings." *Financial Management* 35 (3): 53–79.

Buyske, Susan Gail. 1997. *The Development of Financial Systems in Post-Socialist Economies: Estonia, Russia and Hungary.* New York: Columbia University Press.

Calomiris, Charles W., and Andrew Powell. 2001. "Can Emerging Market Bank Regulators Establish Credible Discipline? The Case of Argentina, 1992–99." In

Prudential Supervision: What Works and What Doesn't, edited by Frederic Mishkin, 147–96. Chicago: University of Chicago Press.

Calvo, Guillermo A. 1986. "Temporary Stabilization: Predetermine Exchange Rates." *Journal of Political Economy* 94 (6): 1319–29.

Calvo, Guillermo A. 1998. "Capital Flows and Capital-Market Crises: The Simple Economics of Sudden Stops." *Journal of Applied Economics* 1 (1): 35–54.

Calvo, Guillermo A., and Enrique G. Mendoza. 2000. "Rational Herd Behavior and the Globalization of Securities Markets." *Journal of International Economics* 51 (1): 79–113.

Calvo, Guillermo, and Frederic Mishkin. 2003. "The Mirage of Exchange Rate Regimes for Emerging Market Countries." *Journal of Economic Perspectives* 17 (4): 98–120.

Calvo, Guillermo, and Carmen Reinhart. 2002. "Fear of Floating." *Quarterly Journal of Economics* 117 (2): 379–408.

Calvo, Guillermo A., and Carlos A. Végh. 1994. "Inflation Stabilization and Nominal Anchors." *Contemporary Economic Policy* 12 (2): 35–45.

Campbell, Carolyn. 2001. "The Impact of EU Association on Industrial Policy Making." *East European Quarterly* 35 (4).

Campello, Daniela. 2015. *The Politics of Market Discipline in Latin America: Globalization and Democracy*. Cambridge: Cambridge University Press.

Canavan, Chris, and Mariano Tommasi. 1997. "On the Credibility of Alternative Exchange Rate Regimes." *Journal of Development Economics* 54 (1): 101–22.

Caporale, Guglielmo Maria, Kalin Hristov, Jeffrey B. Miller, Nikolay Nenovsky, and Boris Petrov. 2002. "The Banking System in Bulgaria." In *Banking Reforms in South-East Europe*, edited by Željko Šević, 219–40. Cheltenham, UK: Edward Elgar.

Caprio, Gerard, Jonathan L. Fiechter, Robert E. Litan, and Michael Pomerleano, eds. 2004. *The Future of State-Owned Financial Institutions*. Washington, DC: Brookings Institution Press.

Cardenas, Juan, Juan Pablo Graf, and Pascual O'Dogherty. 2003. "Foreign Bank Entry in Emerging Market Economies: A Host Country Perspective." Committee on the Global Financial System Working Group Paper. Bank for International Settlements, Basel, Switzerland.

Carlson, John, and Neven Valev. 2001. "Credibility of a New Monetary Regime: The Currency Board in Bulgaria." *Journal of Monetary Economics* 47 (3): 581–94.

Cerutti, Eugenio, and Stijn Claessens. 2014. "The Great Cross-Border Bank Deleveraging: Supply Constraints and Intra-Group Frictions." IMF Working Paper 14/180. IMF, Washington, DC.

Cerutti, Eugenio, Giovanni Dell'Ariccia, and Maria Soledad Martínez Pería. 2007. "How Banks Go Abroad: Branches or Subsidiaries?" *Journal of Banking and Finance* 31 (6): 1669–92.

Cetorelli, Nicola, and Linda S. Goldberg. 2011. "Global Banks and International Shock Transmission: Evidence from the Crisis." *IMF Economic Review* 59: 41–76.

Chang, Roberto, and Andres Velasco. 1998. "Financial Crises in Emerging Markets: A Canonical Model." NBER Working Paper 6606. National Bureau of Economic Research, Cambridge, MA.

Chinn, Menzie D., and Hiro Ito. 2006. "What Matters for Financial Development? Capital Controls, Institutions, and Interactions." *Journal of Development Economics* 81 (1): 163–92.

Choi, Moon Jung, Maria Soledad Martínez Pería, and Eva Gutierrez. 2013. "Dissecting Foreign Bank Lending Behavior during the 2008–2009 Crisis." World Bank Policy Research Working Paper No. 6674.

Christensen, Jacob. 2004. "Capital Inflows, Sterilization, and Commercial Bank Speculation: The Case of the Czech Republic in the Mid-1990s." IMF Working Paper 04/218. IMF, Washington, DC.

Christov, Lubomir. 1997. "A Role for an Independent Central Bank in Transition? The Case of Bulgaria." In *The Bulgarian Economy: Lessons from Reform during Early Transition*, edited by Derek C. Jones and Jeffrey Miller, 129–59. Brookfield, VT: Ashgate.

Claessens, Stijn. 2014. "An Overview of Macroprudential Policy Tools." IMF Working Paper, 14/214. IMF, Washington DC.

Claessens, Stijn, Giovanni Dell'Ariccia, Deniz Igan, and Luc Laeven. 2010. "Cross-Country Experiences and Policy Implications from the Global Financial Crisis." *Economic Policy* 25 (62): 267–93.

Claessens, Stijn, and M. Ayhan Kose. 2013. "Financial Crises Explanations, Types, and Implications." IMF Working Paper No. 13/28. IMF, Washington, DC.

Claessens, Stijn, Ali Demirgüç-Kunt, and Harry Huizinga. 2001. "How Does Foreign Entry Affect Domestic Banking Markets?" *Journal of Banking and Finance* 25 (5): 891–911.

Claessens, Stijn, and Neeltje van Horen. 2012. "Foreign Banks: Trends, Impact and Financial Stability." IMF Working Paper 12/20. IMF, Washington DC.

Claessens, Stijn, and Neeltje van Horen. 2014. "Foreign Banks: Trends and Impact." *Journal of Money, Credit and Banking* 46 (1): 295–326.

Claessens, Stijn, Neeltje van Horen, Tugba Gurcanlar, and Joaquin Mercado Sapiain. 2008. "Foreign Bank Presence in Developing Countries 1995–2006: Data and Trends." Unpublished paper. http://ssrn.com/abstract=1107295. Accessed May 21, 2016.

Clarke, George, Juan Miguel Crivelli, and Robert Cull. 2005. "The Direct and Indirect Impact of Bank Privatization and Foreign Entry on Access to Credit in Argentina's Provinces." *Journal of Banking and Finance* 29 (1): 5–29.

Clarke, George R. G., Robert Cull, and Maria Soledad Martínez Pería. 2006. "Foreign Bank Participation and Access to Credit across Firms in Developing Countries." *Journal of Comparative Economics* 34 (4): 774–95.

Cohen, Benjamin J. 1993. "Beyond EMU: The Problem of Sustainability." *Economics and Politics* 5 (2): 187–202.

Corcoran, Jason. 2013. "J.P. Morgan Is Hired by Russia to Promote Sovereign Credit Rating." *Bloomberg Businessweek*.

Cottarelli, Carlo, and Curzio Giannini. 1997. "Credibility without Rules? Monetary Frameworks in the Post-Bretton Woods Era." IMF Occasional Paper 154, January.

Crespo-Cuaresma, Jesús, Adam Geršl, and Tomáš Slačík. 2010. "Could Markets Have Helped Predict the Puzzling Exchange Rate Path in CESEE Countries During the Current Crisis?" *Focus on European Economic Integration* Q1/10: 32–48.

Crowe, Christopher, and Ellen E. Meade. 2008. "Central Bank Independence and Transparency: Evolution and Effectiveness." *European Journal of Political Economy* 24 (4): 763–77.

Crystal, Jennifer, B. Gerard Dages, and Linda S. Goldberg. 2001. "Does Foreign Ownership Contribute to Sounder Banks in Emerging Markets? The Latin American Experience." *Federal Reserve Bank of New York Staff Reports* 137 (September).

Cukierman, Alex. 1992. *Central Bank Strategy, Credibility, and Independence: Theory and Evidence.* Cambridge, MA: MIT Press.

Cukierman, Alex, Geoffrey P. Miller, and Bilin Neyapti. 2002. "Central Bank Reform, Liberalization and Inflation in Transition Economies-an International Perspective." *Journal of Monetary Economics* 49 (2): 237–64.

Cukierman, Alex, Steven B. Webb, and Bilin Neyapti. 1992. "Measuring the Independence of Central Banks and Its Effect on Policy Outcomes." *World Bank Economic Review* 6 (3): 353–98.

Čulík, Jan. 2000. "Dodgy Bankers." *Central Europe Review* 2 (25), June 26. http://www.ce-review.org/00/25/culik25.html

Cull, Robert, and María Soledad Martínez Pería. 2010. "Foreign Bank Participation in Developing Countries: What Do We Know About the Drivers and Consequences of This Phenomenon?" World Bank Policy Research Working Paper 5398. World Bank, Washington, DC.

Cull, Robert, and María Soledad Martínez Pería. 2012. "Bank Ownership and Lending Patterns During the 2008–2009 Financial Crisis: Evidence from Latin America and Eastern Europe." World Bank Policy Research Working Paper 6195. World Bank, Washington, DC.

Dages, B. Gerard, Linda Goldberg, and Daniel Kinney. 2000. "Foreign and Domestic Bank Participation in Emerging Markets: Lessons from Mexico and Argentina." NBER Working Paper 7714. National Bureau of Economic Research, Cambridge, MA.

Darvas, Szolt. 2011. "Exchange Rate Policy and Economic Growth after the Financial Crisis in Central and Eastern Europe." *Eurasian Geography and Economics* 52 (3): 390–408.

Dědek, Oldřich. 2000. "Měnový otřes '97." Working paper no. 15. Czech National Bank, Monetary Policy Division. http://www.cnb.cz/en/research/research_publications/mp_wp/download/c-vp15–99.pdf. Accessed May 21, 2016.

De Grauwe, Paul. 1992. *The Economics of Monetary Integration.* Oxford: Oxford University Press.

De Grauwe, Paul. 1994. *The Economics of Monetary Integration.* Oxford: Oxford University Press.

De Haas, Ralph, Yevgeniya Korniyenko, Elena Loukoianova, and Alexander Pivovarsky. 2012. "Foreign Banks and the Vienna Initiative: Turning Sinners into Saints?" IMF Working Paper 12/117. IMF, Washington, DC.

De Haas, Ralph, and Ilko Naaborg. 2006. "Foreign Banks in Transition Countries: To Whom Do They Lend and How Are They Financed?" *Financial Markets, Institutions & Instruments* 15 (4): 59–99.

De Haas, Ralph, and Iman van Lelyveld. 2006. "Foreign Banks and Credit Stability in Central and Eastern Europe: Friends or Foes?" *Journal of Banking and Finance* 30 (7): 1927–52.

De Haas, Ralph, and Iman van Lelyveld. 2014. "Multinational Banks and the Global Financial Crisis: Weathering the Perfect Storm?" *Journal of Money, Credit, and Banking* 46 (1): 333–64.

De La Torre, Augusto, Eduardo Levy Yeyati, Sergio L. Schmukler, Alberto Ades, and Graciela Kaminsky. 2003. "Living and Dying with Hard Pegs: The Rise and Fall of Argentina's Currency Board." In *Secondary Living and Dying with Hard Pegs: The Rise and Fall of Argentina's Currency Board*, 43–107 Washington, DC: Brookings Institution Press.

DeLong, J. Brad 1991. "Did J. P. Morgan's Men Add Value? An Economist's Perspective on Financial Capitalism." In *Inside the Business Enterprise: Historical Perspectives on the Use of Information*, edited by Peter Temin, 205–50. Chicago: University of Chicago Press.

De Melo, Martha, Cevdet Denizer, Alan Gelb, and Stoyan Tenev. 2001. "Circumstances and Choice: The Role of Initial Conditions and Policies in Transition Economies." *World Bank Economic Review* 15:1–31.

Del Negro, Marco, and Stephen J. Kay. 2002. "Global Banks, Local Crises: Bad News from Argentina." *Economic Review, Federal Reserve Bank of Atlanta* 87 (3): 1–18.

Demirgüç-Kunt, Asli, and Harry Huizinga. 2010. "Are Banks Too Big to Fail or Too Big to Save? International Evidence from Equity Prices and CDS Spreads." Policy Research Working Paper Series 5360. World Bank, Washington, DC.

Denizer, Cevdet, Raj M. Desai, and Nikolay Gueorguiev. 2006. "Political Competition and Financial Reform in Transition Economies." *Comparative Economic Studies* 48 (4): 563–82.

Desai, Raj. 1995. "Financial Market Reform in the Czech Republic, 1991–1994: The Revival of Repression." Working Paper no. 86, Centre for Economic Research and Graduate Education and Economics Institute, Prague.

Desai, Raj M., and Vladena Plocková. 1997. "Czech Republic." In *Between State and Market: Mass Privatization in Transition Economies, Studies of Economies in Transformation*, edited by Raj M. Desai, Ira W. Lieberman, and Stilpon Nestor, 190–96. Washington, DC: World Bank.

Detragiache, Enrica, and Poonam Gupta. 2006. "Foreign Banks in Emerging Market Crises: Evidence from Malaysia." IMF Working Paper 04/129. IMF, Washington, DC.

Detragiache, Enrica, Thierry Tressel, and Poonam Gupta. 2008. "Foreign Banks in Poor Countries: Theories and Evidence." *Journal of Finance* 63 (5): 2123–60.

Dhonte, Pierre. 1997. "Conditionality as an Instrument of Borrower Credibility." IMF paper on policy analysis and assessment, PPAA/97/2.

Di Giovanni, J., and J. C. Shambaugh. 2008. "The Impact of Foreign Interest Rates on the Economy: The Role of the Exchange Rate Regime." *Journal of International Economics* 74 (2): 341–61.

Dietrich, Diemo, Tobias Knedlik, and Axel Lindner. 2011. "Central and Eastern European Countries in the Global Financial Crisis: A Typical Twin Crisis?" *Post-Communist Economies* 23 (4): 415–32.

Dlouhý, Vladimir. 2004. "Privatization of Komerční Banka." In *Cultivation of Financial Markets in the Czech Republic*, edited by Michal Mejstřík. Prague: Karolinum Press.

Dobrinsky, Roumen. 1994. "The Problem of Bad Loans and Enterprise Indebtedness in Bulgaria." *Moct-Most* 4.

Dobrinsky, Roumen. 2000. "The Transition Crisis in Bulgaria." *Cambridge Journal of Economics* 24 (5): 581–602.

Domaç, Ilker, and Maria Soledad Martínez Pería. 2003. "Banking Crises and Exchange Rate Regimes: Is There a Link?" *Journal of International Economics* 61 (1): 41–72.

Domowitz, Ian, Jack Glen, and Ananth Madhavan. 1998. "Country and Currency Risk Premia in an Emerging Market." *Journal of Financial and Quantitative Analysis* 33 (2): 189–216.

Dornbusch, Rudiger. 1991. "Credibility and Stabilization." *Quarterly Journal of Economics* 106 (3): 837–50.

Dougherty, Carter. 2009. "Sweden Aids Bailout of Baltic Nations." *New York Times*, March 12.

Drábek, Zdenek. 1995. "IMF and IBRD Policies in the Former Czechoslovakia." *Journal of Comparative Economics* 20 (2): 235–64.

Drábek, Zdenek, Kamil Janáček, and Zdenek Tůma. 1994. "Inflation in the Czech and Slovak Republics, 1985–1991." *Journal of Comparative Economics* 18 (2): 146–74.

Drake, Paul W., ed. 1994. *Money Doctors, Foreign Debts, and Economic Reforms in Latin America from the 1890s to the Present.* Wilmington, DE: Scholarly Resources, Inc.

Drazen, Allan, and Paul R. Masson. 1994. "Credibility of Policies versus Credibility of Policymakers." *Quarterly Journal of Economics* 109 (3): 735–54.

Dreher, Axel, and Stefan Voigt. 2011. "Does Membership in International Organizations Increase Governments' Credibility? Testing the Effects of Delegating Powers." *Journal of Comparative Economics* 39 (3): 326–48.

Duenwald, Christoph, Nikolay Georguiev, and Andrea Schaechter. 2005. "Too Much of a Good Thing? Credit Booms in Transition Economies: The Cases of Bulgaria, Romania, and Ukraine." IMF Working Paper 05. IMF, Washington, DC.

Dyba, Karel, and Jan Švejnar. 1995. "A Comparative View of Economic Developments in the Czech Republic." In *The Czech Republic and Economic Transition in Eastern Europe*, edited by Jan Svejnar, 21–45. San Diego: Academic Press.

Edwards, Sebastian. 1986. "The Pricing of Bonds and Bank Loans in International Markets: An Empirical Analysis of Developing Countries' Foreign Borrowing." *European Economic Review* 30 (3): 565–89.

Edwards, Sebastian. 1996. "The Determinants of the Choice between Fixed and Flexible Exchange-Rate Regimes." NBER Working Paper 5756. National Bureau for Economic Research, Cambridge, MA.

Edwards, Sebastian. 2001. "Exchange Rate Regimes, Capital Flows and Crisis Prevention." NBER Working Papers 8529. National Bureau of Economic Research, Cambridge, MA.

Edwards, Sebastian. 2003. "Exchange Rate Regimes, Capital Flows, and Crisis Prevention." In *Economic and Financial Crises in Emerging Market Economies*, edited by Martin Feldstein, 31–78. Chicago: University of Chicago Press.

Edwards, Sebastian. 2005. "Establishing Credibility: The Role of Foreign Advisors." NBER Working Paper 11429. National Bureau of Economic Research, Cambridge, MA.

Eichengreen, Barry. 1992. *Golden Fetters: The Gold Standard and the Great Depression, 1919–1939*. Oxford: Oxford University Press.

Eichengreen, Barry. 1994. *International Monetary Arrangements for the 21st Century*. Washington, DC: Brookings Institution.

Eichengreen, Barry. 2008. *Globalizing Capital: History of the International Monetary System*, 2nd ed. Princeton: Princeton University Press.

Eichengreen, Barry, and Ricardo Hausmann. 1999. *Exchange Rates and Financial Fragility*. NBER Working Paper 7418. National Bureau of Economic Research, Cambridge, MA.

Eichengreen, Barry, and Ashoka Mody. 1998. "What Explains Changing Spreads on Emerging-Market Debt: Fundamentals or Market Sentiment?" NBER Working Paper 6408. National Bureau of Economic Research, Cambridge, MA.

Eichengreen Barry, and Andrew K. Rose. 1998. "Staying Afloat When the Wind Shifts: External Factors and Emerging-Market Banking Crises." NBER Working Paper 6370. National Bureau for Economic Research, Cambridge, MA.

Eichengreen, Barry, Andrew K. Rose, and Charles Wyplosz. 1995. "Exchange Market Mayhem: The Antecedents and Aftermath of Speculative Attacks." *Economic Policy* 21 (October): 251–96.

Einzig, Paul. 1931. *The Fight for Financial Supremacy*. London: Macmillan.

Epstein, Rachel. 2008. "Transnational Actors and Bank Privatization." In *Transnational Actors in Central and East European Transitions*, edited by Mitchell A. Orenstein, Stephen Bloom, and Nicole Lindstrom, 98–117. Pittsburgh: University of Pittsburgh Press.

Epstein, Rachel. 2014. "Assets or Liabilities? The Politics of Bank Ownership." *Review of International Political Economy* 21 (4): 765–89.

Erbenová, Michaela, and Tomáš Holub. 2006. "Czech Trade, Exchange Rate, and

Monetary Policies in the 1990s." In *Can Regional Arrangements Enforce Trade Discipline? The Story of the EU Enlargment*, edited by Zdenek Drabek, 113–53. New York: Palgrave MacMillan.

European Bank for Reconstruction and Development. 2009. Transition Report 2009: Transition in Crisis? (November): 1–268.

Ewing, Jack, and Georgi Kantchev. 2014. "Feud Between Oligarchs Seen as Cause of Bank Run in Bulgaria." *New York Times*, June 30.

Fang, Lily Hua. 2005. "Investment Bank Reputation and the Price and Quality of Underwriting Services." *Journal of Finance* 60 (6): 2729–61.

Faust, Jon, and Lars E. O. Svensson. 2001. "Transparency and Credibility: Monetary Policy with Unobservable Goals." *International Economic Review* 42 (2): 369–97.

Feldmann, Magnus, and Razeen Sally. 2002. "From the Soviet Union to the European Union: Estonian Trade Policy, 1991–2000." *The World Economy* 25 (1): 79–106.

Feldstein, Martin. 2002. "Argentina's Fall: Lessons from the Latest Financial Crisis." *Foreign Affairs*, March/April.

Ferguson, Niall, and Moritz Schularick. 2012. "The 'Thin Film of Gold': Monetary Rules and Policy Credibility." *European Review of Economic History* 16 (4): 384–407.

Fidrmuc, Jan, Julius Horvath, and Jarko Fidrmuc. 1999. "The Stability of Monetary Unions: Lessons from the Breakup of Czechoslovakia." *Journal of Comparative Economics* 27 (4): 753–81.

Fisher, Stanley. 1997. "Moderate Inflation and the Problems Connected with It." In *Five Years of the Estonian Kroon: Papers of the Academic Conference Held in Tallinn on 18 June 1997*. Tallinn: Bank of Estonia.

Fisher, Stanley. 2001. "Exchange Rate Regimes: Is the Bipolar View Correct?" *Journal of Economic Perspectives* 15 (2): 3–24.

Fisher, Stanley, and Ratna Sahay. 2000. "Economies in Transition: Taking Stock." *Finance and Development* 37 (September): 2–6.

Flandreau, Marc. 2003a. *Money Doctors: The Experience of International Financial Advising 1850–2000*. London: Routledge.

Flandreau, Marc, ed. 2003b. "Introduction: Money and Doctors." In *Money Doctors: The Experience of International Financial Advising 1850–2000*, edited by Marc Flandreau. London: Routledge.

Flandreau, Marc, and Juan H. Flores. 2009. "Bonds and Brands: Foundations of Sovereign Debt Markets, 1820–1830." *Journal of Economic History* 69 (3): 646–84.

Flandreau, Marc, and Juan H. Flores. 2012. "The Peaceful Conspiracy: Bond Markets and International Relations During the Pax Britannica." *International Organization* 66 (2): 211–41.

Flandreau, Marc, and Frédéric Zumer. *The Making of Global Finance: 1880–1913*. Paris: OECD, 2004.

Fleming, Alex. 2001. "Banking Sector Restructuring in the Baltics." In *Transitional*

Economies: Banking, Finance, Institutions, edited by Yelena Kalyuzhnova and Michael Taylor. New York: Palgrave.

Fleming, Marcus J. 1962. "Domestic Financial Policies under Fixed and Floating Exchange Rates." *IMF Staff Papers* 9 (November): 369–79.

Freixas, Xavier, Luc Laeven, and José-Luis Peydró. 2015. *Systemic Risk, Crises, and Macroprudential Regulation*. Cambridge, MA: MIT Press.

Focarelli, Dario, and Alberto Pozzolo. 2001. "The Patterns of Cross-Border Bank Mergers and Shareholdings in OECD Countries." *Journal of Banking and Finance* 25 (2): 2305–37.

Focarelli, Dario, and Alberto Pozzolo. 2005. "Where Do Banks Expand Abroad? An Empirical Analysis," *Journal of Business* 79 (1): 2435–63.

Fouejieu, Armand, and Scott Roger. 2013. "Inflation Targeting and Country Risk; an Empirical Investigation." IMF Working Paper 13/21. IMF, Washington, DC.

Frane, Adam, Matevž Tomšič, and Primož Kristan. 2008. "Political Elite, Civil Society, and Type of Capitalism." *East European Quarterly* XLII (1): 43–62.

Frankel, Jeffrey. 1995. "Monetary Regime Choice for a Semi-Open Country." In *Capital Controls, Exchange Rates, and Monetary Policy in the World Economy*, edited by Sebastian Edwards. Cambridge: Cambridge University Press.

Frankel, Jeffrey. 1999. *No Single Currency Regime Is Right for All Countries or at All Times*, Essays in International Finance No. 215. Princeton: Princeton University Press.

Frankel, Jeffrey, and Andrew Rose. 1996. "Currency Crisis in Emerging Markets: Empirical Indicators." NBER Working Paper 5437. Cambridge, MA: National Bureau for Economic Research.

Frankel, Jeffrey, Sergio L. Schmukler, and Luis Servén. 2004. "Global Transmission of Interest Rates: Monetary Independence and Currency Regime." *Journal of International Money and Finance* 23 (5): 701–33.

Fratiani, Michelle, and Jürgen von Hagen. 1992. *The European Monetary System and European Monetary Union*. Boulder: West New Press.

Frieden, Jeffry. 1991. "Invested Interests: The Politics of National Economic Policy in a World of Global Finance." *International Organization* 45 (4): 425–51.

Frieden, Jeffry. 2015. *Currency Politics: The Political Economy of Exchange Rate Policy*. Princeton: Princeton University Press.

Frieden, Jeffry. 2016. "The Governance of International Finance." *Annual Review of Political Science* 19 (1): 33–48.

Frieden, Jeffry, and Ernesto Stein, ed. 2001. *The Currency Game: Exchange Rate Politics in Latin America*. Washington, DC: Inter-American Development Bank.

Friedman, Milton. 1953. "The Case for Flexible Exchange Rates." In Friedman, *Essays in Positive Economics*, 157–203. Chicago: University of Chicago Press.

Frye, Timothy. 2010. *Building States and Markets after Communism: The Perils of Polarized Democracy*. Cambridge: Cambridge University Press.

Fungáčová, Zuzana, and Iikka Korhonen. 2014. Ukrainian Banking Sector in Turmoil. BOFIT Policy Brief. 10. August. Bank of Finland, Helsinki.

Galindo, Arturo J., Alejandro Izquierdo, and Liliana Rojas-Suárez. 2010. "Financial

Integration and Foreign Banks in Latin America: How Do They Impact the Transmission of External Financial Shocks?" IDB Working Paper Series no. IDB-WP-116. Inter-American Development Bank, Washington, DC.

Ganev, Georgy, Marek Jarocinski, Rossitza Lubenova, Przemyslaw Wozniak. 2001. "Credibility of the Exchange Rate Policy in Bulgaria." CASE Report no. 38. Center for Social and Economic Research, Warsaw.

García-Herrero, Alicia, and Maria Soledad Martínez Pería. 2007. "The Mix of International Banks' Foreign Claims: Determinants and Implications." *Journal of Banking and Finance* 31 (6): 1613–31.

Gardó, Sandor, and Reiner Martin. 2010. "The Impact of the Global Economic and Financial Crisis on Central, Eastern and South-Eastern Europe: A Stock-Taking Exercise." ECB Occasional Paper No. 114. Frankfurt: European Central Bank.

Gedeon, Shirley. 2010. "The Political Economy of Currency Boards: Case of Bosnia and Herzegovina." *South East European Journal of Economics and Business* 5 (2): 7–20.

Gelos, Gaston, and Jorge Roldós. 2004. "Consolidation and Market Structure in Emerging Market Banking Systems." *Emerging Markets Review* 5 (1): 39–59.

Gelos, R. Gaston, and Shang-Jin Wei. 2005. "Transparency and International Portfolio Holdings." *The Journal of Finance* 60 (6): 2987–3020.

Gerschenkron, Alexander. 1962. *Economic Backwardness in Historical Perspective: A Book of Essays*. Cambridge, MA: Harvard University Press.

Geršl, Adam. 2006. "Political Pressure on Central Banks: The Case of the Czech National Bank." Working Paper 8/2006, Institute of Economic Studies, Faculty of Social Sciences, Charles University, Prague.

Ghosh, Atish R., Anne-Marie Gulde, and Holger Wolf. 2002. *Exchange Rate Regimes: Choices and Consequences*. Cambridge, MA: MIT Press.

Giannetti, Mariassunta, and Steven Ongena. 2009. "Financial Integration and Firm Performance: Evidence from Foreign Bank Entry in Emerging Markets." *Review of Finance* 13 (2): 181–223.

Giavazzi, Francesco, and Marco Pagano. 1988. "The Advantage of Tying One's Hands: EMS Discipline and Central Bank Credibility." *European Economic Review* 32 (5): 1055–75.

Goldberg, Linda. 2004. "Financial-Sector Foreign Direct Investment and Host Countries: New and Old Lessons." Federal Reserve Bank of New York Staff Reports No. 183.

Goldberg, Linda. 2009. "Understanding Banking Sector Globalisation." International Monetary Fund Staff Papers 56. IMF, Washington, DC.

Goldberg, Linda. 2013. "Banking Globalization, Transmission, and Monetary Policy Autonomy." *Svenges Riksbank Economic Review* 3 (November 2013): 161–93.

Gomulka, Stanislaw. 1993. "The Financial Situation of Polish Enterprises 1992–1993 and Its Impact on Monetary and Fiscal Policies." Center for Social & Economic Research, Warsaw.

Gomulka, Stanislaw. 1995. "The IMF Supported Programs of Poland and Russia,

1990–1994: Principles, Errors, and Results." *Journal of Comparative Economics* 20 (3): 316–46.

Goodhart, Charles, and Gerhard Illing, eds. 2002. *Financial Crises, Contagion, and the Lender of Last Resort: A Reader.* Oxford: Oxford University Press.

Goodman, John B. 1992. *Monetary Sovereignty: The Politics of Central Banking in Western Europe.* Ithaca: Cornell University Press.

Gorton, Garry. 1996. "Reputation Formation in Early Banknotes Markets." *Journal of Political Economy* 104 (2): 346–97.

Grabel, Ilene. 2000. "The Political Economy of 'Policy Credibility': The New-Classical Macroeconomics and the Remaking of Emerging Economies." *Cambridge Journal of Economics* 24 (1): 1–19.

Grabel, Ilene. 2003. "Ideology, Power, and the Rise of Independent Monetary Institutions in Emerging Economies." In *Monetary Orders: Ambiguous Economics, Ubiquitous Politics,* edited by Jonathan Kirshner, 25–54. Ithaca: Cornell University Press.

Gray, Julia. 2009. "International Organization as a Seal of Approval: European Union Accession and Investor Risk." *American Journal of Political Science* 53 (4): 931–49.

Gray, Julia. 2013. *The Company States Keep: International Economic Organizations and Investor Perceptions.* New York: Cambridge University Press.

Grittersová, Jana. 2009. "Taming Financiers: The Political Economy of Exchange Rate Policy in Eastern Europe." PhD dissertation, Cornell University.

Grittersová, Jana. 2014a. "Exchange Rates in Transition Economies." In *The International Political Economy of the International Monetary and Financial System,* edited by Thomas Oatley and W. Kindred Winecoff, Handbooks of Research on International Political Economy, 201–23. Cheltenham, UK: Edward Elgar.

Grittersová, Jana. 2014b. "Transfer of Reputation: Multinational Banks and Perceived Creditworthiness of Transition Countries." *Review of International Political Economy* 21 (4): 878–912.

Grønn, Audun, and Maria Wallin Fredholm. 2013. "Baltic and Icelandic Experiences of Capital Flows and Capital Flow Measures." IMF Working Paper 13/242. IMF, Washington, DC.

Gros, Daniel. 2003. "Who Needs Foreign Banks?" Center for European Studies Working Paper 998. Center for European Policy Studies, Brussels.

Gros, Daniel, and Cinzia Alcidi. 2013. "Country Adjustment to a 'Sudden Stop': Does the Euro Make a Difference?" Economic Papers 492. European Commission, Directorate-General for Economic and Financial Affairs, Brussels.

Grosse, Robert, and Lawrence G. Goldberg. 1991. "Foreign Bank Activity in the United States: An Analysis by Country of Origin." *Journal of Banking & Finance* 15 (6): 1093–1112.

Grubel, Herbert. 1977. "A Theory of Multinational Banking." *Banca Nazionale del Lavoro Quarterly Review* 123: 349–63.

Grzymala-Busse, Anna M. 2002. *Redeeming the Communist Past: The Regeneration of Communist Parties in East Central Europe.* Cambridge: Cambridge University Press.

Guidotti, Pablo, and Carlos Végh. 1999. "Losing Credibility: The Stabilization Blues." *International Economic Review* 40 (1): 23–51.

Guillén, Mauro F., and Adrian E. Tschoegl. 2000. "The Internationalization of Retail Banking: The Case of the Spanish Banks in Latin America." *Transnational Corporations* 9: 63–97.

Guillén, Mauro F., and Adrian Tschoegl. 2008. *Building a Global Bank: The Rise of Banco Santander*. Princeton: Princeton University Press.

Guisinger, Alexandra, and David Andrew Singer. 2010. "Exchange Rate Proclamations and Inflation-Fighting Credibility." *International Organization* 64 (2): 313–37.

Gumus, Inci. 2011. "Exchange Rate Policy and Sovereign Spreads in Emerging Market Economies." *Review of International Economics* 19 (4): 649–63.

Haber, Stephen, and Aldo Musacchio. 2005. "Contract Rights and Risk Aversion: Foreign Banks and the Mexican Economy, 1997–2004." Working Paper, Stanford Center for International Development, Stanford, CA.

Haggard, Stephan, and Robert R. Kaufman. 1995. *The Political Economy of Democratic Transitions*. Princeton: Princeton University Press.

Hagendorff, Jens, Kevin Keasey, and Francesco Vallascas. 2013. *Size, Risk, and Governance in European Banking*. Oxford: Oxford University Press.

Hallerberg, Mark, and Lúcio Vinhas de Souza. 2000. "The Political Business Cycles of EU Accession Countries." Tinbergen Institute Discussion Papers, 00–085/2. Tinbergen Institute, Amsterdam.

Hammermann, Felix, and Mark Flanagan. 2009. "What Explains Persistent Inflation Differentials Across Transition Economies?" *Economics of Transition* 17 (2): 297–328.

Hanke, Steve. 2002. "On Dollarization and Currency Boards: Error and Deception." *Journal of Policy Reform* 5 (4): 203–32.

Hanke Steve H., Lars Jonung, and Kurt Schuler. 1992. *Monetary Reform for a Free Estonia: A Currency Board Solution*. Stockholm: SNS Forlag.

Hanson, Stephen E. 1995. "The Leninist Legacy and Institutional Change." *Comparative Political Studies* 28 (2): 306–14.

Hanson, Stephen E., and Grzegorz Ekiert, eds. 2003. *Capitalism and Democracy in Eastern and Central Europe: Assessing the Legacy of Communist Rule*. Cambridge: Cambridge University Press.

Hansson, Ardo H., and Jeffrey D. Sachs. 1992. "Crowning the Estonian Kroon." *Transition* 3 (3): 1–3. World Bank, Washington, DC.

Harrison, G. B., ed. 1948. *Shakespeare: The Complete Works*. New York: Harcourt, Brace and World.

Hauner, David, Jiri Jonas, and Manmohan S. Kumar. 2007. "Policy Credibility and Sovereign Credit: The Case of the New EU Member States." IMF Working Paper 07/01. IMF, Washington, DC.

Havel, Jiri. 2004. "Czech Banking: The Privatisation Challenge." In *The Cultivation of Czech Financial Markets*, edited by Michal Mejstrik et al., 175–96. Prague: Karolinum Press.

Hefeker, Carsten. 1997. *Interest Groups and Monetary Integration: The Political Economy of Exchange Rate Regime Choice.* Boulder: Westview Press.

Hellman, Joel S. 1998. "Winners Take All: The Politics of Partial Reform in Post-communist Transitions." *World Politics* 50 (2): 203–34.

Henning, C. Randall. 1994. *Currencies and Politics in the United States, Germany, and Japan.* Washington, DC: Institute for International Economics.

Herrmann, Sabine, and Dubravko Mihaljek. 2013. "The Determinants of Cross-Border Bank Flows to Emerging Markets." *Economics of Transition* 21 (3): 479–508.

Hibbs, Douglas A., Jr. 1977. "Political Parties and Macroeconomic Policy." *American Political Science Review* 71 (4): 1467–87.

Higgins, Andrew. 2015. "Despite Assurances, Bulgaria Fears a Spillover of Troubles From Greece." *New York Times,* June 25.

Hirschman, Albert O. 1970. *Exit, Voice, and Loyalty: Responses to Decline in Firms, Organizations and States.* Cambridge, MA: Harvard University Press.

Holden, Steinar, and Birger Vikøren. 1996. "The Credibility of a Fixed Exchange Rate: How Reputation Is Gained or Lost." *Scandinavian Journal of Economics* 98 (4): 485–502.

Hollyer, James R., B. Peter Rosendorff, and James Raymond Vreeland. 2011. "Democracy and Transparency." *Journal of Politics* 73 (4): 1191–1205.

Holub, Tomáš, and Zdeněk Tůma. 2006. "Managing Capital Inflows in the Czech Republic: Experiences, Problems and Questions." Prague, unpublished manuscript.

Horowitz, Shale and Martin Petráš. 2003. "Pride and Prejudice in Prague: Understanding Early Policy Error and Belated Reform in the Czech Economic Transition." *East European Policies and Societies* 1 (2): 231–65.

Horváth, Julius. 1999. "Currency Crisis in the Czech Republic in May 1997." *Post-Communist Economies* 11 (3): 277–98.

Houston, Joel F., Chen Lin, Ping Lin, and Yue Ma. 2010. "Creditor Rights, Information Sharing, and Bank Risk Taking." *Journal of Financial Economics* 96 (3): 485–512.

Hrnčíř, Miroslav. 1999. "The Czech Case: Fixed Exchange Rates through Stages of Transition." In *Exchange-Rate Policies for Emerging Market Economies,* edited by Clas G. Wihlborg, Richard J. Sweeney, and Thomas D. Willett, 309–31. Boulder, CO: Westview Press.

Hutchison, Michael M., and Ilan Noy. 2005. "How Bad Are Twins? Output Costs of Currency and Banking Crises." *Journal of Money, Credit and Banking* 37 (4): 725–52.

Huterski, Robert, Richard Nicholls, and Zenon Wisniewski. 2004. "Central Bank Independence in Poland." In *Central Banking in Eastern Europe,* edited by Nigel Healey and Barry Harrison, 193–224. London: Routledge.

Ilzetzki, Ethan O., Carmen M. Reinhart, and Kenneth S. Rogoff. 2008. "Exchange Rate Arrangements Entering the 21st Century: Which Anchor Will Hold?" Available on Carmen Reinhart's website, http://www.carmenreinhart.com/data/browse-by-topic/topics/11/

Ignatiev, Petar. 2005. *Banking Crisis in Bulgaria during 1996–97* (in Bulgarian). Sofia: Ciela.

Impavido, G., H. Rudolph, and L. Ruggerone. 2013. "Bank Funding in Central, Eastern and South Eastern Europe Post Lehman: A 'New Normal'?" IMF Working Paper 13/148. IMF, Washington, DC.

Ingves, Stefan. 2010. "The Crisis in the Baltics—The Riksbank's Measures, Assessments and Lessons Learned." Speech at the Riksdag Committee of Finance, Stockholm February 10, 2010.

Ingves, Stefan, Göran Lind, Masaaki Shirakawa, Jaime Caruana, and Guillermo Ortiz Martínez. 2009. "Lessons Learned from Previous Banking Crises: Sweden, Japan, Spain and Mexico." Occasional Paper 79. Group of Thirty, Washington, DC.

International Monetary Fund. 1999. "Estonia: Selected Issues and Statistical Appendix." IMF Staff Country Report No. 00/60. IMF, Washington, DC.

International Monetary Fund. 2002. "The Czech Republic." IMF Country Report 02/167. IMF, Washington, DC.

International Monetary Fund. 2006. "Bulgaria: Selected Issues and Statistics." Appendix, IMF Country Report 06/299. IMF: Washington, DC.

International Monetary Fund. 2010. "Czech Republic Staff Report for the 2010 Article IV Consultation." IMF Country Report 10/60. IMF, Washington, DC.

International Monetary Fund. 2011. "Cross-Cutting Themes in Advanced Economies with Emerging Market Banking Links." IMF Policy Paper (November 14). IMF, Washington, DC.

International Monetary Fund. 2013. "Annual Report on Exchange Rate Arrangements and Exchange Restrictions." IMF, Washington, DC.

Irwin, Gregor. 2004. "Currency Boards and Currency Crises." *Oxford Economic Papers* 56 (1): 64–87.

Jahjah, Samir, B. I. N. Wei, and Vivian Zhanwei Yue. 2013. "Exchange Rate Policy and Sovereign Bond Spreads in Developing Countries." *Journal of Money, Credit and Banking* 45 (7): 1275–1300.

Jappelli, Tullio, and Marco Pagano. 2002. "Information Sharing, Lending and Defaults: Cross-Country Evidence." *Journal of Banking & Finance* 26 (10): 2017–45.

Jayaratne, Jith, and Philip E. Strahan. 1996. "The Finance-Growth Nexus: Evidence from Bank Branch Deregulation." *Quarterly Journal of Economics* 111 (3): 639–70.

Johnson, Juliet. 2000. *A Fistful of Rubles: The Rise and Fall of the Russian Banking System.* Ithaca: Cornell University Press.

Johnson, Juliet. 2016. *Priests of Prosperity: How Central Bankers Transformed the Postcommunist World.* Ithaca: Cornell University Press.

Johnson, Juliet, and Andrew Barnes. 2014. "Financial Nationalism and Its International Enablers: The Hungarian Experience." *Review of International Political Economy* 22 (3): 535–69.

Jonas, Jiri, and Frederic S. Mishkin. 2007. "Inflation Targeting in Transition Countries: Experience and Prospects." In *Monetary Policy Strategy*, edited by Frederic Mishkin, 345–403. Cambridge, MA: MIT Press.

Jones, Geoffrey. 1993. *British Multinational Banking*. Oxford: Oxford University Press.

Jones, Geoffrey, ed. 2012. *Banks as Multinationals*. New York: Routledge.

Kallas, Siim. 2002. "Concluding Speech of Mr. Siim Kallas, Prime Minister of the Republic of Estonia." Paper presented at the conference Alternative Exchange Rate Regimes in the Globalized World, Tallinn, Estonia.

Kallas, Siim and Mart Sõrg. 1994. "Currency Reform in Estonia." Working Paper No. 9. Institute of Economics, Tallinn, Estonia.

Kamil, Herman, and Kulwant Rai. 2010. "The Global Credit Crunch and Foreign Banks' Lending to Emerging Markets: Why Did Latin America Fare Better?" IMF Working Paper 10/102. IMF, Washington, DC.

Kamil, Herman, and Kulwant Rai. 2013. "Global Deleveraging and Foreign Banks' Lending to Latin American Countries." *Economía* 13 (2): 1–29.

Kaminski, Antoni Z. 2001. "Poland: Compatibility of External and Internal Democratic Designs." In *Democratic Consolidation in Eastern Europe*, edited by Jan Zielonka and Alex Pravda. Oxford: Oxford University Press.

Kaminsky, Graciela, Saul Lizondo, and Carmen Reinhart. 1998. "Leading Indicators of Currency Crises." *IMF Staff Papers* 45 (1): 1–48.

Kaminsky, Graciela L., and Carmen Reinhart. 1999. "The Twin Crises: The Causes of Banking and Balance-of-Payments Problems." *American Economic Review* 89 (3): 474–500.

Karnitschnig, Matthew, with Hana Lesenarova. 2000. "Meltdown in Prague: A Near-Collapse at IPB Gives a Stark Lesson in How Not to Privatize a Bank." *Business Week*, August 7.

Kawalec, Stefan, and Krzysztof Kluza. 2003. "Two Models of Systemic Bank Restructuring: Independence with Privatization Strategy." Paper presented at the World Bank conference Transforming Public Sector Banks. Washington, DC, April 9–10.

Keefer, Philip, and David Stasavage. 2002. "Checks and Balances, Private Information and the Credibility of Monetary Commitments." *International Organization* 56 (3): 751–74.

Keefer, Philip, and David Stasavage. 2003. "The Limits of Delegation: Veto Players, Central Bank Independence, and the Credibility of Monetary Policy." *American Political Science Review* 97 (3): 407–23.

Kennen, Peter B. 1969. "The Theory of Optimum Currency Areas: An Eclectic View." In *Monetary Problems of the International Economy*, edited by Robert Mundell and Alexander Swoboda. Chicago: University of Chicago Press.

Khoury, Joseph Sarkis, and Clas Wihlborg. 2006. "Outsourcing Central Banking: Lessons from Estonia." *Journal of Policy Reform* 9 (2): 125–44.

Kindleberger, Charles P. 1970. *Power and Money*. New York and London: Basic Books.

Kindleberger, Charles. 1986. *The World in Depression, 1929–1939*. Berkeley: University of California Press.

Kindleberger, Charles, and Robert Z. Aliber. 2005. *Manias, Panics, and Crashes: A History of Financial Crises*. Hoboken, NJ: John Wiley & Sons.

King, Lawrence P., and Aleksandra Sznajder. 2006. "The State-Led Transition to Liberal Capitalism: Neoliberal, Organizational, World-Systems, and Social Structural Explanations of Poland's Economic Success." *American Journal of Sociology* 112 (3): 751–801.

King, Mervyn 2002. "No Money, No Inflation—the Role of Money in the Economy." *Bank of England Quarterly Bulletin* 42 (2): 162–77.

Kirshner, Jonathan. 2007. *Appeasing Bankers: Financial Caution on the Road to War*. Princeton: Princeton University Press.

Klaus, Václav. 1993. "Creating a Stable Monetary Order." *Cato Journal* 12 (September–October): 527–31.

Klaus, Václav. 1994. "Systemic Change: The Delicate Mixture of Intentions and Spontaneity." *Cato Journal* 14 (2): 171–77.

Klaus, Václav. 1997a. "Promoting Financial Stability in the Transition Economies of Central and Eastern Europe." Paper presented at the conference Maintaining Financial Stability in a Global Economy, Federal Reserve Bank of Kansas City, Jackson Hole, WY, August 28–30.

Klaus, Václav. 1997b. *Renaissance: The Rebirth of Liberty in the Heart of Europe*. Washington, DC: CATO Institute.

Klaus, Václav. 2000. "Tři Roky po Měnové Krizi: Rekapitulace Událostí a Jejich Souvislostí, Aby Se Na Některé Veci Nezapomnelo." In Tři Roky od Měnové Krize. *Sborník textů č. 5*, edited by Ivan Kočárník, Václav Klaus, Karel Dyba et al. Vol. 5/2000. Prague: Centrum pro Ekonomiku a Politiku.

Klein, Michael W., and Jay C. Shambaugh. 2010. *Exchange Rate Regimes in the Modern Era*. Cambridge, MA: MIT Press.

Klein, Michael W., and Jay C. Shambaugh. 2013. "Rounding the Corners of the Policy Trilemma." NBER Working Paper 19461. National Bureau of Economic Research, Cambridge, MA.

Knöbl, Adalbert, Andres Sutt, and Basil Zavoico. 2002. "The Estonian Currency Board: Its Introduction and Role in the Early Success of Estonia's Transition to a Market Economy." IMF Working Paper 02/96. IMF, Washington, DC.

Knot, Klaas, Jan-Egbert Sturm, and Jakob de Haan. 1998. "The Credibility of the European Exchange Rate Mechanism." *Oxford Economic Papers* 50 (2): 186–200.

Koch, Elmar B. 1997. "Exchange Rates and Monetary Policy in Central Europe: A Survey of Some Issues." Oesterreichische NationalBank Working Paper 24. Oesterreichische NationalBank, Vienna.

Kochanowicz, Jacek, Piotr Kozarzewski, and Richard Woodward. 2005. "Understanding Reform: The Case of Poland." CASE Report No. 59/2005. Center for Social and Economic Research, Warsaw.

Koford, Kenneth. 2000. "Citizen Restraints on 'Leviathan' Government: Transition Politics in Bulgaria." *European Journal of Political Economy* 16 (2): 307–38.

Koford, Kenneth, and Adrian E. Tschoegl. 2003. "Foreign Banks in Bulgaria, 1875–

2002." William Davidson Working Paper no. 537. William Davidson Institute, University of Michigan Business School, Ann Arbor, MI.

Koleva, Petia, and Caroline Vincensini. 2002. "The Evolution Trajectories of Voucher Funds: Towards Western-Type Institutional Investors? The Case of the Czech Republic and Bulgaria." *Economics of Planning* 35 (1): 79–105.

Konopielko, Lukasz. 1999. "Foreign Banks' Entry into Central and East European Markets: Motives and Activities." *Post-Communist Economies* 11 (4): 463–85.

Korbel, Josef. 1977. *Twentieth-Century Czechoslovakia: The Meaning of its History.* New York: Columbia University Press.

Korhonen, Iikka. 2000. "Currency Boards in the Baltic Countries: What Have We Learned?" *Post-Communist Economies* 12 (1): 25–46.

Kowalski, Tadeusz, and Renata Stawarska. 1999. "Poland's Exchange Rate Policy in the 1990s." In *Exchange Rate Policies for Emerging Market Economies*, edited by R. J. Sweeney, C. Wihlborg, and T. D. Willett, 351–74. Boulder, CO: Westview Press.

Kraft, Vahur. 2002. "Keynote Speech of Mr. Vahur Kraft, Governor of Eesti Pank." Alternative Exchange Rate Regimes in the Globalised World: Conference Dedicated to the 10th Anniversary of the Re-introduction of the Estonian Kroon, Tallinn, Estonia.

Kreps, David M., and Robert Wilson. 1982. "Reputation and Imperfect Information." *Journal of Economic Theory* 27 (2): 253–79.

Kreuzbergova, Eva. 2006. "Banking Socialism in Transition: The Experience of the Czech Republic." *Global Business and Economics Review* 8 (1/2): 161–77.

Krugman, Paul. 1979. "A Model of Balance-of-Payments Crises." *Journal of Money, Credit, and Banking* 11 (3): 311–25.

Krugman, Paul. 1998. "What Happened to Asia." Mimeo (January). MIT.

Krugman, Paul, Maurice Obstfeld, and Marc J. Melitz. 2015. *International Economics: Theory and Policy*, 10th ed. Boston: Pearson.

Krzak, Maciej, and Helmut Ettl. 1999. "Is Direct Inflation Targeting an Alternative for Central Europe? The Case of the Czech Republic and Poland." *Focus in Transition 1/1999*, Oesterreichische Nationalbank.

Kukk, Kalev. 1997. "The Baltic States: Estonia, Latvia and Lithuania." In *Going Global: Transition in the World Economy*, edited by Padma Desai, 243–72. Cambridge, MA: MIT Press.

Kutan, Ali M., and Josef C. Brada. 1998. "The Persistence of Moderate Inflation in the Czech Republic and the Koruna Crisis of May 1997." Working Paper 1998–021A, Federal Reserve Bank of St. Louis.

Kydland, Finn, and Edward Prescott. 1977. "Rules Rather Than Discretion: The Inconsistency of Optimal Plans." *Journal of Political Economy* 85 (3): 473–91.

La Porta, Rafael, Florencio Lopez-de-Silanes, and Andrei Shleifer. 2002. "Government Ownership of Banks." *Journal of Finance* 57 (1): 265–301.

Laar, Mart. 2002. *Little Country That Could.* London: Centre for Research into Post-Communist Economies.

Laar, Mart. 2007. "The Estonian Economic Miracle." Backgrounder no. 2060 on Democracy and Human Rights. Washington, DC: Heritage Foundation.

Laeven, Luc, and Fabian Valencia. 2013. "Systemic Banking Crises Database." *IMF Economic Review* 61 (2).

Lahnsteiner, Mathias. 2011. "The Refinancing Structure of Banks in Selected CE-SEE Countries." *Focus on European Economic Integration* Q1/11: 44–69. Oesterreichische Nationalbank.

Leven, Bozena 2011. "Avoiding Crisis Contagion: Poland's Case." *Communist and Post-Communist Studies* 44 (3): 183–87.

Levine, Ross. 2001. "International Financial Liberalization and Economic Growth." *Review of International Economics* 9 (4): 688–701.

Levy-Yeyati, Eduardo, and Federico Sturzenegger. 2005. "Classifying Exchange Rate Regimes: Deeds vs. Words." *European Economic Review* 49 (6): 1603–35.

Levy-Yeyati, Eduardo, Federico Sturzenegger, and Iliana Reggio. 2010. "On Endogeneity of Exchange Rate Regimes." *European Economic Review* 54 (5): 659–77.

Lewis, Mervyn K. 2002. "Currency Boards and Currency Arrangements in Transition Economies." In *Banking Reforms in South-East Europe,* edited by Željko Šević, 79–99. Cheltenham, UK: Edward Elgar.

Lohmann, Susanne 1992. "Optimal Commitment in Monetary Policy: Credibility versus Flexibility." *American Economic Review* 82(1): 273–86.

Loriaux, Michael, Meredith Woo-Cummings, Kent Calder, Sylvia Maxfield, and Sofia A. Pérez. 1997. *Capital Ungoverned: Liberalizing Finance in Interventionist States.* Ithaca: Cornell University Press.

Łyziak, Tomasz. 2013. "A Note on Central Bank Transparency and Credibility in Poland." NBP Working Paper No. 162. National Bank of Poland, Warsaw.

Łyziak, Tomasz. 2014. "Inflation Expectations in Poland, 2001–2013: Measurement and Macroeconomic Testing." NBP Working Paper No. 178. National Bank of Poland, Warsaw.

Łyziak, Tomasz, Joanna Mackiewicz, and Ewa Stanislawska. 2007. "Central Bank Transparency and Credibility: The Case of Poland, 1998–2004." *European Journal of Political Economy* 23 (1): 67–87.

Marshall, Wesley C. 2008. "Foreign Banks and Political Sovereignty: The Case of Argentina." *Review of Political Economy* 20 (3): 349–66.

Martinez-Diaz, Leonardo. 2009. *Globalizing in Hard Times: The Politics of Banking-Sector Opening in the Emerging World.* Ithaca: Cornell University Press.

Matousek, Roman, and Anita Taci. 2003. "Direct Inflation Targeting and Nominal Convergence: The Czech Case." *Open Economies Review* 14 (3): 269–83.

Mauro, Paolo, Nathan Sussman, and Yishay Yafeh. 2002. "Emerging Market Spreads: Then Versus Now." *Quarterly Journal of Economics* 117 (12): 695–733.

Mayer, Thierry, and Soledad Zignago. 2011. "Notes on CEPII's Distances Measures: The Geodist Database." In CEPII Working Paper 2011–25, CEPII, Paris.

Maxfield, Sylvia. 1997 *Gatekeepers of Growth: The International Political Economy of Central Banking in Developing Countries.* Princeton: Princeton University Press.

McCauley, Robert, Patrick McGuire, and Goetz von Peter. 2010. "The Architecture of Global Banking: From International to Multinational?" *BIS Quarterly Review* (March): 25–37.

McDermott, Gerald A. 2004. "Institutional Change and Firm Creation in East-Central Europe: An Embedded Politics Approach." *Comparative Political Studies* 37 (2): 188–217.

McDermott, Gerald A. 2007. "Politics, Power, and Institution Building: Bank Crises and Supervision in East Central Europe." *Review of International Political Economy* 14 (2): 220–50.

McKinnon, Ronald. 1963. "Optimum Currency Areas." *American Economic Review* 53 (September): 717–25.

McKinnon, Ronald I. 1991. *The Order of Economic Liberalization: Financial Control in the Transition to a Market Economy.* Baltimore: Johns Hopkins University Press.

Meaney, Connie Squires. 1997. "Foreign Experts, Capitalists, and Competing Agendas: Privatization in Poland, the Czech Republic, and Hungary." In *Liberalization and Leninist Legacies: Comparative Perspectives on Democratic Transitions*, edited by Beverly Crawford and Arend Lijphart, 91–125. Berkeley: University of California Press.

Megginson, William L., and Kathleen A. Weiss. 1991. "Venture Capitalists Certification in Initial Public Offerings." *Journal of Finance* 46 (3): 879–903.

Mehl, Arnaud, Cristina Vespro, and Adalbert Winkler. 2006. "Financial Sector Development in South-Eastern Europe: Quality Matters." In *Financial Development, Integration, and Stability-Evidence from Central, Eastern and South-Eastern Europe*, edited by J. Christl K. Liebscher, P. Mosslechner, and D. Ritzberger-Grünwald, 186–206. Cheltenham, UK: Edward Elgar.

Mejstřík, Michal, Anna Dvořáková, and Magda Neprašová. 2004. "Restructuring and Development of the Banking Sector in Advanced Transition Country: The Czech Republic." In *Cultivation of Financial Markets in the Czech Republic*, edited by Michal Mejstřík, 19–113. Prague: Karolinum Press.

Mian, Atif. 2006. "Distance Constraints: The Limits of Foreign Lending in Poor Countries." *Journal of Finance* 63 (1): 1465–1505.

Micco, Alejandro, Ugo Panizza, and M. Yañez. 2007. "Bank Ownership and Performance: Does Politics Matter?" *Journal of Banking and Finance* 31 (1): 219–24.

Miller, Jeffrey B. 2001. "The Bulgarian Currency Board." *Comparative Economic Studies* 43 (1): 53–74.

Miller, Jeffrey B., and Stefan Petranov. 2000. "The First Wave of Mass Privatization in Bulgaria and Its Immediate Aftermath." *Economics of Transition* 8 (1): 225–50.

Miller, Jeffrey B., and Stefan Petranov. 2001. "The Financial System in the Bulgarian Economy." Bulgarian National Bank Discussion Paper 19.

Minassian, Garabed. 1998. "The Road to Economic Disaster in Bulgaria." *Europe-Asia Studies* 50 (2): 331–49.

Minsky, Hyman P. 1975. *John Maynard Keynes.* New York: Columbia University Press.

Mishkin, Frederic S. 1999. "International Experiences with Different Monetary Policy Regimes." *Journal of Monetary Economics* 43 (3): 579–605.

Mishkin, Frederic S. 2004. "Can Inflation Targeting Work in Emerging Market Countries?" NBER Working Paper 10646. National Bureau of Economic Research, Cambridge, MA.

Mishkin, Frederic S. 2006. *The Next Great Globalization: How Disadvantaged Nations Can Harness Their Financial Systems to Get Rich.* Princeton: Princeton University Press.

Mishkin, Frederic S. 2007. "Is Financial Globalization Beneficial?" *Journal of Money, Credit and Banking* 39 (2–3): 259–94.

Mishkin, Frederic, and K. Schmidt-Hebbel. 2007. "Does Inflation Targeting Make a Difference?" NBER Working Paper 12876. National Bureau of Economic Research, Cambridge, MA.

Mitchener, Kris James, and Marc D. Weidenmier. 2009. "Are Hard Pegs Ever Credible in Emerging Markets? Evidence from the Classical Gold Standard." NBER Working Paper 15401. National Bureau of Economic Research, Cambridge, MA.

Mitra, Pradeep, Marcelo Selowsky, and Juan Zalduendo. 2010. *Turmoil at Twenty— Recession, Recovery, and Reform in Central and Eastern Europe and the Former Soviet Union.* Washington, DC: World Bank.

Milgrom, Paul, and John Roberts. 1982. "Limit Pricing and Entry under Incomplete Information: An Equilibrium Analysis." *Econometrica* 50 (2): 443–59.

Montes-Negret, Fernando, and Luca Papi. 1996. "The Polish Experience in Bank and Enterprise Restructuring." *MOST: Economic Policy in Transitional Economies* 7 (1): 79–104.

Mortimer, Kate. 1995. "Banking Privatization Policy in Poland and Czechoslovakia." In *Banking Reform in Central Europe and the Former Soviet Union,* edited by Jacek Rostowski, 80–112. Budapest: Central European University Press.

Moser, Peter. 1999. "Checks and Balances, and the Supply of Central Bank Independence." *European Economic Review* 43 (8): 1569–93.

Mundell, Robert. 1961. "A Theory of Optimum Currency Areas." *American Economic Review* 51 (3): 657–65.

Murphy, Kevin M., Andrei Shleifer, and Robert W. Vishny. 1992. "The Transition to a Market Economy: Pitfalls of Partial Reform." *Quarterly Journal of Economics* 107 (3): 889–906.

Myant, Martin. 2003. *The Rise and Fall of Czech Capitalism: Economic Development in the Czech Republic since 1989.* Northampton, MA: Edward Elgar.

Nash, Nathaniel C. 1995. "A Strong Leash for Currencies on a Rampage." *New York Times,* February 5.

Nenovsky, Nikolay, and Kalin Hristov. 2002. "The New Currency Boards and Discretion: Empirical Evidence from Bulgaria." *Economic Systems* 26 (1): 55–72.

Nenovsky, Nikolay, Kalin Hristov, and Mihail Mihaylov. 2002. "Comparing the Institutional and Organizational Design of Currency Boards in Transition Countries." *Eastern European Economics* 40 (1): 6–35.

Nenovsky, Nikolay, and Gergana Mihaylova. 2007. "Dynamics of the Financial Wealth of the Institutional Sectors in Bulgaria: Empirical Studies of the Post-

Communist Period." William Davidson Institute Working Paper 864. William Davidson Institute, University of Michigan.

Nenovsky, Nikolay, and Yorgos Rizopoulos. 2003. "Extreme Monetary Regime Change: Evidence from Currency Board Introduction in Bulgaria." *Journal of Economic Issues* 37 (4): 909–41.

Nenovsky, Nikolay, Kiril Tochkov, and Camelia Turcu. 2013. "Monetary Regimes, Economic Stability, and EU Accession: Comparing Bulgaria and Romania." *Communist and Post-Communist Studies* 46 (1): 13–23.

Neumann, Sabina, and Michelle Egan. 1999. "Between German and Anglo-Saxon Capitalism: The Czech Financial Markets in Transition." *New Political Economy* 4 (2): 173–94.

Nollen, Stanley, Zdeněk Kudrna, and Roman Pazderník. 2005. "The Troubled Transition of Czech Banks to Competitive Markets." *Post-Communist Economies* 17 (3): 363–80.

Nölke, Andreas, and Arjan Vliegenthart. 2009. "Enlarging the Varieties of Capitalism: The Emergence of Dependent Market Economies in East Central Europe." *World Politics* 61 (4): 670–702.

North, Douglass C., and Barry R. Weingast. 1989. "Constitutions and Commitment: The Evolution of Institutions Governing Public Choice in Seventeenth-Century England." *Journal of Economic History* 44 (3): 803–32.

Obstfeld, Maurice 1986. "Rational and Self-Fulfilling Balance-of-Payments Crises." *American Economic Review* 76 (1): 72–81.

Obstfeld, Maurice. 1996. "Models of Currency Crises with Self-Fulfilling Features." *European Economic Review* 40 (April): 1037–47.

Obstfeld, Maurice 1997. "Destabilizing Effects of Exchange Rate Escape Clauses." *Journal of International Economics* 43 (1–2): 61–77.

Obstfeld, Maurice. 1998. "The Global Capital Market: Benefactor or Menace?" *Journal of Economic Perspectives* 12 (4): 9–30.

Obstfeld, Maurice. 2009. "Lenders of Last Resort in a Globalized World." *Monetary and Economic Studies* 27: 35–52. Bank of Japan, available from http://www.imes.boj.or.jp/english/publication/mes/fmes.html

Obstfeld, Maurice, and Kenneth S. Rogoff. 1995. "The Mirage of Fixed Exchange Rates." NBER Working Paper 5191. National Bureau of Economic Research, Washington DC.

Obstfeld, Maurice, Jay C. Shambaugh, and Alan M. Taylor. 2005. "The Trilemma in History: Tradeoffs among Exchange Rates, Monetary Policies, and Capital Mobility." *Review of Economics and Statistics* 87 (3): 423–38.

Obstfeld, Maurice, and Alan Taylor. 2002. "Globalization and Capital Markets." NBER Working Paper 8846. National Bureau of Economic Research, Washington, DC.

Obstfeld, Maurice, and Alan M Taylor. 2003. "Sovereign Risk, Credibility and the Gold Standard, 1870–1913 versus 1925–1931." *Economic Journal* 113: 1–35.

Orenstein, Mitchell A. 2001. *Out of the Red: Building Capitalism and Democracy in Postcommunist Europe.* Ann Arbor: University of Michigan Press.

Organization for Economic Cooperation and Development. 1999. *Economic Surveys 1998-1999: Bulgaria.* Paris: OECD.

Ötker-Robe, İnci, Zbigniew Polański, Barry Topf, and David Vávra. 2007. "Coping with Capital Inflows: Experiences of Selected European Countries." IMF Working Paper WP/07/190. International Monetary Fund, Washington, DC.

Padilla, A. Jorge, and Marco Pagano. 2000. "Sharing Default Information as a Borrower Discipline Device." *European Economic Review* 44 (10): 1951–80.

Pagano, Marco, and Tullio Jappelli. 1993. "Information Sharing in Credit Markets." *Journal of Finance* 48 (5): 1694–718.

Palda, Kristian. 1997. "Czech Privatization and Corporate Governance." *Communist and Post-Communist Studies* 30 (1): 83–93.

Pauly, Louis. 1988. *Opening Financial Markets: Banking Politics on the Pacific Rim.* Ithaca: Cornell University Press.

Pautola, Niina, and Peter Backé. 1998. "Currency Boards in Central and Eastern Europe: Past Experience and Future Perspectives." *Focus on Transition* 1/1998: 72–103.

Peek, Joe, and Eric S. Rosengren. 2000. "Implications of the Globalization of the Banking Sector: The Latin American Experience." *New England Economic Review* (September/October): 45–63.

Peev, Evgeni. 1995. "Separation of Ownership and Control in Transition: The Case of Bulgaria." *Europe-Asia Studies* 47 (5): 859–75.

Peev, Evgeni. 2002. "Ownership and Control Structures in Transition to "Crony" Capitalism: The Case of Bulgaria." *Eastern European Economics* 40 (5): 73–91.

Persson, Torsten, and Guido Tabellini. 2000. *Political Economics: Explaining Economic Policy.* Cambridge, MA: MIT Press.

Petryk, Oleksandr. 2006. "History of Monetary Development in Ukraine." *Bank I Kredyt* 8: 3–24.

Pistor, Katharina. 2012. "Governing Interdependent Financial Systems: Lessons from the Vienna Initiative." *Journal of Globalization and Development* 2 (2): 1–25.

Polanski, Zbigniew. 1991. "Inflation and the Monetary System in Poland in the 1980s, and the Stabilization Program 1990." *Osteuropa-Wirtschaft* 32 (3): 342–63.

Polanski, Zbigniew. 1994. "Building a Monetary Economy in Poland in the 1990s." National Bank of Poland Working Paper no. 9. National Bank of Poland, Warsaw.

Polanski, Zbigniew. 1997. "Polish Financial System in the 1990s." In *Economic Transition in China and the East European Countries*, edited by Stanislaw Raczkowski. Warsaw: Polish Academy of Sciences and Chinese Academy of Social Sciences.

Polanski, Zbigniew. 1998. Polish Monetary Policy in the 1990s: A Bird's Eye View. In *Financial Market Restructuring in Selected Central European Countries*, edited by Karen S. Vorst, and Willadee Wehmeyer, 7–22. Ashgate: Aldershot.

Polanski, Zbigniew. 2002. "Promoting Financial Development: Lessons from Poland." In *Banking and Monetary Policy in Eastern Europe. The First Ten Years*, edited by A. Winkler. Houndmills: Palgrave.

Pop-Eleches, Grigore. 2009. *From Economic Crisis to Reform: IMF Programs in Latin America and Eastern Europe*. Princeton: Princeton University Press.

Popov, Alexander, and Gregory F. Udell. 2012. "Cross-Border Banking, Credit Access, and the Financial Crisis." *Journal of International Economics* 87 (1): 147–61.

Posen, Adam S. 1993. "Why Central Bank Independence Does Not Cause Low Inflation. There Is No Institutional Fix for Politics." *Finance and the International Economy 7: The AMEX Bank Review Prize Essays*, edited by R. O'Brien. Oxford: Oxford University Press.

Posen, Adam S. 1995. "Declarations Are Not Enough: Financial Sector Sources of Central Bank Independence." In *Macroeconomics Annual*, edited by Ben S. Bernanke and Julio J. Rotemberg, 253–92. Cambridge, MA: MIT Press.

Procházka, Petr. 1996. "Banking Sector Development and Legal Harmonization with EU Standards—the Case of the Czech Republic." In *Monetary Policy in Central and Eastern Europe: Challenges of EU Integration*, edited by Olga Radzyner and Peter Havlik. Vienna: Oesterreichische Nationalbank and the Vienna Institute for Comparative Economic Studies.

Pruski, Jerzy, and Piotr Szpunar. 2005. "Exchange Rate Policy and Foreign Exchange Interventions in Poland." In *Foreign Exchange Market Intervention in Emerging Markets: Motives, Techniques and Implications* 24:255–64. Basel: Bank for International Settlements.

Raiffeisen Research. 2012. *CEE Banking Sector Report*. June. Vienna: Raiffeisen Bank International.

Raiffeisen Research. 2014. *CEE Banking Sector Report*. May. Vienna: Raiffeisen Bank International.

Rao, Hayagreeva, and Paul Hirsch. 2003. "Czechmate: The Old Banking Elite and the Construction of Investment Privatization Funds in the Czech Republic." *Socio-Economic Review* 1 (2): 247–69.

Raudla, Ringa, and Rainer Kattel. 2011. "Why Did Estonia Choose Fiscal Retrenchment after the 2008 Crisis?" *Journal of Public Policy* 31 (2): 163–86.

Ravenna, Federico. 2012. "Why Join a Currency Union? A Note on the Impact of Beliefs on the Choice of Monetary Policy." *Macroeconomic Dynamics* 16 (2): 320–34.

Reinhart, Carmen M., and Kenneth S. Rogoff. 2009. *This Time Is Different: Eight Centuries of Financial Folly*. Princeton: Princeton University Press.

Riley, James C. 1980. *International Government Finance and the Amsterdam Capital Market, 1740–1815*. Cambridge: Cambridge University Press.

Rivera-Batiz, Luis, and Amadou Sy. 2013. "Currency Boards, Credibility, and Macroeconomic Behavior." *Annals of Economics and Finance* 14 (2): 813–52.

Roberts, Andrew. 2003. "Demythologising the Czech Opposition Agreement." *Europe-Asia Studies* 55 (1): 1273–1303.

Rogoff, Kenneth. 1985. "The Optimal Degree of Commitment to an Intermediate Monetary Target." *Quarterly Journal of Economics* 100 (4): 1169–90.

Rojas-Suárez, Liliana, and Sebastian Sotelo. 2007. "The Burden of Debt: An Exploration of Interest Rate Behavior in Latin America." *Contemporary Economic Policy* 25 (3): 387–414.

Roland, Gérard. 2000. *Transition and Economics: Politics: Markets and Firms.* Cambridge, MA: MIT Press.

Romer, David. 1993. "Openness and Inflation: Theory and Evidence." *Quarterly Journal of Economics* 108 (4): 869–903.

Rose, Andrew. 2000. "One Money, One Market: Estimating the Effect of Common Currencies on Trade." *Economic Policy* 15 (30): 7–45.

Rose, Andrew. 2004. "Do We Really Know That the WTO Increases Trade?" *American Economic Review* 94 (1): 98–114.

Rose, Andrew K. 2011. Exchange Rate Regimes in the Modern Era: Fixed, Floating, and Flaky." *Journal of Economic Literature* 49 (3): 652–72.

Rose, Andrew K. 2014. "Surprising Similarities: Recent Monetary Regimes of Small Economies." *Journal of International Money and Finance* 49, Part A (December): 5–27.

Roubini, Nouriel, and Brad Setser. 2004. *Bailouts or Bail-Ins: Responding to Financial Crises in Emerging Markets.* Washington, DC: Peterson Institute for International Economics.

Rousseau, Peter L., and Richard Sylla. 2003. "Financial Systems, Economic Growth, and Globalization." In *Globalization in Historical Perspective,* edited by Alan M. Taylor, Michael D. Bordo, and Jeffrey G. Williamson, 373–413. Chicago: University of Chicago Press.

Rubio, Marco. 2014. "Ukraine Needs a Lifeline—Now." *Wall Street Journal,* May 6.

Sachs, Jeffrey. 1993. *Poland's Jump to the Market Economy.* Cambridge, MA: MIT Press.

Sachs, Jeffrey, Aaron Tornell, and Andres Velasco. 1996. "Financial Crises in Emerging Markets: The Lessons from 1995." *Brookings Papers on Economic Activity* 1: 147–215.

Sapienza, Paola. 2002. "What Do State-Owned Firms Maximize? Evidence from Italian Banks." Unpublished paper. Available at http://papers.ssrn.com/sol3/papers.cfm?abstract_id=303381

Saxonberg, Steven. 1999. "Václav Klaus: The Rise and Fall of and Re-Emergence of a Charismatic Leader." *East European Politics and Society* 13 (2): 96–111.

Schmieding, Holger. 1992. *Lending Stability to Europe's Emerging Market Economies.* Tubingen: J. C. B. Mohr.

Schmukler, Sergio, and Luis Servén. 2002. "Pricing Currency Risk under Currency Boards." *Journal of Development Economics* 69 (2): 367–91.

Schoenmaker, Dirk. 2013. *Governance of International Banking: The Financial Trilemma.* Oxford: Oxford University Press.

Schultz, Kenneth A., and Barry R Weingast. 2003. "The Democratic Advantage." *International Organization* 57 (1): 3–42.

Schumacher, Liliana. 2000. "Bank Runs and Currency Run in a System without a Safety Net: Argentina and the Tequila Shock." *Journal of Monetary Economics* 46 (1): 257–77.

Schwartz, Andrew Harrison. 1997. "The Czech Approach to Residual Share Management." In *Between State and Market: Mass Privatization in Transition Economies*, edited by Ira Lieberman et al. Washington, DC: World Bank.

Schwartz, Andrew Harrison. 2006. *The Politics of Greed: How Privatization Structured Politics in Central and Eastern Europe*. Lanham, MD: Rowman & Littlefield.

Shambaugh, Jay. 2004. "The Effect of Fixed Exchange Rates on Monetary Policy." *Quarterly Journal of Economics* 119 (1): 301–52.

Shleifer, Andrei, and Robert Vishny. 1998. *The Grabbing Hand: Government Pathologies and Their Cures*. Cambridge, MA: Harvard University Press.

Schularick, Moritz, and Alan M. Taylor. 2012. "Credit Booms Gone Bust: Monetary Policy, Leverage Cycles, and Financial Crises, 1870–2008." *American Economic Review* 102 (2): 1029–61.

Simmons, Beth. 1994. *Who Adjusts? Domestic Sources of Foreign Economic Policy during Interwar Years 1924–1939*. Princeton: Princeton University Press.

Šmídková, Kateřina et al. 1998. "Koruna Exchange Rate Turbulence in May 1997." Czech National Bank, Working Paper No. 2. Czech National Bank, Prague. Available at https://www.cnb.cz/miranda2/export/sites/www.cnb.cz/en/research/research_publications/mp_wp/download/a-wp2-98.pdf

Šmídková, Kateřina, and Miroslav Hrnčíř. 2003. "The Czech Approach to Inflation Targeting." *Macroeconomics* 0303019, EconWPA.

Snyder, Edward A., and Roger C. Kormendi. 1997. "Privatization and Performance of the Czech Republic's Komercní Banka." *Journal of Comparative Economics* 25 (1): 97–128.

Sõrg, Mart. 1994. "Banking Reform in Estonia." Institute of Economics, Working Paper No. 10. Tallin Institute of Economics, Tallinn.

Sõrg, Mart. 1998. "Peculiarities of the Corporate Governance in the Banking Sector of Estonia." Paper presented at the 4th Conference on Financial Sector Reform in Emerging Market Economies, Tallinn, Estonia, April 24–26.

Sõrg, Mart, and Janek Uiboupin. 2004. "The Competitiveness of Estonian Banks in EU." In *Integration of Financial Sectors of Baltic States into the European Union: Challenge and Experience*, edited by Mart Sõrg and Vello Vensel, 77–116. Tallin, Estonia: Faculty of Economics and Business Administration, Tallinn University of Technology.

Soukup, Pavel, Anita Taci, and Roman Matoušek. 2004. "Central Bank Independence in the Czech Republic." In *Central Banking in Eastern Europe*, edited by Nigel Healey and Barry Harrison, 167–91. London: Routledge.

Spiegel, Mark M. 2008. "Financial Globalization and Monetary Policy Discipline: A Survey with New Evidence from Financial Remoteness." Federal Reserve Bank of San Francisco Working Paper No. 10. Federal Reserve Bank, San Francisco.

Staehr, Karsten. 2004. "The Economic Transition in Estonia. Background, Reforms and Results." In *Contemporary Change in Estonia*, edited by E. Rindzeviciute, 3:37–67. Södertörn University College.

Staprans, Alda. 1994. "Taking the Politics out of Monetary Policy." *Baltic Observer*, February 3–7.

Stark, David, and László Bruszt. 1998. *Postsocialist Pathways: Transforming Politics and Property in East Central Europe*. New York: Cambridge University Press.

Stasavage, David. 2007. "Cities, Constitutions, and Sovereign Borrowing in Europe, 1274–1785." *International Organization* 61 (3): 489–525.

Stasavage, David. 2011. *States of Credit: Size, Power, and the Development of European Polities*. Princeton: Princeton University Press.

Stasavage, David, and Dominique Guillaume. 2002. "When Are Monetary Commitments Credible? Parallel Agreements and the Sustainability of Currency Unions." *British Journal of Political Science* 32 (1): 119–46.

Steen, Anton, and Juri Ruus. 2002. "Change of Regime-Continuity of Elites? The Case of Estonia." *East European Politics and Societies* 16 (1): 223–48.

Stiglitz, Joseph E. 1994. "The Role of the State in Financial Markets." In *Proceedings of the World Bank Annual Conference on Development Economics, 1993*, edited by Michael Bruno and Boris Pleskovic, 19–52. Washington, DC: World Bank.

Stone, Randall W. 2002. *Lending Credibility: The International Monetary Fund and the Post-Communist Transition*. Princeton: Princeton University Press.

Straumann, Tobias. 2010. *Fixed Ideas of Money: Small States and Exchange Rate Regimes in Twentieth-Century Europe*. Cambridge: Cambridge University Press.

Stroehlein, Andrew, with Jan Culik, Steven Saxonberg, and Kazi Stastna. 1999. "The Czech Republic 1992–1999: From Unintentional Political Birth to Prolonged Political Crisis." *Central Europe Review* 60 (12) (September 13).

Sulling, Anne. 2002. "Should Estonia Euroize?" *Economics of Transition* 10 (2): 469–90.

Svensson, Lars E. O. 1999. "Inflation Targeting as a Monetary Policy Rule." *Journal of Monetary Economics* 43 (3): 607–54.

Svensson, Lars E. O. 2010. "Inflation Targeting." NBER Working Paper 16654. National Bureau of Economic Research, Cambridge, MA.

Szymkiewicz, Krystyna. 2001. "The Second Stage of Banking Transformation in Poland." In *Transitional Economies: Banking, Finance, Institutions*, edited by Yelena Kalyuzhnova and Michael Taylor, 54–84. New York: Palgrave.

Tang, Helena, Edda Zoli, and Irina Klytchnikova. 2000. "Banking Crises in Transition Countries: Fiscal Costs and Related Issues." Policy Research Working Paper 2484. World Bank, Washington, DC.

Tavlas, George S. 1993. "The 'New' Theory of Optimum Currency Areas." *The World Economy* 16 (6): 663–85.

Terk, Erik. 2000. *Privatization in Estonia: Ideas, Process, Results*. Tallinn: Estonian Institute for Future Studies.

Thacker, Strom C. 1999. "The High Politics of IMF Lending." *World Politics* 52 (1): 38–75.

Tomz, Michael. 2007. *Reputation and International Cooperation: Sovereign Debt across Three Centuries*. Princeton: Princeton University Press.

Tornell, Aaron, and Andres Velasco. 2000. "Fixed Versus Flexible Exchange Rates: Which Provides More Fiscal Discipline?" *Journal of Monetary Economics* 45 (2): 399–436.

Truman, Edwin. 2013. "Asian and European Financial Crises Compared." Working

Paper No. 13-9. Peterson Institute for International Economics, Washington, DC.

Tsai, Hsiangping, Yuanchen Chang, and Pei-Hsin Hsiao. 2011. "What Drives Foreign Expansion of the Top 100 Multinational Banks? The Role of the Credit Reporting System." *Journal of Banking & Finance* 35 (3): 588–605.

Tschoegl, Adrian E. 2003. "Financial Crises and the Presence of Foreign Banks." Paper presented at the World Bank conference Systemic Financial Distress: Containment and Resolution, October 7–8.

Tschoegl, Adrian E. 2005. "Financial Crises and the Presence of Foreign Banks." In *Systemic Financial Distress: Containment and Resolution*, edited by Patrick Honohan and Luc Laeven, 197–231. Cambridge: Cambridge University Press.

Tůma, Zdeněk. 2006. "The Banking Sector and Its Regulation in the Czech Republic." Unpublished speech. Czech National Bank, Prague. http://www.cnb.cz/en/pub lic/media_service/conferences/speeches/2006.html. Accessed May 21, 2016.

Ulgenerk, Esen, and Leila Zlaoui. 2000. "From Transition to Accession: Developing Stable and Competitive Financial Markets in Bulgaria." World Bank Technical Paper 473.

Vachudova, Milada Anna. 2001. "The Czech Republic: The Unexpected Force of Institutional Constraints." In *Democratic Consolidation in Eastern Europe*, vol. 2, edited by Laurence Whitehead. Oxford: Oxford University Press.

Vachudova, Milada Anna. 2005. *Europe Undivided: Democracy, Leverage, and Integration after Communism*. Oxford: Oxford University Press.

Valev, Neven, and John Carlson. 2007. "Beliefs about Exchange Rate Stability: Survey Evidence from the Currency Board in Bulgaria." *Journal of Economic Policy Reform* 10 (2): 111–21.

Van Horen, Neeltje. 2007. "Foreign Banking in Developing Countries: Origin Matters." *Emerging Markets Review* 8 (2): 81–105.

Velasco, Andrés. 1996. "Fixed Exchange Rates: Credibility, Flexibility and Multiplicity." *European Economic Review* 40 (April): 1023–35.

Vincelette, Galina Andronova. 2001. "Bulgarian Banking Sector Development, Post-1989." *Southeast European Politics* 2 (1): 4–23.

Vives, Xavier. 2006. "Banking and Regulation in Emerging Markets." *World Bank Research Observer* 21 (2): 79–206.

Vogel, Ursula, and Adalbert Winkler. 2010. "Foreign Banks and Financial Stability in Emerging Markets: Evidence from the Global Financial Crisis." Frankfurt School of Finance and Management Working Papers No. 149. Frankfurt School of Finance and Management.

Vogel, Ursula, and Adalbert Winkler. 2012. "Do Foreign Banks Stabilize Cross-Border Bank Flows and Domestic Lending in Emerging Markets? Evidence from the Global Financial Crisis." *Comparative Economic Studies* 54 (3): 507–30.

Wagner, Nancy, and Dora Iakova. 2001. "Financial Sector Evolution in the Central European Economies: Challenges in Supporting Macroeconomic Stability and Sustainable Growth." IMF Working Paper 01/141. IMF, Washington, DC.

Wagstyl, Stefan, and Neil Buckley. 2011. "Crisis Hits Central and Eastern Europe." *Financial Times*, November 22.

Walter, Stefanie. 2013. *Financial Crises and the Politics of Macroeconomic Adjustment*. New York: Cambridge University Press.

Weber, Axel. 1991. "Reputation and Credibility in the European Monetary System." *Economic Policy* 12 (April): 507–102.

Wellisz, Stanislav. 1997. "Inflation and Stabilization in Poland, 1990–95." In *Macroeconomic Stabilization in Transition Economies*, edited by Mario I. Blejer and Marko Škreb, 157–71. Cambridge: Cambridge University Press.

Williamson, John. 1995. "What Role of Currency Boards?" *Policy Analyses in International Economics* 40 (December). Peterson Institute for International Economics, Washington, DC.

Winkler, Adalbert. 2009. "Southeastern Europe: Financial Deepening, Foreign Banks and Sudden Stops in Capital Flows." *Focus on European Economic Integration* Q1/09: 84–97.

Winkler, Adalbert. 2014. "Finance, Growth and Crisis: A European Perspective." *Intereconomics* 49 (2): 88–94.

Winkler, Alissa M., and Peter R. Haiss. 2010. Post-Crisis Business Models of Austrian Banks in Central and Eastern Europe, European Economics and Finance Society Conference, Athens.

Wittenberger, Tina, Daniela Widhalm, Mathias Lahnsteiner, Stephan Barisitz. 2014. "Macrofinancial Developments in Ukraine, Russia and Turkey from an Austrian Financial Stability Perspective." *Financial Stability Report* 27 (October): 64–73.

World Bank. 2008. The Role of International Banking. Global Development Finance 2008. World Bank, Washington, DC.

World Bank. 2013. Rethinking the Role of the State in Finance. Global Financial Stability Report. World Bank, Washington, DC.

Woodruff, David M. 2005. "Boom, Gloom, Doom: Balance Sheets, Monetary Fragmentation, and the Politics of Financial Crisis in Argentina and Russia." *Politics & Society* 33 (1): 3–46.

Wyzan, Michael. 1998. "Bulgaria's Currency Board Cements Macroeconomic Stability." Radio Free Europe/Radio Liberty Newsline, September 29. Accessible at: http://www.hri.org/news/balkans/rferl/1998/98-09-29.rferl.html

INDEX

1997–98 Asian currency crisis, 211–14
2008 global financial crisis, 179, 181, 194–214, 218
  effect on emerging Europe, 10, 23, 174, 196, 197, 198, 201, 203, 205, 206–15
  effect on Latin America, 198, 201
  role of multinational banks in, 194–97, 198, 203–8

Argentina, 179
  2001 financial crisis, 179, 181–94
  banking reforms in, 185–89, 191
  collapse of currency board, 189–91
  consolidation of banking system, 185
  inflation in, 180, 182, 185, 188, 190
  multinational bank presence in, 188–89, 214
  multinational bank withdrawal from, 191–94
  and sovereign default, 189–91
  and Tequila Crisis, 39, 183, 185–86, 188, 214, 215
Asia, 180
Asian currency crisis of 1997–98. *See* 1997–98 Asian currency crisis
Åslund, Anders, 78, 79, 156, 197, 206, 209
asymmetric information, 30–31, 89, 214. *See also* information asymmetry
asymmetric pesification, 192–94
Austrian banks, presence in emerging Europe, 198–201, 203–4

Balassa-Samuelson effect, 55
Balcerowicz, Leszek, 157, 158
Balcerowicz Plan, 157–58
Banco Central de la Republica Argentina. *See* BCRA

Banco Bilbao Vizcaya Argentaria (BBVA, BBV), 43, 45, 186, 201, 202, 204, 250
Banco Santander, 45, 186, 201, 204, 250
Bank of Estonia (BOE), 96, 97, 100, 101, 102, 107. *See also* Estonia: banking reforms
Bank for International Settlements, 64, 159, 238
bank reputation. *See* reputation: of banks
The Banker, 43–46
banking regulation, 8–10, 28, 36, 38–40, 102, 107, 113–17, 125–26, 143, 148, 166–67, 173, 232. *See also* multinational banks: as providers of regulatory expertise
banking crisis, 215, 220. *See also* currency crisis
  in Argentina, 193, 186
  in Bulgaria, 120–23
  in Czech Republic, 147–56, 221
  in Estonia, 100, 107–8
  preventing, 8, 48, 93, 186
banking socialism, in Czech Republic, 139–43
banking system transparency. *See* financial system transparency
Barro, Robert, 118. *See also* Barro-Gordon model
Barro-Gordon model, 2, 30, 31, 32
BASIC regime, Argentinian, 187
BBVA/BBV. *See* Banco Bilbao Vizcaya Argentaria
BCRA, 182, 183, 185, 186, 190
Bearce, David, 60
Berglöf, Erik, 215, 229
Berov, Lyuben, 113, 114, 117
Bielecki, Jan Krzysztof, 157, 158
Big Four Czech banks, 140–41. *See also* banking socialism

Printed and bound by CPI Group (UK) Ltd, Croydon, CR0 4YY

23/04/2025

14660940-0002